8/16/24

For Judy,
All the best,
Larry Lerton

Trumpism, Bigotry, and the Threat to American Democracy

Trumpism, Bigotry, and the Threat to American Democracy

Larry N. Gerston

LEXINGTON BOOKS
Lanham • Boulder • New York • London

Published by Lexington Books
An imprint of The Rowman & Littlefield Publishing Group, Inc.
4501 Forbes Boulevard, Suite 200, Lanham, Maryland 20706
www.rowman.com

86-90 Paul Street, London EC2A 4NE

Copyright © 2024 by The Rowman & Littlefield Publishing Group, Inc.

All rights reserved. No part of this book may be reproduced in any form or by any electronic or mechanical means, including information storage and retrieval systems, without written permission from the publisher, except by a reviewer who may quote passages in a review.

British Library Cataloguing in Publication Information Available

Library of Congress Cataloging-in-Publication Data Available

ISBN 978-1-66692-087-1 (cloth : alk. paper)
ISBN 978-1-66692-088-8 (electronic)

∞™ The paper used in this publication meets the minimum requirements of American National Standard for Information Sciences—Permanence of Paper for Printed Library Materials, ANSI/NISO Z39.48-1992.

*In memory of
Professor Leslie Lipson
Whose encouragement launched my journey*

Contents

Acknowledgments   ix

Introduction   1

PART I: THE DELICACY OF DEMOCRACY   **5**

1. Democracy's Promise and Performance   7
2. Why Democracies Decline   23

PART II: THE IMPACT OF BIGOTRY   **43**

3. Bigotry as a Threat to Democracy   45
4. Racial Bigotry in the United States: A Brief History   63
5. Donald Trump and Bigotry   91

PART III: TRUMPISM: AN AMERICAN BRAND OF AUTHORITARIANISM   **109**

6. Trump, Bigotry, and the 2016 Presidential Election   111
7. A Bitter Presidency   139
8. Trump, Bigotry, and the 2020 Election   169
9. The January Sixth Insurrection: Before, During, and After   191
10. Trump on the Wane?   221

PART IV: TRUMPISM, BIGOTRY, AND THE THREAT TO AMERICAN DEMOCRACY — **247**

11 Understanding the Threat to American Democracy — 249

12 Saving the American Experiment — 275

Bibliography — 281

Index — 329

About the Author — 343

Acknowledgments

Ask any author, and they will point to the loneliness connected with writing a book. It's a strange journey that only another author truly understands. Still, we go on believing that what we have to say will be a small contribution to our field. And one day, we get to the point where it comes together, but not without help. The team at Lexington has been incredibly helpful and supportive of the project. Thanks go to acquisitions editor Joseph Parry, who saw the value of the project, acquisitions editor Sara Noakes, who nursed the effort to its end, and Mahesh Meiyazhagan and Jessica Thwaite in production. The peer reviewer for this manuscript was generous in their time with a thorough, constructive review, for which I am very grateful. Finally, I offer my heartfelt thanks to Elisa Gerston—spouse, in-house editor, and cheerleader, who helped me work through one issue after another, All the wonderful support notwithstanding, I alone am responsible for the contents of this effort.

Introduction

Sometimes, separate objects, when combined, have a different significance than their original composition. Put two molecules of hydrogen and one molecule of oxygen together, and the result is water, a property vital to the existence of life. Mix the colors blue and yellow on a painter's palette, and you wind up with green. A less desirable outcome arises with the merger of Trumpism, bigotry, and American democracy. Each of these substantive topics has been discussed and written about seemingly as long as one can remember. But put them together and, combined, they take on a dangerous connotation downstream for the American political system.

Trumpism, Bigotry, and the Threat to American Democracy offers a window into the possible future of American politics and government. The book begins by defining and discussing the historical appeal and benefits of democracy, along with the many ways that democracies can disappear. The narrative continues with an examination of bigotry and its relationship to societies both globally and in the United States. The last part of the examination focuses on Donald Trump and his minions, who have employed bigotry in its various forms as a tool for dividing society to the point of potential collapse, from which an authoritarian regime could appear.

But how could the world's oldest continuing democratic nation succumb to such a radical change? Surely, there must be guardrails. That answer is presented in detail throughout the remaining pages of this volume. While much of the analysis is not pleasant, it's vital to those of us committed to the permanence of American democracy with all of its imperfections. If we don't fully understand the cause, effect, and gravity of our present condition—the circumstance that threatens the continuation of our democracy—we'll be hard-pressed to reverse it. Thus, this discussion.

No one source or event can shove a democracy from its historical, political, and cultural moorings in the United States or anywhere else. Various accounts of other democratic failures point to anger over growing wealth gaps, divisions over the proper role of government, cultural or religious chasms, and increasing alienation from the many possible sources of societal decay. Our story has roots, too.

In the United States, bigotry has emerged as a prominent disruptive inroad to the democratic framework of our increasingly multicultural society. Since the colonial period, this scourge has nagged mostly at alienated fringes of the United States with sporadic and tragic outbursts of negativity, but not to the point of turning American democratic governance inside out. Historically, slavery was the most blatant form of bigotry and the justification for Southern succession from the union. Of course, slavery ended with the North's victory in the Civil War and the preservation of the republic. Nevertheless, that political and military victory over the use of slavery notwithstanding, American bigotry, and particularly racism, has persisted through numerous institutional and informal mechanisms not only in the South but in the North as well. In some instances, the plague has been overt, while in other instances, it is covert and almost subtle.

Enter Donald Trump, a provocateur who for years operated in the shadows of American bigotry and racist innuendo. Seizing that dark anti-democratic theme as his currency when joining the national political stage, Trump made bigotry an overt cornerstone of his presidential campaign and subsequent governance dedicated more to authoritarianism than democracy. He exploited the nefarious refrain repeatedly in an effort to divide a multicultural society and divert Americans from attending to long-standing, serious social, economic, and political issues. Under Trump and his followers, racism became an abrasive, ugly instrument for stirring the darkest misdeeds of many Americans. And with that unfortunate political marriage between a would-be-despot and a once-largely suppressed behavior, racism became an openly Trump-promoted value and a key part of the political conduct of a sizable minority of White Americans. Trump didn't invent racism, nor are all Trump voters racists. But it's fair to suggest that most racists have favored Trump.

As demonstrated in the forthcoming pages, Trump successfully seized racism as a political weapon more than any other politician in recent times. In addition, he established an alternate racist-dependent political framework for the Republican Party that has been emulated by others at the national, state, and local levels of politics. Incredibly, Trump has turned an embarrassing historic cultural blemish into a hyper-political epidemic that threatens to overcome the very well-being of the United States.

Once in the presidency, Trump abused his power through firing individuals in key positions of authority, publicly and untruthfully deprecating the value of government institutions, and picking key subordinates on the basis of their loyalty to him rather than competence. Bit by bit, he stripped away democratic norms, replacing them with an authoritarian management style. He maintained popularity largely through his ability to pit elements of society against one another, while presenting himself as the only person capable of saving it from itself.

Donald Trump may have been defeated for re-election in 2020, but a Trump-emboldened racist value system and its encouraged adherents of several million remain a thriving, hate-filled segment of American society. Indeed, openly xenophobic elements were clearly evidenced and endorsed by Trump throughout his presidency, blatantly present during the January 6, 2021, insurrection at the U.S. Capitol, and have been shamelessly demonstrated ever since. Their presence has further exposed the sordid relationship between bigotry and support for would-be undemocratic governance that, by its very existence, could subvert the guarantees and requirements found in the U.S. Constitution.

Regardless of any Trump's role in the 2024 presidential election, bigoted behavior is now front and center in America in public schools, the ballot box, and even the halls of government to an extent not seen in decades. It's often hidden behind claims for "value-free" public education, a "racist-free society," or voter protection laws from unsubstantiated allegations of fraud that are actually intended to suppress minority voters. To be clear, racism was part of America long before Trump and would no doubt be part of America without Trump. But, to cite an old saying, "the genie is out of the bottle" in terms of once-largely marginalized racist values now consuming a sizable portion of the nation, its leaders, and its institutions. What was once quietly discussed and managed is now perpetually present as one of the key issues in American politics. Moreover, legions of racists, including many in high elected positions, have joined in the effort to demonize and minimize non-White, non-Christian populations of American society.

As a result of the marriage of convenience between Trump and racist elements, the United States may now be well down the road to a future with an arbitrary and harmful authoritarian value movement threatening, if not replacing, the world's oldest modern democracy. The threat is real, with its history long before Trump but its modern-day manifestation by Trump. What remains is whether Americans will see through the decadent charade orchestrated by Trump and his growing number of acolytes. The uncertain future of American democracy as we know it hangs in the balance. It's with those stakes in mind that *Trumpism, Bigotry, and the Threat to American Democracy* seeks to shed a little light on the possibilities stemming from this potentially devastating combination.

A final note: If nothing else, the effort here centers on the continuing story of American political history. While numerous dark events and political behaviors have been cited to this point, additional incidents continue to take place, further jeopardizing our future. Yes, it's possible that a democratic resurgence of earth-shaking proportions might reverse the chronicled trend, and that certainly would be a welcome development. But in the current environment, there is a greater likely outcome that more worrisome conduct will be added to the framework described in *Trumpism, Bigotry, and the Threat to American Democracy.*

Part I

THE DELICACY OF DEMOCRACY

Democracies are relatively recent enterprises in the history of societies and nation-building. One account views the past hundred years or so as the period during which most democracies blossomed throughout much of the world, classifying perhaps as much as 60 percent of the world's nations as democratic.[1] For many of us, the advantages of democratic political systems would seem to overwhelm any of the other approaches to governance. Barbara Walter writes that "Citizens of liberal democracies have more political and civil rights than those who live in non-democracies. They participate more in the political life of their nations, have greater protections from discrimination and repression, . . . are happier, wealthier, better educated, and generally have a higher life expectancy than people who live in dictatorships."[2]

Not everyone has such a rosy view, however. Other assessments on the prominence of democracies around the world are less generous than Walter's view. In its Democracy Index covering 167 countries, *The Economist* finds 24 full democracies, followed by 48 flawed democracies, 36 hybrid governments, and 59 authoritarian regimes.[3] Simply put, some nations would appear to be more democratic than others.

Still, the United States has long been regarded as the definitive role model for democracy and long viewed as the country other would-be or even fledgling democracies seek to emulate. With such a reputation, one might ask, why even go with this book?

It may well be that the connection between the United States and democracy is not today what it has been in the recent past, especially given the expanding role of bigotry in an increasingly multicultural society. Numerous studies have found that government protections for residents have not been distributed equally among the nation's diverse population.[4] At the same time, the disproportionate growth of racial minorities and some non-Christian groups relative to White people has become perceived as threats by some White Christians troubled by diminishing percentages of their own race and religions. We also recognize bigotry for its role in oppressing women and others of varying sexual orientations, although the treatment in this work focuses more on the bigoted applications of racism and religious persecution. Regarded as a tool for gaining economic and social advantage, bigotry has also become a carefully planned means through which some candidates have pursued power as well as election to political office.

Racial and religious discrimination have impacted American life throughout the history of the United States, but in recent years, that intersection has taken on an enlarged meaning, particularly in American politics. With respect to elections, Donald Trump exploited racial and religious divisions along the way to becoming a prominent, powerful political figure and, ultimately, president of the United States. Moreover, upon losing a bid for re-election in 2020, Trump played an outsized role in attempting to illegally overturn the result, with much of his argument relying on unsubstantiated claims of votes by undocumented immigrants. This combination of an individual utilizing bigotry as a tool for gain at the expense of others leaves one wondering about the state of American democracy today. It's especially tragic when so many members of the polity ignore, or worse, endorse such behavior.

Defining and understanding the meaning of democracy is the starting point for this book, which proposes to discuss the current state of democracy in the United States, bigotry, and the threat of authoritarianism. Part I focuses on the conditions that promote democracy in chapter 1 as well as those that undermine it in chapter 2. The discussion is important not only for determining the extent to which a democratic foundation exists in today's United States but for understanding the growing number of largely White racist actors willing to rely upon unseemly undemocratic methods as the means to gain political power and undermine our democratic framework.

NOTES

1. Barbara F. Walter, *How Civil Wars Start and How to Stop Them* (New York, NY: Random House, 2022), p. 9.
2. Ibid.
3. *The Economist's* criteria used for defining democratic nations include electoral process and pluralism, functioning of government, political participation, democratic political culture, and civil liberties. See "Democracy Index 2022," *The Economist*, 2022, https://www.eiu.com/n/campaigns/democracy-index-2022/.
4. For recent examinations of this topic, see Marisa Abrajano and Zoltan L. Hajnal, *White Backlash* (Princeton, NJ: Princeton University Press, 2015) and Lafleur Stephens-Dougan, *Race to the Bottom: How Racial Appeals Work in American Politics* (Chicago, IL: University of Chicago Press, 2020).

Chapter 1

Democracy's Promise and Performance

Politically speaking, nations have a lot in common with snowflakes: no two are alike. Physically, demographically, socially, culturally, religiously, and ethnically, nations differ from one another. Nor are most nations static. Most change with evolving values, new economic developments, influences from abroad, technological breakthroughs, populations that migrate in and out, and sometimes from the tragic outcomes associated with wars.

And so it is with governance. Throughout the world, nations are managed by a variety of institutional arrangements, including autocracies, monarchies, theocracies, oligarchies, and democracies. Of these categories, *real* democracy is a relatively rare form of governance compared to the others because of the unique attributes associated with its existence and the endless challenges to maintain it. The reason is simple enough, if the causes aren't: it's much easier to lose a democracy than to keep it. Many political, social, economic, and psychological variables must be aligned in an almost cocoon-like fashion to protect the precious democratic contents from disruption or possible demise.

Combined, the relative rarity and delicate condition of these factors underscore the necessity of understanding the essence of democracies and how they can be nurtured and sustained. As we undergo this exercise, we'll keep in mind not only the requisites of democracy but its existence and role in the United States.

DEFINING DEMOCRACY

Scholars differ on the many political, economic, and social features that comprise democracies.[1] At a minimum, those nations with democratic regimes are dependent upon several key characteristics, among them: a set of agreed-upon and shared values that are honored regardless of who is in power; governments that are elected by citizens without constraints on a regular basis; an independent and free press; civil rights and civil liberties that are enjoyed by all members of society regardless of race, ethnicity, religion, gender, or even citizenship; built-in institutional mechanisms to prevent any one element of government from illegally assuming control at the expense of other competing elements; and a political culture that supports the system under which the people are governed.

The more that all of these elements take root in a nation's political framework, the more likely that they will provide support for an ongoing stable democracy. To the extent that one or more are absent or minimal, a nation's democracy may be unstable, wither, or disappear altogether. Clearly, the multiple moving parts of a democracy are delicate and interdependent. When considering the values of nations claiming to be democratic, we quickly learn that some work better than others.

Agreed-upon Rules between the Governed and the Governors

In a way, democracy is a trade-off of sorts. Citizens willingly cede power to those in positions of authority in accordance with a set of governing rules accepted by society. For their part, those who preside must do so with deference to the same set of rules and concern for the public good. Reinhard Bendix writes that under this arrangement, "A belief in legality means first and foremost that certain formal procedures must be obeyed if the enactment or execution of a law is to be considered legal."[2] This connection represents the collective soul of the polity. It is based on trust between the governed and governors, and that relationship must be consistently nurtured to remain operational.

The rules in a democracy exist beyond any particular moment, emergent set of circumstances, or individual exception. They are enduring and predictable for all to honor all of the time, or at least with great regularity. In his *On the Social Contract*, Jean-Jacques Rousseau refers to laws as "the conditions of civil association"; they bind the people with their government as one.[3] Whereas nondemocratic governments function under the often-changing mindset of the leader or leaders, democracies operate with a fixed set of rules agreed to and abided by the public generation after generation. Leaders also understand that they may be replaced when public sentiment seeks a change for any number of reasons, including disappointing stewardship, changing values, or factors that may have little to do with the performance of those in power. What's important to remember is that historically agreed-upon tenets and procedures set the terms for how the polity functions. Without codified rules accepted by society and those placed temporarily in power, there cannot be a democracy.

There are two ways to assure continuity of the rules in a democracy: First, if citizens feel that those in power have acted in ways contrary to the expectations of those who put them there or abused the rules, they may be replaced in a free election that installs new leaders in office. Second, democratic institutions are known for having several interdependent components, where one part of the government may check another if disagreement or malfeasance of office occurs. Their independence helps keep any one institution from going astray. To that end, Joseph Schumpeter once wrote, "Above all, electorates and parliaments must be on an intellectual and moral level high enough to be proof against the offerings of the crook and the crank, or else men who are neither will be driven into the ways of both."[4]

Democratic governance occurs best when leaders respect well-established values and rules in a political environment of public support. This doesn't mean that citizens necessarily appreciate all decisions and policies. However, they and their elected leaders know that there are routine means via elections to rearrange the assemblage of those in power in a peaceful way. Nor does it mean that democracies are static. Rules may change over time, but general consensus must be part of the evolution.

An Independent and Free Press

In a democracy, journalists and other critics have the unfettered ability to investigate, report, and criticize the ongoing activities of government institutions, those who participate in their operations, and those who interact with them. This role is critical to the well-being of democracy, given that the press serves as a crucial provider to the public of what actually happens in government. Longtime journalist Marvin Kalb writes that "a free press and democracy are tightly intertwined, each sustaining the other. Lose one and you lose the other."[5] In its capacity to provide information, the press serves as a megaphone, making available knowledge about the happenings of governments that most people would otherwise not possess. In the process, the press contributes to an informed public by providing information and differing perspectives on the important issues of the day.[6] By carrying out these responsibilities, the press serves as a valuable linkage institution that links those who make policies with those in society who are impacted by them.[7]

In the United States, the right to report news without permission of or control by government is clearly guaranteed in the First Amendment of the Constitution, which states there should be no law abridging freedom of the press. Other democracies have similar guarantees. For government to otherwise determine the conditions under which the press operates would render the findings of the press useless, impotent, and little more than a tool of those in power. Such a prerequisite does not give journalists and others free rein to carry out their responsibilities. At the same time, journalists do not operate with blank checks; they are obligated to operate in conjunction with the laws protecting individual privacy, national security, and various ethical and institutional boundaries. This arrangement occurs regardless of whether a journalist is reporting on a breach of national security or a robbery at a local convenience store.

There are times when government leaders push back against journalists' investigations in fear of what they may find. This is understandable, if sometimes uncomfortable, tension between the potentially sensitive operations of a government institution and the journalist's effort to inform the public of its activities. Under these circumstances, the courts may be called upon to referee such disputes, providing a reliable way to settle a disagreement. There are also times when individuals or private organizations sue journalists or media establishments for slander or other alleged abuses. These accusations are also then decided in a court of law, considered a neutral source for fairly settling disputed issues. Occasional excesses notwithstanding, in its purest form, the press must be allowed to serve "as a bastion of free expression in a democracy"[8] even if that expression causes personal embarrassment, offends someone in government, or costs the individual his or her job. Without an independent press, society lacks the means to review the actions of government actors.

Civil Rights and Civil Liberties

The discussion of civil rights and civil liberties is sometimes reduced to concern that minorities are not receiving the same opportunities such as others for activities like political expression, voting, representation, employment, and education. True, these are essential elements of equal treatment and should not be trivialized. But civil rights and civil liberties extend to numerous other areas of equal opportunities. Among them are the right to open dissent and free debate, civil disobedience, equal treatment of society's many groups by those in power, and impartial criminal justice. Further, those with claims about their treatment or anything else must have unconstrained access to those in authority or their representatives, as well as the ability to peacefully make such claims without fear of restraint or punishment by those in power.

Particularly for groups who have suffered from a history of discrimination, the demands for these rights are ongoing and evolutionary. It's worth remembering that in the United States, the "universal" founding principles in the Declaration of Independence and Constitution excluded racial minorities and women and were hardly intended for the poor.[9] It was also assumed that society would be Christian. The extension of principles of democratic representation to most White males was generous only compared to life in other political regimes at the time. Clearly, equal rights had a different framework 240 years ago than in modern times. Today, for many groups in the United States, the fight for equality is far from over.[10] The same can be said about minorities in other democracies. Simply put, the pursuits of civil rights and civil liberties are, by necessity, endless struggles for justice and, as such, demonstrate imperfections in almost every democracy. At least in a democracy, these flaws are acknowledged and considered as areas for improvement, although well-intentioned people may differ on solutions.

In authoritarian societies, civil rights and civil liberties movements more often than not fail to achieve substantive change either because of the lack of interest or the brute power enjoyed by those in charge of the government. In more extreme cases (and there are many), those in positions of power have an explicit intent to govern over oppressed groups as part of their authoritarian rule.

In democracies, however, civil rights and civil liberties movements are often warning signs that the political system is not working as well as it should for all. Under these conditions, protest activities function as something akin to cleansing agents in that their existence can underscore the need for political reform in the name of responsive accommodation and compromise.[11] Thus, they serve a valuable role as agents dedicated to pursuing a democracy that works well for all. To the extent that anyone or any group is systemically unfairly denied the basic freedoms associated with civil rights and liberties guaranteed to others, democracy is tarnished and, in many cases, quite likely nonexistent.

Viable Institutional Mechanisms

Democratic governments are much more than political blueprints. They are functional organizations designed to create, direct, and carry out programs and tasks on behalf of the polity. They do so through individuals in institutions and units responsible for considering, making, and managing public policies. In the United States, the best known of these bodies are the legislative, executive, and judicial branches, with their primary roles outlined in the Constitution. Each of these has a connection with the public, although to different degrees. All members of Congress are directly elected by the people.[12] The president gains office through a majority of the votes gathered in the Electoral College, a body that depends upon the vote totals gathered in the individual states,[13] with each state assigned a number depending upon its population. The judiciary, the least connected institution with the public, derives its members from those nominated by the president and confirmed by the Senate. Although it may be indirect, even this branch has a connection with the public by virtue of the elections of officials linked with the other branches.

Other democratic nations have their own sets of institutional mechanisms charged with making public policies. Among them are representation institutions with a variety of names, such as parliaments, councils, assemblies, and diet (in Japan), all of which are commonly associated with an executive such as a prime minister, chief minister, chancellor, or president. The point is that whatever the nomenclature, a key component of democracies lies with a system of dispersed power that discourages the possibility of authoritarian rule. Their judicial networks also have various degrees of independence. In many of these cases, governments exist via elections where the voters directly select their leaders through a system otherwise known as "direct" democracy. They are referred to as direct for the absence of any filtering institutions that might skew the election outcome in a direction other than intended by the voters.

In the American version of democratic institutional mechanisms, the three policy-making bodies have different responsibilities and are designed to be largely independent of one another. Congress considers legislation. The president signs proposed legislation or vetoes it[14]; in the event of a signature, the president may also assign implementation responsibilities to an element of the bureaucracy. The courts may weigh in on the constitutionality of the activities of Congress and the president. This is commonly described as "checks and balances." Over time, the powers of each branch have grown and diminished relative to the others. Regardless of those dynamics, the fact remains that policymaking has the best chance of succeeding when the three agree.

Along with the division of responsibilities, the American democratic system has two important attributes. First, while the three independent branches have separate functions, in most cases, they are dependent upon each other for governing. A simple example might be Congress passing a bill, the president signing it into law, and the Supreme Court upholding the law when it's challenged. Second, the American system is called a "representative" democracy because those who govern are accountable to the people. Is this combination messy? Yes. But *if* the various principals stay in their lanes, representative democracy can work, although it may produce results that differ from the public will such as the presidential elections of 2000 and 2016, where the popular vote and electoral votes differed.[15]

When we consider the Donald Trump presidency, the question of staying in one's lane becomes important. While president, Trump used the powers of his office in ways that went far beyond its boundaries defined by law and tradition. Repeatedly, he violated important norms and, in all likelihood, federal and state laws. He was the only president in American history to be impeached twice by the House of Representatives, although acquitted by the Senate. Upon leaving office, he became the center of several federal and state investigations, some of which will not be resolved for years. Some aspects of the government probes centered on Trump's abusing his power and roles of sycophants in other positions of government authority.

An Open Political Culture

A culture refers to the foundation of a society's collective attributes. Whether primitive, complex, or somewhere in between, all societies contain various shared beliefs, customs, traditions, and habits that function loosely as the basic underpinning of their existence. These patterns of life have developed in previous generations and are inculcated in future generations, although sometimes disposed to societal mutation with discovery, invention, and new traditions. Consider how communication has been transformed in advanced societies. People have shared conversations since the beginning of humanity, but in many societies their methods have changed over time. Think about the past two hundred years alone, where personal interaction methods have advanced from devices such as the telegraph to the telephone, and more recently computers, cell phones, and video conferencing. Those who favor in-person dialogue might wince at the change as a step backward, but it's a phenomenal transformation nonetheless over a relatively short period of time.

Just as societies differ in languages, traditions, and belief systems, so do the political cultures of nations. As with other elements in a society's mores, political cultures in nations reflect an ever-changing mixture of historical and present themes. The more similar the political values in a nation's population, the easier it is for its people to find agreement on economic, social, and political concepts, including the development and maintenance of political institutions.[16] The more diverse the political values of a nation's population, the more challenging it is to secure agreement on these themes, especially in fledgling democracies. Still, those nations with established commitments to tolerance and accommodation of competing themes as part of their values can function reasonably well as democracies.[17]

Sweden

A country like Sweden with a fairly homogeneous population, has more built-in consensus than most other societies. As of 2021, 74 percent of Sweden's population were native-born Swedes. With respect to other data, 60 percent belonged to the Church of Sweden, with Islam, the largest non-Christian religion, representing 1.5 percent. As for residence, 88 percent lived in urban centers, and virtually everyone speaks Swedish. This is not to suggest Sweden is without friction. Since the 1930s, a left-of-center bloc coalition of political parties has governed the country. Over 35 years, Sweden Democrats, a rightwing political party focusing on xenophobic themes, has gained support from as many as 13 percent of the voters, causing concern among some political observers.[18] Principal discontent has focused on rising crime, which Sweden Democrats attribute to Muslim immigrants, a distinct ethnic minority with radically different religious values.[19] Still, despite accepting more migrants than any other European country on a per capita basis, comparatively, Sweden remains a nation emphasizing inclusion, equality, and respect for human rights.[20]

The Democratic Republic of Georgia

On the other hand, some democracies have so many divisions that their future is uncertain. The Democratic Republic of Georgia is a case in point. Freed from communist domination in 1991 after the implosion of the Soviet Union, Georgians struggled over the possibility of adopting democracy. During the 1990s, the country was divided by several civil wars, often because of ethnic, language, and religious divisions.[21] The country's leaders signed agreements with the European Union in 2014, where democracies prevailed. Still, separatist movements largely guided by Russian-oriented groups hindered a smooth transition.[22]

Today, Georgia has regularly scheduled and free elections, hallmarks of a democracy. Nevertheless, ethnic differences have strained the country. Georgia has significant Armenian and Azerbaijani minorities that are poor, speak different languages, and have not been assimilated into the dominant culture. In recent years, accusations of a politicized judiciary, a suppressed media, and harassed candidates have also emerged. The country has its hands full with these potentially disruptive factors.[23] Still, in the post-Soviet era, Georgia's leaders and citizens are working toward a more homogenized democracy.

The United States

Then there is the United States, where rapid demographic change has become a hallmark of concern for some members of the White majority. According to the 2020 census, White people held a majority of 61.6 percent, but that margin was 8.6 percent below the 2010 census, when White people accounted for 70.4 percent of the population. Moreover, demographers predict that the United States will have a majority of ethnic and racial minorities by 2045.[24] This transformation has threatened consensus. Some argue that immigration is part of an ongoing process of redefining the boundaries of an enlarged and evolving community.[25] Others counter that White opposition to the immigration of non-White people reflects self-interest concerns rather than racism.[26] Regardless, the fact remains that the United States has gone through profound demographic shifts in recent years. Moreover, as we will see in future chapters, those strains plague the United States to this day.

Holding It Together

The discussion above underscores the challenges of creating and sustaining democracies. Much like a jigsaw puzzle, each component of democracy must fit precisely in place with the others in order for the system to work. Adjustments must be made constantly to keep the democratic arrangement in place. Even then, democracies are constantly confronted by changing values, competing claims, and evolving internal and external conditions.

THE TROUBLED STATUS OF DEMOCRACY IN THE TWENTY-FIRST CENTURY

Many nations include a version of the word "democracy" in their official name, but few live up to the combination of requirements for that status. The Democratic People's Republic of North Korea and the People's Democratic Republic of Algeria are among those countries that describe themselves as such but fall considerably short of most of the components that characterize "democracy." In fact, North Korea and Algeria are both rigidly authoritarian countries by virtually any impartial standard, irrespective of their official titles.

A review of the political arrangements in today's world reveals that democracies are hard to develop and even harder to keep. In the words of one recent international assessment, "New democracies are often weak and fragile. Older democracies are struggling to guarantee equitable and sustainable economic and social development."[27] Simply put, democracies must be constantly watched for weaknesses and nourished to stay strong, and there is nothing automatic about either behavior.

The Varieties of Democracies Project (also known as V-Dem), a research body located the University of Gothenburg, Sweden, has rich data on this point. The project examines five essential core principles of democracy in nearly two hundred nations; they are electoral, liberal, participatory, deliberative, and egalitarian elements. In its 2021 report, V-Dem estimated that 87 nations, with 68 percent of the world's population, functioned as nondemocratic governments. Moreover, with its criteria, V-Dem calculated that over the past decade, the number of liberal democracies had declined from 41 countries to 32, representing only 14 percent of the world's population. The study concluded that "the level of democracy enjoyed by the average global citizen in 2020 [was] down to levels last found in 1990."[28] Researchers may vary in their methodologies for determining democracies, but overall, many conclude that fewer democracies exist today than in the past.

Backsliding

As noted above, democracies are becoming something of an endangered species. Perhaps even more significant, large numbers of democracies are disintegrating gradually in such a way that their deterioration is hardly noticed until it's too late. This concept is known as "backsliding," which is defined by Stephan Haggard and Robert Kaufmann as "the incremental erosion of democratic institutions, rules that result from the actions of duly elected governments, typically driven by an autocratic leader."[29] That authoritarian regimes can emerge through democratic processes is a troubling development for those observers who worry about democratic decay.

How does this unfortunate reversal occur seemingly in broad daylight? The answer lies with the fact that democratically elected leaders sometimes use their positions of power as platforms for governing as despots. Bit by bit, they cajole fellow leaders with weak democratic moorings to be part of the "cause" typically described as a reform, while eliminating or pushing aside those who object. Bit by bit, they and their growing allies neutralize competing centers of power. And bit by bit, they take over sizable portions of the media and point to a weakened opposition as "enemies of the people." Note the description, "bit by bit." The key to backsliding from democracy to dictatorship is that it occurs slowly over time, leaving the masses unaware of the many undemocratic "pieces" that will become part of a new whole. Historically, weak or flawed democracies often succumbed to backsliding. But in recent times, nations with once strong attachments to democratic norms were viewed as strong political foundations have shown signs of backsliding as well.

Several former countries in the orbit of the former Soviet Union have slowly lost their fledgling democratic footing. Hungary is one such example. Freed from communist domination after the Revolutions of 1989, Hungarians quickly jumped at organizing a democratic government. Viktor Orban, eventually Hungary's leader, was prominent in organizing the country's rebellion against Soviet domination. For a few years after independence, several political parties formed governing coalitions. Concerns with a serious economic recession and government corruption led to several organized public protests between 2007 and 2009, giving a tint to instability. In 2010, Orban's Fidesz, a conservative "reform" political party, joined with the conservative Christian Democrats to win control of the Hungarian Parliament in national elections.

The design of a new constitution in 2011 enabled Fidesz to win narrow control of the government outright. Over time, the party's values shifted from center-right to conservative. Led by Orban, the party was not very popular until a surge of Serbian migrants entered Hungary in 2015. The rest is history. Orban "capitalized on the xenophobic fears of the population."[30] His political party tightened control of major power centers, including the courts, prosecutors, academic institutions, and the media. In 2020, the Hungarian parliament voted for a state of permanent emergency, giving Orban the power to suspend elections. Between 2016 and 2021, the V-Dem Institute downgraded Hungary's democratic standing among nations from 59th to 89th. Ironically, much of Orban's political construction of what he proudly called "the illiberal state" occurred through lavish funding from the European Union,[31] much to the disappointment of Western leaders who had hoped otherwise.[32]

Overcoming Obstacles

All democracies are messy systems because of delicate political arrangements dependent upon the agreement of the people to give power to the government and the obligation of government leaders to provide for the public good. Sometimes, controversy exists over different interpretations of rules of governance and how it should proceed. There are also occasions when rights collide, such as when a zealous reporter's inquiries come up against defensive government officials seeking to keep information from becoming public. Civil rights are sometimes either abridged by government authorities or applied in unequal ways.

There are instances where institutions may not operate as they were designed, although that's often the result of the person or persons who may be managing them in ways contrary to the established rules. Assuming that fair elections exist and that sufficient numbers of voters disagree with the officials' behaviors, these bad actors can be replaced in the next election, but that's not always the case.

Then there is the issue of diversity, a condition where a society suffers from differences so great that they will not congeal. In his *The Great Experiment: Why Diverse Societies Fall Apart and How They Can Endure*, Yascha Mounk writes that diverse societies fall apart from three causes: anarchy, where people are unwilling to accept a central government; domination, where a group claims superiority over the others; and fragmentation, where too many parts of society can't congeal. With respect to the United States, Mounk worries that the danger of ethnic fragmentation may hinder, if not undo, the country's democracy.[33] His concerns are offset by Francis Fukuyama, who argues that over the past few thousand years, the "arc of history" has enabled social evolution to increasingly complex organizations, from families and small groups to states with increasingly complex legal institutions, justice, and equality. All this leads to a liberal society, Fukuyama writes, "which has seen its ups and downs [over time] but has always come back in the end."[34] In the United States, the racial divisions exploited by politicians such as Donald Trump have presented have tested Fukuyama's "come back" theory in ways not seen in decades.

Finally, even in the most culturally similar democracies, the political values are hardly monolithic. In fact, it's common that democracies are havens for competing values; rich debate over issues is a hallmark in itself. The trick is that under such circumstances, the divisions are relatively minor and encased in tolerance and mutual regard. Clearly, there are times when democracies appear more aspirational than operational. Still, when comparing democracies against all other forms of government, they remain the best chance for the people to be heard and respected as the ultimate wells of authority. But that doesn't mean that democracies will always prevail.

A look at the democracies around the world reminds us of the difficulties associated with keeping such systems in place. And for good reason. We're reminded of the words of John Adams, second president of the United States, who cautioned: "Remember, democracy never lasts that long. It soon wastes, exhausts, and murders itself. There was never a democracy yet that did not commit suicide."[35] So far, Adams' words have not been entirely prophetic, yet modern examples of democracies-turned-autocracies abound. As the world's oldest continuing democracy, the United States has avoided such destruction for nearly 250 years. Yet, with the circumstances and potential perils now confronting this country, one wonders if our time has come.

NOTES

1. For example, William Hudson offers four models of democracy: protective, developmental, pluralist, and participatory. See *American Democracy in Peril*, 9th ed. (Thousand Oaks, CA: Sage Publications, 2021), pp. 8–24. Another approach is offered by John Anthony Maltese, Joseph A. Pika and W. Phillips Shively, where they divide democracy into two approaches: direct and indirect. See their *American Democracy in Context* (Thousand Oaks, CA: Sage Publications, 2021), pp. 4–5. Alternatively, Suzanne Mettler and Robert Lieberman speak of democracy as "a system of government in which citizens are able to hold those in power accountable through elections," with those elected being responsible to citizens. See *Four Threats: The Recurring Crises of American Democracy* (New York, NY: St. Martin's Press, 2020), p. 11.

2. Reinhard Bendix, *Nation-Building and Citizenship* (Garden City, NY: Double Day & Company, 1969), p. 135.

3. Jean-Jacques Rousseau, *On the Social Contract* (originally published in 1762, republished by Garden City, NY: Classic Books International, 2010).

4. Joseph Schumpeter, *Capitalism, Socialism and Democracy*, third edition (New York, NY: Harper and Row, Publishers, 1950), p. 294.

5. Marvin Kalb, *Enemy of the People: Trump's War on the Press, the New McCarthyism, and the Threat to American Democracy* (Washington, DC: The Brookings Institution, 2018), p. 7.

6. Shanto Iyengar, *Media Politics: A Citizen's Guide*, fourth edition (New York, NY: W.W. Norton and Company, 2019), p. 21.

7. Jan E. Leighly, *Mass Media and Politics: A Social Science Perspective* (Boston, MA: Houghton Mifflin Company, 2004), p. 8.

8. Michael Schudson, "Why Democracies Need an Unlovable Press," in Doris A. Graber (ed.), *Media Power in Politics*, sixth edition (Washington, DC: CQ Press, 2011), p. 34.

9. Elizabeth Beaumont, *The Civic Constitution: Civic Visions and Struggles in the Path Toward Constitutional Democracy* (New York, NY: Oxford University Press, 2014), p. 22.

10. See Tali Mendelberg, *The Race Card: Campaign Strategy, Implicit Messages, and the Norm of Equality* (Princeton, NJ: Princeton University Press, 2001), pp. 269–276.

11. Barbara F. Walter, *How Civil Wars Start and How to Stop Them* (New York, New York: Random House, 2022), pp. 90–91.

12. Originally, the Constitution provided that election of senators would be the province of state legislatures; however, direct election from the voters came about with the 17th Amendment in 1913.

13. The Electoral College is largely a data-gathering body that collects the electoral votes from each state. In all, there are 538 such "votes." A state's number of electoral votes is determined by a formula driven largely, but not entirely by population. Each state is automatically awarded two votes in recognition of its two U.S. senators. The District of Columbia is awarded electoral votes equivalent to its proportion of the U.S. population, currently three. The remaining 435 votes are awarded commensurate with the state's number of members in the House of Representatives. A presidential candidate must win 270 votes (one more than half) to be elected.

14. Should the president veto a bill, the Congress may overturn the veto through a two-thirds "yes" vote in each chamber.

15. In the 2000 election, Democrat Al Gore collected 500,000 more popular votes than Republican George W. Bush; however, Bush was declared the winner with 271 electoral votes to Gore's 267. In 2016, Democrat Hillary Clinton won 2.9 million more popular votes than Republican Votes, yet Trump enjoyed a decisive electoral vote victory, 306 to 232.

16. For a celebrated comparison of political cultures in different societies, see Gabriel Almond and Sidney Verba, *Civic Culture* (Princeton, NJ: Princeton University Press, 1963).

17. See Gabriel Almond and G. Bingham Powell, Jr., *Comparative Politics: A Developmental Approach* (Boston, MA: Little, Brown and Company, 1966), pp. 258–263.

18. Tino Sanandaji, "The Cost of Sweden's Silent Consensus Culture," *Politico*, September 9, 2018, https://www.politico.eu/article/the-cost-of-swedens-silent-consensus-culture/.

19. Danielle Lee Tomson, "The Rise of Sweden Democrats: Islam, Populism, and the End of Swedish Exceptionalism," The Brookings Institution, Washington, DC, March 25, 2020, https://www.brookings.edu/research/the-rise-of-sweden-democrats-and-the-end-of-swedish-exceptionalism/.

20. "Swedish Cultural," *The Cultural Atlas*, 2022, https://culturalatlas.sbs.com.au/swedish-culture.

21. M. Steven Fish and Matthew Kroenig, "Diversity, Conflict and Democracy: Some Evidence from Eurasia and East Europe," *Democratization*, 13, no. 5 (2006), https://polisci.berkeley.edu/sites/default/files/people/u3833/DiversityConflictandDemocracy.pdf.

22. Katya Soldak, "Two Steps Forward, One Step Backward: Georgia's Path from Soviet Republic to Free Market Democracy," *Forbes*, November 23, 2021, https://www.forbes.com/sites/katyasoldak/2021/11/23/two-steps-forward-one-step-back-georgias-path-from-soviet-republic-to-free-market-democracy/.

23. See Martin Duffy, "Georgia's Democracy Still in Peril," *E-International Relations*, October 9, 2021, and Nino Lejava, "Georgia's Unfinished Search for Its Place in Europe," Carnegie Europe, Brussels, Belgium, April 6, 2021, https://www.e-ir.info/2021/10/09/opinion-georgias-democracy-still-in-peril/.

24. "The U.S. will become 'Minority White' in 2045, Census Projects," Brookings, March 14, 2018, https://www.brookings.edu/blog/the-avenue/2018/03/14/the-us-will-become-minority-white-in-2045-census-projects/.

25. See Justin Gest, "What the 'Majority Minority' Shift Really Means for America," *The New York Times*, August 24, 2021, https://www.nytimes.com/2021/08/24/opinion/us-census-majority-minority.html.

26. See Eric Kaufmann, "Immigration and White Identity in the West: How to Deal with Declining Majorities," *Foreign Affairs*, September 8, 2017, https://www.foreignaffairs.com/articles/united-states/2017-09-08/immigration-and-white-identity-west.

27. "Summary: The Global State of Democracy 2019," International Institute for Democracy and Electoral Assistance, https://www.idea.int/publications/catalogue/summary-global-state-of-democracy-2019?lang=en.

28. "The Global State of Democracy 2021," International Institute for Democracy and Electoral Assistance, Stockholm, Sweden, p. 6, https://static.poder360.com.br/2021/11/integra-the-global-state-of-democracy-2021_0.pdf.

29. Stephan Haggard and Robert Kaufmann, *Backsliding* (New York, NY: Cambridge University Press, 2021), p. 1.

30. Michael Bernhard, "Democratic Backsliding in Poland and Hungary," *Slavic Review*, 80, no. 3, https://www.cambridge.org/core/journals/slavic-review/article/democratic-backsliding-in-poland-and-hungary/8B1C30919DC33C0BC2A66A26BFEE9553.

31. "How the E.U. Standards Allowed Hungary to Become an Illiberal Role Model," *The New York Times,* January 4, 2022, https://www.nytimes.com/2022/01/03/world/europe/hungary-european-union.html.

32. See Peter Kreko and Zsolt Enyedi, "Explaining Eastern Europe: Orban's Laboratory of Illiberalism," *Journal of Democracy*, 29, Issue 3 (July 2018): 39–51, https://www.journalofdemocracy.org/articles/explaining-eastern-europe-orbans-laboratory-of-illiberalism/.

33. Yascha Mounk, *The Great Experiment: Why Diverse Democracies Fall Apart and How They Can Endure* (New York, NY: Penguin Press, 2022), p. 83.

34. See Francis Fukuyama, "The Long Arc of Historical Progress," *The Wall Street Journal,* April 30, 2022, https://www.wsj.com/articles/the-long-arc-of-historical-progress-11651244262.

35. Letter from John Adams to John Taylor, December 17, 1814.

Chapter 2

Why Democracies Decline

Typically, authoritarian systems of governance maintain control through artificial means such as persistent one-party rule, physical domination of the population, and closed hierarchical systems. Under such circumstances, wealth and political power tend to be limited to very few and often connected in a tight web. Moreover, given the closed nature of the authoritarian network and heavy-handed, top-down political control of the levers of government, most of those struggling at the bottom have little opportunity of moving up economically and politically into positions of power.

Our concerns here are about democracies that lose their stride and devolve into authoritarian societies. When modern democracies succumb to less representative forms of governance, it's almost always due to internal conditions. In fact, few are destroyed by foreign powers in a military conflict, although Russia's invasion of Ukraine in 2022 may prove to be a notable, if tragic, modern-day exception. Otherwise, democracies tend to deteriorate over time from a destabilization within the polity.[1] Among the most common factors leading to decay are the failure of leaders to respond to major social issues, economic inequality, ethnic divisions, military coups, and invasions. In many cases, more than one of these categories will be responsible for the erosion of a democracy.

FAILURE TO RESPOND TO MAJOR SOCIAL ISSUES

Democracies sometimes fail because of their inability to deal with issues plaguing society. In these regimes, the "democratic" political system may include most of the elements already discussed—elections, political parties, civil discourse, civilian control, and other traditional basics of democracy, but elections are neither truly free nor fair and one political party tends to win them almost every time. With these weaknesses, the national government may not have the capacity or will to address a systemic problem like poverty, persistent crime, ethnic conflict, or an emergent issue such as economic deterioration.[2] Fragile democracies, those with little history or weak commitment to democratic themes, are particularly vulnerable to becoming failed states. Two prominent factors that lead democracies to lose their status are corruption and weakened societal support for democratic values and institutions.

Corruption

In general terms, corruption refers to the abuse of political office or manipulation for personal gains by those in government or with special access to it. Exploiting or ignoring laws, norms, and official responsibilities as means for securing those gains are all signs of corruption. This malevolence is found to various degrees world over in private enterprises as well as authoritarian forms of government. However, corruption is particularly damaging when found in democracies because it undermines public expectations of fairness, equality, and protection of the public welfare.[3] Often, corruption is particularly pronounced in "transitional societies" attempting to move or have recently transitioned, from authoritarian to new democratic governments. In such regimes, the propensity for corruption is greatest, where the accountability of public officials is neither demanded nor expected by the public.[4] Even new democracies with designated "anti-corruption" offices dedicated to weeding out malevolent forces can be corrupt, their titles notwithstanding, as lofty titled government institutions may be little more than symbolic representations of the public good and little else.[5]

Mexico

Mexico is a case in point. Between 1929 and 2000, Mexico operated with a one-party form of government, which many observers viewed as the source of widespread corruption, or at least tolerating it. Beginning in 2000, one-party government ended. Since then, every successful presidential candidate has run on a platform committed to ending corruption. Administrations from three different political parties successfully labored to install a series of transparent laws and democratic norms, part of which included the weakening of an extremely powerful centralized presidency in favor of decentralized authority. Included in the transformation was a sweeping anti-corruption law, which gave new powers to state and local government officials. Political reformers counted on governments at lower levels of authority to enforce the new democratic themes.

With a weakened executive branch, corruption thrived at new levels of activity, while it continued at the national level.[6] In 2021, Mexican president Andres Manuel Lopez Obrador added to Mexico's corruption problems with his proposal for a national referendum to investigate the previous five presidents, each of whom had been charged with aiding corruption. However, the proposal did not receive enough votes in an awkwardly devised national preelection that asked the voters whether such a proposal should be placed on the ballot; that particular proposal failed for lack of sufficient turnout as required in Mexico's constitution. Critics accused Lopez Obrador of using the referendum as a means to consolidate his own power.[7] Undeterred, he organized another referendum in 2022, this time asking the voters whether they wanted him to stay in power for the remainder of his six-year term. Once again, the turnout was substantially below the 40 percent threshold, although those who voted did so overwhelmingly in rejecting the proposal that Lopez Obrador step down. Meanwhile, opponents continued condemnation of the president's weakening of the once-independent judiciary and media.[8]

In 2021, an international study labeled Mexico the third most corrupt country in the world, just behind Iraq and Colombia and ahead of Brazil and Russia.[9] During the following year, *The Economist* in its annual rankings of nations, downgraded Mexico from "flawed democracy" to "hybrid regime."[10] Thus, despite the breakup of one-party government, corruption remains a mainstay in Mexican society.

Venezuela

A different example of corruption as a source of democratic deterioration can be found with Venezuela. For years during the mid-twentieth century, Venezuela thrived as a democracy largely dependent upon its vast petroleum reserves.[11] Economic and social mobility were mainstays of a relatively flourishing society. But beginning in the late 1970s and over the next decade, reduced oil exports, waning foreign investment and high inflation thrust Venezuela into economic uncertainty. Until that time, corruption existed but was largely ignored; however, once shortages and other misappropriated distribution of valuable resources impacted large swaths of Venezuelan society, the public angered and clamored for change. Neither of the nation's two major political parties, themselves riddled with corruption, moved toward political reform in a way to protect Venezuela's democracy. In fact, during this period, President Jaime Lusinchi (1984–1994) was able to pilfer $36 billion from the economy, according to one report.[12] In 1998, Hugo Chavez, a former military leader once imprisoned for leading a coup d'etat against the government, was elected to the presidency as a minor political party candidate with the promise to eliminate Venezuela's corruption, graft, and patronage. He successfully steered a public vote for a new constitution which enabled the president to dissolve the National Assembly, Venezuela's principal legislative body. The new constitution also allowed the president to declare a national emergency and suspend critical constitutional guarantees, which Chavez did. Over time, the major political parties lost support, largely because of the government's new policy of denying public subsidies for their operations. Critics were exiled or imprisoned and journalists were suppressed. Before long, Chavez was without any significant opposition either in or out of government.[13] Family members gained key positions of power and Chavez's creation of state-owned enterprises yielded a new set of millionaires. Venezuela's democracy was gone and corruption continued.[14]

Weakened Support for Key Democratic Values and Institutions

A democracy can look great "on paper" and still fail. Whatever the constitutional and legislative guardrails against deterioration, without society committed to basic democratic values, democracy can dissipate from within. Societies with sharp differences over basic democratic principles and beliefs such as inclusiveness, pluralism, and tolerance are likely to be polarized with little chance of agreement on how these themes may be operationalized. Much of this can be summed up in what Lucien Pye calls "ordered authority."[15] Yet, reaching that political equilibrium has its own challenges. One recent study found that social polarization "enhances the likelihood that 'anti-system' social movements and political parties gain footholds in the social system."[16] The idea of "we" versus "them" is often found with the emergence of extremist social movements. In such an environment, the reverence for authoritarian leaders may emerge because of their claim to solve society's problems quickly and efficiently, irrespective of established democratic processes.

Ironically, anti-democratic leaders are often elected to power by alienated voters in free and fair elections who turn to them in desperation for change that has eluded the polity. Once secured in their positions, however, authoritarian leaders reject established constitutional guardrails as impediments to "getting things done" and keeping people safe from those elites or collections of despots who would deny them democracy. The "we's," anxious to be safe from the "them's," are all too willing to exchange democratic processes for security.[17] Thus, in fragile democracies, the people often have the primary role in choosing a leader who over time will deny them their basic rights and freedoms. And with that, the hope of democratic stability is dismantled. The International Institute for Democracy and Electoral Assistance estimates that since 2010, democracies representing 30 percent of the world's population have become nondemocratic regimes or suffered democratic erosion.[18]

Turkey

Over the past few decades, Turkey has deteriorated from a democracy to an authoritarian form of government. For many years, the country's democratic status has been tentative, with weak attachments to civil liberties, religious and ethnic divisions, political parties, and independent journalists.[19] For several decades, policies have favored the Sunni Muslims, the dominant religion, over Armenian Christians, Orthodox Christians, and other religious groups, resulting in less than favorable treatment for these minorities. Since 2011, tensions with neighboring Syria have increased, compounded by the migration of 3.7 million refugees from their war-ravaged country to Turkey. In part, the large migration occurred because European countries were sending Syrian refugees, courtesy of an agreement where the European Union agreed to pay Turkey 6 billion Euros (approximately $6.5 billion) for accepting the Syrians.[20] Still, public services for these refugees provided by Turkey have detracted from attention to the native population, complicating resentment in an already xenophobic climate.

Enter Recep Erdogan, Turkey's current president, who was elected prime minister in 2002 as a reformer dedicated to inclusion and stripping power from the country's elites. Erdogan served as prime minister until 2017, at which time he became president in a constitutionally changed system giving extraordinary power to the chief executive. Once he solidified his base, Erdogan portrayed himself as the only leader capable of uniting a fractured nation against its enemies. Instead, he used division as a wedge for dominance. He solidified his position with the conservative Sunni Muslim majority, issued a series of decrees that seized control of the press, rid the government of uncooperative bureaucrats, rounded up political opponents, and weakened potentially competing political parties.[21] He also purged the once-independent judiciary, leaving it little more than a rubber stamp for his policies.[22] After the main opposition party won control of Istanbul in 2019 municipal elections, its leader was charged with insulting the Turkish Republic and sentenced to nearly five years in prison, thereby assuring that she would not play a role in the 2023 presidential election.[23] Her demise was just another example of how Turkey's democracy devolved into an autocracy under Erdogan's control, all emanating from free elections that placed him in power. During the election campaign, Erdogan saw to it that his major opponent had virtually no publicity via the press. Even then, he barely won in a runoff forced because of his inability to secure an outright majority.

ANTI-DEMOCRATIC VALUES

In a democracy, a key function of government is to oversee the management of the economy. The degree of management coincides with the philosophical approach to the reach of government. Thus, in socialist democracies, the government has a major role in connecting the economy with the allocation of wealth. Relatively high taxation policies are employed particularly among the wealthy, from which economic subsidies are disproportionately dispersed to those with lower incomes in an effort to provide acceptable income floors.

In capitalist democracies, governments play a lesser role in redistributing benefits, although today, even the most private sector-oriented capitalist societies such as the United States provide some forms of social welfare for the economically challenged portions of the citizenry. Public education, health care, roads, and other elements of the infrastructure are made available to all citizens, including those with few means to pay what would be "their share." Less publicized but equally important, governments provide subsidies for struggling parts of the economy such as the computer chip industry (national government) and the movie industry (state governments). With capitalist democracies, government institutions work more toward promoting economic opportunity rather than attempting to close income gaps.

Whether socialist or capitalist, the governments of democracies respond to perceived needs of the people, although in different degrees and different ways. The primary difference lies in the extent to which governments make redistribution a larger or smaller part of the relationship. And if enough people feel the responses are unfair or inappropriate, they can express their displeasure through elections.

Economic Inequality

Beyond government assistance, there lies the question of economic mobility, the ease or difficulty for someone to improve his or her economic status. Along with chronic underinvestment in education, skills, public health, and technology, robust economic development will not occur. Many of these portals to success are controlled by those in power. And why is that important? Because economies, political development and governance are all connected. Which takes us to the controls of opportunities. Economist Jeffrey Sachs notes to the extent that authoritarian societies defend the privileges of the rich, democracies can't thrive. Too many obstacles keep those at the bottom of the economic ladder from moving up.[24]

Democracies weaken when the equality issue is ignored, or worse, abandoned. Daron Acemoglu and James A. Robinson describe this as an "extractive" problem, which occurs when elites "design economic institutions in order to enrich themselves and perpetuate their power at the expense of the vast majority of people in society."[25] The extraction of economic resources can occur to such an extent that a democratic government can fail, often leading to a dissatisfied public. Such a circumstance sets the conditions for political unrest or perhaps a revolt, which may result in creation of a repressive regime. Seymour Martin Lipset has noted that when governments fail to live up to economic expectations, they lose their legitimacy.[26] And that trend seems to be increasing. A study by the United Nations of income distribution patterns between 1990 and 2016 found 49 cases of rising economic inequality. Twenty-six of those instances occurred in Europe, Northern America, Oceania, and Japan, areas recently dominated by democracies.[27] Systemic or sudden economic inequality lowers trust in the political system, often leading to political instability that is artificially but successfully managed by the government's monopoly of coercion.[28]

Fragile economies are the enemy of democracy. Economic inequality tends to increase when societies suffer from an economic crisis, or even uncertainty. In their study of 17 European democracies, political scientists Leonardo and Mario Quartana found solid linkage between economic malaise and weakened democracies. Specifically, the authors discovered a general deterioration of the rule of law, growing concerns about what governments can do, and citizen detachment from key institutions. These kinds of negative reactions jeopardize a democracy's capacity to maintain its position in society.[29]

Sometimes, a noneconomic crisis can have a severe impact on the economy, which in turn, can lessen support for democracy, particularly if it is already weak. COVID-19, for example, ravaged governments everywhere; large portions of populations were out of work and businesses throughout the globe suffered greatly. Here again, already embattled democracies lacked the capacity to serve society much more than full democracies. This was particularly the case in "backsliding democracies," such as Hungary, Poland, India, and the Philippines. In all of these cases, loose ties to democracy were already prominently displayed in their parliaments, opposition parties, the courts, and the media.[30] Nevertheless, the executive leaderships in these countries used their nations' difficulties with COVID-19 as justification for expanding and solidifying their power. Thus, even as COVID-19 waned, the leaders continued to maintain expanded control on their populations.

Ethnic Divisions

Ethnic divisions plague almost every nation where the population is less than homogeneous. They can also serve as sources of tension between nations where different groups exist in close proximity, such as Hindu majorities in India and Muslim majorities in neighboring Pakistan. Even more common, ethnic divisions can exist within nations, where different groups struggle against one another for status, economic gains, and power. Sometimes, these rivalries also extend to longstanding disputes between different groups occupying the same territory. They often include violence, such as tensions between Flemish and Walloons in Belgium[31] and Catholics and Protestants in Northern Ireland.[32] Samuel Huntington writes that "Wars between clans, tribes, ethnic groups, religious communities, and nations have been prevalent in every era and every civilization because they are rooted in the identities of people."[33] Ethnic divisions also can keep democracies from thriving or, worse yet, subject democracies to decline.

The African continent serves as ground zero with respect to creating countries with internal ethnic divisions. Many nations that suffer from internal ethnic divisions are artificial creations in the sense that boundaries have been imposed on their populations by occupying countries. In fact, most of the 54 countries on the African continent were shaped out of agreements between a half dozen European nations beginning in 1884 and extending through the early twentieth century. In some cases, these colonial powers assigned boundaries created by rivers, mountains, and jungles. In others, they drew straight lines from one spot to another, with a different European country controlling each side, regardless of where different indigenous populations lived. Thus, many African national boundaries "cut through and enclosed hundreds of diverse and independent groups, with no common history, culture, language, or religion."[34] As a result, in some cases, like-minded populations were split into several European-controlled territories, while in other instances, a single territory contained numerous groups that had nothing in common other than the artificially created territory where they lived. Valuable resources such as rich agricultural land, diamonds, oil, and other precious raw materials also played a role in colonial powers determining boundaries.

Between Nations: The Somali People

Artificial divisions of territory from colonialism can disperse the same groups into different nations. Such movements often disrupt extended families, while weakening the social and economic fabric of a fractured society.

Consider the Somali people who once occupied the same political boundaries on the Horn of Africa. During the late 1800s, the major European colonial powers divided Somalis into what became French Somaliland, British Somalia, Italian Somalia, Ethiopian Somalia, and Kenya. Today, most Somalis live in the countries of Somali, Somaliland (a self-declared independent country from Somalia, although recognized as such by few nations), Ethiopia, Djibouti, and Kenya. The Afar people of Ethiopia suffered similar consequences, with their numbers split among what would become Ethiopia, Eritrea, and Djibouti. These artificial arrangements take a toll on the separated ethnic populations. Instead of groups and their traditions in a single location, their unnatural borders leave them with less commitment to their "homelands."[35] It slows down, if not completely interrupts, the ability for a society to congeal

Within Nations: Splintered Nigeria

The artificial organization of different groups within the same territory can cause a different set of problems. With different cultures occupying the same territory it's difficult to develop a sense of national cohesion.

In Nigeria, three distinctly different groups occupy different portions of the country; Igbo are in the southeast, Yoruba are in the southwest, and Haisa are in the North. But that's only the beginning of Nigeria's fractured status. One review of the three major groups divided them into more than 250 ethnic subgroups and over 500 spoken languages within Nigeria's borders. The author concludes that the country's ethnic compositions are "simply too 'culturally heterogeneous' to ever be cohesive."[37] So fragmented is the nation that presidential elections informally rotate among the three umbrella groups, with little regard for any political stability or continuity.

Given the historical colonialization patterns, it should not be surprising that many African countries suffer from a lack of common traditions, national values, and unified strategic objectives. As a result, it's difficult for democracies to thrive.

Military Coups

Sometimes, a democracy collapses through a coup, often staged by military leaders. For a coup to occur, an actor must seek to overthrow a nation's political head through illegal or unconstitutional force. When that occurs, commonly the affected nation is probably already under some form of stress or division. Weakness may be present in a weak infrastructure, incomplete commitment to democratic tenets, or a divisive controversy. Research shows that historically most military coups have occurred in authoritarian societies; however, since 2000 coup attempts have occurred increasingly in fragile or transitional democracies, where democratic norms are weak.[38] Whatever the preconditions, the inability of those democratically elected into power to persuade sizable elements of society of the benefits from their policies opens the way for revolution to take place.

Chile

An example of a military coup replacing a democratically chosen president occurred in Chile in 1973. Earlier in 1970, socialist candidate Salvador Allende was elected into office over a traditional capitalist conservative by an extraordinarily slim margin. Once in power, Allende carried out his reform promises by nationalizing several key industries, including copper mining and agriculture. Over time, the price of copper, Chile's most important industry, dropped dramatically, reducing the wages of large numbers of workers. Several copper miner-led strikes along with one unsuccessful coup occurred between 1971 and 1973, by which time most leaders of the army had dropped their support for Allende. On September 11, 1973, a military junta led by Chief of Staff General Augusto Pinochet and several key military allies staged a violent coup, which culminated with the assassination of Allende. Pinochet and his team created a temporary constitution in 1980, leading the way for a new constitutional vote in 1988. During this period, the military had to put down several strikes, where opponents were frequently beaten and jailed. The proposed constitution gave new expanded powers to the military and prohibited challenges by political parties to whatever the new president wanted to do, with Pinochet nominated as part of the package. But when the proposal went before the people, 55 percent voted against *Pinochet. In an about face, key military leaders sided with the outcome, and within 18 months,* Pinochet stepped down. However, democratic civilian rule in Chile was not returned until 1998.[39]

Myanmar

Another example of the military overtaking democracy can be seen in Myanmar (formally known as Burma). Freed from British colonial rule in 1948, Myanmar functioned as a democracy until 1962, when a coup launched by the military put the country under its control. From that point on, the military has interrupted democratic rule on several occasions., sometimes directly, other times indirectly. Fast forward to 2011, when the military established a "civilian" government run by a former army member. Four years later, the country had free elections, setting up the re-emergence of democratic rule. Aung San Suu Kyi, at the time a reformer and Nobel Peace Prize recipient under military house arrest for 15 years, emerged as the country's de facto leader in 2017. In 2020, the National League for Democracy, her political party, captured 70 percent of the seats for parliament, and Aung San Suu Kyi continued in her powerful position of State Counselor. However, her tenure was relatively brief. In 2021, the military once again placed Aung Suu Kyi under house arrest and resumed control, asserting that she had committed several crimes against the state.[40] In 2022, she was again convicted of crimes against the state and sentenced to eleven more years in prison. The domination of Myanmar by the military has now lasted over 60 years, with no sign of ending. Her punishment paled compared to the fates of others. Since the 2021 coup, the military rulers have imprisoned more than 12,000 pro-democracy politicians and executed dozens of others.[41]

Invasion

When a democracy is invaded by another nation, such an assault signals the beginning of war. The invader may prevail or be repelled depending on a series of factors including a military power advantage of either side, the intent of the invading nation, dedication of the invaders to the cause, capabilities of the invaded nation, and the commitment of the invaded nation to resist conquest. At its root, the invading nation has undemocratic values, for a nation with democratic principles would not include invasion as part of its relationship with others. This simple formula explains how twentieth-century wars such as World War I and World War II began. In each instance, an authoritarian nation (or collection of authoritarian nations) pursued the conquest of another nation (or nations), many of them democracies.

Sometimes, invasions occur because of the desire for political or territorial expansion; on other occasions, invasions take place because one nation's values are seemingly incompatible with or threatened by those of a nearby neighbor. The point is that invasions are not accidental endeavors. More often than not, they are very costly events in terms of lives, land, and the possible realignment of alliances and enemies. And even though they tend to be carefully planned assaults, invasions do not necessarily produce the expected results for those who undertake the effort.

Russia and Ukraine

The invasion of Ukraine by Russia in 2022 threatened not only the well-being of Ukraine but the security of many of the world's nations, particularly those on the European continent. It was also an unprecedented post–World War II occurrence where an authoritarian leader of an undemocratic nation forcibly attempted to take over a nonthreatening neighbor. As Thomas Friedman declared, "[Russian leader Vladimir] Putin is not only aiming to unilaterally rewrite the rules of the international system that have been in place since World War II—that no nation can just devour the nation next door—he is also out to alter that balance of power that he feels was imposed on Russia after the Cold War."[42]

How did the greatest threat to world peace since World War II come to be? To begin with, Russia and Ukraine have a long history. More than a thousand years ago, Kyiv, now the Ukrainian capital, was actually the capital of what was then greater Russia. For several centuries thereafter, Russian leaders paternalistically referred to Ukraine as "little Russia."[43] During the 1800s, Ukraine struggled without success to become a self-governing entity, although the peoples of the two countries shared many cultural traits and traditions. Fast forward to the days after the Russian Revolution (1917–1923), when Ukraine, a semi-autonomous nation at the time, was swept into the newly formed Union Soviet Socialist Republics. For the next several decades, Ukraine suffered at the hands of Soviet leaders who coveted the region's rich land and imposed harsh treatment on its people. Ukraine remained part of the Soviet bloc until 1991, when it declared independence as the USSR dissolved. Even then, Russia meddled in Ukrainian politics, albeit from a distance.

Governance in the new independent Ukraine was mostly under authoritarian rule until 2014, when a democratic regime assumed power after a series of riots against Russian-supported President Victor Yanukovych, who fled to Russia. However, Russia's Putin had other ideas. Shortly thereafter, the return to Ukrainian democracy, on March 17, 2014, Russian troops seized and annexed Crimea, a sliver of Ukraine, in the southeast part of the country adjacent to Russia. President Putin justified the illegal annexation by claiming without any foundation that "Crimea has always been an integral part of Russia in the hearts and minds of people."[44] With only a small military presence at the time, Ukraine was powerless to do anything about Putin's military move.

Incensed by Putin's hostile takeover of its territory, Ukraine attempted to draw away from Russian influence, with its leaders increasingly expressing the desire to join the European Union and the North Atlantic Treaty Organization (NATO). Such ideas were viewed by Putin as yet further indications of Western powers encroaching on Russia's sphere of influence. In fact, Putin thought they were part of an intentional post-1991 orchestration by the West to extend its influence to nations historically connected to Russia.[45] Several nations previously part of the Soviet Bloc or nearby satellites had joined NATO, confirming Putin's concerns.[46]

Ukraine's Westward drift continued, nevertheless. In 2019, Volodymyr Zelenskyy, running as an anti-establishment political reform candidate, won election to the Ukrainian presidency. Although Zelenskyy sought closer relations with the European Union and NATO, he repeatedly reached out to Putin to improve relations with his eastern neighbor, but the Russian leader had other ideas.[47]

On February 21, 2022, Russia recognized two breakaway eastern regions of Ukraine with large Russian-speaking populations bordering Russia as autonomous republics. Three days later, on February 24, 2022, a full-scale Russian invasion of Ukraine commenced. As to why Putin invaded Ukraine, he said in a speech to his nation, "Ukraine for us is not just a neighboring country, it is an integral part of our own history, cultural and spiritual space."[48] Putin further explained the invasion as a necessary measure to protect Russian security, although no such threat ever occurred. With that justification, Ukraine became the first democracy since World War II to suffer an attempted conquest.

Vladimir Putin drew near universal condemnation for ordering the Russian invasion of Ukraine. NATO, the European Community, and even the United Nations General Assembly, by a margin of 141-to-5 (with 35 abstentions), all stood resolutely against the unwarranted military aggression. By the end of the first year of the Russian invasion, a United States-led coalition had spent more than one hundred billion dollars in providing weapons and training to Ukrainian forces. Within the United States, anger over the Russian movement was largely bipartisan, as seen through the passage of several monetary allocations by one-sided votes in Congress.

Against the widespread denunciation of Putin stood former president Donald Trump, who described the Russian authoritarian as a "genius" who was "savvy" and "brilliant."[49] Trump's praise of Putin was hardly a surprise. The former American president had no qualms about Putin's seizure of Crimea in 2014, saying during the 2016 presidential campaign, "the people of Crimea, from what I've heard, would rather be with Russia than where they were."[50] In response to a Putin-ordered assassination of an ex-Russian spy in the United Kingdom, Trump only slapped modest sanctions against Russia because of intense pressure from Congress.[51] Perhaps most revealing about Trump was his reaction to incontrovertible U.S. intelligence that Russia repeatedly interfered with the 2016 presidential election. Trump publicly rejected the evidence at a press conference following a 2018 Helsinki summit with Putin: "He [Putin] said it's not Russia [that interfered]. I don't see why it would be."[52] As far as Trump was concerned, Putin could do no wrong, as noted in Trump's praise for Putin at the dawn of the Russian invasion of Ukraine. Only after about 10 days of Russia indiscriminately pummeling Ukraine did the former American president finally refer to the slaughter as "a holocaust." Nevertheless, it was Trump's earlier week of constant praise for Putin that fed the Russian propaganda machine.

AN END TO AMERICAN EXCEPTIONALISM OR A BLIP?

Shortly after the end of World War II, much of the world became divided into two camps, democracies and totalitarian forms of government. With the United States assisting a post–World War II group of nations committed to democracy, America became the example for the world of freedom, egalitarianism, and civil society.[53] Writing in the midst of the Cold War, Leslie Lipson noted, "The international responsibility which the United States now manfully shoulders, because ours is the strongest of the democratic states, has made this country the object of attention and curiosity, of envy and attack, from many quarters."[54] Clearly, the United States stood out as a beacon of democracy.

In the wake of a victory over the Axis powers (Germany, Italy, and Japan) and subsequent huge post–World War II immigration influx, Nathan Glazer and Daniel Patrick Moynihan wrote, perhaps proudly, of "the powerful assimilatory influences of American society." They forecasted that the children of immigrants would lead different lives than their parents and become absorbed in a unique, rich multicultural cloth,[55] thereby enriching the nation's political and social fabric. This infusion would bolster the democratic underpinnings of American political culture. That, in turn, would be an asset to maintaining American democracy.

However, an endless series of events in the United States, particularly as they relate to the management of public authority and racial discrimination, suggest the possibility that this once aspirational beacon of democracy may be losing its brilliance. If true, a socio-political devolution may portend unfortunate consequences not only within the United States but for democracies throughout the world. Freedom House, a nonprofit that views democracy as dependent upon political rights and civil liberties, found that over a ten-year period between 2010 and 2020, the United States slipped from a score of 94 out of 100 points to 83. During that time, the United States left the company of France and the Czech Republic (each at 95 on the scale) and joined the likes of Monaco and South Korea (each at 83), followed closely by Poland and Ghana (each at 82). Among the concerns about the United States expressed in the Freedom House report:

- Persistent challenges to the free and fair presidential election outcome
- Attempts to strip some state leaders from constitutional election responsibilities
- New state laws leading to de facto disenfranchisement of racial and ethnic minority communities
- Disruption of transparency
- Harsh criticism of the mainstream media, including violence against journalists
- A spike in religious hate crimes
- Threats to academic freedom
- A series of aggressive and unnecessary police killings of Black civilians
- A widening of the wealth gap and narrowing of access to upward mobility[56]

Much of the Freedom House criticism focused on actions taken throughout the Donald Trump presidential administration, suggesting the possibility of a temporary minor deviation from American tradition. However, numerous studies posit that America's decline has a history extending from well before the Trump years. For example, Steven Levitsky and Daniel Ziblatt trace the beginning of deteriorating American democratic norms back to

1978.⁵⁷ In another assessment, Suzanne Mettler and Robert Lieberman find cracks dating from the 1960s to the present.⁵⁸ The point is that considerable evidence points to anti-democratic factors and conditions in the United States long before Trump created an environment from which Trump profited greatly.

Deviation from the norm can go on for only so long before deviation becomes the new norm. In 2021, an evaluation by *The Economist* placed the United States in the category of "flawed democracy," rather than "full democracy," for the sixth straight year largely due to "long-running cultural wars," polarization, and "the refusal of the outgoing president (Donald Trump) to accept the election result."⁵⁹ During the previous decade, the United States slipped from the 17th most democratic nation to the 25th, and now with a "flawed" designation as part of its description.

Even Americans know something is amiss in American society these days, although they disagree over "what." Asked in early 2021 about "how well is democracy working in the United States," 45 percent agreed that "democracy isn't functioning properly," while 38 percent answered that "democracy is working somewhat well."⁶⁰ Sentiments grew more daunting throughout the year. An NPR/Ipsos poll conducted at the end of 2021 found that 64 percent of Americans believed American democracy "is in a crisis and at the risk of failing."⁶¹ Among America's youth, in a poll of individuals ages 18–29, 13 percent described the United States as "a failed democracy," while 39 percent labeled the American system of governance as "a troubled democracy."⁶² Such sentiments are not exactly ringing endorsements of political conditions in the United States.

And what might we do if American democracy is not working well? A troubling insight into that question emerged in early 2022 with the results from a *Washington Post* poll. With the January 6, 2021, violent insurrection against Congress in the Capitol as a backdrop, a national survey asked respondents, "Do you think it is ever justified for citizens to take violent action against the government?" Thirty-four percent of the respondents answered "yes."⁶³

Clearly, for many Americans, the system no longer works, and they may be ready to do something about it. The question is, why? Clearly, there is no simple answer, but the nation's inability to come to terms with an increasingly pluralistic society and the manipulation of that inability by a would-be authoritarian element plays a huge role.

NOTES

1. Barbara F. Walter, *How Civil Wars Start* (New York, NY: Crown Publishing Company, 2022), p. 34.

2. Larry Diamond, "Empowering the Poor: What Does Democracy Have to Do with It?," Deepa Narayan (ed.), *Measuring Empowerment: Cross-Disciplinary Perspectives* (Washington, DC: The World Bank, 2005), p. 411, https://openknowledge.worldbank.org/entities/publication/847bc88a-b2db-5e7e-b271-cb587bb2bebe.

3. See Alina Mungiu-Pippidi, "Corruption: Diagnosis and Treatment," *The Journal of Democracy*, 17, no. 3 (July 2006): 86–99, https://muse.jhu.edu/pub/1/article/200112.

4. "Anticorruption in Transition: A Contribution to the Policy Debate," The World Bank, Washington, DC, 2000, p. 40, http://web.worldbank.org/archive/website00504/WEB/PDF/TOC-7.PDF.

5. See Katya Gorchinskaya, "A Brief History of Corruption in Ukraine: The Yushchenko Era," *eurasianet*, May 28, 2020, https://eurasianet.org/a-brief-history-of-corruption-in-ukraine-the-yushchenko-era.

6. For a thorough analysis of Mexico's failed experiment, see Vanda Felbab-Brown, "The Ills and Cures of Mexico's Democracy," The Brookings Institution, Washington, DC, March 11, 2019, https://www.brookings.edu/wp-content/uploads/2019/03/FP_20190315_mexico_felbab_brown.pdf.

7. "Mexico Referendum on Former Leaders Has Low Turnout," *The Wall Street Journal*, August 2, 2021, https://www.wsj.com/articles/mexico-referendum-on-former-leaders-has-low-turnout-11627923776.

8. "Mexico: Recall Referendum Ruse Leaves No One Satisfied," *Civicus*, April 22, 2022, https://lens.civicus.org/mexico-recall-referendum-ruse-leaves-no-one-satisfied/.

9. "The 10 Most Corrupt Countries, Ranked by Perception," *U.S. News and World Report*, April 13, 2021 https://www.usnews.com/news/best-countries/articles/10-most-corrupt-countries-ranked-by-perception?slide=10.

10. "A New Low for Global Democracy," *The Economist*, February 2, 2022, https://www.economist.com/graphic-detail/2022/02/09/a-new-low-for-global-democracy.

11. Much of this paragraph comes from Michael Coppedge, "Venezuela: Popular Sovereignty Versus Liberal Democracy," Working Paper #294, April 2002, The Kellogg Institute, University of Notre Dame, Notre Dame, IN, https://kellogg.nd.edu/documents/1587.

12. See Gustavo Coronel, "The Corruption of Democracy in Venezuela," Cato Institute, Washington, DC, March 4, 2008, https://www.cato.org/commentary/corruption-democracy-venezuela.

13. Alisha Holland, "A Decade Under Chavez: Political Intolerance and Lost Opportunities for Advancing Human Rights in Venezuela," Human Rights Watch, New York, NY, 2008, https://www.hrw.org/sites/default/files/reports/venezuela0908web.pdf.

14. Rory Carroll, "Hugo Chavez Revolution Mired by Claims of Corruption," *The Guardian*, April 18, 2010, https://www.theguardian.com/world/2010/apr/18/hugo-chavez-revolution-corruption-claims.

15. Lucien W. Pye, *Aspects of Political Development* (Boston, MA: Little Brown and Company, 1966), p. 88.

16. Ibid., p. 16.

17. Barbara F. Walter elaborates on this linkage in her *How Civil Wars Start*, pp. 19–21.

18. "Global State of Democracy Report 2021," The International Institute for Democracy and Electoral Assistance, Stockholm, Sweden, https://www.idea.int/gsod/global-report.

19. The information in this section comes from Kemal Kirisci and Amanda Sloat, "The Rise and Fall of Liberal Democracy in Turkey: Implications for the West," The Brookings Institution, Washington, DC, February 2019, https://www.brookings.edu/research/the-rise-and-fall-of-liberal-democracy-in-turkey-implications-for-the-west/.

20. "The EU-Turkey Deal, Five Years On: A Frayed and Controversial but Enduring Blueprint," The Migration Policy Institute, April 8, 2021, https://www.migrationpolicy.org/article/eu-turkey-deal-five-years-on.

21. "From Reformer to 'New Sultan': Erdogan's Populist Revolution," *The Guardian*, March 11, 2019, https://www.theguardian.com/world/2019/mar/11/from-reformer-to-new-sultan-erdogans-populist-evolution

22. "Erdogan's Purges Leave Turkey's Justice System Reeling," *The New York Times*, June 21, 2019, https://www.nytimes.com/2019/06/21/world/asia/erdogan-turkey-courts-judiciary-justice.html.

23. "Turkish Court Upholds Politician's Prison Term," *The Wall Street Journal*, May 13, 2022, https://www.wsj.com/articles/turkish-court-upholds-prison-sentence-for-opposition-leader-11652374773.

24. Jeffrey D. Sachs, *Commonwealth: Economics for a Crowded Planet* (New York, NY: Penguin Press, 2008), pp. 223–224.

25. Daron Acemoglu and James A. Robinson, *Why Nations Fail: The Origins of Power, Prosperity, and Poverty* (New York, NY: Crown Publishers, 2012), p. 399.

26. Seymour Martin Lipset, *The First New Nation* (New York, NY: Doubleday Books, 1967), p. 68.

27. See United Nations, Department of Economic and Social Affairs, "World Social Report 2020: Inequality in a Rapidly Changing World," file:///Users/gerstondocs/Downloads/World-Social-Report-2020.pdf.

28. Karen Stenner, *The Authoritarian Dynamic* (New York, NY: Cambridge University Press, 2005), p. 17.

29. Leonardo Morlino and Mario Quaranta, "What is the Impact of the Economic Crisis on Democracy?" *The American Political Science Review*, 37, no. 5 (November 2016), https://www.jstor.org/stable/26556876.

30. Annika Silva-Leander, "Exploring the Impact of COVID-19 on Democracies," Institute for Democracy and Electoral Assistance (IDEA), April 14, 2020, idea.int/news-media/news/devastating-effects-covid-19-democracy-what-if-there-silver-lining.

31. See Chineyer Obari, "Belgium: The Case of Flanders and Wallonia," *Harvard Political Review*, July 22, 2021, https://harvardpolitics.com/flanders-and-wallonia/.

32. "Northern Ireland's Troubles began 50 years ago. Here's why they were so Violent," *The Washington Post*, August 22, 2019, https://www.washingtonpost.com/politics/2019/08/22/why-were-troubles-so-bloody-this-helps-explain/.

33. Samuel P. Huntington, *The Clash of Civilizations and the Remaking of World Order* (New York, NY: Simon and Schuster, 1966), p. 252.

34. Efem Ubi and Vincent Ibonye, "Is Liberal Democracy Failing in Africa or Is Africa Failing under Liberal Democracy?" *Taiwan Journal of Democracy*, 15, no. 2 (December 2019): 147, http://www.tfd.org.tw/export/sites/tfd/files/publication/journal/137-164-Is-Liberal-Democracy-Failing-in-Africa-or-Is-Africa-Failing-under-Liberal-Democracy.pdf.

35. See, Tasew Gashaw, "Colonial Borders in Africa: Improper Design and Its Impact on African Borderland Communities," Africa Up Close, Woodrow Wilson Center, https://africaupclose.wilsoncenter.org/colonial-borders-in-africa-improper-design-and-its-impact-on-african-borderland-communities/.

36. Lucien Pye discusses this in his *Aspects of Political Development* (Boston, MA: Little, Brown and Company, 1970), pp. 6–8 and 78–81.

37. Eniola Anuoluwapo Soyemi, "Failures of a Weak State Are to Blame for Nigeria's Ethnicity Problem," *The Conversation*, August 29, 2016, https://theconversation.com/failures-of-a-weak-state-are-to-blame-for-nigerias-ethnicity-problem-64186.

38. "Annual Risk of Coup Report," *One Earth Future*, Broomfield, CO, April 2019, https://oneearthfuture.org/publication/annual-risk-of-coup-report-2019.

39. See Lester Kurtz, "Chile: Struggle against a Military Dictator (1985-1988)," International Center of Nonviolent Conflict, Washington, DC, June 2009, https://www.nonviolent-conflict.org/chile-struggle-military-dictator-1985-1988/.

40. Lindsay Maizland, "Myanmar's Troubled History: Coups, Military Rule, and Ethnic Conflict," Council on Foreign Relations, Washington, DC, January 31, 2022, https://www.cfr.org/backgrounder/myanmar-history-coup-military-rule-ethnic-conflict-rohingya.

41. "Myanmar Executes Four Pro-Democracy Activists, Defying Foreign Leaders," *The New York Times*, July 25, 2022, https://www.nytimes.com/2022/07/25/world/asia/myanmar-executions.html.

42. Thomas L. Friedman, "We Have Never Been Here Before," *The New York Times*, February 27, 2022, https://www.nytimes.com/2022/02/25/opinion/putin-russia-ukraine.html.

43. For an excellent history of Ukraine and its historical relationship with Russia, see Anne Applebaum, *Red Famine: Stalin's War on Ukraine* (New York, NY: Anchor Books, 2017).

44. "Putin Reclaims Crimea for Russia and Bitterly Denounces the West," *The New York Times*, March 18, 2014, https://www.nytimes.com/2014/03/19/world/europe/ukraine.html.

45. "Putin's Endgame: Undo Post-Cold War Accords," *The Wall Street Journal*, February 22, 2022, https://www.wsj.com/articles/putins-endgame-unravel-the-post-cold-war-agreements-that-humiliated-russia-11645482412.

46. In all, seven previously communist nations joined connected with Russia joined NATO: three Soviet Republics (Estonia, Latvia, and Lithuania) and four members of the Warsaw Pact, the Soviet Union's response to NATO: Bulgaria, Romania, Slovakia, and Slovenia. See "7 Former Communist Countries Join NATO," *The Washington Post*, March 30, 2004, https://www.washingtonpost.com/archive/politics/2004/03/30/7-former-communist-countries-join-nato/476d93dc-e4bd-4f05-9a15-5b66d322d0e6/.

47. For an interesting history of the events leading up to Russia's invasion of Ukraine, see Simon Shuster, "The Road to War," *Time*, February 14-21, 2022, https://time.com/6144109/russia-ukraine-vladimir-putin-viktor-medvedchuk/.

48. Quoted in "Putin Speech Takes Swipe at U.S.-Led International Order," *The Wall Street Journal*, February 22, 2022, https://www.wsj.com/articles/putin-address-takes-swipe-at-u-s-led-world-order-11645485419.

49. "Trump has been on Putin's Side in Ukraine's Long Struggle against Russian Aggression," *CNN*, March 6, 2022, https://www.cnn.com/2022/03/06/politics/trump-putin-ukraine/index.html.

50. Christian Caryl, "Donald Trump's Talking Points on Crimea Are the Same as Vladimir Putin," *The Washington Post*, July 3, 2018, https://www.washingtonpost.com/news/democracy-post/wp/2018/07/03/donald-trumps-talking-points-on-crimea-are-the-same-as-vladimir-putins/.

51. "Under Pressure, Trump Slaps Long-Overdue Sanctions on Russia over Weapons Use," *CNN*, August 2, 2019, https://www.cnn.com/2019/08/02/politics/trump-russia-sanctions-chemical-weapons-spy-poisoning/index.html.

52. "Trump Publicly Sides with Putin on Election Interference," *Politico*, July 16, 2018, https://www.politico.com/story/2018/07/16/trump-russia-putin-summit-722418.

53. Among the various books over the past half century, see Gabriel Almond and G. Bingham Powell, Jr., *Comparative Politics: A Developmental Approach* (New York: Little, Brown and Company, 1966).

54. Leslie Lipson, *The Democratic Civilization* (New York: Oxford University Press, 1964), p. 578.

55. Nathan Glazer and Daniel Patrick Moynihan, *Beyond the Melting Pot* (Cambridge, MA: The M.I.T. Press, 1963), p. 12.

56. "Special Report 2021, From Crisis to Reform: A Call to Strengthen America's Battered Democracy," Freedom House, 2021, p. 3, https://freedomhouse.org/report/special-report/2021/crisis-reform-call-strengthen-americas-battered-democracy.

57. *How Democracies Die* (New York, NY: Penguin Random House LLC, 2019), pp. 146–167.

58. *Four Threats: The Recurring Crises of American* Democracy (New York, NY: St. Martin's Press, 2020), pp. 212–222.

59. "Democracy Index 2020: In Sickness and Health?" *The Economist*, 2021, p, 44, https://www.eiu.com/public/topical_report.aspx?campaignid=democracy2020.

60. "Few in US Say Democracy is Working Well," Associated Press and NORC (Chicago), February 8, 2021, https://apnews.com/article/ap-norc-poll-us-democracy-403434c2e728e42a955c72a652a59318.

61. "6 in 10 Americans Say U.S. Democracy in Crisis as the 'Big Lie' Takes, Root," *NPR*, January 3, 2022.

62. "Harvard Youth Poll," Cambridge, MA, Fall 2021, https://iop.harvard.edu/youth-poll/fall-2021-harvard-youth-poll.

63. "1 in 3 Americans Say Violence against Government can be Justified, Citing Fears of Political Schism, Pandemic," *The Washington Post*, January 1, 2022, https://www.washingtonpost.com/politics/2022/01/01/1-3-americans-say-violence-against-government-can-be-justified-citing-fears-political-schism-pandemic/.

Part II

THE IMPACT OF BIGOTRY

In part I of *Trumpism, Bigotry, and the Threat to American Democracy*, chapters 1 and 2 focused on how democracies thrive and, yet, so easily deteriorate. With those chapters as background, part II centers on racism, a key element of bigotry, and its potential for endangering democracy. We begin in chapter 3 with a definition of racism and its presence in political environments where those in power constitute both majority and minority populations in their countries. Some countries officially classified as "democracies" exhibit racism, which augurs the refrain, can democracies exist as such if large segments of the population are denied the basic tenants of equality? We believe not.

Following this chapter, we build on the deleterious impact of racism in the United States. In chapter 4, we turn to the history of racism in the United States treated by the Congress, federal courts and American presidents. In chapter 5, we turn to the lifelong approach to race by Donald Trump, clearly establishing that his conduct during the 2016 presidential campaign and subsequent years in the presidency was simply an extension of racist behavior exhibited throughout his entire life.

The three chapters in part II clearly show that racism has a long history in governments throughout the world as well as in the United States. Moreover, Donald Trump and Trumpism may be viewed as a continuation of practices and policies in everyday American life. The primary difference with Trump, however, has been the extent to which he has been so open about his prejudices and willing to use them as a vehicle for obtaining power and subverting American democracy.

Chapter 3

Bigotry as a Threat to Democracy

Racism is a commonly discussed subject, yet often without any concrete definition or consensus. To begin, we must distinguish between a *racist* and *racism* as political themes. When an individual systematically acts against another viewed as inferior because of certain physical features, origins or approaches to life, he or she may well be considered a racist for treating such a person as less than equal or even worthless. The demarcating factors may be something like skin color or perhaps the shape of eyes, noses, or lips. More expansively, if one looks down on another because of a religious affiliation or ethnic background, that too, may well be an example of racist behavior regardless of race.

Rather than focusing on an individual's behavior toward another or cluster of individuals, racism is an ongoing condition of discrimination in a widespread and persistent institutional context. It occurs when government actors or others in positions of authority or prominence in the public or private sectors systematically deny benefits and/or opportunities to a group on the basis of perceived inferiority. This may be done through legislation or informal practices. Racism may also occur with government approval of racist groups or organizations that threaten or harm those deemed to be inferior or unworthy of societal participation. Here we refer not to the interaction between one person and another or others presumably on unequal power footings, but rather the explicit or tacit enforcement capabilities of government to deny benefits or opportunities to those who would have them were it not for specific features or behaviors.

At its core, racism is a form of ongoing oppression as well as a tactic for minimizing the psychological, social, and political potential of subordinate individuals or groups.[1] Modern racism has its roots in slavery, which began as early as 6800 BC, when, as a result of their victories, Mesopotamians forced captured enemies to work as slaves.² For centuries thereafter, race and slavery remained largely independent of one another until the late 1300s, when Portuguese traders first brought Africans to Europe by ship to alleviate a labor shortage.

One more consideration: In the strictest sense, racism refers to attitudes about and actions against groups with distinguishing physical and religious characteristics. In today's world, discrimination also occurs against gay members of society as well as those who identify as transgender individuals. Abuse of these groups often accompanies racist behaviors toward others.

Whether in the hands of governments or other power centers, racism underscores, and legitimizes institutionalized inequality. That's because of the power of governments to enforce discriminatory laws, values, and norms. Such aberrant behavior can occur in the workplace, residence, education settings, health care access conditions, and just about any environment where an entity with clout can deny or compel specific behaviors of others. If individuals or groups are denied the same opportunities and guarantees offered to others because of prejudiced assessments or artificially different standards, they may be the victims of racism.

The difference between racist behavior and racism lies with enforcement capability as much as philosophy. Nevertheless, whether individually or institutionally, the intent to deny the dignity of equality to assigned groups presents the same outcome: some are disfavored compared to others. Such behaviors are inherently undemocratic. As Michael Hanchard notes, "Institutions that operate according to racist and xenophobic precepts must ultimately operate in an idiosyncratic, anti-democratic, and highly subjective manner."[3] Where there is such disparity, by definition, democracy cannot exist in societies that practice racism.

BIGOTRY IN A GLOBAL CONTEXT

Institutionalized racism is practiced throughout the world; in fact, it's hard to find where institutionalized racism is not practiced. If racism were a disease, it would be classified as a pandemic; it's that universal and ongoing. We say this knowing that many nations don't acknowledge or keep records of racism. That caveat notwithstanding, in 2021, ongoing racism was officially reported in at least 34 nations, including the United States.[4] In other nations, more times than not, it's not a question of "whether" racism exists as much as it's an issue of "to what extent" and "explicit or implicit." Below, we focus on three cases of racism practiced by a government reflecting the majority population, followed by three cases of racism practiced by governments in the hands of minority populations. Regardless of majority or minority power constructs, all of these examples share the prominence of institutionalized inequality. Collectively, they also illustrate the various conditions under which racism may exist.

Tyranny of the Majority

China

With more than 1.4 billion people, China is the world's most populated country; it's also an exceptionally diverse country. Studies show that within China, there are 56 unique ethnic groups, of which the Han is by far the largest, with 92 percent of the total population and a history that goes back more than 3,000 years. Clearly, in terms of numbers, the Han tower over the remaining 55 ethnic groups.

"Majority" doesn't necessarily mean total dominance when describing the relationship between groups, but that seems to be the case in China when it comes to citizenship and political rights. That's because, in China, the Han ethnicity, national identity, and governance combined are overlapping elements on the question about who the *real* Chinese are—at least as far as the Han are concerned. Typically, the Han obtain the best jobs, political connections, and the most favorable treatment from those in positions of authority. As for the other 55 minority groups, most are marginalized, with their disparaging descriptions running the gamut from "charming and colorful" to "wild and savage."[5] Such depictions do not auger well for political, social, and economic equality in China and, therefore, democracy.

This leads us to a discussion of the Uyghurs, a relatively small ethnic group consisting of about 12,000,000 people, with the largest number dwelling in a remote, autonomous region in the most western part of China. Like the Asian countries immediately to their west, Uyghurs speak their own language, not Mandarin, which is the favored language used by 70 percent of the Chinese population. Uyghurs also abide by ancient Muslim rituals and the worship of Allah, an all-knowing god whose wisdom guides them. They also wear special clothing mirroring ancient Middle Eastern attire found in other Muslim sects. For their part, most Chinese honor Confucianism, Daoism, and Buddhism, which center on rituals, philosophical and ethical teachings, and celebrations of cultural heritage. These beliefs don't center on worshipping any single God as much as they focus on universal concepts such as benevolence, respect, and the balance between humans and nature. To say that Uyghurs don't mesh well with the Han is a gross understatement.

Uyghurs have been targeted by the government since the formation of the Chinese Communist Party in 1949. However, since 2017, the Han have been particularly brutal to Uyghurs. The best estimates are that between

800,000 and 2,000,000 Uyghurs have been detained in concentration camps by Chinese officials, comprising the largest mass internment of any ethnic or religious minority since World War II.[6] The pretexts for detention include unauthorized travel, inadequate identification, and, in many cases, having too many children. But the most common reason lies with the commitment of Uyghurs to the Muslim religion, which government officials argue is an extremist link to separatism and terrorism and, therefore, a threat to the Chinese way of life.

The Chinese government describes the detention camps as government offices for "vocational training" and "thought transformation," but research has chronicled involuntary labor, conversion efforts to the teachings of the Chinese Communist Party, and enforced sterilization in an effort to eliminate the Uyghur population.[7] As a result of the government's strict measures, the Uyghur birth rate declined by 84 percent between 2015 and 2018.[8] With estimates of Uyghur death rates averaging between 5 and 10 percent per year,[9] it's only a matter of time before this minority disappears altogether.

There is nothing accidental about the relationship between the Chinese government and the Uyghur minority. In this situation, an authoritarian government has intentionally adopted a policy to minimize, if not eliminate, a minority with values outside those of the majority. And despite the Chinese government's claim that such persecutions have stopped, there is no independent evidence to support such a claim. In 2021, 43 nations signed on to a statement criticizing China for human rights abuses of the Uyghurs.[10] In March 2022, U.S. Secretary of State Antony Blinken described the Chinese behavior toward the Uyghurs as "ongoing genocide."[11] The institutional racism pattern of the Chinese government toward the Uyghurs is clear; it is a classic, tragic case of ethnic cleansing. Politically, the Chinese government has no room for this minority and the best way to deal with its persistence is by eliminating it.

Turkey

The deterioration of Turkey from a democracy to an authoritarian regime has been discussed in chapter 2. Initially, Recep Erdogan gained high office through a free election. Nevertheless, between 2013 and 2018, he abandoned the very values that allowed him to gain office and used his new power to weaken opponents in the bureaucracy and purge political rivals. He converted a once-independent judiciary into a reliable ally that rubber stamped his policies. Furthermore, he methodically eliminated Turkey's free press. With these efforts, Erdogan strengthened his hold on the Turkish presidency.

Erdogan cleverly took advantage of the times and foreign policy issues to work his will. The inability of Turkey to gain membership into the European Union, ongoing squabbles with nearby Greece over Cyprus, and a loyal xenophobic Islamic base of support all assisted Erdogan's transformation from political reformer to political strong man.[12] Along the way, Erdogan turned on Turkey's small Christian population as a primary source of his country's problems. His target was not new, but rather a revival of past religious tensions in Turkey.

Christians have been part of the area now known as Turkey since the beginning of the Common Era, accounting for about a quarter of the country's population. Collectively, the denominations included Greek Orthodox and Turkish Syriac Christians as well as Catholics and Protestants. That proportion of Turkey's Christian population changed abruptly in 1915 when Turks, staggering from their dissembled Ottoman Empire, murdered 1.5 million Turkish Christian Armenians over the next decade, falsely blaming them for Turkey's demise as a major regional political power.[13]

When the modern country we know as Turkey was formed in 1925, anti-Christian discrimination continued. Meanwhile, during the years following the slaughter, the percentage of Christian Turks slipped to about 5 percent of the population. Recent percentages of Christians have dwindled even more. Christian Turks account for a small fraction of one percent today, estimated by the U.S. State Department at perhaps 50,000.[14] Rather than ignore Christians for their small size, Turkish leaders like Erdogan have made it a mission to pursue Christians as the reasons for Turkey's problems.

But Erdogan hasn't stopped with discrimination of Christians. In 2017, The United Nations Human Rights Commission documented hundreds of killings in Turkey, this time of Kurds, another minority in Turkey, without a single prosecution. One hundred thousand Kurds were dismissed from their jobs because of unsubstantiated government accusations that they were connected with the Kurdistan Workers Party, considered by the government to be a terrorist organization.[15] In 2020, Genocide Watch accused Turkish troops of invading nearby northern Syria and executing thousands of Kurds and Christians.[16] Today, according to a report by the Stockholm Center for Freedom, non-Muslims may not have religious programs or places of worship; may not become part of the judiciary, a military or security professions; and may not even open bank accounts.[17]

Clearly, Recep Erdogan has revealed himself to be a racist authoritarian with no regard for democratic norms, and selected Turkish citizens have suffered for it without any penalty for Erdogan and his government. Still, he is not without enemies, in 2016, several hundred members of the Turkish military attempted a coup against Erdogan on the grounds that he had abandoned his commitment to a secular government and had all but eliminated the checks and balances from other government institutions.[18] The coup was quickly put down, but it nevertheless showed that some Turks were no longer willing to accept Erdogan's rule. For now, however, Erdogan has a grip on Turkeys politics and government.

Colombia

Facing the Pacific Ocean on one side of Panama and the Caribbean Sea on the other side, Colombia has been a nation in one form or another since 1819, when its people broke away from a large Spanish-controlled territory known as New Granada. Subsequent fissures led Colombia to separate from the larger group in the late 1880s. The final change in political geography occurred in 1903 when, with encouragement from the United States, the Panama portion of Colombia seceded and became its own country.

Until the Spanish "conquered" the region in the early 1500s, indigenous people (comparable to Native Americans) comprising about one hundred tribes populated the region. Over the three hundred years that the Spanish governed the area, they brought about one million slaves from Africa. The diversity of Colombia was set, with Mestizos (a combination of Spanish, other European White people, and Indigenous people), true Indigenous natives, and Black individuals (later dubbed Afro-Colombians) comprising almost all of the nation's population. According to government statistics, Mestizos are by far the most dominant group, with 85 percent of the population, followed by Afro-Colombians (10 percent) and true Indigenous people (5 percent). The accuracy of those percentages, however, may be subject to question. Data gathered by the United Nations in 2010 and Freedom House a decade later estimated that Afro-Colombians comprise about 25 percent of the country, a figure considerably higher than that presented by the Colombian government.[19] That kind of distortion in itself lends insight into how the Colombian government feels about its largest minority—not even worth counting. It also helps to explain why Colombia is considered a "partly free" country, according to Freedom House.[20]

Mistreatment of Afro-Colombians by the government has a long history. As far back as the fight for independence in 1822, hero Simón Bolívar excluded Afro-Colombians and Indigenous people from participating in the revolution against Spain.[21] Afro-Colombians were freed from slavery in midcentury, although until well into the twentieth century, most Afro-Colombians worked with little compensation in mines and on tobacco farms. While the government embarked on a policy of assimilation of most people of various ethnicities and races into the large Mestizo majority, Afro-Colombians were intentionally left out as intellectually deficient savages.[22] They were disproportionately poor and frequently displaced from their land despite specific constitutional guarantees written at several points during the twentieth century.[23] Those conditions remain constants for Afro-Colombians. Today, most live in "highly concentrated and geographically segregated communities."[24]

"On paper," the Colombian government has bent over backward to accept Afro-Colombians as equals. Yet, even in recent years, provisions were written into a new Colombian Constitution in 1991 that specifically allow Afro-Colombians, and in some cases, Indigenous people to return to their land, have been ignored.[25] Although the government finally acknowledged the presence of racial discrimination in 1998, literacy rates, health conditions, economic opportunities, and social mobility remain distinctly below those found in the majority. Whether at the national Ministry of Interior or police at local levels of government, discrimination against Afro-Colombians continues to be a mainstay of Colombian life.[26] The government may have settled a half-century-old insurrection with the Revolutionary Armed Forced of Colombia (FARC) in 2016, but it has not come to terms with its largest racial minority.

Tyranny of the Majority in Perspective

China, Turkey, and Colombia represent three cases where majority governments have used their power to keep specific minorities from attaining equality in just about every sense of the term, albeit each case with a different approach. China has sought to eliminate a "disgusting" minority with distinctly different values from the dominant culture. Turkey has denied fairness, justice, and economic opportunities to religious minorities without destroying them or chasing them out of the country, in the process using a more sophisticated approach than its wholesale slaughter of Syriac Christians a century ago. For its part, Colombia, where basic rights seem to exist for only some citizens, has ignored the conditions of its Afro-Colombian minority, despite clear constitutional guarantees and legislation that underscore the importance of equality.

These policies toward discriminated groups may have been different in strategies and tactics, but the outcomes have been strikingly similar—those discriminated against have suffered and continue to suffer at the hands of government authorities. Moreover, in every case, there is no sign that racist practices are about to change.

Tyranny of the Minority

South Africa

A casual glance at the government of modern South Africa might lead one to conclude that relatively recent events of officially ending apartheid have freed the country from historically undemocratic, racist bonds. That glance would only be partially correct. Yes, South Africa today enjoys free elections, and yes, the Black majority holds most of the country's leadership positions, but that's where the story gets interesting. The democratic symbolism of elections and official leadership positions notwithstanding, South Africa is much less of an egalitarian society than appearances suggest.

White European settlers—first Portuguese, then the Dutch, and ultimately the British explored, enslaved, and exploited the black population of what is now South Africa from 1488 until 1834, when the British Parliament officially ended slavery. Out of the mix, Dutch descendants known as Afrikaners dominated the political and economic landscapes. White control of the native population continued without interruption, with the all-White government quickly passing legislation that granted full citizenship to White people only.[27] In 1948, the government officially adopted "apartheid," an Afrikaner word meaning "apartness," a rigid policy of political, social, and economic segregation.

During the 1950s, Black people were assigned to specific residential areas and denied the opportunity to marry White people. Much like the segregationist era in the United States, Black South Africans also were required to use separate public facilities. Black opposition organized, much of it through the African National Congress, and for decades conducted strikes and protests against the apartheid policy. However, apartheid policies continued. Several government-passed acts ultimately assigned about 80 percent of South African land to White people only, with the added provision that the land must remain in White hands for future generations. Later in the decade, the White government further divided South Africa's race classification into four groups: Blacks, with about two-thirds of the population; Whites, about 15 percent; Coloreds, people of mixed races, about 10 percent, and others, mostly Asians, the rest.

South Africa was granted Independence from Great Britain in 1961 with little change in the segregated racial conditions. Shortly thereafter, all elements of citizenship were stripped from Black South Africans altogether. Given an economy that was dependent on cheap labor for mining and farming, the arrangement worked well for White people. Colored people fared slightly better than Black people, often with jobs as domestic workers or, in some cases, skilled trades. Other than a few symbolic concessions to Black people and other minorities, these laws remained in place through the 1980s.

Meanwhile, international pressure on the White South African government grew. During the 1970s, the United Nations officially condemned South African apartheid and ultimately imposed an embargo on the sale of arms to the country. A decade later, Great Britain and the United States imposed strict economic sanctions on the South African government. Then, in 1989, a much more favorable government under F. W. de Klerk began repealing various segregation laws. Finally, in 1994, a new non-White coalition government came to power and quickly ended all elements of apartheid. But the story did not end there.

South Africa's first few decades as a democracy have been bumpy. In the early years after independence from apartheid, the mostly Black national government developed a new constitution dedicated to political, civil, social, and economic rights for all. However, widespread corruption in the government soon developed. Government contracts for mining and other state-owned enterprises were awarded to a few elites, public services suffered, and South Africa remained impoverished. Most significantly, the economic gap between White people and others remained.

A Carnegie Endowment for International Peace Study of South Africa in 2021 found most White people thriving, with most Black people mired in chronic poverty. According to the study, while White people were 9 percent of the population, they represented two-thirds of South Africa's high-income earners.[28] Another study in 2016 found that while Black people accounted for nearly three-fourths of the population, they owned just 4 percent of the country's farmland. Meanwhile, White people, composing 9 percent of the population, owned 72 percent of South Africa's farmland.[29] With respect to the top management positions, two-thirds are held by White people, compared to 14 percent by Black people.[30] Even more important, the Carnegie study pointed to continued political inequality and exclusion of South Africa's Black population because of an "elite bargain" between white elites and the country's Black political leaders.[31] As part of that informal arrangement, "fronting," a tactic where Black people appear to own or manage businesses actually under White control, has added to the perpetuation of inequality.[32]

Political change does not always confer intended results. South Africa's transformation from governance by a minority to governance by the majority at best is a work in progress and at worst is a failure. Minority White control continues to persist, the politics of Black majority rule in government notwithstanding.[33] Apartheid has disappeared in name only. The situation is not entirely bleak: in his study of post-apartheid South Africa, Steven Friedman notes that Black people have abilities to exercise power they did not enjoy prior to 1994. However, he continues, "the state remains bifurcated in ways which sometimes mirror realities before apartheid ended."[34] Still, massive riots by Black people throughout 2021, indicates that majority Black power is a long way from reality.

Syria

It's hard to mention Syria without following (or preceding) it with the word "Assad." Hafez al-Assad and son, Bashar al-Assad have ruled the country without interruption for more than half a century. The Assads are Alawites, a small sect of Shia (non-Sunni) Arabs accounting for about 10 percent of Syria's population. Their group is badly outnumbered by Sunni Arabs, who make up about three-quarters of Syria's population. Whereas Shia claim to be

Muslims, Syrian Sunnis, believe otherwise, and that issue has long explained much of the hostility between the two groups.[35] Non-Arab Kurds and Christians comprise the remaining members of the population. In a country torn by ethnic and religious divisions, the Assads and their fellow Alawites have gained power and ruled ruthlessly in the process.

In some ways, it's not surprising that an autocratic regime would emerge in Syria. At the end of World War I, the Ottoman Empire was split up between France, Britain, and Russia. France gained control of Syria, Lebanon, a region known as Kurdistan, and part of what is now Turkey.[36] Like many of its other possessions, France did little for the future of self-governance in Syria. As Syria historian James Reilly notes, when the French left Syria in 1945, "France had created a Syrian *state* but French policy had discouraged the formation of a Syrian *nation*."[37] Much of the country's disarray showed after Syria's performance in the 1967 war, where Syria lost the Golan Heights region to Israel. The rest was predictable enough. With little political infrastructure, Syria floundered until 1970, when a coup toppled the weak Syrian government. Hafez al-Assad was part of that coup, dubbed "the corrective revolution." Within a year, he emerged as Syria's president and quickly installed fellow Alawites into the most important government and military positions.

Hafez al-Assad ruled Syria with an iron hand. His modest economic reforms were blended with a tradeoff of political repression. Under a state of emergency, al-Assad "restricted virtually all forms of dissent, and prohibited the operation of all independent media;"[38] he justified routine cruelty by Syrian security forces as part of the necessity to keep civil order. By the mid-1970s, Syria's branch of the Muslim Brotherhood, a transnational group dedicated to strict religious governance, became al-Assad's chief domestic enemy, and he treated it accordingly. One particularly brutal event occurred in 1982. For months, the Muslim Brotherhood rebelled against Assad in Hama, a city of about 400,000 people. Al-Assad dispatched 12,000 soldiers to the city, where they massacred more than 10,000 Muslim Brotherhood members and leveled the buildings.[39]

After the Hama atrocity, Syrian opposition to the elder al-Assad quieted; in the words of one authority, "most [opponents] had been killed, jailed, exiled, cowed, or co-opted."[40] When running for a fourth term of office in 1991, he received 99.9 percent of the vote. An observer of Syrian politics at the time claimed, "Even if Allah had run, he wouldn't have done as well."[41] Hafez al-Assad ruled until his death in 2000.

Unlike his father, Bashar al-Assad set his sights on becoming an ophthalmologist. Running Syria would be left to his older brother Bassel al-Assad, but that plan was thwarted because of an automobile accident that ended Bassel's life. Thus, Bashar assumed the Syrian presidency. At first, he showed some signs of liberalizing his country. He released some prisoners, welcomed back exiles and spoke of eliminating corruption and modernizing Syria's institutions in what was described as "Damascus Spring."

But Bashar al-Assad's fresh approach to governance didn't last long. Taking the younger al-Assad at his word, strict Islamists, Kurds, and even secularists, began making demands for various reforms. The government reacted by imprisoning opponents and shooting rioters, but many Syrians persisted in their opposition. By 2011, Bashar al-Assad was in a civil war chiefly against Sunni Muslims. Within a few months, the Sunnis were joined in a loose coalition by Syrian Army defectors and, ultimately, a branch of al-Qaeda, an extremist Muslim organization. The factions had little in common other than the enmity toward al-Assad. The conflict became a proxy war of sorts: Russia and Iran in support of al-Assad, and with the United States, France, the United Kingdom, and Saudi Arabia as well as Syrian Kurds in opposition.[42] Soon after, Turkey jumped into the fray, seizing Syrian land on its border to create a buffer between the two countries.

According to United Nations data, over the next ten years, the Syrian military killed more than 350,000 civilians.[43] As of 2011, Syria had 21 million people. Between 2011 and 2021, 6.8 million sought asylum in other countries, and another 6.7 million were displaced.[44] Most of the refugees fled to Turkey (3 million), Lebanon (1 million), and Jordan (500,000). On several occasions, Bashar al-Assad's soldiers used chemical weapons and barrel bombs, munitions with explosives that destroy large urban populations.[45]

By 2022, al-Assad's forces had reclaimed most of the land lost during the civil war, but at great cost. Of those Syrians remaining in country, more than 90 percent live in poverty. A special United Nations commission investigating the civil war found "grave violations of fundamental human rights and international humanitarian law . . ., including war crimes and ongoing patterns of crimes against humanity."[46] Meanwhile, in May 2021, Bashar al-Assad was "re-elected" to his third term as president with 95.1 percent of the vote. However, given his ruthless domination of the country, the vote was meaningless. No doubt, this explains why Freedom House gives Syria a score of 1 on its 1–100 democracy scale, accompanied only by South Sudan.[47]

Jamaica

At first glance, Jamaica might not seem like a racist society. The country has a two-party system, regular elections, and transparent governance. In its "democracy score," Freedom House rates Jamaica at 80 out of 100 possible points, just below the 83 points awarded to the United States.[48] However, racial discrimination is not always codified or open; in fact, it can seem to be part of a nation's DNA without any open discussion or acknowledgment, and that appears to be the case with Jamaica. Added to the unusual conditions is that virtually all residents of Jamaica—approximately 99 percent—are persons of color. Most discrimination takes place within the dominant Black race, rather than between races, with the shade of one's skin being the determining factor of status and power.

Like many parts of the Americas, Jamaica was born in slavery. "Discovered" by Columbus in 1494 and part of the Spanish Crown, Jamaica was claimed by the British in 1655 as part of the Crown along with many other parts of the Caribbean.[49] The Spanish had brought a few thousand African slaves to work the land after most of the original enslaved inhabitants had died from European diseases and abuses. Over the next 150 years, the number of Black slaves in Jamaica soared to 300,000, most to work the labor-intensive sugarcane fields. Occasional rebellions occurred during this period without success, but the breakthrough came with the Baptist War, a 10-day revolt that included as many as 60,000 slaves. Slavery was abolished in 1834, with limited voting opportunities extended to Black people a few years thereafter and limited self-government by the end of the century.

Throughout the first half of the twentieth-century Black Jamaicans lobbied for full independence, sometimes through political rallies, other times through strikes. After a period of "constitutional decolonization" beginning in 1944, Jamaicans were granted independence from the United Kingdom in 1962. Of the three million people in Jamaica, Black people account for 76.3 percent of the population, followed by Afro-Europeans (15.1 percent), East Indians and Afro-East Indians (3.2 percent), White people (1.2 percent), and Chinese (0.8 percent). African Jamaicans continue to be the dominant racial group.[50] Still, the two percent contingent of White people and Chinese account for much of the economic clout in Jamaica.

At issue is whether all Jamaicans have the same opportunities. Section 24 (3) of the Jamaican Constitution originally adopted in 1962 bans discrimination "by race, place of origin, political opinions, colour, or creed." Yet, in a rather subtle manner, racism divides Jamaica in terms of social status and economic success. While the Jamaican government doesn't provide clear data, several pieces of evidence points to supporting this claim. One study from 1990 found of the 41 companies listed on the Jamaican Stock Exchange, only four had Black chairmen.[51] A 2020 examination of the Jamaican hotel industry found White people and those with light skins dominating management positions with service staff being largely Black.[52] A third research effort on hiring practices found that employers were much more likely to return calls to high-status (and largely White-sounding) names than low-status (and non-White sounding) names.[53] Finally, a 2020 study of skin color and social inequality in Jamaica determined that skin color predicted years of schooling and educational outcomes.[54] As one researcher of Jamaican culture and politics notes, "light skin continues to bestow privilege in both the public and private spheres."[55]

With skin color seemingly a gateway to social and economic advancement, many Jamaicans have adopted the practice of "bleaching," a process where people apply a cream to lighten their skin. The value of being light heralds all the way back to the days of slavery in Jamaica, when skin color often determined one's class within the Black community.

So, is racism part of Jamaican society? It is to the extent that within the dominant Black community, skin color is a determinant for one's place and, therefore, becomes the basis by which people are valued. And that's racism.

Tyranny of the Minority in Perspective

In some respects, discrimination of the majority by minority governments is more remarkable than the cases of majorities humiliating minorities. With majority "rule," at least those in power act in the name of the masses, even if under illegitimate purposes. With minority rule, however, relatively few members of society are able to prevent the majority from participating socially, economically, and politically. The tragedy of inequality, inexcusable in democratic arenas, is all the more wretched under minority rule. In South Africa, where apartheid was officially banned, White people continue to enjoy a disproportionate share of economic success. In Syria, for more than a half-century, one family has kept an overwhelming majority at bay. In Jamaica, where the majority African race rules, the ghost of slavery that created a status by the varying shades of blackness remains a dominant characteristic. As we see from these examples, discrimination manifests in many ways. Whether practiced by a majority or minority, this discrimination continues to be a major factor in denying equality.

GLOBAL RACISM IN THE TWENTY-FIRST CENTURY

The six examples above illustrate the varying conditions and prevalence of racism around the world. They also show the extent to which racism is embedded as a prominent characteristic of human nature. It would be inaccurate to claim that racism is universal, for it is not. It would be just as inaccurate, however, to describe racism as occasional examples of governments or societies gone bad, for it is omnipresent. Additionally, as we have seen, more often than not, racism is not a temporary or whimsical movement. In many cases, its roots extend back for centuries and are not easily removed. With that universality as a backdrop, we turn next to racism in American society.

NOTES

1. Robbie W.C. Tourse, Johnnie Hamilton-Mason, and Nancy Wewiorski, *Systemic Racism in the United States* (Cham, Switzerland: Springer, 2018), p. 9.

2. "Slavery's Roots: War and Economic Domination," https://www.freetheslaves.net/slavery-today-2/slavery-in-history/.

3. Michael G. Hanchard, *The Spectre of Race: How Discrimination Haunts Western Democracy* (Princeton, NJ: Princeton University Press, 2018), p. 105.

4. See "Racist and Xenophobic Hate Crimes," Office for Democratic Institutions and Human Rights: Organization for Democratic Institutions, Warsaw, Poland, 2022, https://hatecrime.osce.org/racist-and-xenophobic-hate-crime.

5. "The Upper Han," *The Economist*, November 19, 2016, https://www.economist.com/briefing/2016/11/19/the-upper-han.

6. "Is China Committing Genocide Against the Uyghurs?" *Smithsonian Magazine*, February 2, 2022, https://www.smithsonianmag.com/history/is-china-committing-genocide-against-the-uyghurs-180979490/.

7. "Chinese Persecution of the Uyghurs," United States Holocaust Museum, https://www.ushmm.org/genocide-prevention/countries/china/case-study/current-risks/chinese-persecution-of-the-uyghurs.

8. "Why Scholars and Activists Increasingly Fear a Uyghur Genocide in Xinjiang," *Journal of Genocide Research*, 23, Issue 3 (2021), https://www.tandfonline.com/doi/full/10.1080/14623528.2020.1848109?scroll=top&needAccess=true.

9. Paula Aceves, "Ilhan Tohti Wants the Uyghurs to Be Free," *The New Yorker*, March 23, 2022, https://nymag.com/intelligencer/2022/03/ilham-tohti-wants-the-uyghurs-to-be-free.html.

10. "Global Condemnation of Chinese Government Abuse in Xinjianing," Human Rights Watch, October 21, 2021, https://www.hrw.org/news/2021/10/21/global-condemnation-chinese-government-abuses-xinjiang.

11. "U.S. Sanctions Officials in China over Persecution of Uyghurs and Other Minorities," *CBS News*, March 22, 2022, https://www.cbsnews.com/news/us-sanctions-china-genocide-persecution-uyghurs-other-religious-minorities/.

12. For a review of Erdogan's emergence, see Kemal Kirisci and Amanda Sloat, "The Rise and Fall of Liberal Democracy in Turkey: Implications for the West," The Brookings Institution, Washington, DC, February 2019, https://www.brookings.edu/wp-content/uploads/2019/02/FP_20190226_turkey_kirisci_sloat.pdf.

13. Daisy Sindelar, "1915: The Crumbling of an Empire, and the Massacre That Ensued," Radio Free Europe, August 23, 2015, https://www.rferl.org/a/crumbling-ottoman-empire-and-armenian-massacres/26974721.html.

14. See "2020 Report on International Religious Freedom: Turkey," Department of State, United States, Government, https://www.state.gov/reports/2020-report-on-international-religious-freedom/turkey/.

15. "Turkey: UN Report Details Allegations of Serious Rights Violations in Country's Southeast," *UN News*, March 10, 2017, https://news.un.org/en/story/2017/03/553062-turkey-un-report-details-allegations-serious-rights-violations-countrys.

16. "Turkey Is Committing War Crimes and Crimes against Humanity in Syria," *Genocide Watch*, June 9, 2020, https://www.genocidewatch.com/single-post/2020/06/08/turkey-is-committing-war-crimes-and-crimes-against-humanity-in-syria.

17. "Hate Speech against Christians in Erdogan's Turkey," Stockholm for Freedom, August 2017, https://usercontent.one/wp/stockholmcf.org/wp-content/uploads

/2017/08/Hate-Speech-Against-Christians-in-Erdog%CC%86an%E2%80%99s-Turkey_21.08.2017.pdf?media=1647703225.

18. See Amb. W. Robert Pearson, "What Caused the Turkish Coup Attempt," *Politico*, July 16, 2016, https://www.politico.com/magazine/story/2016/07/what-caused-the-turkish-coup-attempt-214057/.

19. Gay McDougall, "Report of the Independent Expert on Minority Issues—Addendum," United Nations Human Rights Council, January 25, 2011, https://reliefweb.int/sites/reliefweb.int/files/resources/B7E1E403814947EA85257839005D82AA-Full_Report.pdf and "Freedom in the World 2021," Freedom House, Washington, DC, 2021, https://freedomhouse.org/country/colombia/freedom-world/2021.

20. Freedom House, Ibid. The National Democratic Institute, uses similar language, referring to Colombia as "an undermined democracy." See, "Colombia," The National Democratic Institute, Washington, DC, https://www.ndi.org/latin-america-and-caribbean/colombia.

21. "In Colombia's Mass Protests, Indigenous and Black Activists Find Echoes of Colonial History," *The Washington Post*, June 2, 2021, https://www.washingtonpost.com/politics/2021/06/02/colombias-mass-protests-indigenous-black-activists-find-echoes-colonial-history/.

22. Tianna S. Paschel, *Becoming Black Political Subjects: Movements and Ethno-Rights in Colombia and Brazil* (Princeton, NJ: Princeton University Press, 2016), pp. 41–42.

23. See Rebecca Bratspies, "'Territory is Everything': Afro-Colombian Communities, Human Rights and Illegal land Grabs," *Columbian Human Rights Law Review*, May 27, 2020, https://hrlr.law.columbia.edu/hrlr-online/territory-is-everything-afro-colombian-communities-human-rights-and-illegal-land-grabs/.

24. Ibid.

25. Ibid.

26. "Colombia: Situation of Afro-Colombians, Including Treatment by Society and Authorities; State Protection and Support Services Available (2017-May 2020)," Research Directorate, Immigration and Refugee Board of Canada, https://www.justice.gov/eoir/page/file/1277501/downloa.

27. For a review of early racist policies in South Africa, see Andrew Tzvi Farkash, "The Ghosts of Colonialism: Economic Inequality in Post-Apartheid South Africa," *Global Studies Journal* (2015), https://escholarship.org/content/qt9p08t856/qt9p08t856.pdf?t=o1vgqz.

28. Brian Levy, Alan Hirsch, Vinothan Naidoo, and Musa Nxele, "South Africa: When Strong Institutions and Massive Inequalities Collide," Carnegie Endowment for International Peace, Washington, DC, March 18, 2021, https://carnegieendowment.org/2021/03/18/south-africa-when-strong-institutions-and-massive-inequalities-collide-pub-84063.

29. John Dasche, "Land Reform in South Africa: How Can the U.S. Respond?" The Wilson Center, November 23, 2021.

30. "South Africa Elections: Who Controls the Country's Business Sector?" *BBC*, May 2019, https://www.bbc.com/news/world-africa-48123937.

31. Ibid.

32. David Thomas, "Is South African Transformation Dead?" *African Business*, September 1, 2020, https://african.business/2020/09/economy/black-economic-power-matters-is-south-african-transformation-dead/.

33. Steven Friedman, *Prisoners of the Past* (Johannesburg: WITS University Press, 2021), p. 45.

34. Ibid.

35. See Miiad Hassan, "Ethnic Politics in Minority Dominant Regimes," *Ethnic Studies Review*, 43, no. 1 (Spring 2020): 56–57, https://online.ucpress.edu/esr/article-abstract/43/1/43/107097/Ethnic-Politics-in-Minority-Dominant-RegimesThree?redirectedFrom=PDF.

36. The arrangement was known as the Sykes-Picot agreement. For an analysis, see Robin Wright, "How the Curse of Sykes-Picot Still Haunts the Middle East," *The New Yorker*, April 30, 2016, https://www.newyorker.com/news/news-desk/how-the-curse-of-sykes-picot-still-haunts-the-middle-east.

37. James A. Reilly, *Fragile Nation, Shattered Land: The Modern History of Syria* (Boulder, CO: Lynne Reiner Publishers, 2019), p. 2.

38. Radwan Ziadeh, "Countries at the Crossroads 2011: Syria," Freedom House, Washington, DC, 2012, https://www.freedomhouse.org/sites/default/files/inline_images/SYRIAFinal.pdf.

39. The Muslim Brotherhood claimed that as many as 40,000 members were killed, with 15,000 no accounted for and 100,000 expelled from the area. See "30 Years Later, Photos Emerge From Killings in Syria," *NPR*, February 2, 2012, https://www.npr.org/2012/02/01/146235292/30-years-later-photos-emerge-from-killings-in-syria.

40. James A. Reilly, op. cit., p. 162.

41. Quoted in Neil MacFarquhar, "Hafez al-Assad, Who Turned Syria into a Power in the Middle East, Dies at 69," *The New York Times*, June 11, 2000, https://www.nytimes.com/2000/06/11/world/hafez-al-assad-who-turned-syria-into-a-power-in-the-middle-east-dies-at-69.html.

42. President Donald Trump withdrew U.S. involvement in 2019.

43. "Syria: 10 years of War has Left at least 350,000 Dead," *United Nations News*, September 24, 2021, https://news.un.org/en/story/2021/09/1101162.

44. "Syrian Refugee Crisis: Facts, FAQs, and How to Help," *World View*, July 13, 2021, https://www.worldvision.org/refugees-news-stories/syrian-refugee-crisis-facts.

45. "8 Reminders of How Horrible Syrian President Bashar al-Assad has been to His People," *GlobalPost*, September 24, 2014, https://theworld.org/stories/2014-09-24/8-reminders-how-horrible-syrian-president-bashar-al-assad-has-been-his-people.

46. "Fears Grow for Syria Amid Rising Violence, Deepening Humanitarian Crisis," *UN News*, March 9, 2022, https://news.un.org/en/story/2022/03/1113592.

47. "Global Freedom Scores: Countries and Territories," 2021, Freedom House, Washington, DC, https://freedomhouse.org/countries/freedom-world/scores.

48. See "Jamaica," Freedom House, Washington, DC, 2021, https://freedomhouse.org/country/jamaica/freedom-world/2021 and "United States," Freedom House, Washington, DC, 2021, https://freedomhouse.org/country/united-states/freedom-world/2021.

49. Much of the material in this section comes from "Black History Month 2022: History of Jamaica," https://www.blackhistorymonth.org.uk/article/section/jamaica/history-of-jamaica/.

50. "Jamaica Population 2022, World Population Review," https://worldpopulationreview.com/countries/jamaica-population.

51. Lee Hockstader, "Jamaican Racial Harmony Challenged on Issue of Black Role in Economy," *The Washington Post*, July 4, 1990, https://www.washingtonpost.com/archive/politics/1990/07/04/jamaican-racial-harmony-challenged-on-issue-of-black-role-in-economy/e268b21e-f668-4051-831e-ad856de547e8/.

52. Henrice Altink, "Out of Place: Race and Color in Jamaican Hotels, 1962-2020," *New West Indian Guide*, 95, Issue 3–4 (2021), file:///Users/gerstondocs/Downloads/[22134360%20-%20New%20West%20Indian%20Guide%20_%20Nieuwe%20West-Indische%20Gids]%20Out%20of%20Place%20(1).pdf.

53. Nekeisha Spencer, Mikhail-Ann Orquhart, and Patrice Whitely, "Class Discrimination? Evidence from Jamaica: A Racially Homogeneous Labor Market," *Review of Radical Political Economics*, 52, no. 1 (2020): 77–95, https://journals.sagepub.com/doi/full/10.1177/0486613419832674.

54. Monique D.A. Kelly, "Examining Race in Jamaica: How Racial Category and Skin Color Structure Social Inequality," *Race and Social Problems,* March 18, 2020, https://link.springer.com/article/10.1007/s12552-020-09287-z?utm_source=toc.

55. Henrice Altink, "Black Lives Matter in Jamaica: Debates about Colourism Follow Anger at Police Brutality," *The Conversation*, June 22, 2020, https://theconversation.com/black-lives-matter-in-jamaica-debates-about-colourism-follow-anger-at-police-brutality-140754.

Chapter 4

Racial Bigotry in the United States
A Brief History

Racism is not unique to the United States or, for that matter, the colonies that preceded formation of the United States. As we noted in the preceding chapter, racism is ubiquitous. The large numbers of African-American slaves and now citizens led some people to view modern-day racism in the United States basically as unlawful discrimination of Black people by White people. This view is only partly true for two reasons.

First, African Americans are not the only group facing racial discrimination. Others include Latinos, now the largest minority in the United States, Asian Americans, and Native Americans. Religious denominations, notably Jews and Muslims, may not have the same physical characteristics as racial and ethnic groups, but they, too, have suffered from discrimination. Beyond race and religion, members of the LGBTQ community have also experienced discrimination. They, like the others, have suffered from varying combinations of exploitation, marginalization, powerlessness, cultural imperialism, and violence.[1] It's in this broader context that we approach the history of racism in the United States, particularly because of the way that has been expropriated by Trumpism.

Second, discrimination in the United States is not simply a White/nonwhite conflict. For example, African Americans have been known to discriminate against Asian Americans, while Asian Americans have been accused of discriminating against Latinos and African Americans. Even a few Native American tribes have histories of discriminating against African Americans, who in some areas of the country were actually slaves to them.[2] There also have been instances where members of a given group discriminate against others with the same characteristics. The second category pales in contrast with the first and doesn't attract the same attention, but it shows that racism is more universal in the United States than we might think.

Racism, as we have learned, comes in many forms and is exercised in numerous ways. In some instances, policymakers have developed legislative schemes to keep certain groups from coming to the United States; in other situations, policymakers have created programs to control those people of color and minority ethnicities already here. Both approaches have been geared to keep various minorities from enjoying the benefits and opportunities routinely experienced by others.

In the United States, racist language is often employed without any awareness of those using it. The term "off the reservation" today refers to someone who has gone astray or off the mark in an analysis or behavior, yet its origin refers to Indigenous Americans[3] daring to leave their "place" in society (the reservation) to be part of the larger population. Reference to someone as a "welfare queen" is often attributed to Black single mothers receiving government aid through fraud or because they are too lazy to find work. "Wetback," sometimes used to describe Latinos, originates from the efforts of Mexicans to enter the United States illegally after swimming or wading across the Rio Grande. White people haven't escaped racial slurs, either. "WASP," an acronym for White Anglo-Saxon Protestants, stems from critics of White people with money, power, and connections that others don't have. We could go on and on, but the point is that racism and racist terminology are endemic in our culture to the point that Americans sometimes don't even realize their impact, which has become part of our contemporary descriptive vocabulary.

Still, we are all too aware of racism employed as a tool by individuals, leaders, and institutions as a means to subjugate groups to positions of artificial inferiority and powerlessness. Further, there are indications that this activity has increased in recent years, jeopardizing America's position as a tolerant democracy. To this point, institutions can be far more powerful than individuals in controlling the behavior of society through racist laws and corporate policies that become almost foundational in American culture. The bottom line is that racism serves as justification for an individual or group to exercise a power over other individuals or groups characterized as unworthy simply because of their physical appearances or personal values.

PRACTICING INEQUALITY

We turn now to a discussion of American institutional practices of racism at the national level of government. For almost 200 years, little was done at the national level to provide any semblance of equality for non-White people. Yes, the 13th Amendment to the Constitution officially ended slavery, the 14th Amendment assured African-Americans citizenship, and the 15th Amendment stipulated that the right to vote shall not be denied "on account of race" and actually provided Congress the power to enforce that guarantee through legislation, but little was done to secure the right in any meaningful way until the Voting Rights Act of 1965. Otherwise, there were baby steps toward equality such as President Harry Truman's Executive Order to desegregate the military in 1948,[4] but they were just that—baby steps. However, the Voting Rights Act was a major effort toward substantiating equality, at least in the voting booth.

This is not to say that states and local governments have not employed racist practices. In fact, depending on the latitude given to them by national institutions, particularly the federal courts, states often have created incredibly racist policies, which will be discussed later. For now, we will focus on the many groups victimized by racist policies originated by federal institutions, where the concept has a history as old, or in some instances older, than the country itself. The persistence of this treatment over such a long period gives little indication of it going away. Furthermore, as we will see later on, racism fits in well with autocracies, in that authoritarian leaders use its elements to pit groups against one another as a strategy of keeping their power.

African Americans

The fundamental values of freedom and equality were embedded in the founding of the United States. Ironically, the Framers espousing such themes were overwhelmingly White, Protestant, and privileged; in addition, many were slave or former slave owners. After all, that's the way things had been in the colonies. Thus, the Framers of the U.S. Constitution never included universal suffrage—a bedrock of equality—as a constitutional right. They worried that the masses might be unrepresentative of their values and, therefore, a threat to a carefully assembled set of rules protecting the individual rights of elites.[5] Perhaps that's part of the reason why racism has never disappeared from the United States; there's a link that is yet to be severed.

With respect to racial minorities already in the United States, Congress was largely quiet for the first hundred years or so of the American experience. The legislative branch first acted on the slavery issue in 1807 by passing The Act Prohibiting the Importation of Slavery, which took effect the next year. However, slave importation continued until the Civil War, which left the 1807 Act meaningless. Otherwise, Congress didn't act on the slavery issue until 1850, when it passed the Fugitive Slave Act, which required the federal government to take responsibility for returning runaway slaves to their states of origin. In that legislation, penalties were created for any federal, state, and local law enforcement agency that refused to arrest a runaway slave for return to its owner.[6]

In the midst of the Civil War, President Abraham Lincoln issued his Emancipation Proclamation in 1863. Nearly 4,000,000 slaves were freed, at least in terms of the president's order. Another 400,000 had been freed earlier, most as a reward for serving alongside Northern troops in the Civil War. Of course, ending slavery did not halt racism. The termination of slavery, however, did stop the overt version of racial oppression as a government-sanctioned policy.

After the Civil War, the Civil Rights Amendments to the United States Constitution codified the equality of African Americans. Now, instead of working the land as slaves in the South, Black people were sharecroppers who leased land from White owners at exorbitant prices.[7] Their "place" in society was routinely enforced by the Ku Klux Klan and other White supremacist groups, which roamed the South and some areas of the North from the end of the Civil War through the 1930s. While most of the Klan's attention focused on Black people, they and other supremacists had plenty of disdain for Jews and Catholics. In its heyday, Klan membership estimates were as high as 8,000,000.[8]

Between Reconstruction and the Civil Rights Amendments, Black participation in the franchise increased. But once Reconstruction ended in 1877, White-dominated Southern legislatures wasted little time in passing laws making it difficult for Black people to vote.[9] Then, as now, state leaders officially expressed concern for voter fraud as the basis for their laws, but the real motivation was race, period. As one Mississippi White leader put it at a state constitutional convention in 1890, "This ballot system must be so arranged as to effect one object: we find the two races now together, the rule of one which has always meant economic and moral ruin; we find another race whose rule has always meant prosperity and happiness to all races."[10] Such imperatives were not only commonplace but supported through *Plessy v. Ferguson* in 1896, where the U.S. Supreme Court ruled that the "separate but equal" relationship between Black people and White people would satisfy the "equal protection of the laws" provision in the 14th Amendment of the U.S. Constitution. Thus, in Plessy's case, he could be assigned a segregated seat in a train in as much as Black people and White people were both going to the same place and would arrive at the same time. That very concept allowed states to establish separate facilities for Black people and White people, including voting places and conditions.

In the South, Democrats used various techniques to prevent the Black vote. Poll taxes, literacy tests, and citizenship proof were given to all voters in various combinations, depending on the state, with disproportionate negative impacts on Black people. "Grandfather clauses," state rules that allowed the descendants of White citizens prior to Reconstruction to vote without going through any literacy tests or poll taxes, were commonplace. By the turn of the century, Black voters had been all but eviscerated from the South; for example, only 2 percent of Black people in Alabama and 6 percent in Mississippi were registered to vote.[11] Restrictive covenants, rules stipulating where Black people could vote, typified cities whether in the North or South.

Beyond voting, African Americans in the post–Civil War world lived in segregated environments. Equally qualified African Americans were frequently paid less than White people in the same jobs, and many states passed laws requiring segregated housing, transportation, prisons and public education. Redlining, the process of banks employing color-coded maps to define where African Americans would be serviced by loans, was universally applied throughout the nation. That process assured that the races would live separately from one another. Public schools were segregated, with White schools generally providing better educations than their Black counterparts. Marriages between White people and African Americans were out of the question in most states. Even the U.S. military was segregated until President Harry Truman's Executive Order in 1948.

Few substantive efforts to assure equality for African Americans occurred between the end of the nineteenth century and the 1960s. Perhaps the most significant structural adjustment came in 1944, when the U.S. Supreme Court overturned White primary elections used by Democrats in southern states.[12] Otherwise, major change didn't come until the Voting Rights Act of 1965. With that landmark legislation, Black registration and voting soared. In Mississippi, for example, Black registration went from 6.7 percent in 1965 to 59.8 percent in 1967—still 30 points below White people but a huge jump nonetheless.[13] And given that Black people identified overwhelmingly with Democrats, suppression of their vote would go a long way toward helping White Republicans succeed in future elections.

In the 2020 presidential election, Black voter turnout was still below White people, 63 percent compared to 71 percent. However, recent state laws threaten that progress. But new evidence suggests that the new round of state-sanctioned "voter fraud" laws have placed new burdens disproportionately on people of color, thereby making it harder for them to participate in the franchise.[14] We'll discuss that in chapter 11.

Native Americans

African Americans were the primary minority group to face discrimination during the first century of United States nationhood. However, they weren't the only group. Indigenous Americans (also referred to as Native Americans), the only other group of significant notoriety during the early period, also suffered from wars with White Americans coupled with their lack of immunity to Western diseases. Between 1778 and 1871, Indigenous Americans signed 368 treaties with federal and state governments. Most carried the same theme: the promise of sovereignty for Native Americans in exchange for their moving to reservations, usually far from where they lived.

As a general rule, treaties were valid until the U.S. government decided to break them, especially if the new Native American lands were later determined to be valuable for White purposes, such as mining gold or growing crops on valuable soil.[15] How is it that Native Americans suffered such a fate? Despite the 14th Amendment granting citizenship to Black Americans, Indigenous Americans were without American citizenship until Congress passed the Indian Citizenship Act of 1924.

Even with citizenship, wherever they lived Native Americans were treated as second-class citizens. For example, in the same year they were granted citizenship, the California State Supreme Court approved a state law requiring "Indian children or others in whom racial differences exist, to attend separate schools, provided such schools are equal . . . with those furnished for children of the white race."[16] Of course, as later declared in *Brown v. Board of Education*, separate but equal is not equal. With respect to the right to vote, the franchise was not fully guaranteed to Indigenous Americans until the Voting Rights Act of 1965.[17] Even then, Native American suffrage was hardly a given.

In fact, it's still an issue. There are 5,000,000 Native Americans today who are members of approximately 500 tribes. About half of that number still live on reservations, which are often far from urban areas. There have been moments when Native Americans have played a critical role in political events. For example, of the 67,000 eligible Native American voters in Arizona, an overwhelming majority voted for Democrat Joe Biden in 2020, a state that Biden won by 10,500 votes. Many rode on horseback as much as 30 miles to the polls.[18] Still, the future for Native Americans looks bleak. In 2021, the U.S. Supreme Court upheld two Arizona laws, one banning a vote gathering process derisively described as "ballot harvesting," and the other dismissing ballots cast in the wrong precinct. Attorneys for the Native American community argued that disallowing collection of ballots by a representative would keep Native Americans from voting and that rejected ballots from incorrect precincts would harm turnout. The Supreme Court decided otherwise.[19]

Problems continue in other states as well. Native American voters in Montana and South Dakota, for example, have been thwarted by ballot drop boxes and election officials that are 100 miles or more away from their reservations, thus reducing turnout in elections.[20] Such decisions have had the effect of minimizing Native American turnout.

Latinos

While African Americans spent the first 200 years of their presence on U.S. soil in the eastern and southern portions of the country, Latinos were present primarily in the west and southwest portions.[21] In fact, many were already here at the time of the American Revolution. They had no standing as citizens, however, by virtue of the fact that the areas where they lived were not incorporated into the United States first as territories, then states, from 1848 through 1912. With the signing of the Treaty of Guadalupe Hildalgo in 1848, Mexico ceded 55 percent of its territory to the United States, which included parts of present-day Arizona, California, New Mexico, Colorado, Nevada, and Utah. With that transfer of territory, approximately 50,000 people of Mexican-origin became citizens of the United States overnight.

For the first few decades of the rearranged boundary between the United States and Mexico, Mexicans came and went to the United States as conditions dictated. Families often straddled both sides of the border. Most of those who stayed worked as laborers, farmworkers and housecleaners, and later garment makers in California. As their numbers grew, their lots in life worsened. In California, most large agricultural land grants issued by the Mexican government somehow drifted into White ownership.[22] Similar activity occurred in Texas, where public officials used newly conferred statehood in 1848 to strip away Mexican land ownership.[23]

By 1930, approximately 1.5 million Mexicans had immigrated to the United States, mostly to Texas, Arizona, and California. Typically, they lived in segregated neighborhoods with dilapidated schools and other decrepit public facilities. Few were permitted to vote, and those who were rarely did so because the ballots were not translated into Spanish. With the onset of the Great Depression during the 1930s and few jobs available, U.S. authorities deported thousands of Mexicans to Mexico; in some cases, Mexicans who were American citizens were deported as well.[24] Ironically, at the same time, many Mexican American citizens enlisted in the military with the onset of World War II.

Mexican immigration resumed during World War II largely to fill the farm labor shortage in the western United States. It continued thereafter under the auspices of the bracero (Spanish for manual laborer) program, which allowed Mexicans to come and go with harvest times. Still, many nativist Americans demanded Mexican removal altogether, leading the U.S. Immigration and Naturalization Services to institute "Operation Wetback" a racial cleansing program that deported 3.5 million Mexicans, including one million in 1954 alone, the height of the program.[25] As was often the case with racial minorities, White people wanted the benefits of inexpensive immigration labor while rejecting any thought of acknowledging the same immigrants as equals.

Over the past half-century, little has been done in the states to end Latino discrimination. A Pew Research poll conducted among Latinos in 2021 found that about one-third had experienced discrimination in the past 12 months. With respect to voting, Latino turnout in the 2020 presidential election was

54 percent, 17 points lower than the turnout of White people. But the biggest hurdle for Latinos lies with the large number of unauthorized immigrants who are in limbo because of Congressional inaction on immigration policy. One recent survey of the 11.4 million unauthorized immigrants in the United States found that 7.4 million were from Mexico, Venezuela, and Central America.[26] For these people, their uncertain status presents its own discrimination stigma.

Asians

For nearly the entirety of American history, Asians from throughout the region have moved to the United States. Hardly homogeneous, they include Japanese, Chinese, Koreans, Filipinos, Indians, Pakistanis, and Vietnamese, and others. Vietnamese and Chinese have been particularly prevalent in recent years. However, with respect to being recently victimized by racism, Chinese and Japanese immigrants stand out the most.

Chinese immigrants first came to the United States during the 1840s, when formal relations between the two governments began. During the California Gold Rush, the Chinese worked in mining camps. In an early sign of institutional racial discrimination, the state legislature tried to exclude the Chinese in 1853, but mining companies persuaded legislators otherwise.[27] In 1854, the California State Supreme Court held that Chinese would not be allowed to testify in legal procedures, thereby giving a blank check to discrimination and harsh treatment. Another Asian wave occurred between 1863 and 1869 when the Central Pacific Company brought 15,000 Chinese to construct the western portion of the transcontinental railroad.

After their railroad work ended, many of the Chinese looked for work in Los Angeles and San Francisco. There, they repeatedly suffered at the hands of White gangs with local government authorities looking the other way.[28] Shortly thereafter, Congress passed the Chinese Exclusion Acts, the first national legislation restricting immigration into the United States. Along with hatred toward African Americans, the animus toward the Chinese in the United States became a plank of the Populist (sometimes called Peoples) party, which lasted from the early 1880s until 1896, when it was absorbed into the Democratic Party. Organized labor also came down on the Chinese, in fear that they might replace White workers. In 1900, San Francisco gangs erroneously blamed Chinese residents for bringing the Bubonic Plague to American shores.

In 1904, Congress passed legislation banning Chinese immigration because of their race, the first time that Congress explicitly used race as the explicit basis of denying admission to the United States. Chinese immigrants were not allowed to apply for U.S. citizenship until 1943. But Congress wasn't through. Various forms of quotas for Chinese admission to the United States existed until 1965, when they ended a racially based quota system. In reviewing the long-term pattern of prohibiting Chinese immigration, historian Beth Lew-Williams warns, "If the history of Chinese exclusion teaches us about the perils of racial discrimination, it also should warn us about the dangerous inequalities produced by alienage."[29] It wouldn't be a stretch to extend that counsel to all non-White groups in the United States.

With the Chinese blocked from further entry, American policymakers turned their attention to Japanese immigrants, who represented the second major immigration wave to the United States. Between the mid-1880s and 1910, approximately 400,000 Japanese immigrated to the United States. Much of the impetus for immigration came from warmed relations between the two nations, with a trade treaty in 1895 that included a provision permitting Japanese to eventually gain citizenship in the United States. Most relocated in Hawaii, then a U.S. territory, or California.

As with the Chinese, opposition to Japanese immigrants came from organized labor and an isolationist political party, the Progressives. Philosophical successors to the Populists, Progressives viewed Japanese immigrants as threats to the United States, especially to the agricultural industry. But there was more. At about the turn of the twentieth century, a term known as "racial science" took root in the American polity. Those who subscribed to the term believed that intelligence corresponded with whiteness of skin.

Nowhere was opposition to the Japanese greater than in California. In 1905, the Asiatic Exclusion League was formed in San Francisco with the expressed commitment to separate Japanese students from White people in public schools. In 1922, the U.S. Supreme Court handed down a decision denying citizenship to Japanese immigrants, a ban that existed until 1952.[30] But the biggest insult came with Executive Order 9066 issued by President Franklin Roosevelt in 1942, which commanded 120,000 Japanese-American citizens and residents in California to live in internment camps for the duration of the war, lest any of them be Japanese spies. There was no proof of such accusations. In what might have been the greatest incongruity of the massive relocation, 33,000 Japanese Americans enlisted in the U.S. military to fight for democracy! Moreover, it turned out that the 442nd regimental combat team, a segregated unit, was the most decorated combat team for its size.[31]

In recent times, Asian Americans have been attacked particularly in moments of international stress. In 1982, a Chinese American was beaten to death by two White autoworkers in Detroit who mistakenly took him for a Japanese American. Their anger stemmed from anguish over the Japanese automobile industry successfully penetrating the American market, leading the autoworkers to believe their jobs were in jeopardy.[32] Similar reactions against Asian Americans occurred following the September 11, 2001 Muslim terrorist attacks. Shortly after the tragedy, a turbaned Sikh American was attacked by White people who mistakenly believed his clothing was connected with the Muslim religion. Attacks against American Sikhs with South Asian origins spiked for the first week after the 9/11 attacks.[33]

The point is that historically Asian Americans have been blamed for events not of their doing simply because of their different appearances and values. Often living in a fearful environment, many have continued to feel dismissed and intimated when they have sought to vote. A study in 2008 found endless examples of segregated voting lines, extraordinarily long voting times, racist and untrained poll workers, improper Chinese-American identification checks, and unavailable ballots in Chinese languages.[34]

Hostility toward Asians has increased dramatically in recent years, with the renewed focus particularly on the Chinese-American community. Much of the recent wave of animus stems from President Donald Trump's description of COVID-19 as "the Chinese virus," implying that the Chinese government was responsible for the pandemic.[35] That comment was immediately picked up by key Republican leaders who, in many cases, conflated Trump's false claim with blame for the virus on Chinese-American citizens.[36] Trump later explained that Chinese Americans were innocent of any involvement, but the damage was done. A poll published by *USA Today* a year after the debunked Trump allegation revealed that one in four Americans and nearly half of all Asian Americans had seen someone accuse Asian people of bringing about COVID-19.[37] Another survey by Pew Research found that 39 percent of Americans had expressed racist views against Asians since the coronavirus outbreak.[38] Finally, a separate study conducted in 2020 found that anti-Asian hate crimes in America's 16 largest cities soared by 149 percent in the past year, offering further evidence of racist behavior.[39]

In fact, in recent years American hostility toward Asian Americans has been a constant. A national poll conducted in 2001 found results similar to the 2021 data. In that survey, 25 percent of those surveyed had negative attitudes toward Chinese Americans, with one-third of the respondents believing that Chinese Americans were more loyal to China than the United States.[40] Anti-Asian sentiment is alive and well in the United States.

Institutionalized Racism in Perspective

Three statements may be made with certainty about racial minorities in the United States: First, their numbers have grown disproportionately to those of White people. Second, each group has experienced a long history of racial and/or ethnic discrimination. And third, each group has voted disproportionately for Democratic candidates, particularly since the 1930s when political party realignment occurred among voters in the United States.[41] To the extent that particular groups are excluded from the electorate, the poor and people of color suffer disproportionately.[42] Of course, there are exceptions in each of these cases, but it's impossible to ignore the generalizations.

RESTRICTING THE ENTRY OF IMMIGRANTS

Racism in the United States has a history of implementation through discrimination against the entry of immigrants. For the first 150 years of U.S. existence, Congress concentrated on immigration policies which, in most cases, struggled to control the flow of non-White people into the United States. Much of these efforts occurred between the 1870s and 1930s. Two waves of immigration control laws focused on Asians. The Page Act (1875) banned all Chinese women from the United States. A few years later the Chinese Exclusion Act (1882) suspended all Chinese immigration. The second wave of anti-Asian legislation came toward the end of World War I, when the Immigrant Control Act (1917), which barred immigrants from most of Asia except Japan and the Philippines.

During the 1920s, Congress passed three laws dedicated to establishing immigration quotas by continent. Increasingly, they skewed larger percentages of the immigrant quotas toward Europeans, thereby assuring disproportionate admissions of White people.

Congress changed its attitude toward immigration a bit after World War II and the onset of the Cold War with the Soviet Union. The combination of World War II refugees and large numbers of people attempting to escape Soviet rule precipitated re-opening the immigration door for refugees, although the moment of embrace was relatively brief. The key pieces of legislation during this period included the Immigration and Naturalization Act (1952), which liberalized quotas and repealed the racial ban denying citizenship; and the Immigration and Nationality Act (1965), which allowed immediate relatives of immigrants living outside the United States to move to the United States for purposes of family unification.

The last period of substantive immigration legislation took place during the 1980s. In The Refugee Act (1980), the meaning of "refugee" was expanded from political, racial and religious persecution to include economic deprivation. Finally, in 1986, Congress passed the Immigration Reform and Control Act (1986), which required employers to confirm employees' immigration status and legalized 60,000 immigrants who had entered the United States before January 1, 1982. Remarkably, Congress has not passed any comprehensive immigration since 1986.

As a result of these laws and programs, several demographic changes in American society—some anticipated, some not—occurred. Among them:

- Millions of immediate families have been reunited, many from non-Hispanic White countries; in fact, about two-thirds of all immigrants since 1965 have been admitted on this basis;[43]
- A huge talent pool of foreign scientists and innovators has come to the United States and remained;[44]
- Millions of low-skilled workers have assumed relatively menial and other undesirable jobs eschewed by native-born White Americans;
- The proportions of non-Hispanic White people to non-White people decreased relatively quickly from 84 percent to 16 percent in 1965 to 61 percent to 39 percent in 2020;[45]
- Moreover, the U.S. Bureau of the Census has predicted that recent demographic trends project an America with a majority of non-Hispanic White people by 2044.[46]

The last point is perhaps particularly important in terms of American racism. While Americans have benefited immensely from immigrant talent and participation in the national economy, a sizable swath of White people see harm to society from the demographic change. They argue that immigrants harm the employment opportunities of low-skilled White Americans, take disproportionate government assistance and can't fit into America's culture, which has a distinctly White history and appearance.[47] Yet, studies show immigrants add to the U.S. economy, receive little government assistance, and actually complement the existing workforce by taking jobs others don't.[48] So, the issue is more than economic disruption. Judging from the types of legislation passed, it's more likely to be about race. More on this later.

CONGRESS AND RACISM

No serious action on racial equality was undertaken by Congress until the 1957 Civil Rights Act, the first legislation on the topic since 1875. Riding on the coattails of *Brown v. Board of Education,* an historic and unanimous desegregation decision by the U.S. Supreme Court in 1954, Congress established a Commission of Civil Rights to investigate civil rights complaints as a Civil Rights division in the Department of Justice. In 1960, Congress moved again with the Civil Rights Act of 1960, which provided federal referees to examine state voter registration and voting procedures. The act was fairly toothless, however, since it did not provide any concrete basis for documenting examples of Black voter discrimination or doing much about it, which later became essential to the discussion leading to the Voting Rights Act of 1965.[49]

The first substantive Congressional commitment to racial equality came with the Civil Rights Act of 1964, which prohibited discrimination in public places such as theaters, restaurants, public transportation, and hotels, as well as in the workplace. For the first time, the act also prohibited gender discrimination. By taking on discrimination directly, the 1964 act was described as "a knockout punch for the old Civil War alignment," which had divided North from South.[50]

In the wake of a massive electoral landslide in 1964, the following year, the overwhelmingly Democratic Congress went to work on voting. In the Voting Rights Act of 1965, Congress stripped away the power of southern states to deny registration and voting opportunities to racial minorities. Among the most important parts, the act prohibited states (mostly southern) with histories of discrimination from changing any election rules without approval from the U.S. Department of Justice; the Attorney General was also empowered to investigate and sue any states accused of denying anyone the franchise. The 1965 act was reauthorized in 1970, 1975, 1982, 1992, and 2006—the last time by a vote of 390–33 in the House of Representatives and 98–0 in the U.S. Senate. The 1975 reauthorization added a new dimension with penalties for states or localities that discriminated against people who spoke foreign languages, a codicil that has grown in importance given the significant numbers of Latinos who rely on Spanish as their first language.

As concern about excessive immigration developed in some portions of American society, second thoughts emerged about continuing the Voting Rights Act. When a similar version of the 1965 act and its subsequent amendments was introduced in the U.S. Senate in 2022, it stalled. Republican critics there claimed the proposed legislation went beyond the intentions in 1965; in fact, the only parts of the act later eliminated by the U.S. Supreme Court in 2013 and 2021 were original portions of the 1965 legislation.[51] Nevertheless, as noted in the next section, the actions by the Supreme Court gave Senate Republicans the leeway to dramatically reduce voting rights guarantees without taking a vote on restoring the provisions excised by the Court. Sixteen Senate Republicans who voted to extend the Voting Rights Act in 2006 turned away from the 2022 version intended to restore the provisions stripped by the Supreme Court.[52]

THE COURTS AND RACISM

The federal judiciary offered little guidance on race until *Dred Scott v. Sandford* in 1856. In response to the Fugitive Slave Act of 1850, several northern states enacted legislation offering sanctuary to runaway slaves, including an opportunity to gain their freedom. However, in the *Dred Scott* case, the U.S. Supreme Court declared that Black people "have for more than a century been regarded as beings of an inferior order," and thus "had no rights which white men were bound to respect."[53] African Americans, it seemed, were viewed as property rather than people and the approaches of the northern states were overruled.

Judicial Minimalism

After the Civil War, the U.S. Supreme Court maintained its "hands off" attitude toward guaranteeing Black civil rights. In 1871, the Court overturned the 1871 Enforcement Acts which protected the rights of African Americans to vote and hold office and forbade meetings of Ku Klux Klan members—this despite the fact that the 14th and 15th Amendments had been ratified; the principal case was *United States vs. Cruikshank*. But there was more judicial minimalism.

In *The Civil Rights Cases* (1883), the U.S. Supreme Court overturned the Civil Rights Act of 1875, which protected all citizens from discrimination when they sought public accommodations or transportation. Then there was *Plessy v. Ferguson*, which upheld the right of states and local governments to segregate citizens, as long as their treatment was "separate but equal;" Finally, the U.S, Supreme Court was particularly willing to deny basic civil rights to Japanese-American citizens in *Korematsu v. U.S*. In the case, the justices decided that President Franklin Roosevelt had the right during World War II to relocate 120,000 Japanese Americans on the west coast from their homes to "internment" camps.[54]

As a result of these cases, the Court basically made a farce of Reconstruction and the 13th, 14th, and 15th Amendments designed to put an end to racial discrimination. In the words of one account, the Supreme Court's decisions during the period "not only fully validated the blatant ploys to disfranchise Black Americans and relegate them to some shadow existence between freedom and slavery, but also threw open the door to a more codified approach removing African Americans first from the voting rolls and then from mainstream civil life."[55] Moreover, while not addressing African-American civil rights per se, *Korematsu* extended the denial of equality to Japanese Americans for similar reasons.

One case favoring African-American rights stood out during the first half of the twentieth century. Beginning in the 1880s, shortly after the end of the Reconstruction Era, most southern states enacted all-White political party primaries, which assured that the nominees of all parties would be White. In *Smith v. Allwright* (1944), the U.S. Supreme Court declared the all-White political party primary unconstitutional because of the 14th Amendment's equal protection clause. That's how matters stood with the federal judiciary until 1954.

An Interlude of Activism

For a few years, beginning in 1954, the U.S. Supreme Court changed course on race and equality. Starting with the stunning *Brown v. Board of Education* decision in 1954, the Court declared that "separate but equal" was on its face not equal, and as such, the Court ordered public schools to desegregate "with all deliberate speed." Then, during the 1960s and 1970s, the U.S. Supreme Court upheld a series of civil rights cases, many of which stemmed from the Civil Rights and Voting Rights laws of 1964 and 1965.

In *Baker v. Carr*, the U.S. Supreme Court addressed the issue of malapportionment, which tended to pack large numbers of minorities into congressional and state legislative districts that had the effect of reducing their numerical clout elsewhere. In that case and subsequent cases over the next decade, the Court insisted on the concept of "one person, one vote." Included was the additional interpretation that redistricting could not be done in such a way as to artificially segregate voters into districts on the basis of race.[56] In *Loving v. Virginia* (1967), the Court struck down a Virginia law that barred interracial marriage, citing the 14th Amendment's equal protection and due process clauses.

As a means of promoting minority inclusion in society, the Court also accepted "Affirmative Action," a controversial formulaic approach that improved the chances for racial minorities and women to university admissions. But the justices were extremely careful (and divided) about the way such inclusion could take place. In *Regents of the University of California v. Bakke* (1978), the Supreme Court actually handed down two decisions, each by 5-to-4 votes. In the first, the Court wrote that race could be considered as a factor for determining university admission. In the second, the Court decided that formal quotas, guaranteed spots for various groups, would not be permitted. With those two decisions, the Supreme Court began a new direction in interpreting civil rights guarantees.

The Return to Minimalism

Then, the collective approach of the changing Supreme Court justices changed yet again. The twin decisions in the Bakke case were a precursor of the Court's new direction on racial discrimination, which was really a return to leaving the states as arbitrators of equality. In 1991, the U.S. Supreme Court agreed with a lower federal court order that ended school busing to provide educational parity, even if the schools remained segregated.[57] Moving beyond schools and employment issues, the U.S. Supreme Court next excised the most important parts of the Voting Rights Act of 1965. In 2013, the Court, through *Shelby County v. Holder,* nullified Sections 4 and 5 of the Act, which had required seven southern states and localities in three other states with historical patterns of racial discrimination to obtain U. S. Department of Justice approval before changing any laws.[58]

In 2021, the Court struck down Section 2 of the 1965 act in *Brnovich v. Democratic National Committee*, by narrowing the scope of provisions allowing citizens to challenge discriminatory voting laws. The impact of the decision reduced the abilities of the Department of Justice to rectify acts of voter discrimination promulgated by state legislation or judicial decisions. Together, the *Shelby County* and *Brnovich* cases freed states to create their own redistricting laws without any federal oversight, once again opening the possibility that equality would have different definitions and applications.

Lastly, in 2023, the Supreme Court rejected the concept of affirmative action. For years, the Court had reduced the utility of affirmative action at the margins, but now, with a firm 6-to-3 conservative majority, the justices declared that universities could no longer consider race as part of the admissions process. Writing for the majority, Chief Justice Roberts declared that "For too long, universities have concluded, wrongly, that the touchstone of an individual's identity is not the challenges bested, skills built, or lessons learned but the color of their skin. Our constitutional history does not tolerate that choice."[59] With that, the justices declared that minorities no longer needed any special consideration for college admission and that past injustices no longer existed.

Critics of the U.S. Supreme Court often cited, and sometimes complained about, the Warren Era, the years when Earl Warren served as Chief Justice (1953–1969), as a period when the Court exhibited interpretive activism through its decisions that expanded several individual rights and federal powers. They looked forward to a time when the Court would be more rigorous in its assessments of Constitutional issues. With the recent appointments of three "originalist" justices by former president Donald Trump, that day has come. But it would be a mischaracterization to declare the Court under Chief Justice John Roberts (2005–present) has been less activist than the Warren Court. Rather, it can be argued that the majority, beginning in the late 1990s, has been just as activist as the previous generation through its willingness to change the status quo by paring back individual guarantees and federal obligations.[60]

As a result of several Supreme Court decisions during the first quarter of the twenty-first century, federal judicial protection for those alleging racial discrimination has weakened and, in some cases, all but disappeared. Further, it's abundantly clear that the Warren Era stands out as the exception of Court's decisions on race over the past 200 years, rather than the rule.

ACTION (OR THE LACK THEREOF) IN THE EXECUTIVE BRANCH

Whatever the original carefully balanced power design of the Constitution, the American presidency has emerged clearly as the nation's most dominant institution and source of moral authority. In their book on the American presidency, George Edwards III and Stephen Wayne confirm as much in writing that the American presidency has become "the prime initiator and coordinator among separate and independent institutions sharing power, the foremost mobilizer among disparate and competing interests, and the principal communications link among a multitude of groups and individuals."[61] Thus, it behooves us to examine the role of the American presidency on the issue of racism post-Civil War through the Barack Obama administration. The activities of Donald Trump will be assessed separately in subsequent chapters.

The record is mixed at best. We begin our assessment of presidents after the Civil War, when the issue of freedom for African Americans purportedly was "settled," yet it was anything but. One review of presidents and race cites several instances underscoring presidential disdain for African Americans. As noted above, upon assuming the presidency in 1877, Rutherford Hayes (1877–1881), who referred to himself as a "friend" of Black people, withdrew federal troops from Southern states where they had been protecting African Americans from white supremacist organizations.[62] Theodore Roosevelt (1901–1909), the famous Progressive who promoted public education for all, once wrote that Black people "are altogether inferior to whites." And Woodrow Wilson (1913–1921), strong League of Nations proponent for its intended ability to resolve international conflicts, once wrote to an African-American leader that "segregation is not a humiliation but a benefit."

There are other examples. When Jews were fleeing Nazi murderers in 1939 during the early days of the Holocaust, President Franklin Roosevelt (1933–1945) refused to allow 937 mostly Jewish passengers on the ocean liner St. Louis to disembark in Miami for one of two reasons: either because the passengers were a "threat to national security" or because their numbers exceeded the German immigration for that year. Neither reason speaks to courage. During the St. Louis crisis, Roosevelt also refused to support a bill in Congress that would have added an additional 20,000 people to the German immigration quota for the year, thereby providing the means for admission.[63] Upon the return of the St. Louis to Europe, more than 200 Jews died at the hands of the Nazis.

For his time, President Harry Truman (1945–1953) appeared somewhat enlightened on race, although he didn't start out that way. Throughout much of his life, Truman expressed disdain toward Black people, Asians, Jews, and just about every group other than White Protestants.[64] To that end, Democratic Southerners were reasonably satisfied when the Missouri-born vice president became president after the death of FDR in 1945. As noted earlier, in July 1948, shortly before beginning his campaign for a full four-year term, Truman, through an Executive Order, desegregated the military. Just three months earlier, then-General Dwight Eisenhower, the highest-ranking officer of the military at the time, argued before a congressional committee that a segregated military was necessary to "protect unit cohesion,"[65] but Truman decided the time had come to desegregate. Even then, most accounts point to Truman's use of racist language throughout the rest of his life.[66]

A few years later, President Dwight Eisenhower (1953–1961) basically avoided the race issue, even though he presided over the nation during massive Black marches, lunch counter and bus protests, and the historic U.S. Supreme Court *Brown v. Board of Education* desegregation decision. His one concession to change came in 1957, when Eisenhower ordered federal troops to accompany students to a segregated Arkansas high school after Orval Faubus, the state's governor and avowed segregationist, had blocked their admission with national guardsmen blocking the entrances. Nevertheless, Eisenhower, a former general, not only believed in a segregated army but insisted that, as a general rule, civil rights issues should be managed on a state-by-state basis.[67]

During his campaign for the presidency, John F. Kennedy (1961–1963) spoke passionately for civil rights. However, he spent most of his three years in office reacting to racial crises rather than promoting policies to end them. Protests, demonstrations, and conflicts between civil rights leaders and segregationists were commonplace during Kennedy's presidency. Most of his efforts to solve discrimination issues occurred on a piecemeal basis, despite the fact that Kennedy called civil rights a "moral crisis." For example, when African-American James Meredith attempted to attend the segregated University of Mississippi in 1962, Kennedy assigned federal marshals to assist Meredith's entry but offered little else in terms of setting broad national policy. Shaken by violence and demonstrations in the South, in 1963 Kennedy gave a national address pledging tough legislation to end segregation and provide economic and political equality for African Americans. However, Congress wasn't moved, at least before Kennedy's assassination in November 1963. Meanwhile, key African-American leaders who had looked to Kennedy for a holistic approach to racism remained disappointed with what they perceived as spotty attention to the most critical issue of the day.[68]

If there is a bright spot in presidential behavior for racism opponents, it lies with Lyndon Johnson (1963–1969). As Senate Majority Leader during the last years of the Eisenhower administration, the Texan pushed through the Civil Rights Act of 1957, which allowed federal prosecution of anyone who interfered with an individual's attempt to vote. His leadership role changed considerably after being selected as John F. Kennedy's vice-presidential running mate in 1960. Thrust into the presidency in 1963 after Kennedy's assassination, and Johnson leveraged his new position to strengthen a modest civil rights bill and secure its passage from Congress in 1964. He promoted a much more robust civil rights package a year later with the 1965 Voting

Rights Act, which became the most important voting rights legislation since the Civil Rights Amendments.[69]

Two examples of presidential attitudes on race occurred with then-Republican President Richard Nixon (1969–1974) and future President Ronald Reagan (1981–1989). In a taped telephone conversation about the United Nations votes from several African nations, Reagan is recorded as having said to Nixon, "To see those, those monkeys from those African countries—damn them, they're still uncomfortable wearing shoes!" To that, Nixon let out a robust laugh.[70] But the exchange was more than casual bad humor—it was insight into Nixon's values. In a subsequent taped conversation with a confidant, Nixon used similar language about Africans. Still reacting to the U.N. vote, Nixon told his friend that the actions of African delegates proved "how they ought to be still hanging from the trees by their tails." Tim Naftali, the first Director of the Nixon Presidential Library and Museum, summarized Nixon's behavior as follows: "Nixon believed in a hierarchy of races, with whites and Asians much higher up than people of African descent and Latinos."[71]

Serving as president for only slightly more than two years, Gerald Ford (1974–1977) had little opportunity to lead on race-related issues. While in Congress, he voted for the Voting Rights Act of 1965 and signed a seven-year extension of the act shortly after he assumed office in August 1974. Otherwise, Ford was rather passive on race.

As a Democratic Southerner from Georgia, Jimmy Carter (1977–1981) presented a different attitude on race than fellow Southerner Lyndon Johnson. In fact, Carter, known later in his life as a humanitarian, took a rather conservative approach to race-related issues. With respect to desegregation, Carter was anything but a proponent. During his 1976 campaign for the office, he lauded African Americans for "trying to maintain the ethnic purity of their neighborhoods" at a time when the civil rights movement was urging just the opposite[72] (he apologized for those words five days later). Towing the line in this manner, Carter was able to secure a majority of the White vote in 1976 while still capturing more than 90 percent of the African-American vote. When the Bakke case came before the U.S. Supreme Court in 1978, Carter advocated for Affirmative Action. Still, his civil rights record *after* his presidency was more proactive than during his presidency.

George H. W. Bush (1989–1993) revealed his approach to race while running for the presidency, when he ran a campaign ad focusing on a Black murderer who raped a White woman. The symbolism behind the ad was that Democratic opponent Michael Dukakis would allow African Americans to pulverize the White community.[73] Once in the Oval Office, Bush was cautious about race. He vetoed a civil rights act in 1990, which was designed to stop employment discrimination, but signed a weaker version the next year.

President Bill Clinton (1993–2001) had a less-than-stellar record on race and discrimination. Regarding the latter, Clinton ran on a platform that would allow gays to serve openly in the military, which would have been a step toward equality for the LGBTQ community. But he backed down on the issue by signing a law promoting "Don't Ask, Don't Tell," where gay military members could remain in their positions as long as they didn't go public about their lives, at which point they would be separated from the service. Regarding race, Clinton was popular with the Black community for his preaching of racial reconciliation. Acclaimed Black novelist Toni Morrison even dubbed Clinton "the nation's first Black president" for his commitment to ending racial injustice, but little substance accompanied Clinton's extensive symbolism.[74]

Much of George W. Bush's presidency (2001–2009) centered on foreign policy, beginning with the September 11, 2001 Muslim terrorist attacks on the United States. Bush quickly committed to crushing Al Qaida, the Afghan-based extremist organization claiming responsibility for the attacks. He and Congress quickly conceived the 342-page USA Patriot Act that restricted civil liberties of many Muslim U.S. citizens and residents. Civil libertarians called the Bush presidency "the Islamophobic administration."[75] Regarding Latinos, Bush strongly supported the attempt by a coalition of Senate Republicans and Democrats to pass the DREAM Act (Development, Relief, and Education for Alien Minors), the first major immigration act since 1986. Nevertheless, the effort failed for lack of Republican support in the U.S Senate, even though Republicans controlled that body at the time.

Lastly, we focus on the Barrack Obama administration (2009–2017). As the nation's first African-American president, Democrat Obama knew well the pains of discrimination and racism. Indeed, he was directly confronted by it. Many opponents, including future President Donald Trump, questioned whether Obama was born in the United States, although Trump tersely reversed years of promoting the false claim in the last days of his 2016 campaign.[76]

Soon after he assumed office, Obama proposed that Congress reconsider the abandoned DREAM Act. Hope emerged, given that Democratic majorities controlled both chambers of Congress, but once again the effort missed the mark. This time, Senate Democrats failed to hold their 60 members together, and were therefore unable to overcome a Republican filibuster against the proposal. Nevertheless, Obama pursued relief for immigrants through an executive order to create the Deferred Action for Childhood Arrivals program (DACA), which allowed 800,000 foreign-born children to remain in the United States until Congress came up with a legislative solution. That program remains in place to this day, although its presence via executive order leaves it vulnerable to demise either through congressional legislation or federal court decisions.[77]

On matters concerning African Americans, Obama was less direct, perhaps because of a fear that he would be accused of promoting African Americans to the exclusion of others. For example, early in his presidency, Black members of Congress pressed Obama to promote legislation alleviating Black unemployment, which was more than twice the rate of White unemployment. To that request Obama replied, "I can't pass laws that say I'm just helping Black folks."[78] On the other hand, Obama did successfully promote passage of the Fair Sentencing Act of 2010, which adjusted harsh sentencing for Black people compared to White people for similar drug-related crimes. Clearly, Obama felt the need to be measured in his leadership of race-related issues.

The foregoing paragraphs reveal much about the history of presidential activity with respect to racism, discrimination, and immigration. Other than clear national crises usually precipitated by tragic incidents of great violence, for the most part presidents have shown little substantive willingness to take positions dedicated to repairing the nation's racism problems. Even then, the responses have been limited and almost transactional in scope, as in "what do I have to do to get through this so I can go on to something else?" For the most part, leaders of the executive branch have shied away from tackling racism and its causes in any holistic manner. Looking back, only Presidents Lyndon Johnson and Barrack Obama showed serious commitment to taking on racism directly. The efforts of virtually all others were nonexistent, weak, or ineffective. In some cases, they walked away from the issue altogether.

NATIONAL INSTITUTIONS AND ACTORS IN PERSPECTIVE

As with many sweeping issues, key leaders in the national government have had opportunities to chart a definitive course for combating racism in American society. But more times than not, they haven't done so, at least not in any clear-cut, consistent, and ongoing manner. Yes, there have been occasional moments of clear outrage at specific events, such as when President Eisenhower ordered federal marshals to escort James Meredith into the University of Mississippi or when Congress passed the Voting Rights Act of 1965. Nevertheless, the overall record of national commitment to racial, ethnic, and religious tolerance has been rather muddy.

SHIFTING RACE POLICY TO THE STATES

The lack of authoritative moral clarity at the national level has allowed the race issue and its management to fall into the unsteady hands of state and local governments, which has brought on a different set of problems. Predictably, given extensive powers at these levels and a lack of agreement, a rather ragged patchwork-quilt-like series of approaches to race has emerged.

Forty-nine states have hate crime laws, but many are of token value with poor reporting procedures, insensitive law enforcement, or both. Worse yet, only 31 states collect hate crime data for the Federal Bureau of Investigation archives, despite a national law in 1990 requiring such. In 2020, the last available year for national data, 71 cities with populations over 100,000 did not report *any* hate crimes from the previous year, not because they were safe but because they had no mechanisms for doing so.[79] Another problem is that states have different definitions of hate crimes and the penalties for them. For example, an assault on a Black person in one state may be labeled a hate crime but not in another.

The information above clearly shows that hate crimes are a major component of racist practices in American society. Like racism in general, these acts of discrimination existed in the United States long before Donald Trump's presidency. But their numbers grew considerably during the four years of Trump's presidency, raising the question of whether his inflammatory racial rhetoric encouraged those with racial animus. Given Trump's exhortations to dismiss non-White people, it's difficult to see any other answer. An examination of hate crime homicides between 2004 and 2019 shows the annual numbers soaring from 4 in 2013 to 51 in 2019.[80] At the same time, the number of mass shootings (classified by the FBI as events or four or more people are injured or killed) between 2017 and 2021 was the largest of any half-decade going back to 1966.[81]

There's more. Young White males play the largest role in mass shootings. An investigation by the *New York Times* found that young men aged 21 and under were responsible for six of the nine largest mass shootings between 2018 and 2022.[82] In a larger study of 113 mass shootings between 1982 and July 2022 where the shooter's race could be identified, 62 percent of the shooters were White.[83] Clearly, not all mass shootings are carried out by young White supremacists. That said, it's obvious that they have a major role in these activities and their increasing numbers—a role that gathered steam during the Trump administration. But it hasn't stopped. Their anger has spilled over to the Biden administration, particularly since so many believe that the presidential election was "stolen," including large numbers of congressional Republicans.

Discrimination, always an underpinning in American culture, but more exposed than at other times during the civil rights period, is once again front and center in the nation's politics. It has reemerged stronger than ever, with a huge assist from Donald Trump. He is an individual with the uncanny ability to widen the nation's racial wounds largely through appeals to disgruntled White people and White supremacists, while increasing his power in the process. Along the way, steps by Trump and his racist minions have threatened the nation's democracy. We turn to that discussion in part III.

NOTES

1. These elements are discussed at length in Robbie W.C. Tourse, Johnnie Hamilton-Mason, and Nancy J. Wewiorski, *Systemic Racism in the United States* (Cham, Switzerland: Springer, 2018), pp. 9–11.

2. "Descendants if Black Slaves in Some Native American Tribes—Know as Freedmen—Struggle for Recognition as Tribal Citizens," *Chicago Tribune*, May 1, 2021, https://www.chicagotribune.com/nation-world/ct-aud-nw-freedmen-native-american-tribes-20210501-zxsby5vrmbgmpo37a7x6y4cvpe-story.html.

3. The terms Indigenous Americans and Native Americans are used interchangeably in this book.

4. Executive Order 9971 was signed July 26, 1948,

5. Morgan Marietta, "The Right to Vote is not in the Constitution," *The Conversation*, August 26, 2020, https://theconversation.com/the-right-to-vote-is-not-in-the-constitution-144531.

6. David M. Potter, *The Impending Crisis, 1848-1861* (New York, NY: Harper and Row, 1976), pp. 90–120.

7. "Sharecropping, Black Land Acquisition, and White Supremacy, (1868-1900)," Duke Stanford World Food Policy Center, https://wfpc.sanford.duke.edu/durham-food-history/sharecropping-black-land-acquisition-and-white-supremacy-1868-1900.

8. "The Ku Klux Klan in the 1920s," American Experience, PBS.org, https://www.pbs.org/wgbh/americanexperience/films/klansville/. https://www.pbs.org/wgbh/americanexperience/features/flood-klan/.

9. Terry H. Anderson, *The Pursuit of Fairness: A History of Affirmative Action* (New York, NY: Oxford University Press, 2004), p. 5.

10. Quoted in Amy McKeever, "Voter Suppression has Haunted America since it was Founded," *National Geographic*, August 21, 2020, https://www.nationalgeographic.com/history/article/voter-suppression-haunted-united-states-since-founded.

11. Anderson, *The Pursuit of Fairness*, p. 5, and "A History of Voter Suppression," National Low Income Housing Coalition, September 2020, https://nlihc.org/resource/history-voter-suppression.

12. The case was *Smith v. Allwright*.

13. "How the Voting Rights Act Transformed Black Voting in the South, in One Chart," *Vox*, August 6, 2015, https://www.vox.com/2015/3/6/8163229/voting-rights-act-1965.

14. "The Impact of Voter Suppression on Communities of Color," The Brennan Center, January 10, 2022, https://www.brennancenter.org/our-work/research-reports/impact-voter-suppression-communities-color.

15. For a case study, see Kimbra Cutlip, "In 1868, Two Nations Made a Treaty, the U.S. Broke It and Plains Indians Tribes are Still Seeking Justice," *The Smithsonian*, November 7, 2018, https://www.smithsonianmag.com/smithsonian-institution/1868-two-nations-made-treaty-us-broke-it-and-plains-indian-tribes-are-still-seeking-justice-180970741/.

16. Quoted in Kunal M. Parker, *Making Foreigners: Immigration and Citizenship Law in America, 1600-2000* (New York, NY: Cambridge University Press, 2015), p. 174. The case was *Piper et al v. Big Pine School District of Inyo County et al*.

17. "How Voter Suppression Laws Target Native Americans," The Brennan Center for Justice, May 23, 2022, https://www.brennancenter.org/our-work/research-reports/how-voter-suppression-laws-target-native-americans.

18. "Native American Votes Helped Secure Biden's Win in Arizona," *APNews*, November 19, 2020, https://apnews.com/article/election-2020-joe-biden-flagstaff-arizona-voting-rights-fa452fbd546fa00535679d78ac40b890.

19. The case was *Arizona v. Inter Tribal Council of Arizona, Inc*.

20. "How Voter Suppression Laws Target Native Americans," The Brennan Center for Justice.

21. The term "Latino" can be misleading because of its breadth. Technically, "Latino" refers to people from Latin America, including Mexico, the countries in Central America, and the countries in South America. Latinos share the same language with "Hispanics," those whose ancestors hail from the Iberian Peninsula, which is largely Spain. Then there are Puerto Ricans, Cubans, Dominicanos (people from the Dominican Republic), and a few Caribbean areas who speak Spanish but identify as Hispanics. Inasmuch as about 78 percent of all of the first group have roots in the Americas, we use the term "Latino" for the entire Spanish-speaking immigrant bloc.

22. Stephanie S. Pimcetl, *Transforming California* (Baltimore, MD: The Johns Hopkins Press, 1999), p. 5.

23. Monica Muñoz Martinez, "Oversight of the Trump Administration's Border Policies and the Relationship between Anti-Immigrant Rhetoric and Domestic Terrorism," Testimony before Congress, September 6, 2019.

24. Tomás R. Jiménez, *Replenished Ethnicity: Mexican Americans, Immigration, and Identity* (Berkeley, CA: University of California Press, 2010), p. 37.

25. Ibid., p. 40.

26. "Estimates of the Unauthorized Immigrant Population Residing in the United States January 2015-January 2018," Department of Homeland Security, January 2021, https://www.dhs.gov/sites/default/files/publications/immigration-statistics/Pop_Estimate/UnauthImmigrant/unauthorized_immigrant_population_estimates_2015_-_2018.pdf.

27. Lon Kurashige, *Two Faces of Exclusion: The Untold History of Anti-Asian Racism in the United States* (Chapel Hill, NC: University of North Carolina Press, 2016), p. 22.

28. Kevin Starr, *Inventing the Dream* (New York, NY: Oxford University Press, 1985), pp. 42–43.

29. Beth Lew-Williams, *The Chinese Must Go* (Cambridge, MA: Harvard University Press, 2018), p. 234.

30. The decision was *Ozawa v. United States.* Parker, *Making Foreigners*, p. 152.

31. "Going for Broke: The 442nd Regimental Combat Team," The National World War II Museum, New Orleans, September 24, 2020, https://www.nationalww2museum.org/war/articles/442nd-regimental-combat-team.

32. "Decades after Infamous Beating Death, Recent Attacks Haunt Asian Americans," *The New York Times,* June 17, 2022, https://www.nytimes.com/2022/06/16/us/vincent-chin-anti-asian-attack-detroit.html.

33. "A Citizen Fights for His Civil Rights after 9/11: Amric Singh Rathour," Advancing Justice, https://archive.advancingjustice-la.org/sites/default/files/UCRS%2013_Amric_Singh_Rathour_story%20r2.pdf.

34. "Asian American Access to Democracy in the 2008 Elections," Asian American Legal Defense Fund, 2008, https://www.aaldef.org/uploads/pdf/AALDEF_Election_2008_Report.pdf.

35. "Trump Sparks Anger by Calling Coronavirus the 'Chinese Virus,'" *The Guardian*, March 17, 2020, https://www.theguardian.com/world/2020/mar/17/trump-calls-covid-19-the-chinese-virus-as-rift-with-coronavirus-beijing-escalates.

36. "How Asian-American Leaders Are Grappling With Xenophobia Amid Coronavirus," *The New York Times*, April 10, 2020, https://www.nytimes.com/2020/03/29/us/politics/coronavirus-asian-americans.html.

37. "Exclusive: 43% of Americans Say a Specific Organization or People to Blame for COVID-19," *USA Today*, March 21, 2021, https://www.usatoday.com/story/news/politics/2021/03/21/poll-1-4-americans-has-seen-asians-blamed-covid-19/4740043001/.

38. "Many Black and Asian Americans Say They Have Experienced Discrimination Amid the COVID-19 Outbreak," Pew Research, https://www.pewresearch.org/social-trends/2020/07/01/many-black-and-asian-americans-say-they-have-experienced-discrimination-amid-the-covid-19-outbreak/.

39. "Anti-Asian Hate Crime Reported to Police in America's 16 Largest Cities," Center for the Study of Hate and Extremism, California State University, San Bernardino, March 21, 2021, https://www.csusb.edu/sites/default/files/FACT%20SHEET-%20Anti-Asian%20Hate%202020%20rev%203.21.21.pdf.

40. "Survey: 1 in 4 in U.S. Have Asian-American Bias," *ABC News*, April 26, 2001, https://abcnews.go.com/US/story?id=93457.

41. In his *Critical Elections and the Mainstreams of American Politics*, Walter Dean Burnham writes about the unique conditions leading to mass realignments of voter behavior. Most political scientists consider the 1960s as one such period largely due to the passage of the Democrat-sponsored Civil Rights Acts of 1963 and 1964 along with Voting Rights Act of 1965. Published in 1970 by W.W. Norton Company, New York, New York.

42. Tova Andrea Wang, *The Politics of Voter Suppression* (New York, NY: Cornell University Press, 2012), p. 125.

43. See "Family-Based Immigration Backlogs: 5 Things to Know," February 10, 2022, fwd.us, San Francisco and Washington, DC, https://www.fwd.us/news/family-based-immigration-backlogs/.

44. "One-Third of Innovators in U.S. Are Immigrants," VOA Learning English, Washington, DC, https://learningenglish.voanews.com/a/more-than-one-third-of-inventors-discoverers-in-us-are-foreign-born/3242494.html and "The Impact of International Scientists, Engineers, and Students on Research Outputs and Global Competitiveness," *MIT Science Policy Review*, August 30, 2021, https://sciencepolicyreview.org/2021/08/impact-international-scientists-engineers-students-us-research-output/#:~:text=International%20scientists%20and%20engineers%20f.

45. See "Modern Immigration Wave Brings 59 Million to U.S., Driving Population Growth and Change Through 2065," September 28, 1965, https://www.pewresearch.org/hispanic/2015/09/28/modern-immigration-wave-brings-59-million-to-u-s-driving-population-growth-and-change-through-2065/#:~:text=As%20a%20result%20of%20its,Americans%20were%20non%2DHispanic%20whites and "Most Americans Say the Declining Share of White People in the U.S. is neither Good nor Bad for Society," Pew Research Center, August 23, 2021, https://www.pewresearch.org/fact-tank/2021/08/23/most-americans-say-the-declining-share-of-white-people-in-the-u-s-is-neither-good-nor-bad-for-society/.

46. "Projecting Majority-Minority," U.S. Census Bureau, Washington, DC, 2014, https://www.census.gov/content/dam/Census/newsroom/releases/2015/cb15-tps16_graphic.pdf.

47. For example, see George J. Borjas, "Yes, Immigration Hurts American Workers," *Politico Magazine*, September/October 2016, https://www.politico.com/magazine/story/2016/09/trump-clinton-immigration-economy-unemployment-jobs-214216/.

48. "Immigration Facts: The Positive Economic Impact of Immigration," Fwd. US, 2020, https://www.fwd.us/wp-content/uploads/2020/09/Immigration-Facts-The-Positive-Impact-of-Immigration-2020-Fact-Sheet.pdf.

49. William Sturkey, "The Hidden History of the Civil Rights Act of 1960," *Black Perspectives*, https://www.aaihs.org/the-hidden-history-of-the-civil-rights-act-of-1960/.

50. Anderson, *The Pursuit of Fairness*, p. 82.

51. See Andrew Garber, "Debunking False Claims about the John Lewis Voting Act," The Brennan Center for Justice, January 13, 2022, https://www.brennancenter.org/our-work/research-reports/debunking-false-claims-about-john-lewis-voting-rights-act.

52. "Republicans Who Supported Voting Rights Act Now Oppose Bill Democrats say Would Strengthen Its Provisions," *The Washington Post*, January 19, 2022, https://www.washingtonpost.com/politics/2022/01/19/republicans-voting-rights/.

53. Quoted in David Brian Robertson, *Federalism and the Making of America* (New York, NY: Routledge, 2012), pp. 62–63.

54. For a discussion on the issues surrounding Roosevelt's order, see Kurashige, *Two Faces of Exclusion*, pp. 171–183.

55. Lawrence Goldstone, *Inherently Unequal: The Betrayal of Equal Rights By the Supreme Court, 1865–1903*, (New York, NewYork: Walker & Company), 2020, p. 155.

56. See *Shaw v. Reno*, 1993.

57. "Mandatory Busing May Go, Even If Races Stay Apart," *The New York Times*, January 6, 1991, https://www.nytimes.com/1991/01/16/us/justices-rule-mandatory-busing-may-go-even-if-races-stay-apart.html.

58. The seven states included Alabama, Georgia, Louisiana, Mississippi, North Carolina (most), South Carolina, and Virginia. The three states with affected portions by the law were Alaska, Arizona, and Virginia.

59. See "Supreme Court Strikes down Affirmative Action in College Admissions," *The Wall Street Journal*, June 29, 2023, https://www.wsj.com/articles/supreme-court-rules-against-affirmative-action-c94b5a9c. The case was *Students for Fair Admission, Inc. v. President and Fellows of Harvard College*.

60. Aziz Huq, "When Was Judicial Self-Restraint?" *California Law Review* 579 (2012), https://chicagounbound.uchicago.edu/cgi/viewcontent.cgi?article=2520&context=journal_articles.

61. George C. Edwards III and Stephen J. Wayne, *Presidential Leadership*, 8th ed. (Boston, MA: Cengage Wadsworth, 2010), p. 1.

62. This and the remaining examples in this paragraph come from Stephen A. Jones and Eric Freedman, "Presidents have a Long History of Condescension, Indifference and Outright Racism toward Black Americans," in *The Conversation*, August 26, 2020, https://theconversation.com/presidents-have-a-long-history-of-condescension-indifference-and-outright-racism-toward-black-americans-143166. For a much more comprehensive discussion, see their *Presidents and Black America: A Documentary History* (Thousand Oaks, CA: Sage Press, 2021).

63. See Daniel A. Gross, "The U.S. Government Turned Away Thousands of Jewish Refugees, Fearing That They Were Nazi Spies," *Smithsonian Magazine*, November 18, 2015, https://www.smithsonianmag.com/history/us-government-turned-away-thousands-jewish-refugees-fearing-they-were-nazi-spies-180957324/ and Dara Lind, "How America's Rejection of Jews Fleeing Nazi Germany Haunts Our Refugee Policy Today," *Vox*, January 27, 2017, https://www.vox.com/policy-and-politics/2017/1/27/14412082/refugees-history-holocaust.

64. See "How Harry S. Truman went from being a Racist to Desegregating the Military," *The Washington Post*, July 26, 2018, https://www.washingtonpost.com/news/retropolis/wp/2018/07/26/how-harry-s-truman-went-from-being-a-racist-to-desegregating-the-military/.

65. John R. Allen, "Like Truman's Military Desegregation Order, Leadership against Racism begins at the Top," Brookings, July 26, 2019, https://www.brookings.edu/blog/up-front/2019/07/26/like-trumans-military-desegregation-order-leadership-against-racism-starts-at-the-top/.

66. "Truman's Racist Talk Cited by Historian," *The Seattle Times*, November 3, 1991, https://archive.seattletimes.com/archive/?date=19911103&slug=1314805.

67. H. Prentice Baptiste and Blanca Araujo, "American Presidents and Their Attitudes, Beliefs, and Actions Surrounding Education and Multiculturalism," Multicultural Education, Spring, 2004, https://files.eric.ed.gov/fulltext/EJ783087.pdf.

68. See Daniel Ruprecht, "Executive Inaction: John F. Kennedy and the Civil Rights Crisis," January 1, 2016, https://ir.vanderbilt.edu/bitstream/handle/1803/8351/Executive-Inaction.pdf?sequence=1&isAllowed=y.

69. See James MacGregor Burns, *Leadership* (New York, NY: Harper and Row, 1978), pp. 345–356.

70. Tim Naftali, "Ronald Reagan's Long-Hidden Racist Conversation with Richard Nixon," *The Atlantic*, July 30, 2019, https://www.theatlantic.com/ideas/archive/2019/07/ronald-reagans-racist-conversation-richard-nixon/595102/.

71. Ibid.

72. Quoted in Ian Haney-Lopez, "The Racism at the Heart of the Reagan Presidency," *Salon*, January 11, 2014, https://www.salon.com/2014/01/11/the_racism_at_the_heart_of_the_reagan_presidency/.

73. "What Was George H.W. Bush's Record on Race?" *PBS News Hour*, December 4, 2018, https://www.pbs.org/newshour/politics/what-was-george-h-w-bushs-record-on-race.

74. Jim M. Weber, "William Jefferson Clinton, 'Racism in the United States,' (16 October 1995)," *Voices of Democracy* 1 (2006): 228–229, http://voicesofdemocracy.umd.edu/wp-content/uploads/2010/07/weber-clinton.pdf.

75. "The Islamophobic Administration," Brennan Center for Justice, April 19, 2017, https://www.brennancenter.org/our-work/research-reports/islamophobic-administration.

76. "What Donald Trump has said through the years about where President Obama was Born," *Los Angeles Times*, September 16, 2016, https://www.latimes.com/politics/la-na-pol-trump-birther-timeline-20160916-snap-htmlstory.html.

77. For a discussion of DACA, see "Deferred Action for Childhood Arrivals (DACA)," *Immigration Equality*, August 30, 2020, https://immigrationequality.org/legal/legal-help/other-paths-to-status/deferred-action-for-childhood-arrivals-daca/.

78. Quoted in Randell Kennedy, "Did Obama Fail Black America," *Politico Magazine*, July/August 2014, https://www.politico.com/magazine/story/2014/06/black-president-black-attorney-general-so-what-108017/.

79. "Biden Signed a New Hate Crimes Law—But there's a Big Flaw," *Politico*, May 20, 2021, https://www.politico.com/interactives/2021/state-hate-crime-laws/.

80. "Hate Crime Homicides," *Report to the Nation: Illustrated Almanac*, Center for the Study of Hate and Extremism, California State University, San Bernardino, November 22, 2020, https://www.csusb.edu/sites/default/files/Special%20Status%20Report%20Nov%202020%2011.22.20%20combined.pdf.

81. "What You Need to Know about the Rise in U.S. Mass Shootings," The Marshall Project, July 6, 2022, https://www.themarshallproject.org/2022/07/06/what-you-need-to-know-about-the-rise-in-u-s-mass-shootings.

82. "A Disturbing New Pattern in Mass Shootings: Young Assailants," *The New York Times*, June 2, 2022, https://www.nytimes.com/2022/06/02/us/politics/mass-shootings-young-men-guns.html.

83. "Number of Mass Shootings in the United States between 1982 and July 2022. Bu Shooter's Race or Ethnicity," statista.com, https://www.statista.com/statistics/476456/mass-shootings-in-the-us-by-shooter-s-race/.

Chapter 5

Donald Trump and Bigotry

Some aspirants for elected office have longer documented histories than others. Regardless, there is a general rule of thumb regarding the attention paid to political candidates: the higher the office under discussion, the more that journalists, opponents, and the public will vet the candidate because of the responsibilities connected with the position. It stands to reason, therefore, that in the United States, candidates who pursue the presidency, the pinnacle of all elected offices and the most powerful position in the world, will draw the most scrutiny. And they do.

This takes us to Donald Trump, who has long maintained that he is "the least racist person that you've ever encountered."[1] Because of his appetite for notice long before his candidacy for the presidency, Trump has a rich history of drawing attention from the press—much of it not particularly positive. Hungry for publicity throughout his business career and social life, Trump was the closest thing to an open book when it came to the issue of race. In fact, often, he was downright blunt, and often cruelly so. In his view, African Americans were lazy; Jews, otherwise suspicious, were excellent managers of money; and El Salvadorans lived in "shithole" countries. For Trump, these sweeping observations represented his summary of humanity's components.[2] As his political persona developed, Trump's original prejudices were joined by negative characterizations of Latinos (also referred to as Hispanics), Asians, Muslims, and in some cases, women. His crass generalizations may have been acceptable to some people in the 1950s, 1960s, and 1970s, but they weren't nearly as welcome on a mass level by 2016 when Trump ran for the presidency.

For presidential candidate Donald Trump, however, his insensitive observations about race as a young man were no different 50 years after his earliest days in business, and they were easily authenticated for public scrutiny. Nevertheless, when presented with the revolving list of 2016 presidential election candidates, enough voters were willing to choose Trump or Democratic opponent Hillary Clinton, overlooking what otherwise had become unacceptable social behavior. The question is, why?

Some voters considered Trump's racist statements as simply rough edges around an otherwise remarkably forthright candidate who blended conservative principles and populist appeals; as such, they disregarded those indelicacies or considered them as meaningless attempts to attract voter support. Others, however, weren't the slightest offended by Trump's rather blunt comments; in actuality, Trump's assessments about race were closer to their own feelings than they'd publicly admit. Indeed, the history of racism in this country suggests much more support for Trump's bigoted comments about the topic than we might think. Thus, sporadic racist assertions and all, Donald Trump was still able to secure nomination from the Republican party, followed by a majority of electoral votes, and become the nation's 45th president.

This chapter centers on Donald Trump's attitude toward race from his childhood through the days leading up to his presidency. Despite token presidential gestures opposing racist language and behavior, from young adulthood on to his bigger-than-life business career, Trump espoused a continuous distinctly negative position and rhetoric about race. As will be chronicled in chapter 6, racist language became a fixture throughout his presidency, along with crude diatribes against Jews, Muslims, Chinese, and women. His negative stereotypes about various groups existed then and persist now as key elements of his lexicon.

But the issue here is not simply Trump's crass approach to race. The fact remains that many Americans weren't offended by his public statements on race then—and perhaps even now—sufficiently to oppose the flamboyant business person-turned-politician. In the long run, this lack of concern may be even more significant for America's future than the behavior of Trump before, during and after his presidency.

CHILDHOOD

Relatively little is known about Donald Trump's approach to race during his formative years. We do know, however, that he grew up in a highly structured environment dominated by his father who seemed more concerned with tending to his business than his wife and children. We also know that young Trump had a temperamental, rebellious side that he expressed especially toward authority figures, which left him feeling somewhat like an outsider.

This combination is important when considering that years later, particularly in his run for the presidency, Donald Trump repeatedly espoused an "us" versus "them" attitude, with the "us" group claiming poor treatment of the general public by elites, otherwise known as the "them." Such an approach was totally artificially contrived and inauthentic, given that by adulthood, he clearly presented himself as a member of the elite establishment.

Life in Queens

Donald Trump grew up in Queens, 45 minutes and a world away from Manhattan. Years later, the suburban-like New York borough became a racially mixed community, but during Trump's youth it was, according to one longtime resident, "a borough defined by tribalism, racial segregation, and simmering resentments,"[3] which was divided into various isolated neighborhoods. Father and patriarch Fred Trump, a developer by trade, built many single family homes and apartments in Queens.

For most of Donald Trump's childhood, Fred, mother Mary Trump and their brood of five children lived in a 23-room home safely surrounded by upper middle-class residences. Years later, while Donald Trump noted some rough spots in Queens, he nevertheless described Jamaica Estates as "an oasis" that was "safe and family oriented."[4] In fact, the Trumps lived in a sort of enclave, safely sealed off from the rest of the other racial and ethnic communities. Greeks, Irish Catholics and Jews resided in segregated sectors; still, at least they were all thankfully White and politically conservative, except for a small Black section whose residents stuck to themselves.

In fact, the divisions in Queens exposed some of the same characteristics, vulnerabilities and opportunities for Trump in his approach to national audiences. Maria Budhos, a well-known observer of contemporary issues and former Queens resident, once described the neighborhood as a sort of social petri dish from which wealthy Donald Trump could stir passions of the less affluent: "The Trump franchise has always been about promising the masses access to a very particular brand of wealth and glamour. That's a potent mixture for the disenfranchised whites drawn to his rallies: Trump offers entry into a distant world, yet he's simultaneously disdainful of elites."[5] In this sense, Trump's isolation in an enclave of a segregated community was a social experiment of sorts where he first learned how to manipulate those who hoped for a better life that in all likelihood would never be realized.

Reports suggest that Donald Trump's childhood may have been a bit less than idyllic. According to Mary Trump, a psychologist, niece of Donald Trump, and granddaughter of Fred Trump, the patriarch Trump was constantly demanding and punished his children for being kind and generous instead of making money and passion to "succeed at all costs." The Trump children, including Donald, received little affection from their father, while their mother was often sidelined with serious emotional issues. Mary Trump also described her grandfather as callous and indifferent, with little time for his children. Instead he was laser-focused on his business, where he viewed people around him as expendable. To that end, Trump children were urged to concentrate on doing "anything to get attention, financial rewards, and to 'win.'"[6]

As a child, Donald Trump seemed to have serious issues with authority. With friends, he was carefree enough, but dealing with power relationships was another matter. He was described as ill-behaved in a respected, upscale private school and something of a hothead. An arrogant attitude often found Trump bullying others in class without reason.[7] In fact, he was sufficiently incorrigible in his classes that at the age of 13, his father sent Donald to New York Military Academy to learn respect and order. It was there that Trump was toughened up for the competitive business world that would follow in due course,[8] although he excelled much more in sports than in the academic world. As the captain of the baseball team, he carried a healthy .350 batting average.

Mary Trump adds another childhood psychological observation that future President Trump inherited from his father, which was avoiding being a loser at all costs: "In life, there can be only one winner and everybody else is a loser."[9] Mary Trump subsequently tangled with Donald and cousins in a lawsuit she filed over Fred Trump's estate, so her motives might be suspect. Nevertheless, the "expendability" concept attributed to Donald Trump by his niece was clearly observable through his associations with staff throughout his presidency.

Another account described Donald Trump's childhood as an unfortunate outcome of his father's cold and demanding attitude toward his children. The elder Trump's dour behavior at home paralleled his behavior toward the business world.[10] Fred Trump's children were useful only to the extent that they helped with his projects. From niece Mary Trump's point of view, Donald Trump emerged from his childhood pretty much with a personality much like that of his father: an architect of intentional division that "continues to benefit him at the expense of everybody else."[11]

Others saw a dark side of young Donald Trump that continued into adulthood. One assessment pointed to a troubling series of characteristics during his youth. Early on, the account goes, Donald showed signs of a brooding person not to be trifled with. He was described as incorrigible, swaggering, and unwilling to ever acknowledge mistakes—another trait later observed in his presidency. He was also termed a bully with a temper to match that also led to more than his share of fights. At one point during his military school years, the report continues, Trump was so incensed about an issue that he tried to push a fellow cadet out a second floor window, only to be stopped by his classmates.[12]

Donald Trump, himself, offers some insight into his assertive personality in his *Trump: The Art of the Deal*. In the book, Trump reveals an early arrogance when he discusses a heated disagreement with his piano teacher, an authority figure. He writes, "Even in elementary school, I was a very assertive, aggressive kid. In the second grade I actually gave a teacher a black eye—I punched my music teacher because I didn't think he knew anything about music and I almost got expelled."[13] Trump prides his behavior in that confrontation as "standing up" for himself, but it also could be viewed as a blatant rejection of authority. Put these childhood traits together—brash assertiveness, rejection of authority, arrogance, and a sense of entitlement--and we have an individual committed to winning at all costs regardless of who or what might be in his way or disagree with him.

Years later, the Trump philosophy of life would be represented by Donald Trump's closest allies. As recently as 2022, sometime-Trump political strategist Steve Bannon commenting on the 2020 presidential election, wrote in a forthcoming book that the former president "would lie about anything to win."[14] Likewise, in the aftermath of the same election, then-Trump Chief of Staff Mark Meadows repeatedly pushed the Trump lie that the election had been stolen when he knew otherwise.[15] "Do whatever it takes," the Trump childhood motto, framed his political work ethic. Then, there was Stephen Miller, a special assistant who with Trump in deliberately enraging White men, "rode that rage to the White House."[16] All the pieces of Trump's adult behavior had an early beginning.

College Years

His decent high school grades at the New York Military Academy led Trump to Fordham, a small Catholic university in the Bronx, after he failed to gain admission elsewhere, according to Mary Trump. Once again, he seemed more intent on sports than a solid education. Wayne Barrett, a reporter who wrote about Trump for decades, describes his two years at Fordham as "an uneventful mix of a light and undistinguished course load, combined with a sporting menu that ranged from squash to football."[17] But Fordham was only a bridge to bigger things. In his junior year, Trump transferred to the prestigious Wharton school (part of the University of Pennsylvania), where he continued his education with a largely under-the-radar existence, other than participation in sports and social activities. He graduated in 1968, a critical year and troubling time for many Americans, given the Vietnam War controversy and civil rights anguish, without publicly saying much about either.

Two controversies about Trump's tenure at Wharton emerged later when he climbed up the public political figure ladder. The first centered on the Vietnam War. Trump drew a high number in the national lottery that determined the order of conscription (355 of 366), virtually guaranteeing that he would not be drafted into military service. Still, he wanted to avoid involvement in the war, which in itself was understandable, considering its controversy. However, his alleged method of avoidance was provocative and may have bordered on illegality. Somehow, the longtime athlete managed to obtain a medical deferment from the military draft on the basis of bone spurs. Although the always physically competitive Trump denied it, interviews with the daughters of a deceased New York podiatrist years later suggested that the physician "wrote a letter for Trump and his physical impairment" as a favor to Fred Trump, in whose building he rented space for his medical practice.[18] The incident might not have even crossed anyone's mind except that as he came into view on the national stage, Trump didn't miss an opportunity to criticize people who shaded their own Vietnam Era records. For example, when U.S. Senator Richard Blumenthal falsely claimed that he served in Vietnam, Trump tore into the Connecticut Senator about his military "experience" which, by the way, Trump totally mischaracterized.[19]

The second Wharton misadventure revolved around Trump's alleged academic prowess at an institution known for producing superior graduates. In the years after his attendance as a student in the real estate program at the Ivy League school, Trump has repeatedly boasted of his presence on the Dean's List, a collection recognizing the best students who have completed their undergraduate education with distinction. Despite the claim, the Dean's list from 1968, the year of Trump's graduation, does not contain Trump's name. Yet, Trump has made the claim again and again without foundation throughout his adulthood to the present day.[20] Indeed, repeating a claim again and again, regardless of its inaccuracy, became a *modus operandi* for Trump when he continued his protest of the 2020 presidential election results: "If you say it long enough, hard enough, often enough, people will start to believe you," he once said.[21]

Viewed as isolated instances, these issues could easily be cast aside as youthful errors or poor judgment. But when considered in the context of Trump's overall career, they take on a much more serious tone. In both cases, Trump has emphasized his version of the "facts" again and again, much the same way that years later, he claimed again and again that his "victory" in the 2020 presidential election was "stolen"—also without foundation. There's more than a little irony in the comparison, although the 2020 misrepresentation takes on much graver meaning.

RACISM IN ADULTHOOD

Filled with a combined sense of entitlement and superiority, Donald Trump did not hesitate to compare his position in life with others. Nowhere was the contrast more distinct than in the subject of race, a pattern that followed him through his adult life all the way to the White House. For now, however, we limit our examination of Trump and race to his adult years leading up to the 2016 presidential election.

In the late 1970s, Trump completed his first major Manhattan construction project, the Grand Hyatt Hotel. By the 1980s, Trump had become a social fixture in Manhattan, the societal heart of New York City. His first blockbuster success, the 68-story Trump Tower, was heralded for its architecture and grandeur, despite a few scandals that occurred during construction.[22] *The New York Times* concluded as much about Trump's ascendance in a 1983 article. After recounting the city's most famous business families, the newspaper wrote: "And now there is Trump, a name that has in the last few years become an internationally recognized symbol of New York City as a mecca for the world's super rich."[23] That sense of entitlement placed Trump well beyond the world of construction, real estate, and finance.

The Central Park Five

He began to insert himself into political and social realms, often creating controversy along the way, especially in matters related to race. In 1989, Trump voiced critical comments about a New York tragedy centering on an attack of a 28-year-old White female investment banker while jogging in Central Park. The unknown assailant became known as "the Central Park Jogger." Two weeks after the attack, the New York police arrested five boys between the ages of 14 and 16. Four were African American; the fifth was Hispanic. Shortly thereafter, a full-page ad purchased by Donald Trump appeared in New York's major newspapers. Referring to "roving bands of wild criminals" that roam through parks intending to rape and murder innocent victims, the ad declared that they "should be executed for their crimes." The ad didn't mention Central Park or the victim, but the timing and subject matter made it clear that the reference was to the Central Park incident and the arrested participants.

African-American leaders characterized the ad as racist and demanded that Trump apologize. Trump refused. After a trial, the five accused teenagers were convicted and sent to prison. Years later, a longtime criminal confessed to the Central Park crime, and shortly thereafter the prisoners were released, with the City paying them $41 million for a wrongful conviction and imprisonment. Despite the facts, even then Trump refused to admit his poor judgment. Instead, he called the settlement a disgrace, and declared that "settling doesn't mean innocence."[24] Rather than admit error, Trump chose to double down.

Still there were times even then that Trump needed non-White people. In her book on Trump, Maggie Haberman references a conversation between Trump and mentor Roy Cohn where, in a real estate legal matter, Cohn advised Trump to hope for a Black judge because "they could be manipulated,"[25] a description Trump seemed to appreciate.

Miss Universe

Between 1996 and 2015, Donald Trump owned the Miss Universe Organization. In addition to the Miss Universe Pageant, the business included Miss USA and Miss Teen USA. Trump's problems with the parent organization began the first year he owned it. The winner in 1996, Alicia Machado, was from Venezuela. Shortly after Machado won the pageant, she began to gain weight. That physical change was particularly bothersome to Trump inasmuch as the pageant winner carried out various public functions for the coming year. Repeatedly, according to Machado, Trump belittled her for her weight, calling her "Miss Piggy" and "Miss Housekeeper." Machado soon became bulimic in attempting to deal with her weight gain, putting herself in physical jeopardy.[26]

But Trump's concerns were about more than weight. Miss Universe Pageant staffers complained that Trump, who had the right to reject and replace finalists, opposed too many women of color, often because they looked "too ethnic or dark skinned."[27] Over time, Univision, the Spanish-speaking television network airing Miss Universe pageants, severed its association with Trump because of his disparaging comments about Mexican immigrants and Mexican Americans. When asked if he would withdraw his false claims that Mexico allowed undesirable people to enter the country, Trump replied, "They're (immigrants) criminals in many cases, why would I change that statement?"[28] With his ownership of the Miss Universe Pageant, Trump revealed his attitudes about misogyny, racism and immigrants.

Birtherism

As with so many aspects of his political life, Donald Trump didn't invent birtherism; however, he was a master at utilizing the concept to his advantage. Birtherism was created early in 2008 during Barack Obama's campaign for the presidency. Subscribers to birtherism claimed without any evidence that Obama was born outside of the United States, namely Kenya, an African country.[29] The term was a not-so-subtle way of reminding the voters of

Obama's race. Moreover, if true, Obama would have never been eligible for the presidency, inasmuch as the U.S. Constitution clearly requires that the president be American-born.[30] In fact, Obama was born in Hawaii in 1961, as attested to by Honolulu hospital records, but that wasn't enough for Trump. The birthplace accusation haunted Obama to the point that he released a copy of his birth certificate in the months leading up to the 2008 election. But that wasn't the official state form, and therefore not satisfactory for the birthers.

Even after Obama's victory, the birther rumors continued. Donald Trump latched on to the movement and took it a step further. In March 2011, Trump said about Obama, "I have a birth certificate. . . . He (Obama) doesn't have a birth certificate. He may have one but there is something on that birth certificate—maybe religion, maybe it says he's a Muslim." A few weeks later, Trump upped the ante: "If [the birth certificate] weren't an issue, why wouldn't he (Obama) just solve it? . . . If he doesn't, it's one of the greatest scams in the history of politics . . . Right now, I have real doubts."[31] So, now Trump was questioning Obama's Christianity in addition to his race. In fact, the Muslim attribution to Obama also was false, but that didn't Trump stop from making it again and again.

In 2011, as he prepared for his re-election campaign, Obama released the longer birth certificate form. Meanwhile, Trump continued to fan the birtherism flame until September 2016, weeks before the general election, when he simply stated, "President Obama was born in the United States—period," without an apology for his lies over the preceding few years. With that, Trump went on his next set of grievances.

Mexican Rapists

Disparaging Hispanic Miss Universe candidates was not an outlier remark by Donald Trump; rather, it was part of a pattern. As with African Americans, Trump's animus for non-White people had no limits. He revealed as much on June 16, 2015 when he declared his candidacy for the Republican nomination to the presidency. The United States, he asserted, had become the punching bag of the world, with other nations taking advantage of us at every turn. Mexico had become enemy number one, he went on: "When Mexico sends its people, they're not sending their best. . . . They're sending people that have lots of problems, and they're bringing those problems with [them]. They're bringing drugs. They're bringing crime. They're bringing rapists."[32] In short, the Mexican government was responsible for harming the United States and its people by supporting Mexican immigrants who illegally came into this country.

Like so many other sweeping generalizations, Trump offered no proof then, or reliable data at any other time when he discussed immigration and Mexico. As Trump's campaign gathered steam in 2015, he repeatedly turned to illegal immigration as the source of the problems suffered by everyday Americans, a divisive tactic that summarized America's condition as "us versus them." Over time, the list of undesirable countries grew, almost all of which were comprised of non-White people or non-Christians.

RACE IN TRUMP'S BUSINESS AFFAIRS

During his teenage years, Donald Trump became increasingly involved in his father's construction business. He regularly participated in the Trump Management company's policy of rejecting the applications of would be-Black tenants because of their race, although such a reason was never offered.[33] Later, while in college first at Fordham, then at Penn's Wharton School, he continued to work for his father on weekends, shuttling back and forth between Philadelphia and Queens.

After graduation, Donald Trump went to work with his father full time. By the age of 25, he was made president of Trump Management, with the responsibility of overseeing the management of thousands of Trump apartments. Fred Trump assumed the role of chairman. Until the early 1970s, the father had found himself in a couple of controversies with local public housing authorities over building profits, but nothing threatening to the wellbeing of his company. Shortly after assuming the presidency of the family organization, Donald Trump took the company in a new direction that revealed openly racist policies. Clearly, the way he conducted himself foreshadowed his behavior approaching and after winning in the 2016 presidential election.

Civil Rights Abuse Allegations at Trump Village

Trouble regarding allegations of racial discrimination began for Donald Trump in 1973. The year before, several undercover agents working for the City of New York had applied for apartments in Trump Village, a large working-class housing project with 3,800 units in Brooklyn. The Urban League, a prominent civil rights organization, had received several complaints of discrimination against Black people, and that such treatment violated the Fair Housing Act of 1969. In order to validate the complaints, the Urban League created "Operation Open City," an undercover mission where White and Black couples separately applied to rent vacant apartments. Repeatedly, White applications were approved, while Black applicants were repeatedly told there were no vacancies.

Upon assessing the evidence, the U.S. Department of Justice sued Trump Management. Shortly after charges were filed alleging racial bias, Trump Management President Donald Trump responded, "[The charges] are absolutely ridiculous. We have never discriminated, and never would."[34] Trump denied knowing anything about federal law and the rental policies at his apartments. He actually tried to sue the United States for $100,000,000 in damages, the first of many $100,000,000 lawsuits, for falsely accusing his company of racial discrimination against African Americans. The lawsuit was quickly dismissed by the judge in the case.

Despite Trump's denial, the DOJ was convinced they had a case. Elyse Goldweber, the prosecuting attorney for the Civil Rights Division of DOJ at the time, reflected on the obvious discrimination from a check on applications: "If you came and you were a person of color, your application would be marked with a big 'C.' . . . I was pretty young and naïve. But that was a really strong thing, finding the 'C' on people of color's applications."[35] The evidence was unmistakable. Nevertheless, the case dragged on in the courts for nearly two years, with the matter settled after Trump Management agreed to a consent decree that his company would not discriminate. Part of the agreement included an order to advertise in local newspapers that Trump Management would rent to any qualified person irrespective of race; however, there was no monetary penalty or admission of guilt. Trump presented the outcome as a "victory over the federal government" even though he signed a consent decree.

Three years later, the Justice Department found Trump in contempt of the 1973 order. The department brought Trump and his company back to court, alleging that the consent agreement had been breached. Seeing no substantive changes in Trump Management's renting practices, the DOJ charged that the company's discriminatory conduct had continued "with such frequency that it has created substantial impediment to the full enjoyment of equal opportunity."[36] The Court cited testimony by several Trump building superintendents confirming that rental applications were distinguished by race. Once again, Trump was ordered to abide by the original consent decree and federal law.

Race Discrimination Charges at Atlantic City

By the late 1970s, Donald Trump's businesses had taken him first to building skyscrapers in Manhattan, and then to Atlantic City. It's at Atlantic City where Trump saw the potential for huge profits. For a quarter century (1984–2009), Trump was active in the gaming city, and at one time owned three of its casinos. There was good reason for the fast-moving Trump to be involved in the East Coast gambling mecca. Said Trump, "I like the casino business. I like the scale, which is huge, I like the glamor, and most of all, I like the cash flow."[37] But along with the glamor and the money, Trump needed a staff, and once again, he found himself in trouble on the race issue.

The problem stemmed from the treatment of his employees at the Trump Plaza Hotel. According to a complaint filed with the New Jersey Casino Control Commission, a big gambler at the Trump Plaza insisted on having White male dealers. With that demand, casino managers removed African American and female personnel at whatever table the gambler played, which precipitated a complaint to the New Jersey Casino Control Commission. After a hearing, the Commission fined the Trump Plaza Hotel for abiding by the high-roller's demand to transfer Black and female dealers. In assessing the penalty, one disgusted commissioner commented, "There are, or ought to be, certain things that a casino hotel cannot sell or provide to a customer in order to assure his continued patronage. Those things include honor and decency and human courtesy."[38] An appeal by the Trump organization was subsequently denied.

Beyond the specific case, at issue in the Trump Plaza Hotel was the matter of corporate culture. That element typically begins at the top of the organization, which means Donald Trump. So, it shouldn't be too much of a surprise to learn that Trump himself had issues with Black people throughout his business career, as evidenced by the information above. But more to the point, Trump was known to avoid African Americans wherever possible during his Atlantic City years. He once said to John O'Connell, at the time Trump's president of the Trump Plaza, "I've got Black accountants at Trump Castle and Trump Plaza. Black accountants counting my money! I hate it. The only people I want counting my money are short guys wearing beanies everyday (referring to Orthodox Jews who wear yarmulkes)."[39] In one fell swoop, Trump managed to use racist language against two minorities! That attitude was prevalent throughout Trump's Atlantic City properties. In the words of one Black Trump Plaza employee at the time, "When Donald and Ivana (spouse) came to the casino, the bosses would order all the Black people off the floor. It was the eighties, I was a teenager, but I remember it: they put us in the back."[40]

Trump's approach to African Americans extended well beyond the 1980s. By the early 2000s, Trump was operating several different companies with few minorities in high-level positions. As Randal Pinkett, a former Trump executive, recalls, "I was the only person of color that I saw in my entire year with the Trump Organization. And to put that into context, this was 2006."[41]

Trump never apologized for his racist comments or actions; if anything, he acknowledged them with little concern. When asked in a 1999 interview about O'Donnell's allegations, for example, Trump answered, "the stuff O'Donnell wrote about me is probably true,"[42] and then went on to attack his former president of one of Trump's Atlantic City casinos as irresponsible.

Other Incidents

For Donald Trump, it was hard to find a group that escaped his scorn filled with bigoted and unsupported claims. The issues below further illustrate Trump's endless, and often, petty grievances and behaviors.

Native Americans

While much of Trump's published racial disregard centers on African Americans, they were not the only ones in his cross-hairs. In early 1993, with his own casinos nearby, Trump publicly opposed planned construction of Native American casinos in New England. In a testimony before a committee in the House of Representatives, he spoke against development on the grounds that the Native Americans applying for the rights "don't look like Indians to me."[43] To make matters worse, he went on to say, "A couple of these Indians up in Connecticut look like Michael Jordan," a well-known African-American basketball player.[44] Part of Trump's argument stemmed from the fact that Native Americans don't pay federal taxes if they live on reservations courtesy of long-standing historical treaties with the federal government. Ironically, during much of his business career, Trump hasn't paid federal income taxes either, including 1993.[45]

Muslims

Trump has also clashed with Muslims. When, in 2010, a group of American Muslim religious leaders purchased land near Ground Zero in New York City for development of a community center, Trump offered to buy the land at a profit to the owners. Noting that the land was adjacent to the World Trade Center buildings destroyed by Muslim terrorists on September 11, 2001, Trump viewed the development as an insult to all Americans. He wrote in his proposal that he was making the offer "not because I think the location is a spectacular one [because it is not] but because it will end a very serious, inflammatory, and highly divisive situation that is destined, in my opinion, to only get worse."[46] For many observers, the "offer" reflected negativity toward Muslims more than any sincere concern for overcoming divisiveness and was nothing other than gratuitous.

But Trump's disdain for Muslims didn't stop there. In 2015, he called for a "total and complete shutdown of Muslims entering" the United States until our country's representatives can figure out what's going on."[47] In other words, Trump chose to punish all Muslims for the crimes committed by a few.

Women and Teenage Girls

Discrimination is not necessarily limited to the categories of race or religion, although Donald Trump has exhibited evidence of derogatory behavior toward both groups. To those categories, we can add women. This detour is important because it adds to the way Trump used his power for personal gain at the expense of others. In his own words, Trump viewed women as objects and little more. Just before the 2016 presidential election, a 2005 videotape of Trump discussing how he exercised his position of power for sex was made public. In the tape, he said to a male acquaintance, "You know, I'm automatically attracted to beautiful [women]—I just start kissing them. It's like a magnet. Just kiss. I don't even wait. And when you're a star, they let you do it. You can do anything."[48] By the election, more than a dozen women had publicly charged Trump with a variety of unwanted sexual advances; Trump responded, calling his accusers "horrible, horrible liars."[49] Incredibly, he won the presidency in spite of the claims.

Trump's humiliating attitude toward women extended to teenage girls. When he owned the Miss Teen USA beauty pageant, Trump boasted about his sense of entitlement through visits to the contestants' dressing room: "I'll tell you the funniest thing is that I'll go backstage [at the pageant] before a show and everyone's getting dressed. No men anywhere, and I'm allowed to go in, because I'm the owner of the pageant and therefore I'm inspecting it. . . . You know, they're standing there with no clothes. 'Is everyone OK'-[they ask]? And you see these incredible looking women, so I sort of get away with things like that."[50] Trump was proud that he could "get away with things like that," behavior he knew was wrong. A *New York Times* in-depth study of Trump's association with more than fifty women concluded, "In many cases there was an unmistakable dynamic at play: Mr. Trump had the power, and the women did not. He had celebrity. He had wealth. He had connections. Even after he had behaved crudely toward them, some of the women sought his assistance with their careers or remained at his side."[51] How much self-worth they had is another matter.

A HISTORY THAT IS INDISPUTABLE

In life, no one is perfect, and that includes the ways we treat those around us. Unfortunately, racism is such a large part of American culture that sometimes a person will say a racist comment without thinking or unintentionally. Of course, such a mistake can occur anywhere and by anyone. However, in a democracy, widespread bigotry is not acceptable because it's not only divisive and unkind; it refuses to acknowledge equality for those who suffer from the behavior.

But this chapter is not only about an individual's poorly constructed phrases, thoughtless remarks, or awkwardly stated comments. It points to a pattern that has defined Donald Trump's life for decades. It's central to his character and his propensity to position groups against one another while he thrives. As we will see shortly, that pattern only intensified during Trump's presidency as he rallied like-minded people around him to carry out his mission.

Per the discussion in chapter 4, we know that Trump is not the only president to ever exhibit racist language or behavior. But whatever the poor judgment of his predecessors, on this issue, Donald Trump's relentless consistency places him in a class by himself.

Still there are more consequences than society putting up with a foul-mouthed, ill-mannered, individual with a racist comportment. Trump's behavior gave White racists throughout America permission to express themselves openly about their view of American society and in many cases, justification for violence. As one observer wrote, his words and behavior "moved racism from the euphemistic and plausibly deniable to the overt and freely acclaimed."[52] He opened the door for people—millions of them—who had wanted to walk through without suffering the condemnation from others in society or even arrest from authorities. And walked they have.

NOTES

1. "Six Times President Trump Said He is the Least Racist Person," *The Washington Post*, January 17, 2018, https://www.washingtonpost.com/news/the-fix/wp/2018/01/17/six-times-president-trump-said-he-is-the-least-racist-person/.

2. See John O'Donnell and James Rutherford, *Trumped! The Inside Story of the Real Donald Trump—His Cunning Rise and Spectacular Fall* (New York, NY: Simon and Schuster, 1991), pp. 114–115.

3. Marina Budhos, "Donald Trump's Childhood in Queens can Explain His Obsession with Borders," *Quartz*, October 20, 2016, https://qz.com/814851/donald-trumps-childhood-in-queens-can-explain-his-obsession-with-borders/.

4. Katie Warren, "I Visited Trump's Childhood Neighborhood on the Outskirts of NYC and it didn't Take Too Long to See Why He's called it an 'Oasis'," *Business Insider*, August 19, 2020, https://www.businessinsider.com/donald-trump-childhood-neighborhood-queens-new-york-city-photos-2018-11.

5. Marina Butros, "Donald Trump's Childhood in Queens can Explain His Obsession with Borders," *Quartz*, October 20, 2016, https://qz.com/814851/donald-trumps-childhood-in-queens-can-explain-his-obsession-with-borders.

6. "President Trump's 'Dysfunctional' Upbringing Created 'Dangerous Situation' for America, Niece Claims," *ABC News*, July 15, 2020, https://abcnews.go.com/Politics/president-trumps-dysfunctional-upbringing-created-dangerous-situation-america/story?id=71788912.

7. Michael Kranish and Marc Fisher, *Trump Revealed* (New York, New York: Simon & Schuster, 2016), pp. 34–35.

8. Timothy L. O'Brien, *Trump Nation: The Art of Being the Donald* (New York, NY: Warner Business Books, 2005), p. 50.

9. Mary L. Trump, *Too Much and Never Enough* (New York, NY: Simon & Schuster, 2020), p. 43.

10. Kranish and Fisher, *Trump Revealed*, p. 37.

11. Trump, *Too Much and Never Enough*, p. 15.

12. "Confident. Incorrigible. Bully. Little Donny was a lot like Candidate Donald Trump," *The Washington Post*, June 22, 2016, https://www.washingtonpost.com/lifestyle/style/young-donald-trump-military-school/2016/06/22/f0b3b164-317c-11e6-8758-d58e76e11b12_story.html.

13. Donald J. Trump with Tony Schwartz, *Trump: The Art of the Deal* (New York, NY: Ballentine Books, 1987), p. 71.

14. Quoted in Joshua Zitser, "Steve Bannon said Trump 'Would Lie about Anything' to Win, New Book Says," *Business Insider*, July 16, 2022, https://www.businessinsider.com/trump-lie-about-anything-win-arguments-steve-bannon-book-2022-7.

15. "Inside Mark Meadows's Final Push to Keep Trump in Power," *The Washington Post*, May 9, 2022, https://www.washingtonpost.com/politics/2022/05/09/inside-mark-meadowss-final-push-keep-trump-power/.

16. Jean Guerrero, *Hatemonger: Stephen Miller, Donald Trump, and the White Nationalist Agenda* (New York, NY: William Morrow, 2022), p. 9.

17. Wayne Barrett, *Trump: The Deals & The Downfall* (New York, NY: HarperCollins, 1992), p. 74.

18. "Did a Queens Podiatrist Hep Donald Trump Avoid Vietnam," *The New York Times*, December 26, 2018, https://www.nytimes.com/2018/12/26/us/politics/trump-vietnam-draft-exemption.html.

19. "President Trump's 90-Second Rant on Richard Blumenthal and Vietnam," *The Washington Post*, October 3, 3028, https://www.washingtonpost.com/politics/2018/10/03/president-trumps-second-rant-richard-blumenthal-vietnam/.

20. See "Questions Linger about Trump's Academic at Wharton," *Philadelphia Inquirer*, February 17, 2017, https://www.inquirer.com/philly/blogs/real-time/Questions-linger-Donald-Trump-academic-record-Wharton.html&outputType=app-web-view.

21. Trump post-2020 news conference, video displayed in Chris Cillizza, "Donald Trump just Accidentally Told the Truth about His Disinformation," *CNN*, July 5, 2022, https://www.cnn.com/2021/07/05/politics/trump-disinformation-strategy/index.html.

22. See Barrett, *Trump*, pp. 171–195.

23. "The Empire and Ego of Donald Trump," *The New York Times,* August 7, 1983, https://www.nytimes.com/1983/08/07/business/the-empire-and-ego-of-donald-trump.html.

24. "Central Park Five: Money was not the Issue in Settlement with NYC," *Los Angeles Times*, June 27, 2014, https://www.latimes.com/nation/nationnow/la-na-nn-central-park-five-jogger-20140627-story.html.

25. Maggie Haberman, *Confidence Man* (New York, NY: Penguin Press, 2022), p. 63.

26. "Alicia Machado, the Woman Trump called Miss Housing, is Ready to Vote against Donald Trump," *The Washington Post*, September 2016, https://www.washingtonpost.com/news/the-fix/wp/2016/09/27/alicia-machado-the-woman-trump-called-miss-housekeeping-is-ready-to-vote-against-donald-trump/.

27. David Corn and Michael Isikoff, "What Happened in Moscow: The Inside Story of How Trump's Obsession with Putin Began," *Mother Jones*, March 8, 2018, https://www.motherjones.com/politics/2018/03/russian-connection-what-happened-moscow-inside-story-trump-obsession-putin-david-corn-michael-isikoff/.

28. "Trump's Racist Comments Jeopardize His Miss Universe Pageant," *Vanity Fair*, June 25, 2015, https://www.vanityfair.com/news/2015/06/univision-drops-miss-universe-trump-comments.

29. For more on the origins of birtherism, see Adam Serwer, "Birtherism of a Nation," *The Atlantic*, May 13, 2020, https://www.theatlantic.com/ideas/archive/2020/05/birtherism-and-trump/610978/.

30. The language is in Article II, Section 1.

31. See "A Look at Trump's 'Birther' Statements," *The Washington Post*, April 28, 2011, https://www.theatlantic.com/ideas/archive/2020/05/birtherism-and-trump/610978/.

32. Quoted in Guerrero, *Hatemonger*, p. 145.

33. "'No Vacancies' for Blacks: How Donald Trump Got His Start, and Was First Accused of Bias," *The New York Times*, August 27, 2016, https://www.nytimes.com/2016/08/28/us/politics/donald-trump-housing-race.html.

34. "Major Landlord Accused of Antiblack Bias in City," *The New York Times*, October 16, 1973, https://www.nytimes.com/1973/10/16/archives/major-landlord-accused-of-antiblack-bias-in-city-us-accuses-major.html.

35. "Trump's Showdown," *Frontline*, PBS.org, May 23, 2018, https://www.pbs.org/wgbh/frontline/interview/elyse-goldweber/.

36. "Trump Charged with Rental Bias," *The New York Times*, March 7, 1978, https://www.nytimes.com/1978/03/07/archives/trump-charged-with-rental-bias.html.

37. Quoted in John R. O'Donnell with James Rutherford, *Trumped!* (Hertford, NC: Crossroad Press, 1991), p. 3.

38. "Trump Plaza Fined $200,000 for Discrimination," *UPI*, June 6, 1991, https://www.upi.com/Archives/1991/06/06/Trump-Plaza-fined-200000-for-discrimination/2869676180800/.

39. O'Connell and Rutherford, *Trumped!*, p. 115.

40. Nick Paumgarten, "The Death and Life of Atlantic City," *The New Yorker*, August 31, 2015, https://www.newyorker.com/magazine/2015/09/07/the-death-and-life-of-atlantic-city.

41. "An Oral History of Trump's Bigotry," *The Atlantic,* June 2019, https://www.theatlantic.com/magazine/archive/2019/06/trump-racism-comments/588067/.

42. "Fact Check: Trump had been Accused of Racism by Contemporaries Prior to Presidential Campaign," *Reuters*, May 6, 2021, https://www.reuters.com/article/factcheck-trump-racism/fact-check-trump-had-been-accused-of-racism-by-contemporaries-prior-to-presidential-campaign-idUSL1N2MT312.

43. Quoted in "How Donald Trump's 1993 Comments about 'Indians' Previewed Much of His 2016 Campaign," *The Washington Post*, July 1, 2016, https://www.washingtonpost.com/news/the-fix/wp/2016/07/01/how-donald-trumps-1993-comments-about-indians-previewed-much-of-his-2016-campaign/.

44. Kranish and Fisher, *Trump Revealed*, p. 281.

45. "What we know about Donald Trump's Income Tax History, by Year," *The Washington Post*, March 14, 2017, https://www.washingtonpost.com/news/the-fix/wp/2016/10/01/what-we-know-about-donald-trumps-income-tax-history-by-year/.

46. Quoted in "Trump Offers to Buy Out Islamic Center Investor," *The Wall Street Journal*, September 9, 2010, https://www.wsj.com/articles/SB10001424052748704644404575482093330879912.

47. "Trump Calls for a 'Total and Complete Shutdown of Muslims Entering' U.S.," *NPR*, December 7, 2015, https://www.npr.org/2015/12/07/458836388/trump-calls-for-total-and-complete-shutdown-of-muslims-entering-u-s?utm_source=twitter.com&utm_campaign=politics&utm_medium=social&utm_term=nprnews.

48. "Transcript: Donald Trump's Taped Comments About Women," *The New York Times*, October 8, 2016, https://www.google.com/search?q=trump%27s+statements+about+women&rlz=1C5CHFA_enUS773US773&ei=9CTfYuWkA8mfkPIPhuaVoAE&start=10&sa=N&ved=2ahUKEwjl7vPMlpX5AhXJD0QIHQZzBRQQ8NMDegQIARBC&biw=1440&bih=719&dpr=1.

49. "Trump Calls Women's Claims of Sexual Advances 'Vicious' and 'Absolutely False,'" *The Washington Post*, October 13, 2016, https://www.washingtonpost.com/politics/multiple-women-accuse-donald-trump-of-making-sexual-advances/2016/10/13/3862fab0-9140-11e6-9c52-0b10449e33c4_story.html.

50. "Teen Beauty Queens Say Trump Walked in on Them Changing," *Buzzfeed*, October 12, 2016, https://www.buzzfeednews.com/article/kendalltaggart/teen-beauty-queens-say-trump-walked-in-on-them-changing.

51. "Crossing the Line: How Donald Trump Behaved with Women in Private," *The New York Times*, May 14, 2016, https://www.nytimes.com/2016/05/15/us/politics/donald-trump-women.html.

52. Ta-Nehisi Coats, "The First White President," *The Atlantic*, October 2017, https://www.theatlantic.com/magazine/archive/2017/10/the-first-white-president-ta-nehisi-coates/537909/.

Part III

TRUMPISM

AN AMERICAN BRAND OF AUTHORITARIANISM

We'd like to believe that candidates for political office are guided by a well-developed set of core values; descriptions such as "conservative," "moderate," and "liberal" often explain that framework of ideas. Of course, there are others not as well known; among them, "libertarian," "neo-conservative," "institutionalist," and lately, "progressive" have also appeared at various times. These depictions not only outline the candidates' philosophies but are also shortcuts for the electorate to connect their own belief sets with those of the candidates as voters prepare to select their choices in elections.

Along with political values, leaders can be analyzed through their approach to governing. As we read in chapter 1, democracies depend on several factors including the agreement of shared rules between the governed and their governors, an open political culture that welcomes people of different backgrounds, and peaceful dissent. In chapter 2, we discussed the reasons why democracies decline, including open ethnic divisions, the illegal seizure of public institutions, and the failure of leaders to respond to major social factors.

This takes us to the United States, where the populous and leaders alike have long wrestled over the collision between discrimination and democracy. That tension reverberates in a complicated political system full of checks and balances, multiple levels of government, and frequent elections, which amplify numerous variables including, Karen Stenner notes, "conflict, the propagation of adversaries, and the constant airing of disagreement."[1] For the most part, our system has managed conflict through these outlets.

The system is challenged the most in moments of crisis, when the public searches for answers in the hope of returning to less burdensome moments. Particularly in troubled times, a problematic condition provides opportunities for someone to assert that they "alone can fix it," which is exactly what

Donald Trump claimed to sustained applause in his acceptance speech at the 2016 Republican National Convention.

An unsteady democracy can create instability which, in turn, opens the possibility of authoritarianism, a condition where Marc Herrington and Jonathan Weiler write, leaders "make stronger than average distinctions between in-groups—the groups they identify with—and out-groups—the groups that they (the leaders) perceive challenge them."[2] In seizing upon those distinctions, authoritarian leaders encourage, and in some cases incite, the circumstances under which they are able to rule at the expense of those they have singled out as a means of perpetuating their positions of power. This is the framework of part III.

In chapter 6, we examine the relationship between Donald Trump, his approach to race, his campaign for election, and the presidency in 2016. Chapter 7 builds on the racism patterns of the Trump administration as the driving force for maintaining his presidency. Chapter 8 delves into Trump's ill-fated bid for re-election in 2020. Upon failing to win, he promoted the January 6 insurrection at the Capitol, as chronicled in chapter 9—an activity that came perilously close to overturning not only the election but the nation's democracy as well. The incredible sequence of events from Trump's 2016 race to 2020 demise was not due to Trump alone but rather from the connection Trump nurtured with powerful racist groups and willing individuals throughout the nation.

NOTES

1. Karen Stenner, *The Authoritarian Dynamic* (New York, NY: Cambridge University Press, 2009), p. 18.

2. Marc J. Hetherington and Jonathan D. Weiler, *Authoritarianism & Polarization of American Politics* (New York, NY: Cambridge University Press, 2009), p. 4.

Chapter 6

Trump, Bigotry, and the 2016 Presidential Election

With his growing number of flashy Manhattan projects, Atlantic City casinos, and frequent radio talk radio appearances, Donald Trump presented himself as the consummate American success story. Add to these elements a string of self-written (more accurately ghost-authored) books on topics ranging from self-help to finance, and Trump became something of a national personality. He sponsored boxing matches and briefly owned the Miss Universe pageant. At one point, he even owned a team in the short-lived United States Football League. Oddly enough, six bankruptcies did little to damage his national reputation as a successful businessperson.

Yet, all of these steps paled to Trump's success with *The Apprentice*, a weekly national television show that aired between 2004 and 2015, where Trump and invited guests judged contestants vying for approval of, and interest, in their business propositions. Beyond its entertainment value, the show "was built as a virtually nonstop advertisement for the Trump empire and lifestyle."[1] Endless references by Trump to his business acumen and enterprises were virtual co-stars of the weekly show. With success of *The Apprentice*, Trump completed his journey to widespread national recognition.

SEARCHING FOR A LANDING SPOT IN PRESIDENTIAL POLITICS

Most of us have core values, basic beliefs that stay with us as we move through life's challenges and triumphs. On rare occasion, events, or experiences may lead us to reconsider or amend a particular principle, but such moments are infrequent once we have settled on a general political framework to guide us through life.[2] That hasn't been the case with Donald Trump, who has operated through life without settling on core political principles. Perhaps the best example would be political party affiliation, where Trump has bounced back and forth between the Democrats, Independents, and Republicans, his current political residence. At other moments, he has also flirted with the Reform party and the Independence Party of America. A kind assessment of this behavior would offer that Trump has spent his life searching for a political party that truly reflects his values; a less charitable appraisal would be that over time Trump has aligned himself with the political party where he might find the best temporary connection for his own transactional objectives.

But there's more. At various times, Trump has been pro-choice and pro-life; for extending background checks on gun purchases and against them; for fighting the Iraq war and opposing U.S. involvement; and for universal healthcare and dead set against it, to name a few examples of his unpredictable political style. Such erratic behavior might leave one to wonder just what he really does and does not believe.[3] Given such inconsistencies, it would seem that Donald Trump has no substantive political core. Somehow, none of that has stopped Trump from seeking office or kept his followers from supporting him.

Long before his official run for the presidency in 2016, Trump toyed with running for president. As early as 1999, he was urged by longtime advisor Roger Stone to consider running for the 2000 presidential nomination of the Reform Party,[4] which had served as the political perch of candidate Ross Perot in 1992 and 1996. Perot had actually secured 19 percent of the vote in 1992 as a Reform Party candidate, and may well have affected the outcome, which ended with Democratic candidate Bill Clinton defeating Republican incumbent George H. W. Bush for the presidency with only 43 percent of the popular vote.

Trump set up an exploratory committee and toyed with the possibility of running, but key leaders of the Reform Party wanted nothing to do with him. As then-Reform Party chairman Russ Verney reflected in 2018, midway through Trump's presidency, "I strongly discouraged him (Trump) from getting involved with the Reform Party. . . . He was just a hustler, just an egomaniac. And I think events have proved me right on that point."[5] For whatever reason, Trump decided to pass on the prospect in 2000, yet the possibility remained foremost in his mind. Less clear for Trump, however, was any real vision or philosophy of governing. Then again, Trump focused more on the possibility of gaining presidential power than the ways he might use it. That would come later.

THE 2012 ELECTION OPPORTUNITY

In Donald Trump's mind, the 2012 presidential election offered a better opportunity than 2000 to seek the presidency. Trump had spent a good deal of time bashing President Barack Obama over his place of birth and connected with some voters on the issue. In 2011, a national poll sponsored by *Politico* found that 51 percent of Republicans believed that Obama was born in another country; only 28 percent trusted that Obama was born in the United States.[6] Even after Obama released his official and complete birth certificate in April 2011, one-quarter of Republicans still believed that he was definitely or probably born in another country.[7] For Trump, the unmitigated birther proponent, those were good numbers to begin a presidential nomination campaign, should he be interested in doing so. Meanwhile, the now-prominent television figure continued to pursue his "us" versus "them" list of grievances. Along with his thinly veiled anti-Black statements couched in birtherism, he criticized China for unfair trade, the OPEC nations for holding the United States hostage with high oil prices and other countries taking advantage of the United States.[8] America should come first, he would constantly say. His criticisms notwithstanding, Trump offered few, if any, substantive policy proposals. He was much better at criticizing what was wrong with American politics than advancing any programmatic plans to improve a bad situation.

Still, there was potentially positive news for Trump. In the first few months of 2011, the polls showed Trump at or near the top of Republican presidential candidates. A national poll for ABC in early April of that year showed Trump tied for second with former Arkansas governor Mike Huckabee at 17 percent; only Mitt Romney had more support with a 21 percent share.[9] And Trump's popularity wasn't a fluke. A Gallup national poll conducted in late April 2011 had Trump tied for first with Huckabee, each with 16 percent, followed by eventual nominee Mitt Romney with 12 percent.[10] The nomination was anything but settled and Trump was clearly in the mix.

One month later, Trump dropped out of the 2012 presidential race that he officially had never been in. In announcing his departure from the field, he cited the need to return full time to his business, even though earlier he had expressed no hesitation to turn his business over to his three adult children.[11] Left without mention in his withdrawal from the campaign was a two-year renewal offer by NBC to continue his popular television program, now called *Celebrity Apprentice*, for which Trump would reportedly receive $65 million each year.[12] Ironically, the good times for Trump on network television ended in June 2015 when, during his 2016 presidential candidacy announcement, Trump made his infamous statement about Mexico sending rapists to the United States, after which NBC ended its relationship with him. Rather than apologize for a racist remark, Trump blamed the network for the contract termination. He complained that "NBC is weak, and like everybody else trying to be politically correct—that is why our country is in serious trouble."[13] Now the media was added to the "them" category in the "us" versus "them" grievance list.

Trump's nomination interest in 2012 may have been aborted because of various personal and political considerations, but it nevertheless revealed early signs of Trumpism. Ultimately authoritarian in nature, Trumpism developed as a blend of several negative characteristics best described by longtime Trump observer Tim O'Brien as resentment against institutions and elites combined with us-versus-them identity politics peddled through bigotry and racism.[14] Add to that an "America first" touch of nationalism that can only be protected by minimizing the influence of "others" (non-White people and non-Christians) and we have the basic formula for Trumpism. Over time, it became clear that this combination had a powerful staying power, something has been demonstrated by the approaches of some leaders beyond Trump's presidency.

Trump viewed disarray as a necessary and valued precondition for his success. Whenever possible, he feathered chaos by encouraging violence against opponents at his rallies and in other venues such as protests against police brutality.[15] And of course, Trump would say, that only he was qualified to lead the nation out of the dark period that had enveloped us. We hasten to add that all of these concerns have been part of the American political tapestry at various moments in the nation's history, but Trump managed to package them in a way that led many to accept these themes as particularly threatening to the wellbeing of American society.

GOING FOR ALL THE MARBLES IN 2016

In the "us" versus "them" fight, the "thems" were growing. Now included were minorities, elites, and the media as chunks of the great conspiracy to deny the people ("us") their rightful place in politics and society. That was the overarching theme articulated by Donald Trump in June 2015 when after descending a glittery escalator in Trump Tower, he announced his candidacy for the Republican nomination. In his speech, Trump began by saying the United States had lost its global leadership. Other countries are "laughing at our stupidity," he said, because the United States has no leadership, and American politicians were controlled by lobbyists, donors, and special interests.

Beyond the international picture, much of Trump's candidacy announcement focused on the perils that minorities and immigrants brought to American society. With respect to arrivals from Mexico, Trump warned that Mexico was "sending people that have lots of problems. . . . They're bringing drugs. They're bringing crime. They're rapists."[16] He went on that the same problems were "coming from all over South and Latin America, and it's coming—probably—from the Middle East." Trump tied uncontrolled immigration to American unemployment, alleging without any evidence that Americans can't get jobs "because China has our jobs and Mexico has our jobs." In other words, outsiders were bringing America to its knees because of a poor immigration policy.

Throughout his speech, Trump criticized the leaders of both political parties. Wherever you look, he said, "We have losers. We have people that don't have it. We have people that are morally corrupt." How do we solve our problems, Trump asked? "We need somebody that can take the brand of the United States and make it great again. . . . So, ladies and gentlemen, I am running for president of the United States, and we are going to make America great again. . . . I will be the greatest jobs president that God ever created." And so began Donald Trump's quest for the American presidency: one laden with unsubstantiated claims, blame, criticism and an early version of how he was the only person who would be capable of saving the United States from certain doom.

Along the way to his first presidential campaign, Trump picked up two key ideological allies. Over the years, Trump occasionally had turned to Roger Stone, the former Nixon adviser and self-described anti-elitist, sometimes for lobbying work, other times for political advice. But Stone was not always reliable because of questionable antics, and at one point, was even described by Trump as a "cold-stone loser." Still, Stone had some value as an "us" versus "them" provocateur, but Trump needed more.

Steve Bannon, a provocative far right media strategist, became a Trump confidant in 2010. Before Trump announced his candidacy in 2015, he and Bannon had forged a relationship promoting "America first" nationalism and condemning illegal immigration. Bannon also provided Trump an entry to conservative organizations,[17] thereby widening Trump's potential political and financial infrastructure.

Bannon rode the Trump train all the way to the 2016 presidential election. More important, Bannon introduced Trump to Stephen Miller, who he first met in 2013 when Miller was a young aid to then U.S. Senator Jeff Sessions—the same Jeff Sessions who would become Trump's first Attorney General. His youth notwithstanding, Miller had developed a reputation for despising immigration, whether legal or illegal, as the source of America's problems, ranging from inner city decay to the loss of American jobs.[18] After Trump declared his presidential candidacy, Miller became a key speech writer, with much of his outrage focused in the immigration question. Miller stayed as a presidential adviser once Trump was elected and made immigration the centerpiece of his policy portfolio.

There were others who had roles in the first Trump presidential campaign. But with respect to the political architecture bolstering the race issue— namely globalism and immigration—Bannon and Miller were key to Trump.

The Presidential Primary Campaign

Donald Trump began his presidential quest with a bit of an uphill struggle. He had never been an elected official, eschewed the niceties and nuanced statements that candidates typically make, and focused on grievances as the foundation of his campaign. People of color, ethnic minorities, women, and some religious denominations were prominent on his list of those responsible for the nation's problems. Such an approach of singling out purportedly unworthy segments of the population as the nation's enemies has long been rejected by mainstream candidates as a death knell. In fact, historically, most mainstream candidates have bent over backward to underscore equality, inclusion, respect, and hope as core components of their campaigns rather than race and divisiveness.

Recall the 2008 presidential campaign when at a town hall meeting, a member of the audience said to then-Republican presidential nominee John McCain, "I can't trust Obama. I have read about him and he's . . . an Arab." To which McCain quickly responded, "No ma'am. He's a decent family man [and] a citizen that I just happen to have disagreements with . . . and that's what this campaign is all about. He's not [an Arab]."[19] The crowds at McCain's political events often booed him for that comment at other times during his campaign when he defended Obama's birth and American citizenship, but McCain never backed down. For Trump, however, non-White people, ethnic minorities, and people with non-Christian religions offered the opportunity with largely White Christian audiences to distinguish "us" from "them" in a mocking and often attacking fashion. The "thems" threatened real Americans and didn't belong with the rest of us.

Racist Rallies

Throughout the 2016 presidential campaign, Donald Trump thrived on large rally crowds. The exchange of energy was incredible, Trump to the crowd and the crowd to Trump. And he wasn't afraid to build his candidacy on race-related issues. Trump's taunts had begun with his candidacy announcement in June 2015, when he complained about Mexican rapists and his promise to build a great wall separating Mexico from the United States that would end illegal immigration once and for all. Typically, the largely White crowd would roar with approval.

But Trump's racist bravado was not universally accepted. The moderate-to-conservative Republican Establishment had fits over Trump's crude approach to issues, particularly as it related to racism. They had good reason for their consternation. A Republican party "autopsy" of the loss to Democrat Barack Obama in 2012 had found that "Public perception of the Party is at record lows . . . and many minorities wrongly think that Republicans do not like them or want them in the country." To that condition, the report concluded, "If we want ethnic minority voters to support Republicans, we have to engage them and show our sincerity."[20] But Trump had little regard for the new proposal to bring minorities into the Republican tent; they were, after all, the source of much of his wrath. To that end, his campaign rallies were filled with racist remarks, to which the audiences roared with approval.[21]

Trump's confrontational stances not only distinguished him from his Republican opponents but also defined him as he acquired growing numbers of followers. It became clear that his rallies were welcome to White people only, and many of those in his audience responded accordingly with taunts at minorities.[22] His rallies often hinted at violent confrontations with minorities, only for Trump to then condemn such ideas with a wink. Some examples: At an October 2015 rally in Miami, Florida, Trump supporters kicked and dragged to the ground a Hispanic protester.[23] Shortly thereafter at a Richmond, Virginia rally, Trump supporters shouted to nearby immigration activists, "Go back where you came from."[24] At a November 2015 rally in Birmingham, Alabama, Trump supporters assaulted a Black protester, chanting "Black lives matter."[25] At a Rock Hill, South Carolina rally on January 8, 2016, a 56-year old woman standing silently in a shirt inscribed "Salam, I come in peace" was assaulted after Trump criticized President Barack Obama for not using the term "radical Islamic terrorism" to describe Muslims.[26] On February 29, 2016 at a Georgia campaign rally, several Black university students stood silently, waiting for Trump; they were asked to leave, according to a reporter observing the incident.[27] The next day, at a Louisville, Kentucky rally, when Black protesters arrived, Trump called his security to "get them out of here;" supporters responded by shoving and then forcibly removing a young Black female protester from the premises. "They were pushing and shoving me, cursing at me, yelled at me, called me every name in the book," a Black female University of Louisville student declared after being forcibly removed by Trump supporters she called "disgusting and dangerous."[28] And at a March 2016, rally in Fayetteville, North Carolina, police escorted a young Black protester from the event after an older White man punched him in the face. After the disturbance quieted, Trump asked rhetorically, "Why are they (Black protestors) allowed to do the things that we're not allowed to do? Really a disgrace." And, seemingly disappointed that only one person was ejected from the crowd, Trump asked, "Can't we have a little more action than this?"[29]

Trump would often say he wanted peaceful rallies—those were his words, anyway. Yet, more often his calls for action against protesters of color suggest he was hardly an innocent bystander. At a Las Vegas rally in February 2016, where he longed for the "good old days" of beating up protesters, he asked the crowd, "So if you see somebody getting ready to throw a tomato, knock the crap out of 'em, would you?" At another rally in Iowa after a fracas, he assured his supporters tangling with protesters, "I promise you, I will pay for the legal fees. I promise, I promise."[30] Clearly, Trump's racist-laced rallies had become revival assemblies and non-believers in attendance would suffer the consequences of their nonconformity.

Trump was even more direct on other occasions. At the Las Vegas rally, Trump said in response to a removed protester, "You know what they used to do to guys when they were in a place like this? They'd be carried out in a stretcher. . . . I'd like to punch him in the face, I tell ya."[31] Indeed, Trump was proud to be the leader of violence, feeling there would never be any recrimination from his actions or urging of violence. Perhaps the clearest example of Trump's self-confidence with respect to violence came at a January 2016 rally in Iowa when he said, "I could stand in the middle of Fifth Avenue and shoot someone and I wouldn't lose voters."[32] Among Trump's followers, that claim may have seemed more correct than his adversaries would care to admit. What it says about leadership in a democratic society, however, is another question altogether.

Rather than tone down his rhetoric after winning the Republican Party nomination for president, Trump amped up his crowds as the 2016 election neared. Looking ahead to November, he warned of repercussions if he lost the election because he would only lose if it was "rigged." He suggested that his followers should carefully monitor voting sites to prevent illegal voting. Moreover, he added, his followers just might rely on their Second Amendment rights in response to a rigged election.[33] The rigged election notion, of course, was reprised during his 2020 campaign.

Displays of anger and violence at the Trump rallies did not occur in a vacuum. In fact, they literally spilled over to the communities where they were held. A study of the impact of Trump rallies during 2016 found that cities where they occurred actually experienced 2.3 times more assaults than average on days when they had Trump election events.[34] The violence "appeared to be a phenomenon that's unique to Donald Trump's rally," the study's author concluded.[35] The report found no similar spillover effects with the Hillary Clinton campaign rallies. Clearly, Trump followers, or at least many of them, viewed his calls for action as a general command for violence anywhere it was needed, and they were eager to comply.

Republican Debates and Intra-Party Republican Struggles

With no incumbent seeking re-election to the presidency in 2016, Republicans saw this as a golden opportunity to win the nation's most important elected office. As such, the field was incredibly crowded, with 17 announced candidates. Least likely to succeed, according to a survey among Republicans in June 2015, would be Donald Trump. A FiveThirtyEight poll of Republicans found that Trump was disliked by a whopping 57 percent of the respondents; no other Republican candidate had been as offensive in the 36 years the polling company had asked the question.[36] Nonpartisan observers dismissed Trump as well. Nathan Gonzales, editor of the nonpartisan and highly respected *Rothenberg and Gonzales Political Report* called Trump everything but a fraud: "Donald Trump is not going to be the Republican nominee for President. . . . Any time he consumes on the debate stage and in the media, he's taking away from a legitimate contender."[37] Trump was underestimated from all sides of the political spectrum and wasn't about to go away. Nevertheless, Trump's unique approach to campaigning would be tested in a series of Republican debates during the summer and fall of 2015.

The first Republican presidential candidate debate took place in Cleveland, Ohio, on August 5, 2015, where Trump appeared with 16 other candidates. There, Trump cited his grievances ranging from trouble-causing immigrants to stupid American leaders. But his first personal attack focused on Fox co-moderator Megyn Kelly with intemperate answers to her question about his references to women. When she asked Trump if he wanted to reconsider his unflattering characterizations of women as "fat pigs, dogs, slobs and disgusting animals," Trump abruptly responded, "I don't have time for political correctness and neither does the country."[38]

The next night on CNN, he lit into a description of Kelly, with his infamous comment, "You could see there was blood coming out of her eyes, blood coming out of her whatever," with the latter description likely referring to her menstrual cycle. Trump's remarks led critics to complain about his demeaning treatment of a woman interviewer. While his detractors grumbled about his seemingly anti-female demeanor and comments about race, Trump had won the audience over with ovation after ovation with every insult that came from his mouth.[39] On the subject of violence at his rallies, Trump defended the mayhem, saying "We have 25 [thousand], 30,000 people . . . [who] come with tremendous passion and love for the country, and . . . when they see what's going on in this country, they have anger that's unbelievable."[40]

Over the next several months, during about a dozen intra-party Republican debates, Trump insisted that all immigrants in the United States should be made to learn English (September 16, 2015, in Simi Valley, California); all Muslims should be banned from the United States and illegal immigrants are flooding across the border (January 14, 2016, in North Charleston, South Carolina); and in reference about racial violence to his rallies, unruly protesters "have got to be taken out" (March 10, 2016 in Miami, Florida). We have no leadership, Trump would continuously assert, and these changes would be steps toward returning greatness to America.

Republican Presidential Convention

After the March 10 debate in Miami, Trump declared that he was finished with the events. He was substantially ahead both in delegates and Republican public opinion. Many of his competitors had dropped out before March, while most of the rest conceded before the July Republican National Convention in Cleveland. Only Ted Cruz quixotically decided to face Trump for the remaining convention delegates where he asked the delegates to vote their conscience, only to be repeatedly booed by the largely pro-Trump audience during his presentation. In fact, Cruz's defeat was sealed long before he arrived. Donald Trump would be the Republican nominee for president.

So, how was Trump the last Republican presidential candidate standing in Cleveland? Virtually all the candidates took their shots at incumbent Democrat Barack Obama which, while an outgoing incumbent, is always standard fare for the other party's challengers. And of course, there were the usual the concerns about America's economy, our global leadership (or lack thereof), and the traditional conservative approach to social issues like abortion, guns, and states' rights. Trump discussed all those things at various points plus the one-two punch of immigration and race, which he billed as the most important problems facing America.

He had good reason to take that approach. A Pew Research Poll conducted in May 2015 just before Trump's announcement pointed the way. One question in the survey asked if immigrants burden the country or strengthen it. Overall, respondents cited "strengthen" over "burden" 51 percent to 41 percent. When divided by political party, however, only 27 percent of Republicans answered "strengthen" against 63 percent who answered "burden." In another question, the survey asked whether the Constitution should be changed to bar citizenship for children of illegal immigrants. Overall, 39 percent went with "change," compared to 57 percent who wanted to leave the Constitution as is. Among Republicans, 47 percent advocated "change," compared with 49 percent who favored the status quo. And among self-defined "Tea Party Republicans," the most conservative wing of the Republican Party, 57 percent wanted "change," whereas only 38 percent opted to keep the Constitution in its present form.[41] Given that of the more than 11 million undocumented immigrants at the time were people of color, it doesn't take a rocket scientist to put immigration and race together. Trump preached to that cohort and they supported him *en masse*.

With internal competition behind him, it was time to unite his party. He was only partially successful. Most traditional Republican leaders were nowhere to be found at the convention, no doubt because of Trump's divisive approach to the issues and the way he verbally slashed his opponents.

Former president George W. Bush, the last Republican to hold the office, did not attend, nor did 2008 Republican presidential nominee John McCain and 2012 Republican presidential nominee Mitt Romney. Generally, at national party conventions, the nominee works with the party leadership to mold the platform (a treatise elucidating key values, themes and propositions) along his or her lines of thinking. Trump did little with the document in progress other than soften the party's hard line attitude toward Russia. That offended mainstream conservative Republicans who supported a traditional get-tough policy with Russia.

As for Trump's acceptance speech, typically the high point of a national political party convention, the Republican nominee cited street violence and chaos in the nation's communities largely the result of "illegal immigrants . . . being released by the tens of thousands into our communities with no regard for the impact on public safety or resources."[42] He claimed the nation was adrift with Americans feeling "neglected, ignored, and abandoned." Former Secretary of State and Democratic opponent Hillary Clinton plus incumbent Democratic President Barack Obama were responsible for putting the nation in such a perilous position. Trump said. Because of them, hope was something of the past, and the powerful had prevailed over the people. No longer was there anyone to look out for the nation, to which, he declared "I am your voice!"[43] His plan, Trump said, "will begin with safety at home—which means safe neighborhoods, secure borders, and protection from terrorism."[44] Only at the end of his 75-minute speech did Trump invoke the "we" with "We will make America strong again. We will make America proud again. We will make America safe again. We will make America great again." In reviewing Trump's speech, one neutral observer described it as a "dystopian portrait of a country riven by division and grievances."[45] For America, there was little light at the end of the tunnel except the single beam provided by one Donald Trump. It was a "trust me" update equivalent to the "I alone can fix it" moment that came with his announcement of candidacy in 2015.

Lost in the buzz over Trump's nomination was the masterful way through which his allies took over the national Republican party and its political machinery. Aided by loyalists on the Republican National Committee, Trump's campaign personnel quickly seized ownership of the Party's voter files and fund-raising structure. These data and networks were not only important for Trump's 2016 campaign; they became the foundation of the 2020 Trump presidential re-election campaign as well. Control of the party's financial apparatus also allowed Trump campaign personnel to bill the Republican National Committee for an array of activities ranging from law suit costs to his impeachment defense in 2020.[46]

The Presidential Debates

Trump's isolationist framework that combined racist-tinged sentiments with anti-immigration and America first statements clearly separated him from Hillary Clinton, his Democratic opponent for the 2016 presidential election. Couple these elements with his contempt for elites and an "only I can save you" attitude and he offered himself as a candidate with unusual characteristics. For those Americans who were tired of feeling at the bottom of the economic ladder, angered at those they perceived as taking their jobs, and contemptuous of unresponsive political leaders, Trump—and only Trump—would be the answer to their problems. He told them what they wanted to hear and they roared for more. These themes would be expressed in various combinations throughout the three debates with Democrat nominee Hillary Clinton.

In the first debate, moderator Lester Holt asked the candidates how they would heal the racial divide in the United States. Clinton replied the problem stemmed from mistrust between minorities and the police, easy access to guns, and poorly trained police to deal with bias and mental health issues. In fact, Clinton added, racial bias is a problem that sweeps across America. For his part, Trump responded that communities need more "stop and frisk" policing, where police question someone who "looks" like a would-be criminal. Historically, such treatment has overwhelmingly been applied to racial minorities. As for his leadership in the birtherism movement directed toward then-president Barack Obama, Trump took credit for getting to the bottom of the issue.[47]

The second debate yielded more sparring between the two candidates than the first. Trump was asked about the infamous tape about women and Clinton was questioned about her email management which led to thousands of lost communications when she was Secretary of State. On race-related issues, Trump continued to criticize the arrival of Muslims to the United States because so many were murderers and drug lords, that if president, Clinton would see to hundreds of thousands of Muslims being admitted to the United States. "We take care of illegal immigrants . . . better than we take care of our vets," Trump claimed. Clinton countered that the United States has had Muslims living here for centuries without problems. She accused Trump of being demagogic about Muslims for putting them all in one terrorist basket simply because of their religion.

In some respects, the third presidential debate on October 19, 2016 was the most significant not only for the issues discussed but Donald Trump's answer to the question on whether he would accept the results of the election. The two candidates tussled over the kinds of justices who should be nominated to the U.S. Supreme Court, the Second Amendment, foreign policy, and abortion. On immigration, the candidate differences were particularly stark. Clinton pointed out "we're a nation of immigrants" and that the government needs to be careful in deporting innocent people just because they were immigrants. Trump accused Clinton of proposing open borders that would allow criminals to flow in from places like Syria and repeated his belief that a wall would keep out sordid, illegal immigrant Mexican drug dealers who were poisoning the country.

But the biggest moment in the third debate came when moderator Chris Wallace cited Trump's claims at rallies that the election was rigged and that could be why he would lose. To that, Wallace asked Trump if he would accept the 2016 election result. In declaring his concerns about the "corrupt media" and an expectation that votes for him would not be counted, Trump replied, "I will look at it (the outcome) at the time." Those eight words had immense implications and also foreshadowed Trump's contention after the 2020 presidential election. In effect, Trump was saying that his judgment alone would determine the election result, a direct indication of an authoritarian and yet further evidence of his "I alone can save it" referring to the nation's condition. No major political candidate in the nation's history had ever offered such a condition.

Election Victory

The remainder of the 2016 campaign yielded an improbable victory for Donald Trump, although not by much. Clinton actually captured 2.9 million votes more than Trump, but in our system electoral votes determine the winner. On that score, Trump received 306 electoral votes to 232 for Clinton. One by one, the "Blue Wall" of Democratic states gave way to an improbable Trump election result. The only presidential candidate with no governmental or military experience now found himself about to preside over the most powerful office of the most powerful nation in the world.

In retrospect, the outcome shouldn't have been a total surprise. A Pew Research poll in July 2016 found widespread dissatisfaction with both Donald Trump and Hilary Clinton. More than 4 in 10 voters said it would be difficult to choose either candidate because "neither would be a good president."[48] Nevertheless, by the end of election day, enough of the voters sided with Trump.

There were other factors in addition to general discomfort. While political party breakdowns of the vote remained predictable (89 percent of Democrats voted for Clinton, 90 percent of Republicans voted for Trump), Independents broke for Trump, 48 percent to 42 percent. When analyzed by gender, 51 percent of men voted for Trump, while 39 percent cast their votes for Clinton. In a close race, these data become important.[49]

Finally, there was the issue of the public's division on race. Postelection surveys indicated that a sizable segment of White Barack Obama voters defected from would-be successor Hillary Clinton in 2016.[50] Polling showed that as many as half of the White Obama voters were not sympathetic to the contention that Black people face widespread discrimination. Many also favored the death penalty (generally opposed by African-Americans) and believed that illegal immigrants were harmful to the American economy. Recall the extent that Trump constantly focused either directly or indirectly on race, an issue, he would repeatedly claim, that was harmful to mainstream American culture and values. To that, a major study found, the candidates' distinctly different positions on race became an important source of voter decision making in the 2016 presidential election.[51] On that question, Trump charted a racially tinged course in presidential elections, different from the sixteen candidates in his political party. He touched a nerve with millions of Americans who had similar feelings, but no one to be their champion. That "someone" was Donald Trump.[52]

Almost immediately after his victory, Trump's racist followers expressed both their satisfaction and expectations. The Loyal White Knights of the Ku Klux Klan, a white nationalist group based in North Carolina, posted a picture on its website showing "TRUMP=TRUMP'S RACE UNITED MY PEOPLE."[53] In his summary of the 2016 presidential election's outcome, Jared Taylor, head of the American Renaissance, a magazine-turned alt-right website, said "The sleeping giant (Whites) has been stirring for some time and Mr. Trump gave it a voice and a reason to act." He continued, the best thing for America would be "voluntary separation of the races."[54] Andrew Anglin, founder of the *Daily Stormer* website dubbed by civil rights groups as neo-Nazi, added "Our glorious leader (Trump) has ascended to God Emperor. Make no mistake about it: we did this. . . . Much, much, much more work [is] to be done. But the White race is back in the game."[55]

Confronted with these claims, Trump passively "disavowed" White nationalists, at least in words. But his deeds proved otherwise.[56] At the same time, he claimed no involvement with racist groups, Trump hired former Breitbart News editor and alt-right advocate Steve Bannon as the chief strategist in his administration. He brought in Stephen Miller to lead the charge against racial minorities and would-be immigrants. The very fact that Trump didn't fully condemn these groups and others showed his heart and affiliation lay with those determined to divide American society.

THE BIGOTED PRESIDENCY

President Donald Trump wasted little time in exercising his power with race-related issues. Using the various levers at his disposal from his bully pulpit to executive orders, he directed much of his energy to race-related issues, and he often carried out his efforts with little concern for their constitutionality or political controversy. In the process, during his four years in office, Trump satisfied his new core constituency—particularly working-class White males, while angering large segments of the minority population as well as White moderates and liberals. These were not the only groups that approved and disapproved of Trump's actions. For example, evangelicals and the anti-immigration Congressional Freedom Caucus played important roles in Trump's victory. But in considering how Trump won the 2016 election, the defection of working-class White males was particularly important in securing his victory. Now, it would be Trump's job to fulfill his responsibilities (and their hopes) as president.

As documented in earlier chapters, Trump's use of racial resentment for political gain in 2016 was hardly new. His approach to race and racist-thinking went back to his earliest days of adulthood. Nor was race as a political tool new to the Republican party, or national politics in general. Some accounts go back to 2010 when with the success of the first Tea Party candidates, "the GOP began to play to a populist base that would prove dangerous, first to Democrats, but then to the traditional Republican elite."[57] Others detected the change in concert with the 1964 Civil Rights Act and Voting Rights of 1965 when as Lawrence Glickman wrote, White people were in fear "of losing jobs to Negroes; fear that neighborhood schools will be flooded by Negro kids 'bussed in' from across town; fear that homeowners will be forced to sell, if they wish to sell at all, to Negro newcomers."[58] The point is that racism has deep roots in American society, but rarely has it been weaponized to the extent that Donald Trump did as an open course of doing business.

Once in office, Trump frequently used the megaphone of his office to criticize the shortcomings of various groups, and he wasted little time in doing so. He began with an element of a favorite grievance: the notion of a rigged election, despite his electoral college vote victory. Of his 2.9 million popular vote loss to Hillary Clinton, Trump falsely blamed the difference on between three and five million undocumented residents who illegally voted in the presidential election; otherwise, Trump said, he would have had a popular vote majority. Almost immediately, Republican congressional sycophants followed suit with their revisionist histories.[59] From that day forward, he routinely faulted minority groups for the problems they brought to American society. While his rhetoric was no doubt offensive to those he belittled, it served to prove his value to those who elected Trump to office. "Unity" was a foreign word to Trump; rather he preyed on the politics of divisiveness as an insurance policy for keeping power. The cavalcade of his racist claims as well as the resulting presidential action steps follow below.

Muslims

Trump's open anger toward Muslims was expressed first after 9/11 when he claimed without evidence that he watched thousands of Muslims in New Jersey celebrating the terrorist-orchestrated crashes of two passenger planes into two World Trade Center towers. When asked about the allegation shortly after he his declared candidacy for the presidency, Trump insisted the event happened.[60] There were no television accounts, written news stories, or police reports of such an activity. Given an unfair attribution to local Muslims, most local officials were angered by Trump's lie. Trump persisted with Muslim celebration allegation through his presidential campaign.

Even when the truth was clearly not on Trump's side, those who knew better would not correct the record. At one point, in August 2015, fellow Republican presidential aspirant Chris Christie, New Jersey's governor at the time of the Twin Towers tragedy, shied away from a direct answer about the celebratory role of Muslims, saying to a reporter, "I do not remember . . . but, you know, there could be things I forget, too." Really? The Governor of New Jersey didn't recall whether thousands of Muslims were celebrating the disaster? Christie's "forgetfulness" was his escape from confronting Trump's lie, not exactly a badge of courage. As a result, Christie's unwillingness to correct the record gave room for Trump to continue his unproven allegation.

As President, Trump ratcheted his anti-Muslim diatribe. During his campaign, he promised, if elected, to ban all Muslims from coming to the United States and track those already here. Within days of taking office, Trump signed a toned-down version of his original promise, an executive order that denied entry of Muslims from seven countries to the United States. The federal courts struck down that version as well as another. In Trump's modified third effort, the U.S. Supreme Court, by a 5-to-4 vote, allowed the ban to proceed while new arguments wended their way through the federal courts. The constitutionality of the ban was never officially adjudicated by the nation's highest Court because on January 20, 2021, his first day in office, President Biden reversed Trump's executive order. Nevertheless, Trump's ban prevailed virtually the entire time during his presidency. Significantly, most Americans endorsed the ban. According to a Reuters poll taken in July 2017, 60 percent agreed with Trump's effort,[61] giving support for Trump's nationalism. Trump's outrage toward Muslims continued through much of his presidency.[62]

Like so many aspects of racism in America, Trump didn't create Islamophobia, the fear of Islam. But he didn't dismiss the bigotry of Islamophobia either. With the opportunity presented from 9/11, it's clear that he used the nation's animus toward Muslims as part of his "us versus them" strategy.

Latinos/Hispanics

Trump has a history of despising undocumented immigrants, except when they have been useful to him. That was especially the case with Latinos. As he neared the Republican presidential nomination in June 2016, Trump picked a fight with a federal district court judge handling civil suits against his Trump University, which was a real estate training program. He accused the judge, Gonzalo Curiel, of having "an absolute conflict" because Curiel's "Mexican heritage" was at odds with Trump's campaign against illegal immigration.[63] Earlier, in a speech before the Conservative Political Action Conference (CPAC) in 2014 he warned the attendees about Mexicans, "They're taking your jobs." He also criticized Florida Republican U.S. Senator and future campaign opponent Marco Rubio for his attempt to negotiate a comprehensive immigration reform plan.[64] At one point during his presidential campaign, Trump promised to deport all 11,000,000 undocumented immigrants; later he changed his plan to deporting only the "bad dudes." Left out of his many speeches about undocumented immigrants was that Trump himself employed them—a practice that continued well into his presidency! When asked about an investigation that showed a widespread practice of employing undocumented immigrants at his many properties, President Trump responded, "Well, that I don't know, because I don't run it (his businesses). But I would say this: Probably every [golf] club in the United States has that [undocumented immigrants] because it seems to me, from what I understand, [it's] a way people did business."[65]

Trump had two answers to the illegal immigration issue: build a $25 billion, 1,900-mile-long wall that would be paid for by Mexico and do everything possible to keep immigrants from entering the United States, especially those coming from Mexico, by employing harsh tactics at the border. With respect to the wall, the United States never received as much as a dollar from Mexico. Instead, the U.S. spent $14 billion to reinforce existing barriers and build a total of 52 miles of new construction.[66] Most of the money, it turns out, came from original allocations to the Department of Defense for more than one hundred different projects. Members of Congress howled over Trump redirecting the funds—an activity long considered a congressional prerogative. The Sierra Club and the Southern Border Communities Coalition sued over the recommitment, but the cases bounced back and forth between federal judicial levels through the rest of Trump's tenure.[67] However, the Supreme Court allowed Trump to move the funds until the case was decided by the nine jurists. With the election of Joe Biden to the presidency and his stated intention to reject Trump's funding approach, the new administration asked the court to vacate the case.

The southern border tactics of the Trump administration had equally calamitous results. With respect to preventing immigration, Trump declared or authorized 472 Executive Branch actions during his four years in office. They included the highest number of migrant border apprehensions since 2007; drastically reduced asylum admissions; an overhaul of the immigration court system, which led to a dramatic increase in removal orders and voluntary departures; and a program that separated parents from their children while awaiting adjudication of their requests to remain in the United States. The latter was designed as a means to discourage family migration—families would remain apart or leave.[68]

In a bizarre way, the COVID-19 pandemic was an anti-immigration gift of sorts to Trump. Given the contagiousness of the virus, the Trump administration contended that everyone seeking admission to the United States would have to wait until the virus abated. Said Ken Cuccinelli, the acting deputy of the Department of Homeland Security, "When you're talking about a pandemic, and you overlay that on a border crisis . . . [t]his creates a new wrinkle to the crisis where we have to look at ways to bar entry."[69] And they did; Trump invoked Title 42, a portion of a law passed in 1944 that permits denying entry of individuals if there is a danger that they might bring communicable diseases into the country.

Trump's fixation on illegal immigration issues had a hand-in-glove fit with his penchant for race-related complaints. One review of Trump's comments went so far as to describe him as "the only presidential candidate in modern U.S. history to run and win on an immigration-centered platform."[70] To be sure, there were other elements to Trump's candidacy, but few brought the anger and anguish that appeared with race-immigration combination.

Black People

As with other groups, Donald Trump's animus toward Black people began well before he moved into the White House. His days in business from building apartments to running casinos were tarnished with anti-Black sentiments, some of which brought trouble with the government. He even sought to create a season of *The Apprentice* pitting Black contestants against White contestants, which was flatly rejected by NBC.[71] And so it continued in politics. During a 2016 campaign visit to Little Haiti in Miami, Bob Woodward recounts that Trump expressed sympathy for Haitian residents, saying, "I feel sorry for these people. They came from such a shithole."[72]

Those words would return in a 2018 meeting about immigration with congressional leaders. As they attempted to hammer out how a policy on treating immigrants from Haiti, El Salvador, and African countries, Trump blurted out, "Why are we having all these people from shithole countries come here? Why do we need more Haitians? Take them out [of any immigration legislation]."[73] In the same conversation, he said, "we should have more people from Norway."

Asians wouldn't be so bad either, he went on to say, because they would contribute to the economy.[74] He would later change his mind about Asians when Trump blamed China for bringing COVID-19 to the United States.

Trump's attitude toward Black people became particularly crude and public during the second half of his term. A series of shootings of unarmed African-Americans by largely White police officers throughout the country led to a raft of public protests. In some cases, city leaders painted "Black Lives Matter" on key streets or intersections in honor of the deaths and injuries from police brutality. Trump called the "Black Lives Matter" slogan a "symbol of hate,"[75] distancing himself from any concern about what many saw as systemic racism by the police.

Rather than engage Black leaders over their issues, Trump angrily warned against any public outbursts, with threats of sending federal troops to cities with protests that sometimes turned violent. In a 2020 interview over why so many African-Americans had been killed by White police, Trump dismissed the claim by responding that more White people were killed by police than Black people.[76] Trump was correct that more White people had been killed than Black people by almost a two-to-one margin. But he failed to note there were five times *more* White than Black people. Those two data points clearly showed that, proportionately, Black people were killed by police much more than White people.[77]

Trump also defended the Confederate flag as a reasonable symbol of free speech and rejected the idea that it would offend African-Americans whose ancestors in all likelihood would have been enslaved in states bearing the standard. On a related issue, Confederate statues, a Quinnipiac poll in 2020 found agreement by a margin of 52 percent to 44 percent. However, the divisions among race were stark. Whereas only 44 percent of White people favored removal, 84 percent of African-American people and 58 percent Hispanic people approved of the proposal.[78] Trump's racist opinions took a toll on two large segments of voters.

We don't know how much Trump disliked Black people, but the pattern of disfavor with them was clear. Moreover, he showed little inclination over time to alter his behavior with Black people as well as every other major non-Christian White racial or ethnic group.

Jews

Donald Trump found himself in a quandary over American Jews. In one sense, Trump showed deep loyalty to Israel, the home to millions of Jews after World War II and the Holocaust. That Trump picked Israel over potentially hostile Arab neighbors endeared him not only to many Israelis but to Christian evangelicals who had a special reverence for Israel. For evangelical

Protestants, the largest religious group in the United States, a Jewish Israel is essential to keeping the Judeo-Christian creed.[79] As he prepared for his 2016 presidential campaign, Trump, never particularly religious, understood the value of this segment's vote and aligned himself with the evangelical community on Israel and abortion, also a late conversion issue by Trump.[80] Couple his relationship with evangelicals and the clout of fiscal conservatives, and Trump had the makings of a sizable political base.

Trump's alliance with evangelicals was a world away from his relationship with American Jews. Oddly enough, his daughter, Ivanka converted to Judaism when she married Jared Kushner. In fact, any time Trump was accused of being anti-Semitic, he would point to his daughter and Jewish grandchildren as evidence of his comfort with Jews. Still, numerous comments by Trump about Jews over the years suggest that he had a good deal of contempt for this sector of American society.

Even before he was nominated as the Republican party's standard bearer, Trump made his feelings about Jews known. In early June 2016, he tweeted a caricature from a prominent anti-Semitic website showing a picture of Hillary Clinton set inside of a six-point Star of David with a backdrop of 100 dollar bills and the slogan, "the most corrupt candidate ever." Critics immediately condemned the post as anti-Semitism. Trump said that the display consisted of a Sheriff's star, not a Star of David. The problem was that Sheriff's badges typically have little circles near the tips of each spike on a star; no such element appeared on the star in Trump's post. But it was the combination of alleged corruption, money, and the Star of David that led critics to slam the post as a stereotypical view that Jews control money and politics that convinced opponents of Trump's real intention.[81]

The next year in Charlottesville, Virginia, gave further insight into Trump's sentiment about Jews. A movement had begun in the South to remove Confederate statues from well-known public places because of their connection to slavery. One night in August 2017, more than 200 young self-described White supremacist men dressed in fatigues with torches and weapons snaked through a part of the University of Virginia campus displaying a statute of Confederate General Robert E. Lee. As they marched, the group, organized by prominent Nazi sympathizer Richard Spencer, shouted over and over in unison, "Jews will not replace us" along with "White lives matter" and other anti-Black slogans. University students and others nearby found themselves fighting with the White nationalists in a brawl where many were hurt. The next day at a counter-protest rally, one of the White agitators rammed his car into the crowd, killing a counter-protester.

That evening, President Trump spoke of the previous night's altercation, saying, "We condemn in the strongest possible terms this egregious display of hatred, bigotry and violence on many sides" suggesting that both groups shared responsibility for the attack. The following day, however, he changed his posture on the weekend's events, declaring that were "very fine people on both sides" of the altercation.][82] Sensing approbation from the president, White supremacist leaders were beyond glee.

Trump's disdain for Jews continued throughout his presidency. In 2019, he questioned Jewish patriotism when at a meeting with reporters, Trump declared, "Any Jewish people that vote for a Democrat, I think it shows either a total lack of knowledge or great disloyalty."[83] He also said that Jews who vote for Democrats are disloyal to Israel. In other words, loyalty to Trump superseded dedication to anything other than Trump. Most Jewish leaders and civil libertarians strongly disagreed with the president's description of American Jewish voters. Oddly enough, however, the Republican Jewish Coalition, a small group of Trump loyalists, actually agreed with Trump, no doubt a sign of total devotion no matter the issue. For Trump, in his "us versus them" mindset, however, most Jews were the "them" and therefore unredeemable. Apparently, that approach didn't sit well with most American Jews. A national poll of Jews taken at the time of the 2016 presidential election found that 72 percent viewed Trump's personality unfavorable, compared with 18 percent who viewed him favorably.[84] Those data corresponded remarkably with the actual vote, 71 percent of which went for Clinton, compared with 25 percent for Trump.

THE POWER OF GRIEVANCE: TRUMP'S SECRET WEAPON

In his work, *Devil's Bargain*, Joshua Green contends that Trump's seemingly disorganized style interfered with this campaign messages. He writes, "one weakness of Trump's campaign is that it was guided almost entirely by the candidate's impulses."[85] Green is on the mark in that Trump was and remains famously known for going off script. However, how much of that stemmed from disorganization versus how much from understanding the anger of his audience is another question. Trump used the explosive power of grievance to connect with his audiences, energize his audiences, and dispatch them as soldiers of revenge. They were his army committed to election renewal and he was their General. Protesting about the loss of "American culture" because of those who don't rightfully belong here was Trump's ammunition, and his believers used it.

We must be reminded that racism was not the only factor that led to Trump's 2016 presidential victory. Strong support from Christian evangelicals and an inept Hillary Clinton presidential candidacy, and a last-minute FBI allegation that proved wrong were among the myriad factors that helped

Trump win the election. But amidst the cacophony of a close campaign, Trump's racist-oriented political operation can't be ignored as a powerful weapon for mobilizing a slice of electorate who saw the election as their moment for an overdue redirection of the country.

NOTES

1. Michael Kranish and Marc Fisher, *Trump Revealed* (New York, NY: Simon & Schuster, 2016), p. 213.
2. See Russell Brooker and Todd Schaefer, *Public Opinion in the 21st Century: Let the People Speak* (Boston, MA: Houghton Mifflin Company, 2006), pp. 113–114.
3. See "The Many Ways in which Donald Trump was Once a Liberal's Liberal," *The Washington Post*, July 9, 2015, https://www.washingtonpost.com/news/the-fix/wp/2015/07/09/ths-many-ways-in-which-donald-trump-was-once-a-liberals-liberal/.
4. David Freedlander, "An Oral History of Donald Trump's Almost-Run for President in 2000," *New York Magazine*, October 11, 2018, https://nymag.com/intelligencer/2018/10/trumps-almost-run-for-president-in-2000-an-oral-history.html.
5. Ibid.
6. "51% of Republican Voters: Obama Foreign," *Politico*, February 15, 2011, https://www.politico.com/story/2011/02/51-of-gop-voters-obama-foreign-049554.
7. "Obama's Birth Certificate Convinces Some, but Not All, Skeptics," *Gallup Poll*, May 13, 2011, https://news.gallup.com/poll/147530/obama-birth-certificate-convinces-not-skeptics.aspx.
8. Keren Blankfield, "Donald Trump for President 2012? A Conversation with the Donald," *Forbes Magazine*, January 5, 2021, https://www.forbes.com/sites/kerenblankfeld/2011/01/05/donald-trump-for-president-2012-a-conversation-with-the-donald/?sh=5861f5e51e28.
9. "Donald Trump Runs Second in Poll: Can He Win Republican Nomination," *ABC News*, April 7, 2011, https://abcnews.go.com/Politics/poll-donald-trump-catapults-place-2012-gop-field/story?id=13318814.
10. "Huckabee, Trump, Romney Set Pace for 2012 GOP Field," *Gallup Poll*, April 22, 2012, https://news.gallup.com/poll/147233/huckabee-trump-romney-pace-gop-field-2012.aspx.
11. Blankfield, "Donald Trump for President 2012?"
12. "NBC gives Donald a Trump-Sized Raise to $160M," *New York Post*, June 22, 2011, https://nypost.com/2011/06/22/nbc-gives-donald-a-trump-sized-raise-to-160m/#ixzz1Q08fudIS.
13. Quoted in "NBC Fires Donald Trump over 'Derogatory Statements about Immigrants'," *PBS News Hour*, June 29, 2015, https://www.pbs.org/newshour/politics/nbc-fires-donald-trump-moguls-derogatory-statements.
14. Timothy L. O'Brien, "Trumpism is a Dish Republicans Can Serve without Trump," *Bloomberg Opinion*, November 9, 2022, https://www.bloomberg.com/opinion/articles/2022-11-09/midterm-elections-trumpism-doesn-t-need-trump.

15. See Samira Saramo, "The Meta-violence of Trumpism," *European Journal of American Studies*, Summer 2017, https://journals.openedition.org/ejas/12129.

16. The comments here and in the following paragraph are all found in "Here's Donald Trump's Presidential Announcement Speech," *Time*, June 16, 2015, https://time.com/3923128/donald-trump-announcement-speech/.

17. Joshua Green, *Devil's Bargain: Steve Bannon, Donald Trump, and the Storming of the Presidency* (New York, NY: Penguin Press, 2017), pp. 46–47.

18. Jean Guerrero, *Hate Monger: Stephen Miller, Donald Trump, and the White Nationalist Agenda* (New York, NY: HarperCollins Publishers, 2020), p. 158.

19. See "McCain: Obama not an Arab, Crowd Boos," *Politico*, October 10, 2008, https://www.politico.com/story/2008/10/mccain-obama-not-an-arab-crowd-boos-014479.

20. "RNC Autopsy," December 2012, https://www.documentcloud.org/documents/624581-rnc-autopsy.

21. "GOP Leaders Fear Damage to Party's Image as Donald Trump Doubles Down," *The Washington Post*, July 8, 2015, https://www.washingtonpost.com/politics/trump-could-damage-the-republican-image-party-leaders-worry/2015/07/08/2ec75b4c-25ab-11e5-b72c-2b7d516e1e0e_story.html.

22. The information in this paragraph comes from Willa Frej, "Here's a Running List of Racist Things That Have Happened at Trump Rallies," *HuffPost*, March 16, 2016, https://www.huffpost.com/entry/list-racist-things-trump-rallies_n_56d7019ae4b0871f60ed519f.

23. *Ibid.*

24. Ibid.

25. Ibid.

26. "Muslim Woman Gets Kicked of Trump Rally—For Protesting Silently," *The Washington Post*, January 9, 2016, https://www.washingtonpost.com/news/post-politics/wp/2016/01/08/muslim-woman-escorted-out-of-trump-rally-in-south-carolina/.

27. Ibid.

28. Ibid.

29. David A. Graham, "The Lurking Menace of a Trump Rally," *The Atlantic*, March 10, 2016, https://www.theatlantic.com/politics/archive/2016/03/donald-trump-fayetteville/473169/.

30. Tina Nguyen, "Donald Trump's Rallies Are becoming Increasingly Violent," *Vanity Fair*, March 16, 2016, https://www.vanityfair.com/news/2016/03/donald-trump-protesters-rally-violence.

31. "'Get 'em out!' Racial Tensions Explode at Trump Rallies," *The Washington Post*, March 12, 2016, https://www.huffpost.com/entry/list-racist-things-trump-rallies_n_56d7019ae4b0871f60ed519f.

32. Fabiola Cineas, "Donald Trump is the Accelerant," January 9, 2021, https://www.vox.com/21506029/trump-violence-tweets-racist-hate-speech.

33. "Feds Concerned about Risk of Violence as Election Day Nears," *NBC News*, October 26, 2016, https://www.nbcnews.com/news/us-news/feds-concerned-about-risk-violence-election-day-nears-n672821.

34. "Assaults Spiked on Trump Rally Days during 2016 Election," *Penn Medicine News*, University of Pennsylvania, March 16, 2018, https://www.pennmedicine.org/news/news-releases/2018/march/assaults-spiked-on-trump-rally-days-during-2016-election.

35. "Assaults Increased When Cities Hosted Trump Rallies, Study Finds," *The New York Times*, March 16, 2018, https://www.nytimes.com/2018/03/16/us/trump-rally-violence.html.

36. "Why Donald Trump Isn't a Real Candidate, in One Chart," *FiveThirtyEight.com*, June 16, 2015, https://fivethirtyeight.com/features/why-donald-trump-isnt-a-real-candidate-in-one-chart/#fn-1.

37. "This Time, Donald Trump Says He's Running," *USA Today*, June 16, 2015, https://www.usatoday.com/story/news/politics/elections/2015/06/16/donald-trump-announcement-president/28782433/.

38. "Trump to Megyn Kelly: I Don't Have Time for Political Correctness and Neither Does the Country," *Real Clear Politics*, August 6, 2015, https://www.realclearpolitics.com/video/2015/08/06/trump_to_megyn_kelly_i_dont_have_time_for_political_correctness_and_neither_does_this_country.html.

39. Green, *Devil's Bargain*, pp. 170–171.

40. Graham, "The Lurking Menace."

41. These data come from "Broad Public Support for Legal Status for Undocumented Immigrants," Pew Research Center, June 4, 2015, https://www.pewresearch.org/politics/2015/06/04/broad-public-support-for-legal-status-for-undocumented-immigrants/.

42. "Donald Trump 2016 RNC Draft Speech Transcript," July 21, 2016.

43. Ibid.

44. Ibid.

45. Eli Stokols, "Trump's Four Dysfunctional Days in Cleveland," *Politico*, July 22, 2016, https://www.politico.com/story/2016/07/rnc-2016-donald-trump-dysfunction-226001.

46. "How the Trump Campaign Took Control of the G.O.P.," *The New York Times*, December 24, 2020, https://www.nytimes.com/2020/03/09/us/trump-campaign-brad-parscale.html.

47. See "Donald Trump's Big Debate Problem: Hillary Clinton Hit the Right Note on Race; Donald Trump Went off the Rails," *Salon*, September 27, pp. 2–16, https://www.salon.com/2016/09/27/placeholder-for-simon-debate-cover/.

48. "2016 Campaign: Strong Interest, Widespread Dissatisfaction," Pew Research Center, July 7, 2016, https://www.pewresearch.org/politics/2016/07/07/2016-campaign-strong-interest-widespread-dissatisfaction/.

49. See Rachel Bitecofer, *The Unprecedented 2016 Presidential Election* (Cham, Switzerland: Palgrave Publisher, 2018), pp. 170–173.

50. "Behind Trump's victory: Divisions by Race, Gender, Education," Pew Research Center, November 9, 2016, https://www.pewresearch.org/short-reads/2016/11/09/behind-trumps-victory-divisions-by-race-gender-education/.

51. These data and assessments come from John Sides, Michael Tesler, and Lynn Vavreck, *Identity Crisis: The 2016 Presidential Campaign and the Battle for the Meaning of America* (Princeton, NJ: Princeton University Press, 2018), pp. 165–169.

52. Lafleur Stephens-Dougan, *Race to the Bottom: How Racial Appeals Work in American Politics* (Chicago, IL: University of Chicago Press, 2020), p. 176.

53. "The Alt-Right Supported Trump. Now its Members Want Him to Satisfy their Demands," *The Washington Post*, November 10, 2016, https://www.washingtonpost.com/national/the-alt-right-used-to-be-ignored-now-theyre-courting-a-president-elect/2016/11/10/746341d8-a75b-11e6-8fc0-7be8f848c492_story.html.

54. "What this White Separatist Expects from the Trump Administration," *On the Media*, WNYC Public Radio, November 17, 2016, https://www.wnycstudios.org/podcasts/otm/segments/what-white-separatist-expects-trump-administration.

55. Quoted in Morgan Winsor, "Trump's Victory Buoying White Nationalists, Anti-Discrimination Advocates Say," *ABC News*, November 11, 2016, https://abcnews.go.com/Politics/trumps-victory-buoying-white-nationalists-anti-discrimination-advocates/story?id=43467300.

56. "Trump Disavows the White Nationalist 'Alt-Right' but Defends Steve Bannon Hire," *The Guardian*, November 22, 2016, https://www.theguardian.com/us-news/2016/nov/22/donald-trump-steve-bannon-alt-right-white-nationalist-disavow.

57. Sidney Tarrow, *Movements and Parties* (New York, NY: Cambridge University Press, 2021), p. 179.

58. Lawrence Glickman, "How White Backlash Controls American Progress," *The Atlantic*, May 21, 2020, https://www.theatlantic.com/ideas/archive/2020/05/white-backlash-nothing-new/611914/.

59. "The Tale of a Trump Falsehood: How His Voter Fraud Claim Spread like a Virus," *The Washington Post*, January 31, 2071, https://www.washingtonpost.com/politics/the-tale-of-a-trump-falsehood-how-his-voter-fraud-claim-spread-like-a-virus/2017/01/30/47081e32-e4ed-11e6-ba11-63c4b4fb5a63_story.html.

60. "Trump's Outrageous Claim that 'Thousands' of New Jersey Muslims Celebrated the 9/11 Attacks," *The Washington Post*, November 22, 2015, https://www.washingtonpost.com/news/fact-checker/wp/2015/11/22/donald-trumps-outrageous-claim-that-thousands-of-new-jersey-muslims-celebrated-the-911-attacks/.

61. "Most American Voters Support Limited Travel Ban: Poll," *Reuters*, July 5, 2017, https://www.reuters.com/article/us-usa-immigration-poll/most-american-voters-support-limited-travel-ban-poll-idUSKBN19Q2FW.

62. "86 Times Donald Trump Displayed or Promoted Islamophobia," *Medium*, April 19, 2018, https://medium.com/nilc/86-times-donald-trump-displayed-or-promoted-islamophobia-49e67584ac10.

63. "Trump Says Judge's Mexican Heritage Presents 'Absolute Conflict,'" *The Wall Street Journal*, June 3, 2016, https://www.google.com/search?q=trump+university&rlz=1C5CHFA_enUS773US773&oq=trump+university&aqs=chrome..69i57j46i131i199i433i465i512j0i512j0i131.

64. "Trump Warns GOP on Immigration: 'They're Taking Your Jobs,'" *The Washington Post*, March 6, 2014, https://www.washingtonpost.com/news/post-politics/wp/2014/03/06/trump-warns-gop-on-immigration-theyre-taking-your-jobs/.

65. "'If you're a Good Worker, Papers Don't Matter': How a Trump Construction Crew has Relied on Immigrants without Legal Status," *The Washington Post*, August 9, 2019, https://time.com/4386240/donald-trump-immigration-arguments/.

66. "Most of Pentagon Billions Moved to Border Not Recoverable," *Roll Call*, May 7, 2021, https://rollcall.com/2021/05/07/most-of-pentagon-billions-moved-to-border-wall-not-recoverable/.

67. The case was *Trump v. Sierra Club*.

68. Guerrero, *Hate Monger*, p. 192.

69. "Trump Restricts Immigration Amid the Pandemic. Critics see it as an Excuse to Push His Own Agenda," *PBS News Hour,* July 28, 2020, https://www.pbs.org/newshour/politics/trump-restricts-immigration-amid-the-pandemic-critics-see-it-as-an-excuse-to-push-his-own-agenda.

70. "Four Years of Profound Change: Immigration Policy during the Trump Presidency," Migration Policy Institute, Washington, DC, February 2022, https://www.migrationpolicy.org/sites/default/files/publications/mpi-trump-at-4-report-final.pdf.

71. "Trump Suggested 'Black vs Whites' Games in *The Apprentice*," *The Independent*, July 22, 2019, https://www.independent.co.uk/news/world/americas/us-politics/trump-apprentice-black-vs-white-contest-howard-stern-interview-a9015701.html.

72. Bob Woodward, *Fear: Trump in the White House* (New York, NY: Simon & Schuster, 2018), p. 321.

73. "Trump Derides Protections for Immigrants from 'Shithole' Countries," *The Washington Post*, January 12, 2018, https://www.washingtonpost.com/politics/trump-attacks-protections-for-immigrants-from-shithole-countries-in-oval-office-meeting/2018/01/11/bfc0725c-f711-11e7-91af-31ac729add94_story.html.

74. "Trump Wishes We Had More Immigration From Norway. Turns Out We Once Did," *NPR*, January 12, 2018, https://www.npr.org/sections/goatsandsoda/2018/01/12/577673191/trump-wishes-we-had-more-immigrants-from-norway-turns-out-we-once-did.

75. See "Trump: Black Lives Matter is a 'Symbol of Hate,'" *Politico*, July 1, 2020, https://www.politico.com/news/2020/07/01/trump-black-lives-matter-347051.

76. "Trump Downplays Police Violence, Deaths of Black Americans," *NPR*, July 14, 2020, https://www.npr.org/sections/live-updates-protests-for-racial-justice/2020/07/14/891144579/trump-says-more-white-people-killed-by-police-violence-than-blacks.

77. According to the 2020 U.S. Census, African-Americans represented 75.8% of the U.S. population, compared to African-Americans at 13.6%, a ratio of better than 5-to-1.

78. "68% Say Discrimination against Black Americans a 'Serious Problem,' Quinnipiac University National Poll Finds; Slight Majority Supports Removing Confederate Statues," Quinnipiac Poll, June 17, 2020, https://poll.qu.edu/Poll-Release?releaseid=3786.

79. See "The Biggest Fans of President Trump's Israel Policy? Evangelical Christians," *The Washington Post*, December 18, 2017, https://www.washingtonpost.com/news/made-by-history/wp/2017/12/18/the-biggest-fans-of-president-trumps-israel-policy-evangelical-christians/.

80. Elizabeth Dias, "How Evangelicals Helped Donald Trump Win," *Time*, November 9, 2017, https://time.com/4565010/donald-trump-evangelicals-win/.

81. Jeremy Diamond, "Donald Trump's 'Star of David' Tweet Controversy, Explained," *CNN*, July 5, 2016, https://www.cnn.com/2016/07/04/politics/donald-trump-star-of-david-tweet-explained.

82. "Trump Gives White Supremacists an Unequivocal Boost," *The New York Times*, August 15, 2017, https://www.nytimes.com/2017/08/15/us/politics/trump-charlottesville-white-nationalists.html.

83. "Donald Trump Courts Jews by Peddling Anti-Semitic 'Disloyalty' Tropes: Today's Talker," *USA Today*, August 21, 2019, https://www.google.com/search?q=Donald+Trump+courts+Jews+by+peddling+anti-Semitic+%27disloyalty%27+tropes%3A+Today%27s+talker&rlz=1C5CHFA_enUS773US.

84. "2016 Post-election Jewish Surveys Summary Findings," Report by GBA Strategies, Presented to J Street, November 9, 2016, https://jstreet.org/wp-content/uploads/2016/11/J-Street-Election-Night-Survey-Analysis-110916.pdf.

85. Joshua Green, *Devil's Bargain: Steve Bannon, Donald Trump, and the Storming of the White House* (New York, New York: Penguin Press), p. 209.

Chapter 7

A Bitter Presidency

In his ground-breaking work, *The Presidential Character*, James David Barber is quick to point out that every president's personality is unique from the others, including their adaptation to the office, use of power, and view of the surrounding environment. Appreciating their differences, Barber outlines four types of presidential character: active-positive, consisting of high self-esteem and rational behavior; active-negative, entailing intense emotion and great difficulty in managing aggressive feelings; passive-positive, involving other-directed characteristics with low self-esteem; and passive-negative, comprising the desire to serve the polity but not lead it.

In Barber's view, the prime threat to the active-negative personality is the other people in society. A president with such disposition, Barber Writes, "tends to divide humanity into the weak and grasping. . . . In struggling to understand social causality, he restricts the explanations to conspiracy and chaos." Further, the active-negative personality "is taken up with his own performance [and] continually seeks confirmation of his self-esteem from other people."[1] The leader's consistent need for adoration from crowds would seem to fit in with this description.

To be sure, no president fits perfectly into one of Barber's categories, but it's difficult to imagine Donald Trump as being in any other category than that of an active-negative personality. The evidence is overwhelming. Consider that thus far, we've discussed Trump's penchant to divide humanity through his attitude and behavior toward racial, ethnic, and religious minorities. Recall his "us" versus "them" attitude to divide society, his penchant for calling enemies "losers," and constant expectation of adoration. Trump's aggressive conduct has been chronicled through the way he exhorts his followers in rallies to violence, his belligerent presidential debate performances, and in this chapter, we'll include these observations with his treatment of the press and staff members who leave him because of Trump's unwillingness to entertain thoughts and proposals contrary to his own.

As for conspiracy, all we have to do is recall Trump's distrustful comments surrounding the 2016 presidential election. Should he lose, Trump often stated, it would be because of a "rigged" election system. When he actually won the 2016 election, Trump quickly dropped the objection. Nevertheless, Trump raised the same grievance four years later when, after he lost his reelection bid, he again alleged his defeat happened because the election was "rigged." Similar allegations occurred during the 2022 midterm election campaigns. Asked to speak on behalf of Republican candidates in key races, Trump used his appearances to resume his protests with promises of retribution with his own reelection, only to cause losses for the candidates he was supposed to help.[2]

In pledging stern rule if re-elected on 2024, Trump often expressed adoration for authoritarian leaders as role models for governing. Repeatedly, he praised Russia's Vladimir Putin, North Korea's Kim Jong-Un, Turkey's Recep Erdogan, and China's Xi Jinping for their ability to rule their countries without question or political challenges.[3] In an interview with then-Fox anchor Tucker Carlson in April 2023, Trump described Kim Jung-Un as "very smart . . . He took over the country (North Korea) at a very young age. And he has total dominate control."[4] Total domination was part of Trump's "win at any cost" mentality locked in his mindset ever since his childhood.

Throughout this chapter, examples of Trump's active-negative personality will be provided again and again. More important will be the extent to which Trump's behavior and that of his followers threaten American democracy.

DISTRUSTING MANAGEMENT STYLE

Donald Trump's presidential administration was not rigged as much as it was ragged. Few key appointees stayed very long and many managed their executive responsibilities in an "acting" capacity that limited their influence internally as well as with other government agencies. Combined, these two aspects of Trump's administration contributed to an erratic, fumbling bureaucracy that suited Trump just fine. A weakened federal bureaucracy was less likely to check a burgeoning presidency.

High Turnover

Over his four years in the presidency, Donald Trump had a higher turnover rate of key Executive Office decision-makers than his five predecessors.[5] His 92 percent resignation rate of key officials easily exceeded the rates of recent presidents Barack Obama (50 percent), George W. Bush (64 percent), Bill Clinton (77 percent), George H.W. Bush (65 percent), and Ronald Reagan (78 percent).[6] The record of excessive resignations was important for two reasons: first, because mass departures of key staff members undermined coherence of the executive branch, and second, because the revolving door of exits left unquestioned power with Trump and his inner circle.[7]

As to the explanations for so many departures, toward the end of Trump's presidency CNN compiled a list of reasons provided by former Executive Office and Cabinet officials. Former Defense Secretary James Mattis left because his strategic advice no longer resonated with Trump.[8] Former White House Chief of Staff John Kelly departed because of Trump's penchant for "yes" men. Former Special Assistant to the President Cliff Sims claimed that Trump had compiled an "enemies" list of members of his own administration. Former National Economic Council Director Gary Cohn noted that there was no one in Trump's staff to tell him "what he didn't want to hear." Former Secretary of State Rex Tillerson called Trump "undisciplined" and complained that Trump asked for personal favors during his interaction with Ukrainian President Volodymyr Zelinksyy that included using U.S. assets as collateral." It's worth remembering that all of these individuals were personally recruited by Trump.

Along these lines, it's important to recall the interaction between President Trump and James Comey, the FBI director he inherited from the Biden administration. According to Comey, in a private meeting the two had shortly after Trump's inauguration, Trump demanded personal allegiance as a condition for Comey keeping his job. "I need loyalty. I expect loyalty," Comey remembers the president insisting. Uncomfortable with the expectation, Comey promised the president "honesty."[9] Of course, the FBI as part of the Department of Justice is loyal to laws of the United States, not to the president or any individual. Over the next few weeks after their initial meeting, Trump asked Comey for personal loyalty in a manner that would have Comey abandon nonpolitical status; he refused Trump's request, and within four months was publicly fired by Trump for his "poor leadership" of the FBI.[10]

The irony is that in every case except Comey's, Trump was responsible for hiring his executive team. But when they left, Trump turned on virtually all of them with a series of pejorative assessments. A few examples: Trump criticized John Kelly, his choice for Chief of Staff for not following through with Trump's agenda.[11] He accused James Mattis, also his hand-picked Chief of Staff, as being "way over his head,"[12] and described another departed Chief of Staff, Mick Mulvaney, as being "a born loser."[13] As for other appointees, Trump characterized former Secretary of State Rex Tillerson as "dumb as a rock."[14]

But the most ironic Trump condemnation was reserved for former Attorney General William Barr. Early on in his tenure with Trump, Barr pre-empted Special Counsel Robert Mueller's congressionally mandated critical report on Trump's early years in office[15] with his own soft-pedaled assessment, thereby deflecting considerable criticism, which delighted Trump.[16] But that wasn't enough. After the 2020 election, Barr resigned in the wake of Trump's pressure to overturn the result, after which Trump called Barr "a coward who didn't do his job."[17] For Trump, total loyalty was the number one requirement for being on his team.

Time after time, Trump considered himself the smartest, most capable chief executive, while those who left him were dumb, lazy, disloyal, or not following through. He elevated himself on the shoulders of those who left him, yet consistently belittled the value of his employees once they left.

The "Acting" Executive Branch

Quite often in government, when an appointee departs from his or her position, an acting administrator fills the post until a permanent leader is selected. That's the case with respect to the key management positions in the U.S. national government such as the Cabinet and key regulatory agencies. By definition, an acting official is a placeholder until the replacement is appointed, and in most cases at the highest policymaking levels, confirmed by the U.S. Senate.

During his first three years in office, President Donald Trump used acting officials for 22 Cabinet and Cabinet-level posts, with permanent appointments not made for months and sometimes not at all. Trump viewed this approach as beneficial because it gave him "flexibility;"[18] acting officials could be moved in and out of office without going through sometimes painful Senate hearings. However, his "interpretation" of the use of acting officials conflicted with the Federal Vacancy Reform Act of 1998, which limited acting appointments to no more than 210 days. According to one study, Trump had violated the Federal Vacancy Reform Act with at least 15 appointments that had gone beyond the 210-day limit.[19] In one case alone, the Department of Homeland Security, the most important federal agency dealing with undocumented immigrants and the southern border with Mexico, went without a Senate-confirmed leader for almost 500 days.

Trump's use of acting executives avoided entanglements with—and possible rejection by—the U.S. Senate. It also weakened the ability of acting administrators to carry out the functions of their offices because of the sense that they were temporary employees. As a result of Trump's disregard for the law, his approach to governing interfered with the Senate's rightful role to confirm or deny confirmation. Only late in Trump's presidency did a federal court issue an order denying him the ability to make excessively long "acting" appointments. It always left key departments and agencies without any firm guidance. For almost his entire administration, however, Interestingly, few Republican members challenged Trump.

Loyalty to Trump Above the Constitution

Not all of Trump's key administrative officials were "acting," however. Trump's Attorneys General, first Jeff Sessions and later William Barr, were trusted allies. Of course, if they violated the Trump loyalty pledge by doing something untoward the president, they were dismissed, as was the case with Sessions recusing himself in the Mueller investigation. As noted above, FBI Director James Comey also flunked the Trump loyalty promise and was quickly fired after Trump assumed office in 2017.

One administration loyalist of great value to Trump was Charles Rettig, Trump's Internal Revenue Service (IRS) Commissioner appointee. Trump, it should be noted, never released his income tax documents while running for office, becoming the first presidential candidate in modern times to refrain from doing so since voluntary disclosures began with the Richard Nixon administration. The reason, Trump said, stemmed from the fact that he was under audit by the IRS, and that, as such, he would not be able to make his records available until the audit ended. Throughout his entire presidency Trump repeatedly offered his IRS audit explanation, declaring that he would be happy to release his records once the investigation ended. But that simply wasn't the case. Trump's tax records subpoenaed by the House Ways and Means Committee in 2019 later revealed that he had not been under investigation by the IRS during his candidacy.

Despite a law mandating the IRS to audit every president, the agency failed to audit Trump until 2019, just after the House of Representatives subpoenaed the president's tax records. That effort led to a bitter court fight between the Democratic Congress and Trump until November 2022, when the U.S. Supreme Court declared the House was entitled to examine the tax returns. One other fact of interest: Charles Rettig, Trump's nominee for the IRS Commissioner position in 2018, wrote an op-ed piece in 2016 defending Trump's resistance to releasing his IRS records.[20] Clearly, Trump had an appointee willing to defy his own agency's rules.

Trump's fixation with enemies didn't end with the Executive Branch. Even before taking office, Trump was at work compiling an enemies list of elected officials who had opposed him either before the nomination or during the 2016 campaign. Traditionally, presidents refrain from taking on congressional members in their own party once nominated, and certainly upon election; after all, presidents rely on Congress for carrying out their legislative agenda. But there was little "traditional" about Trump. Once in power, he wasn't hesitant of using his clout to chase opponents out of office in subsequent elections by threatening to endorse others in his political party.[21] It worked more times than not.

ENDLESS TANGLING WITH THE PRESS

News stories and other reports by the press bring information to the public and provide a level of transparency in government. Such capability is specifically mentioned in the First Amendment of the U.S. Constitution, which stipulates that "Congress shall make no law . . . abridging the freedom of speech, or freedom of the press." There are few constitutional guarantees as specific as the First Amendment, and few as important as sources of political information.

The Press and Democracy

Whether from a distant Amazon jungle or a nearby U.S. city, the communication of events by the media gives us the opportunity to learn more about our world that we wouldn't have otherwise. Some of us really have little concern about events and circumstances outside of our immediate surroundings; others of us can't get enough news. Through print, electronic means and television, the press provides information to the public and other interested parties. As an informal linkage institution, the value of the press lies in its role as an information conduit between elected public officials and the mass public.[22] To that end, no connection is more important than information stemming from the president to the body politic. A two-way arrangement occurs where the president seeks to disseminate information via the press and where the press with reporters asks questions on behalf of the public. However, journalists can't report events and other circumstances if they are denied access to government officials who possess information potentially vital for public consumption.

All of this points to what Doris Graber describes as a traditional "rocky marriage" between the president and the press.[23] On the one hand, the president wants to make available information on his or her terms; on the other hand, reporters may ask questions the president does not particularly want to deal with, lest that information put the president in a somewhat less than favorable light or reveal details the president feels the public shouldn't know. If journalists are not granted access to public information on a regular basis, they are unable to do their jobs and we are left without the opportunity to know what is happening. Finding the right midpoint for these two different objectives can be tasking under any circumstances.

Trump's Relationship with the Press

Donald Trump had a particularly thorny relationship with most reporters. From the earliest days during his campaign for the presidency, Trump made the press his enemy and, in his words, "an enemy of the American people."[24] At various times, without any evidence, he accused reporters of being "very dishonest people" and claimed that their coverage of him was "an outrage." Whenever a story was written about Trump that conflicted with his interpretation of the facts, Trump wrote it off as "fake news." Trump's ongoing tirades against the press continued throughout his term of office. His spokesperson assumed the same adversarial approach to reporters. When reporters wrote that pictures of the crowd at Trump's inauguration revealed attendance considerably smaller than the first Obama inauguration, Trump Press Secretary Sean Spicer accused the press of writing "deliberate falsehoods."[25] Then, when NBC *Meet the Press* moderator Chuck Todd asked Trump's presidential adviser Kellyanne Conway on how the president could stick to an attendance claim that was obviously a lie, she responded that Spicer had simply provided reporters with "alternative facts."[26] Such re-interpretations of information based on anything but truth persisted throughout the Trump presidency. When a reporter challenged Trump on a falsehood, Trump would simply explain that the reporter was part of the "deep state," that mysterious underground collection of bureaucrats, reporters, and special interests dedicated to undermining the truth and his presidency. The irony, of course, was that in defending an outright lie, Trump would falsely accuse the challenging reporter with just that—a lie!

The Weakening of Public Trust

Earlier (chapter 2), we discussed the importance of authoritarians having control of the information dissemination process. One step toward that end is persuading the public of the press's depravity. Accordingly, Trump's hostile relationship with the press served as an invitation for Trump rally attendees to boo the press and occasionally rough up a reporter. It's important to recall that at his rallies, Trump would often make hostile comments about the press; accordingly, attendees viewed such statements as encouragement for attacking reporters.[27] In 2018, Trump even praised a Republican congressional candidate for body-slamming a reporter.[28] During press conferences, sometimes Trump would simply walk out when reporters asked a question he didn't want to answer."[29] Trump's hostility toward the press gave sympathizers an excuse to act against his enemies. *The Boston Globe* and *CNN* received death threats; in 2018, a pipe bomb was sent to *CNN's* New York office.[30]

Donald Trump's endless berating of the media was not lost on those who supported him the most. In fact, his constant belittling of the press provided results that left his base trusting him more than the press. The Pew Research Center routinely polls on attitudes toward basic American institutions, the very instruments designed to protect our democracy. One such topic centers on public trust in the media, historically a guardrail against the demise of democracy. A question routinely asked is, "Do you have trust in national organizations?" The press is one such organization on the list. In 2016, just before the onset of Donald Trump's presidency, 76 percent expressed support for national media organizations; by 2021, support dropped to 58 percent, some slippage but not dramatically so. However, the real shock came with dramatically different answers from Democrats and Republicans. Democratic trust in the media between 2016 and 2021 dipped slightly from 83 percent to 78 percent. Republican trust plummeted from 70 percent to 35 percent.[31] With distrust of the press baked into the Trump message, more than ever they counted on their leader to save them and "Make America Great Again." And with that, support for a free press suffered as sizable chunks of the electorate began to believe Trump over press reports.

DETERIORATED PRESIDENTIAL NORMS

"Norms" are part of the informal, generally acceptable behaviors found in society. There are customs in every culture, although the same behavior may be viewed as a norm in one but not another. Lining up in single file to board a bus may be an acceptable norm in one society and totally unimportant in another. Similarly, in some cultures, people greet one another by shaking hands; in others, they acknowledge one another with a bow or curtsy. It's important to note that norms are not laws. For example, many people may believe that helping an elderly person cross a street is a good deed, yet choosing not to help that individual would not be breaking the law even though critics might consider the lack of concern poor behavior.

In the world of politics, norms help explain what is generally viewed as desirable behavior from undesirable behavior. For example, in the United States, it's polite to address the president as Mr. President. Likewise, it's considered proper for an elected official holding a press conference to let the reporter complete his or her question before answering it or even declining to respond.

This takes us to the behavior of Donald Trump during his presidency. Highly unorthodox in his style, Trump has been described as a leader responsible for breaking many social norms, ranging from being the first president in modern times to refrain from disclosing his income tax returns to publicly attacking American intelligence agencies.[32] Our concern, however, centers on the norms violated by the president as they relate to racism and related issues. For example, earlier, we discussed the confrontation between violent White nationalists and counter-protesters, after which President Trump declared, "there were very fine people on both sides." Most Americans do not like White nationalists. In fact, a poll immediately after the Charlottesville tragedy found that only 9 percent approved of Neo-Nazis/White supremacists, while 83 percent found them unacceptable. Yet, Trump offered approbation of both, giving a sense of parity, which was clearly outside of American norms.[33] That sense of equality conferred by the President boosted the respectability of anti-democratic groups for their followers.[34]

Other examples of Trump behavior outside American norms abound. In 2019, Trump complained about four Progressive Democratic Congresswomen of color "who originally came from countries whose governments are a complete and total catastrophe . . . now loudly and viciously telling the people of the United States . . . how our government is to be run." Later he added that the four Progressive congresswomen should "go back and help fix the totally broken and crime infested places from which they came."[35] In the cases of three of the four members, the country they "came from" was the United States! And even if they were all born elsewhere, these four were citizens of the United States elected by the voters to the legislative branch of national government.

Then, there was Trump's behavior regarding undocumented migrants who entered the United States from Mexico. At one point, he ordered the Immigration and Customs Enforcement Agency to separate children from parents until the parents agreed to leave or the case was settled in Immigration Court, which could take months or even years. The policy, which separated as many as 5,600 children from their parents, was halted only when ordered by a federal judge.[36] It's hard to imagine many parents that would favor separating children from them upon illegal entry into the United States, or any strange place for that matter, but that was the case.

When it comes to race, Trump's violations of social norms were almost endless. Among the other comments he made about minorities during his presidency are: "These aren't people. They are animals" (referring to migrants coming to the United States through the southern border); "Proud boys: Stand back and standby" (urging members of a White nationalist, semi-fascist group to be ready to violently confront minorities); and "these thugs" (describing protesters peacefully assembling in response to the unprovoked murder of African-American George Floyd by Minneapolis policemen).[37] Given his proclivity for fostering division among the races, the evidence suggests that these comments and more by Trump were intentional provocations to gin up the base, and on several occasions they succeeded. That he was criticized and rebuked from those impacted by Trump's inflammatory remarks didn't matter for they weren't part of his base. And when the press dared to question Trump on such statements, their objections were quickly dismissed as "fake news."

REPUBLICANS: WHAT TO DO?

Differences between Democrats and Republicans are hardly new in American politics. For fifty years or so, between the early 1960s and second decade of the twenty-first century, the political parties were relatively stable. Most Democrats stretched from the far left to the political center and a tad to the right, covering a wide swath of views on various issues. Republicans were more homogeneous, ranging from right of center to the far right. Each side had its share of extremists—for example, small numbers of Socialists among Democrats and a few libertarians among Republicans. When the extreme of one political party would capture control of the presidential nomination and lose the general election badly, party leaders would conduct a sort of political autopsy and the party would snap back toward less controversial positions closer to the center. That's what happened to the Republicans in 1964 when the nation overwhelmingly spurned staunch conservative Barry Goldwater; a similar instance transpired in 1972 when the electorate rebuffed ultra-liberal Democrat George McGovern. All the rules changed, however, with the candidacy and election of Donald Trump.

Recall that much of Trump's campaign focused on grievances against minorities who, increasingly, were eating away at "our culture," a euphemism for an allegedly oppressed White majority. Given their connection with Trump over race, conspiracy, and elitism, rightwing extremist groups catered to the political wounds of those who felt left out and urged their loyalty to Trump and the Republican Party.

A Reconfigured Republican Party

American political parties are complex institutions. Historically, they have been described as containing three distinct units. The party-in-government contains the elected and major appointed office holders. The party organization consists of the party convention with the party platform which discusses the party's values and objectives, meetings, fundraising, and bureaucratic activities that occur both during and between elections. Last, the party-in-the-electorate, entailing the voters who consider themselves "Democrats," "Republicans," or even small-party members.[38]

Traditional literature on American political parties posits that on rare occasions, extraordinary circumstances fundamentally alter the political landscape so much that the party coalitions and their voters change and adopt new core values. Known as political party "realignment," political scientist Jeffrey Stonecash refers to this shift as "the gradual 're-sorting' of the electoral coalitions."[39] Such occurrences have occurred perhaps a half dozen times in the history of American political parties. Political scientists differ on precisely when these political earthquakes begin and end, but they usually agree on general time frames. A case in point would be the partisan realignment that took place during the 1960s, when in the wake of major national civil rights and voting rights legislation, a large swath of White Southern Democrats gravitated to the Republican Party as Democrats simultaneously consolidated support among the cities and racial minorities.

The Trump phenomenon and growth of the modern presidency have given us reason to question the classic three-part division of political parties, at least in the short term, for two reasons: First, while Trump refers to himself as a Republican, his adherents extend beyond the traditional Republican Party core to White working-class Democrats and voters who have no real attachment to any political party. A post-2016 election voter analysis found that almost one out of every four White working-class Democrats defected from Democrat Barack Obama to Donald Trump in 2016 or a third-party candidate.[40] With a slice of the Democratic Party in its camp, at least for the moment, the Republican Party exhibited a slightly different look in the Trump 2016 campaign and had just enough to win. Whether that new configuration becomes permanent remains to be seen.

Second, the Trump political operation successfully replaced the national Republican Party organization with its own unit specifically loyal to Trump, not the traditional Republican Party brand. He did so with the help of evangelicals, the pivotal foot soldiers of the Republican Party, which he received by agreeing to support all their basic social values, including the appointments of conservative federal judges who would likely vote to reverse previous Supreme Court decisions on abortion.[41] Thus, traditional Republican themes like balanced budgets, less government, and a strong international presence disappeared from the site. When the Republicans held their 2020 nominating convention, they not only re-nominated Trump as expected but declared the party platform as follows: "RESOLVED, That the Republican Party has and will continue to enthusiastically support the President's America-first agenda."[42] At least for the moment, we now divide the Republican Party as follows: Trumpism, Republican Party leaders, and the reconfigured Republican electorate.

Trumpism

As discussed in the last chapter, Donald Trump has shown no consistent set of core values. Of course, many candidates alter or shade their opinions about particular issues from time to time, but the number of Trump changes on traditional Republican Party themes (some several times) have been phenomenal. For example, Republican Party positions have been largely pro-life, anti-Obamacare, and pro-strong defense. As the 2016 campaign took shape, for the most part Trump realigned his values with basic Republican themes. During the Republican debates leading up to the nomination, opponents pointed out Trump's glaring policy inconsistencies.[43] Amazingly, many supporters seemed to take Trump's policy changes in stride, thus choosing an individual over a set of political principles which just didn't seem to matter.

Trump has had at least one consistent set of values, however: grievances against groups that oppose him, otherwise deemed to be "unAmerican." For decades, Trump has berated various racial and religious minorities, distancing them from White Christians as part of his "them" versus "us" narrative. His "Make American Great Again" theme was a slick twist of an "America First" refrain long pushed by isolationists. In modern terms, the update was a convenient phrase for attacking immigrants, globalists, and elites who perverted White Christian values and who no longer cared about traditional "American culture," in itself a euphemism for the need to prevent immigrants from taking jobs otherwise belonging to White people. To pre-election rallies of thousands of people, he would avoid discussing major policy issues and instead would invoke the "we" against "them" concept with exhortations such as "The silent majority is back, and we're going to take our country back."[44] The rest of the country, non-White people, were not welcome.

At his rallies, Trump wasn't arguing traditional Republican themes *per se*; policies and traditional approaches just didn't seem to matter. Rather, routinely, he played to fears, particularly with respect to the changing U.S. demography, and promised the crowds he would find a way for them to regain their rightful place in a White-dominated society. His approach was simple, to the point, and the crowd loved it. There may have been an "R" next to Trump's name, but he was speaking to all who had felt left out with a plan that would heal their wounds. In her work, *The Authoritarian Dynamic*, Karen Stenner writes that "Conditions of social threat, especially normative threat, dramatically magnify the impact of authoritarianism on intolerant attitudes."[45] For Trump's followers, his focus on race, the alleged inundation of immigration, and the loss of White national leadership have stood as the combination of concerns that have compelled followers to support their leader. As such, fear of the "them" ruining American society was the fuel of his authoritarian engine.

Republican Party Leaders Fall into Line

By the time Donald Trump became president in 2016, almost all of the Republican leadership had joined in his support. Their conversion was anything but seamless or natural. At first, key national Republican leaders laughed off Trump's candidacy. They had good reason. A Gallup poll released in July 2015, found that only about one-quarter of Republicans took Trump's candidacy seriously. At about the same time, a *Washington Post* study found that of nine declared Republican candidates (at the time) in 2021, Trump had the largest negative rating by far—23 percent viewed him positively, compared to 65 percent who viewed him negatively.

On the campaign trail, most of these leaders had chastised Trump for his attitudes toward racial minorities, women, and his proposal to ban all Muslims from entering the United States, but they ultimately became part of his political network nonetheless. South Carolina Republican U.S. Senator Lindsey Graham had called Trump a "jackass" for the way that he had ridiculed former Vietnam prisoner and U.S. Senator John McCain. U.S. Senator Ted Cruz from Texas who campaigned against Trump called him "a pathological liar." Then South Carolina Republican Governor Nikki Haley who later became Trump's ambassador to the United Nations said, Trump represented "everything a governor doesn't want in a president." Florida Republican U.S. Senator Marco Rubio called Trump a "con man." We could go on, but the point is that these and countless other Republicans who condemned Trump went on to become his most endearing supporters.

We know what happened from there: Trump sliced and diced his way through twelve Republican debates to capture the Republican nomination, and went on to win the presidency after that. Given Trump's outrageous behavior, what would the party leaders do after he won the presidency? How would they go forward, given Trump's departure from traditional Republicanism?

Incredibly, most Republican leaders seemed to think they had little choice. A few, notably former Republican presidential nominee and later Utah U.S. Senator Mitt Romney, then-Governor John Kasich, and Maine U.S. Senator Susan Collins condemned Trump before his election and remained largely opposed to him after. Others such as then-Arizona U.S. Senator Jeff Flake were all but drummed out of office at the next election because of Trump's opposition to him. Still, most Republican leaders found ways to work with Trump. Even the traditional conservative talk radio hosts dedicated to immigration reform, strong defense alliances, and free trade converted to Trumpism.[46] The acquiescence of so many Republican leaders helped Trump solidify his grip on the Republican Party with remarkably little opposition. Perhaps that said as much about the Republican Party as it did about Trump.

As for governing, even after Trump vacated his office in 2021, Republican legislators voted against proposed legislation that would have guaranteed the franchise to minorities, no longer a certainty courtesy of the U.S. Supreme Court's decisions. This may have been a sign that on matters related to race, Republicans weren't overcome by Trump as much as they became soulmates with him on the issue. The best indication of that theory may have been found when national Republican elected officials had the opportunity to codify voting rights. As noted earlier, after the U.S. Supreme Court negated two key portions of the Voting Rights Act of 1965 with strong national government enforcement provisions, about two dozen states enacted bills that made it harder to vote. When Democrats proposed a bill preventing discrimination in states with a history of racial intolerance, all 50 Senate Republicans voted "no," in effect a successful filibuster against the bill and voting rights.[47]

As an aside, it's important to note that Democrats, particularly those associated with the Hillary Clinton presidential campaign, helped bring about their own demise. Early on in the Republican primary struggle, the Clinton team intentionally refrained from criticizing the most conservative Republican candidates with the hope that they would push each other to the right. Trump, Ted Cruz and Ben Carson were dubbed the "Pied Piper" candidates most likely to pull the collection of candidates to the right, a place, the Clinton team thought, that would make it easier for Democrats to marginalize Republicans and defeat them in the 2016 election.[48] How much that strategy contributed to a Trump victory remains unknown. Nevertheless, the Clinton team did their best to make Trump look like a bigot, and yet he won!

Republican Voters: An Expanded Constituency?

On November 8, 2016, American voters had a virtually binary choice for president, as they typically do: Democratic candidate Hillary Clinton or Republican candidate Donald Trump. By this time, Trump made his divisive approach on race very clear; there was little nuance and plenty of anger.

Exit polls from the 2016 election revealed some interesting statistics, particularly when compared with the 2012 presidential election vote. The biggest changes from 2012 occurred with race and education. Regarding race, Trump received 58 percent of the White vote, up 5 points. With respect to education, those with no college degree voted for Trump over Clinton, 67 percent to 28 percent, also up 5 points from 2012. Combined, less educated White people were the biggest sources of the changing constellation of votes for Republican candidate Trump. All this occurred through Trump's use of racist language as a tool for victory. A Republican National Committee autopsy after the 2012 loss specifically pointed out glaring problems with minority voters. One of the recommendations moving forward focused on minority outreach: "If we want ethnic minority voters to support Republicans, we have to engage them and show our sincerity," including comprehensive immigration reform.[49] Yet, according to one analysis, Trump went in the opposite direction and "capitalized on deep concern about immigration, Islam, and racial diversity among Republicans."[50] Plainly speaking, Trump's racist-oriented campaign drew increasing numbers of White working classes voters and his plan led to an unexpected election victory.

Why is this important? Historically the economy and an individual's financial condition were key points of reference for determining an individual's political party orientation. They weren't the only political benchmarks but clearly among the most important indicators. For these reasons, White working-class people tended to align with the Democrats, who paid more attention to the needs of those at or near the bottom of the economic ladder.[51] But no more. This group has become disproportionately Republican, particularly as racial minorities have gravitated in growing numbers to the Democratic Party. This isn't true for every voter, but the movement is undeniable.

A slightly different explanation of the Republican change centers on the significant numbers of the White working class feeling closer to the views presented by Trump instead of Hillary Clinton. In this view, the group in question feels a threat to their status by current conditions, including immigration and preferential policies for non-White people. Recall Trump's continuous concerns with the pending loss of "American culture," in other words dominant White values.[52] Either way, a sizable block of working-class White people viewed Trump as closer to their values than Clinton, and immigration was a key issue.

GAINING SUPPORT FROM THE ALT-RIGHT

As he campaigned for and then worked his way through the presidency, Donald Trump made his share of friends and enemies in the voter universe. On the latter, his approach to race and minorities in general left Trump with precious little support from minorities, a political distance that only hardened during his term of office. Without that support, Trump now knew more than ever that he had to increase his White base as much as possible, and he did so by making non-White people and non-Christians the enemy while cultivating the far-right element of the American political spectrum.

Given his historical disdain for minorities, Trump had little difficulty in courting those largely White males who viewed themselves as marginalized in an increasingly racially diverse society. This segment of voters believes that government benefits and jobs have accrued disproportionately to racial minorities, immigrants, and Jews. Many have come to identify themselves as members of the "alt-right," short for alternative right. Included are White nationalists, White supremacists, and neo-Nazis who share disdain for non-Christian Americans and people of color. They have at times also found common ground with libertarians, those who seek minimal government, and men's rights groups, those who feel that women have too much control in society. They are called "alt" because they view themselves as different than mainstream conservatives who, as they see it, "have sold out white people as a group."[53] Their coming of age has taken its place in American society to the relief of those who have felt left behind and ignored. That said, these groups are housed under an umbrella of racist behavior and distrust in conventional American political institutions.

Many alt-right groups have paramilitary and anarchist components; many also have strong anti-government beliefs. Politically, most consider themselves politically aligned either with Independents or Republicans. Most important, they looked to Donald Trump as their savior. Trump brilliantly tapped into this alienated and angry segment of American society.

History of the Alt-Right

Experts disagree over when the alt-right evolved into a political force in the American polity. Some consider the election of 2008 and the ascendance of African-American Barack Obama as the starting point, when White nationalist Richard Spencer coined the term, "alt-right."[54] Others go back to the 1990s when authors like Richard Herrnstein and Charles Murray pontificated intelligence differences between White and non-White people, which, in their view, accounted for the superiority of White people.[55] Others still go even further back to Europe in the 1960s where ethno-nationalistic and anti-immigrant attitudes connected with a defined cultural hierarchy with White people at the top.[56] We can, however, identify a few key points and actors whose activities were fundamental to stirring the alt-right pot to a heightened level of racist behavior. Richard Spencer, a self-identified White supremacist, coined the term "alternative right" in 2008 as a way of distinguishing conservatives against equality, affirmative action, multiculturalism and open immigration from traditional Republican conservatives. The head of the National Policy Institute, a White nationalist think tank, Spencer developed a following through a series of online publications and speeches that attracted racists, anti-semites, and those committed to preserving what Spencer referred to as the European-American culture.[57] At an alt-right gathering in Washington, DC, shortly after Trump's 2016 presidential victory, Spencer exhorted the crowd to "party like it's 1933," referring to the time when Hitler was appointed Germany's Chancellor, after which he began the country's anti-Semitic ethnic cleansing.[58]

Spencer, of course, wasn't alone in the effort to purge minorities from American society. In 2007, Andrew Breitbart, a young provocateur in California, founded *Breitbart News*, an online publication that carried syndicated news columns along with a healthy dose of stories described by Breitbart as "the underground conservative movement."[59] Much of his online tabloid focused on criticizing what he viewed as hypocrisy stemming from anti-White behavior, the policies of liberals in the national government, and embarrassing situations for Democratic leaders. By the time Donald Trump assumed office in 2017, *Breitbart News* had more than 17 million followers. Indeed, the online paper had become a huge booster for Trump.[60] Andrew Breitbart never lived to see the extent of that success, however, as he died suddenly from a heart condition in 2012.

Breitbart's work was carried on by Steve Bannon. Born in an Irish-Catholic working-class family, Bannon bounced around in several careers before hooking up with Breitbart. A college graduate, he served in the U.S. Navy, graduated Harvard's MBA program and, worked on Wall Street before landing in Hollywood. There, he produced a few rightwing movies, one of which was seen by Andrew Breitbart. From that connection, Bannon went to work for *Breitbart News*. There Bannon's stories focused on failed immigration policies, concluding that the United States would never be great without dispensing of immigrants. The alt-right vessel also concentrated on related issues such as race-related problems and radical Islam.

After Bannon met Donald Trump in 2012, the two joined forces on birtherism and began outreach efforts to conservatives dedicated to defeating Democrat Hillary Clinton's bid for the presidency in 2016. The rest is history. Bannon managed Trump's 2016 presidential campaign, and upon Trump's victory became senior strategist in the White House, where he promoted alt-right policies from the heart of American government.

Spencer, Breitbart, and Bannon deserve attention as architects in the development of the alt-right and its connection with Donald Trump. Of course, many others were critical during this fertile political period, some better known than others, but virtually all committed to overturning what they see as a "failed nation" from catering to non-Christian racial and ethnic minorities. Nowadays, alt-right links extend to college campuses, rightwing evangelists, various online "news" organizations, and numerous entities disguising themselves as "think tanks," "institutes" and "public policy" entities.[61] Most of all, the alt-right has become a focal point for a swath of White people with racist attitudes longing for representation on their terms.

Key Alt-Right Groups

It's hard to underestimate the influence of social media in politics, particularly as megaphones for alt-right groups. Commerce marketplaces, communications amenities, and payment systems are but a few of the better known opportunities available through this way of connecting people who would not have connected otherwise, whether on an individual or group biases.[62] Denied access to traditional media because of contentious and offensive topics, alt-right groups such as those discussed below have made phenomenal use of social media platforms through distributing their messages and facilitating communication to extensive audiences. Because of their toxic political positions and threats of violence to those deemed "unAmerican," many alt-right groups have been either suspended or banned outright from major social media platforms from which to spew their hate.

Next, we turn to some of the most prominent alt-right organizations that have embraced and been embraced by Donald Trump. They became his vigilante warriors. With their actions and his approval, they also threatened American democracy.

Three Percenters

Founded in 2008 in response to the election of Democrat and African-American Barack Obama to the United States presidency, the Three Percenters began as an anti-government, pro-gun, white supremacist organization. Its name comes from the unsubstantiated notion that it took only three percent of the public to successfully oppose and defeat the British during the American Revolution. In other words, a few people can go a long way in changing politics and policies in American society.

Loosely organized, Three Percenters operate in a paramilitary militia fashion with survival training to defend against Muslims, Black Lives Matter, illegal immigration, "fake" news, far leftists, and corrupt politicians. The group has been particularly active against Muslims, often threatening violence to those living in the United States. For example, responding to increased Muslim presence in Texas, one Three Percenter leader promised, "We will interfere with every move they (Muslims) make towards taking over our country."[63] Three Percenters have also operated as armed protectors for individuals in standoffs with the federal government over taxes, land ownership and land use.[64] With little formal hierarchy, numerous autonomous chapters have begun to operate throughout the United States. They are bonded through their mutual need to protect themselves from government overreach and its ugly byproducts such as the threats to the nation from endless immigration, gun control, and Islamization.

During the 2016 presidential election campaign, the Three Percenters officially supported Donald Trump. While Trump's election left the White citizens group less antagonized against the federal government, Three Percenters focused more on left-wing extremists and Antifa activists as well as concerns with "intrusive" policies of state governments in areas such as gun control and COVID-19 protocols. With a prominent internet presence, they urged people to attend Trump rallies, where the group often provided armed "security" against anti-Trump protesters. During the Trump presidency, they also conducted vigilante patrols along the United States border with Mexico to apprehend migrants.

Members of the Three Percenters were present at the 2017 "Unite the Right" rally in Charlottesville. Unlike other groups, the organization ceased involvement in the Charlottesville confrontation after an alt-right individual in a car ran down and killed a peaceful demonstrator. Three percenter members issued a statement saying, "We cannot have this organization tainted by new(s) outlets as they will most certainly report that we have aligned ourselves with white supremacists and Nazis."[65] But the turn away from violence was temporary. In August 2018, an offshoot of the Three Percenter group was charged with bombing a Mosque in Minnesota following a failed bombing attempt at an Illinois abortion clinic.[66] Given other violent Three Percenter activities before and after Charlottesville, it's likely that the organization was concerned about bad publicity at the time rather than becoming peaceful in its operations.

Oath Keepers

Pledging to protect the United States from government overreach, the Oath Keepers was founded in 2009 by former paratrooper and lawyer Stewart Rhodes, who doubled as a libertarian blogger. He organized the group because of his concern about the election of African-American Barack Obama to the presidency, believing that Obama intended to eliminate Constitutional liberties in the United States. The alt-right militia specializes in recruiting military veterans and law enforcement personnel, which has helped the organization immensely with weapons training and discipline. The Oath Keepers routinely preach white supremacy. A leaked Oath Keepers roster in 2022 revealed a national membership of 38,000, although some federal government experts believe the actual numbers of active participants are considerably less. According to the organization's data, about two-thirds of the members had backgrounds in law enforcement, with about 10 percent currently employed.[67] Such qualities helped to ensure preparedness and obedience in the field.

The Oath Keepers have a long history of illegal activities often connected with violence. Members have been arrested for crimes including threats on the lives of government officials, illegal possession of explosives, and obstructing justice as well as charges on perjury, illegal drugs, and possessing child pornography.[68] They have a particular antipathy for government. In 2014, they joined with others in Nevada to support Cliven Bundy, a rancher who faced off against federal authorities because of his unwillingness to pay grazing fees. During that period, Oath Keepers were prominent in a number of federal confrontations throughout the West, with the theme typically focusing on overreaching government activities.[69]

Oath Keepers activity on race issues has grown with protests in support of police homicides of unarmed Black people and the suppression of the Black Lives Matter movement which, Stewart Rhodes believes, is little more than "well-funded Marxist and racist agitators."[70] Ostensibly, the Oath Keepers have turned up to protect property and constitutional guarantees of citizens, but in fact the organization has routinely tussled with law-abiding demonstrators, often causing great harm.[71] The leaders frequently have dispatched members to protests that have emerged after unarmed Black residents have been killed by police.[72] About antifa and protesters, Rhodes once said to colleagues, "They are insurrectionists, and we have to suppress insurrectionists."[73] Thus, these days, wherever justice equality protesters, the Oath Keepers are almost sure to follow.

According to one well documented report, during the 2016 presidential campaign, Rhodes sent Oath Keepers to Trump rallies to "protect" (detractors said "intimidate") Trump supporters. When Trump claimed that migrants were illegally crossing over the southern border, Oath Keepers appeared to "patrol" the border. And when Trump claimed that the 2016 presidential was "rigged," Rhodes dispatched Oath Keepers to monitor selected voting sites to "protect" the vote.[74]

Proud Boys

Islamophobic, antisemitic, and misogynistic, the all-male, anti-immigrant Proud Boys were established during the 2016 presidential election. Founded by Gavin McInnes, the group describes itself as a fun-loving men's club, but their actions show an entirely different behavior. The organization has been particularly adept at using social media platforms to recruit, indoctrinate, and organize members.[75] Willing to use violent tactics at protests and rallies, the Proud Boys have been dubbed the "Alt-right fight club" by the Southern Poverty Law Center.[76] That's because of the group's willingness to physically tangle with supporters and journalists at anti-race protests.[77] In fact, one of the rituals of participation in Proud Boys is for a member to prove his worth by physically fighting for the group's values.[78]

The Proud Boys achieved public notoriety with its participation in the racist march and violence at Charlottesville in 2017 dubbed "Unite the Right." Members took particular comfort when then-President Donald Trump pronounced that there were "fine people on both sides" at the ensuing battle between peaceful protesters and the violent counter-protesters. From that point on, the group's violence against their self-proclaimed enemies increased considerably.[79] Peaceful Black-led urban protests against police brutality often became violent when the Proud Boys came upon the scene with disruptive tactics.[80]

Much of the Proud Boys' self-defined legitimacy comes from photos with high profile Republicans such as U.S. Senator Ted Cruz of Texas, then-Governor (and now U.S. Senator) Rick Scott of Florida, several members of the House of Representatives, and Donald Trump, Jr.[81] In 2018, the FBI classified the Proud Boys as an extremist organization because of its ties to white nationalism.

After the 2020 election defeat of Donald Trump, the Proud Boys declared their total loyalty to him, at one point circulating a message among members stating, "Hail Emperor Trump." But their loyalty became less certain after Trump willingly left office. Some members worried that Trump was weak.[82]

QAnon

Operating underground for several years, QAnon gained public visibility during the Barack Obama administration, when its messages referred to Obama as "Hussein," his middle name, in an effort to emphasize a foreign-sounding name as evidence Obama's birth in Africa. QAnon's antisemitic values include the claim that Jews use children's blood for various rituals. Jews, particularly, are singled out as for "scheming among themselves in evil cliques to hoard the riches of the world and destroy those who oppose them."[83] Q, the alleged leader of the organization, is described as a Pentagon insider and the person who purportedly guides followers and promotes various anti-social activities, all intended to destroy the "deep state." However, Q has never been revealed, although, among other quests, his followers believe that they have been called to destroy a group of Satanic cannibalistic sexual abusers of children.

QAnon followers rely on endless Twitter feeds, called "drops," from Q for guidance; many adherents share thoughts and reinforce one another in chat and group texts. Some messages have been hard to believe, others totally without evidence altogether. Among them: Prominent Democrats had hidden children in the basement of a Washington, D.C. pizzeria; John F. Kennedy, Jr. was alive; and Jews murdered Christian children for their rituals. We need not worry about such terrible people, however, because QAnon messages say that Donald Trump was put on earth to save us from these and other outrageous disasters.

QAnon concepts contain a variety of radical negative dogmas about the "deep state," which is the source of all control. The belief system describes a clandestine network of bureaucrats, industrialists, traditional media, Jews, and celebrities who have conspired to run America and the world, while keeping the truth of their activities from the rest of us. Many who subscribe to QAnon tenets are convinced that their enemies drink children's blood for sustenance. In a 2020 public opinion poll conducted by Ipsos, 17 percent of the respondents agreed with a QAnon claim that "a group of Satan-worshipping elites who run a child sex ring are trying to control our politics and media."[84] Concerns about the threats to "American culture" and an emphasis on antisemitism are also frequent themes. Other QAnon messages have blamed China for COVID-19 and focused on people of color as responsible for kidnapping White children.[85]

Assessing the Alt-Right as a New Element in American Politics

Let's be clear: not all White males are members of the alt-right; in fact, only a small but outspoken portion of society identify with the alt-right category—somewhere between 6 percent and 10 percent, according to recent estimates.[86] Nevertheless, their loud voices, social media presence, and hostile physical attacks on their "enemies" seem to gain them recognition well beyond their numbers. In addition, not all alt-right members are part of antigovernment groups; some are plainly angry with society or hold government responsible for their plight. But their kinship with Trump is clearly evident. That loyalty has developed to the dismay of those who feel that the moorings of our democracy have become threatened by fanatics all too willing to forego traditional forms of political participation to reset governance with White people permanently at the top of the political food chain.

The point is the alt-right has become a force in American politics for some time, only in different forms. Sidney Tarrow explains that "appeals to racial resentment—which had been beneath the surface of Republican strategy for decades—were brought to the surface in Trump's campaign." Moreover, by his statements and actions, Trump legitimized this anger.[87] Think of it as someone opening a carbonated beverage after shaking its contents—the liquid-treated gas must escape the container and therefore flows over. That "someone" was Donald Trump.

There is a branding benefit from the alt-right that many people have missed: namely, that this hostile and hate-driven group could now promote racist tenets without being viewed as racists, at least to the extent that pure racism preaches hate of minority targets clearly and without reservation. As Zoe Hyman notes, the "purposeful repackaging of white supremacy into . . . intellectual spaces as the so-called 'alt-right' . . . enabled racists to normalize the ideology of white supremacy. In doing so, they claimed middle-class respectability and political legitimacy."[88] That's why Trump's explanation of the behavior of alt-right White nationalists as peaceful counter-protesters in Charlottesville in 2017 is so important: he defended both as respectable groups. In the process, Trump gave the White supremacy groups approval and, as such, equal stature with nonviolent groups.

Experts also disagree about the extent to which the alt-right impacted the 2016 election. One camp believes that the alt-right "swayed" the election to a Trump victory over Hillary Clinton.[89] Others say it was Clinton's characterization of Trump supporters as "deplorables" that moved undecideds into the Trump camp.[90] Regardless, by the end of the 2016 presidential campaign, the love fest between Trump and the alt-right was palpable and now part of his presidency.

Within days of Trump's 2016 victory, the alt-right began to cash in on its growing clout. In North Carolina, the Loyal White Knights of the Ku Klux Klan, posted a picture of Trump on its website accompanied by "Trump=Trump's Race United My People."[91] Trump supporter William Daniel Johnson of the fringe American Freedom Party, said "In the past. Presidents have reached out to all peoples, except those whites who are proud of their heritage and want to preserve Western civilization. Our hope is that his large tent will include us who have been despised for generations."[92] In Washington, DC, where 150 attendees of the self-described White nationalist, alt-right National Policy Institute, leader Richard Spencer said to the mostly young White male group that they had a "psychic connection" with Trump that they don't have with any other Republicans. Spencer ended his address to the group with, "For us (the White race), it's conquer or die." He ended his address by holding out his right hand in a Nazi-like salute and saying, "Hail Trump, hail our people, hail victory." The attendees followed this gesture by raising their hands in the same fashion.[93] Not in any of these examples was there finger-pointing at Black people, Latinos, Muslims, Jews, or other targets of hate, yet their hope for regaining White superiority was clearly evident.

The alt-right has been a huge gift for Trump, and he for them. At times, this mutual relationship has not always been clear, however, as Trump has talked from both sides of his mouth. For example, in an interview with *The New York Times* shortly after his 2016 election victory, then President-elect Trump rejected the politics of the alt-right, saying "I condemn them, I disavow and I condemn them." Later, in the same interview, he said about Steve Bannon, alt-right leader and latter chief strategist in the Trump administration, "If I thought he was a racist or alt-right or any of those things, I wouldn't even think about hiring him (Bannon)"[94] as part of his administration.

Yet, Bannon's approach to the 2016 election was patently clear. He sought to "run a nationalist, divisive (presidential) campaign in which issues of race, immigration, culture, and identity were put front and center."[95] So are we to think that Trump didn't know the strategy of his own campaign? This is the same Steve Bannon who was quoted in 2018 as saying being called a racist is "badge of honor."[96] And this is the same Trump who used the term "Kung Flu" to describe COVID-19, called Mexican migrants "rapists," referred to all Muslims as "terrorists," described Black people as "lazy," and preferred Jews to "count his money." The likes of Steve Bannon and other alt-right leaders clearly were part of Trump's worldview and coalition, regardless of how Trump might obfuscate the worth of the alt-right to his presidency.

THE REVISIONIST FORMULA FOR "GOVERNING" AMERICA

Trumpism, the alt-right, malleable Republican Party leaders, and angry voters created a new powerful segment of the Republican Party. No longer was the GOP the party of globalism, free trade, balanced budgets, and small government; under Trump's leadership, the party eschewed long-established military commitments and multi-lateral economic agreements while embracing trade protectionism. The budget commitments of the federal government actually grew substantially as well.

However, traditional guardrails against authoritarianism such as the mainstream media were unjustly and consistently berated, making it difficult for reporters to question presidential behavior. Historic norms were twisted, maligned and/or ignored by Trump as those who knew better looked the other way. Millions of leaders and voters approved of his policies, even to the extent that they were divisive, discriminatory, and harmful to various minorities.

With respect to race, no longer was the Republican Party playing down racism; instead many of the party's supporters either accepted Trump's condemnation of minorities outright or remained eerily silent as Trump endlessly pursued the politics of divisiveness and hate. Those who espoused racist sentiments quietly with others now felt emboldened to speak out publicly. Worse yet, because of Trump's racist behavior, large numbers of people who were overtly racist felt that they had a sponsor of sorts to carry out anti-minority activities, many of which were violent. None of these conditions and activities bode well for American democracy, and as bad as they were, more troublesome days lay ahead.

NOTES

1. James David Barber, *The Presidential Character: Predicting Performance in the White House*, 4th ed. (Englewood Cliffs, NJ: Prentice Hall, 1992), p. 82.

2. "Far-Right Candidates Struggled in Mid-Term Election. Who's to Blame? Experts say Trump, GOP," *USA Today*, November 12, 2022, https://www.usatoday.com/story/news/politics/2022/11/12/far-right-midterms-trump/8295708001/.

3. "15 Times Donald Trump Praised Authoritarian Rulers," https://www.cnn.com/2019/07/02/politics/donald-trump-dictators-kim-jong-un-vladimir-putin/index.html.

4. "Top of the Line! Trump Absolutely FAWNS Over Brutal Dictators Putin, Xi, and Kim Jung-Un to Tucker Carlson," *Mediaite*, April 12, 2023, https://www.mediaite.com/trump/top-of-the-line-trump-absolutely-fawns-over-brutal-dictators-putin-xi-and-kim-jong-un-to-tucker-carlson/.

5. A study by the Brookings Institution defined key Executive Office decision-makers as non-Cabinet officials holding positions of authority in the Executive Office of the president. The areas include but are not limited to communications, domestic policy, economic affairs, national security, outreach, and personnel administration. See Kathryn Dunn Tenpas, "Tracking Turnover in the Trump Administration," Brookings, January 2021, https://www.brookings.edu/research/tracking-turnover-in-the-trump-administration/.

6. Ibid.

7. See Richard Neustadt, *Presidential Power*, 2nd ed. (New York, NY: John Wiley & Sons, 1980), pp. 195 and 213.

8. The references in the remainder of this paragraph come from "The Long List of Trump Administration Officials Turned Critics," *CNN*, June 5, 2020, https://www.cnn.com/2020/06/04/politics/officials-who-criticized-donald-trump/index.html.

9. James Comey, *A Higher Loyalty: Truth, Lies, and Leadership* (New York, NY: Flatiron Books, 2018), p. 237.

10. "Suspicious Timing and Convenient Reasoning for Trump's Firing of Comey," *NPR*, May 10, 2017, https://www.cnn.com/2020/06/04/politics/officials-who-criticized-donald-trump/index.html.

11. "Trump Accuses John Kelly of 'Missing the Action' after Scathing Criticism," *Politico*, February 13, 2020, https://www.politico.com/news/2020/02/13/donald-trump-john-kelly-114861.

12. "Trump says He 'Essentially' Fired Mattis (Who Actually Resigned in Protest)," *CNN*, January 2, 2019, https://www.usatoday.com/story/news/politics/2018/12/07/rex-tillerson-donald-trump-remarks/2237327002/.

13. "Trump Calls Ex-chief of Staff Mick Mulvaney 'a Born Loser'," *The Hill*, April 18, 2023, https://thehill.com/blogs/blog-briefing-room/3956541-trump-calls-ex-chief-of-staff-mick-mulvaney-a-born-loser/.

14. "'He was Dumb as a Rock:' Trump Responds to Rex Tillerson Calling Him 'Undisciplined,'" *USA Today*, December 7, 2018, https://www.usatoday.com/story/news/politics/2018/12/07/rex-tillerson-donald-trump-remarks/2237327002/.

15. See The Mueller Report, *The Washington Post*, published by *The Washington Post* in 2019.

16. "Barr's Summary of the Mueller Report Seems Good for Trump," *FiveThirtyEight.com*, March 24, 2019, https://fivethirtyeight.com/features/barrs-summary-of-the-mueller-report-seems-good-for-trump/.

17. "Trump Slams Bill Barr as 'a Coward Who Didn't Do His Job,'" *The Hill*, June 11, 2023, https://thehill.com/blogs/blog-briefing-room/4044744-trump-slams-bill-barr-as-a-coward-who-didnt-do-his-job/.

18. "President Trump Likes Acting Cabinet Members. Research Shows They May Hurt Them," *Time*, April 9, 2019, https://time.com/5566733/trump-acting-secretary-concerns-scholars/.

19. See "At Least 15 Trump Officials Do Not Hold Their Positions Lawfully," *Just Security*, September 17, 2020, https://www.justsecurity.org/72456/at-least-15-trump-officials-do-not-hold-their-positions-lawfully/.

20. Charles Rettig, "No Ordinary Audit: Donald Trump Is Facing the IRS 'Wealth Squad'," *Forbes*, February 28, 2016, https://www.forbes.com/sites/irswatch/2016/02/28/no-ordinary-audit-donald-trump-is-facing-the-irs-wealth-squad/#1658bd2c4d71.

21. "President Trump's Enemies List," *Politico*, July 10, 2017, https://www.politico.com/story/2017/07/10/president-trump-enemies-list-240344.

22. Jan E. Leighley, *Mass Media and Politics: A Social Science Perspective* (Boston, MA: Houghton Mifflin Company, 2004), p. 206.

23. See Doris Graber, *Mass Media and American Politics*, 8th ed. (Washington, DC: CQ Press, 2010), pp. 232–240.

24. Quoted in Marvin Kalb, "Trump's Troubling Relationship with the Press," Brookings, February 21, 2017, https://www.brookings.edu/blog/up-front/2017/02/21/trumps-troubling-relationship-with-the-press/.

25. "Trump's Media Relations Get Rocky Quickly," *Politico*, January 1, 2021, https://www.politico.com/story/2017/01/trump-media-relations-233981.

26. "Kellyanne Conway Defends White House's Falsehoods—'Alternative Facts,'" *Time*, January 22, 2017, https://time.com/4642689/kellyanne-conway-sean-spicer-donald-trump-alternative-facts/.

27. "A Week on the Trail with 'Disgusting Reporters' Covering Trump," *Slate*, March 20, 2016, https://www.washingtonpost.com/blogs/erik-wemple/wp/2018/09/07/president-trump-celebrates-the-body-slam-of-a-reporter-in-montana/.

28. "President Trump Celebrates the Body-Slam of a Reporter in Montana," *The Washington Post*, September 17, 2018, https://www.washingtonpost.com/blogs/erik-wemple/wp/2018/09/07/president-trump-celebrates-the-body-slam-of-a-reporter-in-montana/.

29. "Trump Abruptly Ends Press Conference after Contentious Exchange," *CNN*, May 12, 2020, https://www.cnn.com/2020/05/11/media/trump-press-briefing-weijia-jian-kaitlan-collins/index.html.

30. See "Trump Attacks on Press Effective, New Study Finds," *VOANews*, April 17, 2020, https://www.voanews.com/a/press-freedom_trump-attacks-press-effective-new-study-finds/6187774.html.

31. "Partisan Divides on Media Trust Widen, Driven by a Decline among Republicans," Pew Research Center, August 31, 2021, https://www.pewresearch.org/fact-tank/2021/08/30/partisan-divides-in-media-trust-widen-driven-by-a-decline-among-republicans/.

32. For example, see "The Abnormal Presidency," *The Washington Post*, November 10, 2020, https://www.washingtonpost.com/graphics/2020/lifestyle/magazine/trump-presidential-norm-breaking-list/.

33. *Washington Post/ABC Poll*, August 20–23, 2017, http://apps.washingtonpost.com/g/page/politics/washington-post-abc-news-poll-aug-16-20-2017/2235/.

34. "Trump Gives White Supremacists an Unequivocal Boost," *The New York Times*, August 15, 2017, https://www.nytimes.com/2017/08/15/us/politics/trump-charlottesville-white-nationalists.html.

35. "Trump Tells Four Liberal Congresswomen to 'Go Back' to their Countries, Prompting Pelosi to Defend Them," *The Washington Post,* July 14, 2019, https://www.washingtonpost.com/politics/trump-says-four-liberal-congresswomen-should

-go-back-to-the-crime-infested-places-from-which-they-came/2019/07/14/b8bf140e-a638-11e9-a3a6-ab670962db05_story.html.

36. "Federal Judge Rules Children, Parents Separated at Border must be Reunited within 30 Days," *ABC News*, https://abcnews.go.com/Politics/federal-judge-rules-children-parents-separated-border-reunited/story?id=56192051,

37. "Fact Check: 12 of 28 Comments Deemed Racist on Viral List are Trump's Direct Speech," *USA Today*, October 30, 2016, https://abcnews.go.com/Politics/federal-judge-rules-children-parents-separated-border-reunited/story?id=56192051.

38. This model was originally developed by Ralph M. Goldman. See his "Party Chairmen and Party Faction, 1789-1900" (Ph.D. dissertation, University of Chicago, 1951).

39. Jeffrey M. Stonecash, *Political Parties Matter: Realignment and the Return of Partisan Voting* (Boulder, CO: Lynne Rienner Publishers, 2006), p. 14.

40. "A 2016 Review: Turnout Wasn't the Driver of Clinton's Defeat," *The New York Times*, March 28, 2017, https://www.nytimes.com/2017/03/28/upshot/a-2016-review-turnout-wasnt-the-driver-of-clintons-defeat.html.

41. See Alex Morris, "False Idol—Why the Christian Right Worships Donald Trump," *Rolling Stone*, December 2, 2019, https://www.rollingstone.com/politics/politics-features/christian-right-worships-donald-trump-915381/.

42. Quoted in Tom Wheeler, "The Republican Party Platform: 'L'etat, c'est moi,'" Brookings, August 25, 2020, https://www.brookings.edu/blog/up-front/2020/08/25/the-2020-republican-party-platform-letat-cest-moi/.

43. For example, see "Republican Debate Raises Voices, Name Calling, and Personal Attacks," *The Washington Post,* February 13, 2016, https://www.washingtonpost.com/politics/all-eyes-will-be-on-trump-at-republican-debate/2016/02/13/bd30bae2-d274-11e5-abc9-ea152f0b9561_story.html.

44. "Donald Trump Defiantly Rallies a New 'Silent Majority' in a Visit to Arizona," *The New York Times*, July 11, 2015, https://www.nytimes.com/2015/07/12/us/politics/donald-trump-defiantly-rallies-a-new-silent-majority-in-a-visit-to-arizona.html.

45. Karen Stenner, *The Authoritarian Dynamic* (New York, NY: Cambridge University Press, 2005), p. 31.

46. Jeremy W. Peters, *Insurgency: How Republicans Lost Their Party and Got Everything They Ever Wanted* (New York, NY: Crown Books, 2021), p. 297.

47. The Bill was HR4, The John Lewis Voting Rights Advancement Act. See "After a Day of Debate, the Voting Rights Bill is Blocked in the Senate," *The New York Times*, January 19, 2022, https://www.nytimes.com/2022/01/19/us/politics/senate-voting-rights-filibuster.html.

48. See "How the Hillary Clinton Campaign Deliberately 'Elevated' Donald Trump with its 'Pied Piper' Strategy," *Salon*, November 9, 2016, https://www.salon.com/2016/11/09/the-hillary-clinton-campaign-intentionally-created-donald-trump-with-its-pied-piper-strategy/.

49. Republican National Committee, "Growth and Opportunity Project," printed in the *Washington Post*, December 2012, https://www.washingtonpost.com/politics/all-eyes-will-be-on-trump-at-republican-debate/2016/02/13/bd30bae2-d274-11e5-abc9-ea152f0b9561_story.html.

50. John Sides, Michael Tesler, and Lynn Vavreck, *Identity Crisis: The 2016 Presidential Campaign and the Battle for the Meaning of America* (Princeton, NJ: Princeton University Press, 2018), p. 35.

51. Tyler T. Reny, Loren Collingwood, and Ali A. Valenzuela, "Vote Switching in the 2016 Election: How Racial and Immigration Attitudes, Not Economics, Explain Shifts in White Voting," *Public Opinion Quarterly*, 83 (Spring 2019), http://tylerreny.github.io/pdf/pubs/final_submission_reny_etal_poq_public.pdf.

52. Diana C. Mutz, "Status Threat, Not Economic Hardship, Explains the 2016 Presidential Vote," *Proceedings of the National Academy of Sciences of the United States of America*, 115, no. 19 (2018), https://www.pnas.org/doi/10.1073/pnas.1718155115.

53. Niko Heikkila, "Online Antagonism of the Alt-Right in the 2016 Election," *European Journal of American Studies*, Summer 2017, https://ifstudies.org/blog/the-demography-of-the-alt-right.

54. Mark Potok, "The Radical Right's Reaction to the Election of Barak Obama," *Intelligence Report*, The Southern Poverty Law Center, November 30, 2008, https://www.splcenter.org/fighting-hate/intelligence-report/2008/radical-right%E2%80%99s-reaction-election-barack-obama,

55. Charles A. Murray and Richard Hernnstein, *The Bell Curve: Intelligence and Class Structure in American Life* (New York, NY: Simon & Schuster, 1994).

56. See Daniel Steinmetz-Jenkins, "The European Intellectual Origins of the Alt-Right," Istanbul University Press, pp. 255–266, https://dergipark.org.tr/tr/download/article-file/679543.

57. "Alt Right: A Primer on the New White Supremacy," ADL.org, February 10, 2016, https://www.adl.org/resources/backgrounders/alt-right-a-primer-on-the-new-white-supremacy.

58. "'Let's Party Like It's 1933': Inside the Alt-Right World of Richard Spencer," *The Washington Post*, November 22, 2016, https://www.washingtonpost.com/local/lets-party-like-its-1933-inside-the-disturbing-alt-right-world-of-richard-spencer/2016/11/22/cf81dc74-aff7-11e6-840f-e3ebab6bcdd3_story.html.

59. Quoted in Joshua Green, *Devil's Bargain: Steve Bannon, Donald Trump, and the Storming of the Presidency* (New York, NY: Penguin Press, 2017), p. 89.

60. "Breibart News Helped Trump Win. Under Steve Bannon, It Might Also Help Him Lose," *Daily Beast*, December 20, 2017, https://www.thedailybeast.com/breitbart-news-helped-trump-win-under-steve-bannon-it-might-also-help-him-lose.

61. For discussion on alt-right origins and its breadth, see Cynthia Miller-Idriss, *Hate in the Homeland* (Princeton, NJ: Princeton University Press, 2020).

62. For a discussion on social media platforms, see Anne Helmond, "The Platformization of the Web: Making Web Data Platform Ready," *Social Media + Society*, July–December 2015, https://www.readcube.com/articles/10.1177%2F2056305115603080.

63. "Armed 'Three Percenters' Turn Protests toward Muslim Americans," *Chicago Tribune*, December 11, 2015, https://www.chicagotribune.com/nation-world/ct-protests-toward-muslim-americans-20151211-story.html.

64. "The Three Percenters: A Look inside an Anti-Government Militia," *New Lines Institute for Strategy and Policy*, February 2021, https://newlinesinstitute.org/wp-content/uploads/20210225-Three-Percenter-PR-NISAP-rev051021.pdf.

65. "The Hate Report: Get to know the Three Percenters," *RevealNews*, March 18, 2018, https://revealnews.org/blog/hate-report-get-to-know-the-three-percenters/.

66. Alt Right: A Primer on the New White Supremacy," February 10, 2016, ADL.org, https://www.adl.org/resources/backgrounders/alt-right-a-primer-on-the-new-white-supremacy.

67. "New from ADL: Leaked Oath Keepers' Membership List Reveals Hundreds of Current & Former Law Enforcement Officers, Members of Military, and Elected Officials," ADL, September 6, 2022, https://www.theatlantic.com/magazine/archive/2020/11/right-wing-militias-civil-war/616473/.

68. "Oath Keepers," Southern Poverty Law Center, 2017, https://www.splcenter.org/fighting-hate/extremist-files/group/oath-keepers.

69. Sarah Childress, "The Battle over Bunkerville: The Bundys, the Federal Government, and the New Militia Movement," *Frontline*, May 16, 2017, https://www.pbs.org/wgbh/frontline/article/the-battle-over-bunkerville/.

70. "Behind the Armor: Men Seek 'Purpose' in Protecting Property Despite Charges of Racism," *The Washington Post*, October 5, 2020, https://www.washingtonpost.com/national/behind-the-armor-men-seek-purpose-in-protecting-property-despite-charges-of-racism/2020/10/05/b8496fec-001e-11eb-9ceb-061d646d9c67_story.html.

71. "'Civil War Is Here, Right Now,': Patriots' Urge Trump to Empower Militias to Fight Antifa in Streets," *Daily Kos*, August 31, 2020, https://www.dailykos.com/stories/2020/8/31/1974015/-Oath-Keepers-to-Trump-Send-out-the-militias-to-stop-antifascists-Marxist-takeover-of-America.

72. For example, see "Behind the Armor: Men Seek 'Purpose' in Protecting Property despite Charges of Racism."

73. Quoted in Mike Giglio, "A Pro-Trump Group Has Recruited Thousands of Police, Soldiers, and Veterans," *The Atlantic*, November 2020, https://www.theatlantic.com/magazine/archive/2020/11/right-wing-militias-civil-war/616473/.

74. Ibid.

75. "The Proud Boys: Chauvinist Poster Child of Far-Right Extremism," *European Center for Populism Studies*, February 1, 2021, https://www.populismstudies.org/the-proud-boys-chauvinist-poster-child-of-far-right-extremism/.

76. "New Alt-Right 'Fight Club' Ready for Street Violence," *Intelligence Report*, Fall 2017, Southern Poverty Law Center, https://www.splcenter.org/fighting-hate/intelligence-report/2017/new-alt-right-%E2%80%9Cfight-club%E2%80%9D-ready-street-violence.

77. Miller-Idriss, *Hate in the Homeland*, p. 100.

78. "The Proud Boys."

79. Daniel Rothbart and David Stebbins, "The Proud Boys Raging Righteously at the U.S. Capitol on January 6, 2021: A Hate Group in Action," *Peace and Conflict: Journal of Peace Psychology*, September 1, 2022, https://psycnet.apa.org/fulltext/2022-95009-001.pdf.

80. Shannon E. Reid and Matthew Valasik, *Alt-Right Gangs* (Oakland, CA: University of California Press, 2020), p.118.

81. "The Proud Boys: Chauvinist Poster Child of Far-Right Extremism."
82. "The Patriot Boys."
83. Mike Rothchild, *The Storm Is Upon Us* (Brooklyn, NY: Melville Press, 2021), p. 50.
84. "More than 1 in 3 Americans Believe that the 'Deep State' is Working to Undermine Trump," *Ipsos*, December 30, 2020, https://www.ipsos.com/sites/default/files/ct/news/documents/2020-12/topline_npr_misinformation_poll_123020.pdf.
85. See "QAnon Pushes Alarming Conspiracy Myths Targeting China and Jewish People," *Los Angeles Times*, March 23, 2021, https://www.latimes.com/california/story/2021-03-23/qanon-conspiracy-evolves-new-world-order-china-jewish-people and "We knew that QAnon is Anti-Semitic. Now we know it's Racist, Too," *Bulletin of the Atomic Scientists*, July 5, 2021, https://www.latimes.com/california/story/2021-03-23/qanon-conspiracy-evolves-new-world-order-china-jewish-people.
86. See George Hawley, "The Demography of the Alt-Right," Institute for Family Studies, August 19, 2018, https://ifstudies.org/blog/the-demography-of-the-alt-right.
87. Sidney Tarrow, *Movements and Parties: Critical Connections in American Political Development* (New York, NY: Cambridge University Press, 2021), p. 180.
88. Zoe Hyman, "Transatlantic White Supremacy: American Segregationists and International Racism and Civil Rights," in Daniel Geary, Camilla Schofield, and Jennifer Sutton, *Global White Nationalism: Frim Apartheid to Trump* (Manchester, MI: Manchester University Press, 2020), p. 190.
89. Heikkila, "Online Antagonism of the Alt-Right in the 2016 Election."
90. See "President Trump Thanks 'Deplorables' for Helping Him Win the 2016 Election," *USA Today*, November 8, 2017, https://www.usatoday.com/story/news/politics/onpolitics/2017/11/08/president-trump-thanks-deplorables-helping-him-win-2016-election/844744001/.
91. "The Alt-Right Supported Trump. Now its Members Want Him to Satisfy their Demands," *The Washington Post*, November 10, 2016, https://www.washingtonpost.com/national/the-alt-right-used-to-be-ignored-now-theyre-courting-a-president-elect/2016/11/10/746341d8-a75b-11e6-8fc0-7be8f848c492_story.html.
92. Ibid.
93. "Energized By Trump's Win, White Nationalists Gather to 'Change The World," *NPR*, November 2016, https://www.npr.org/2016/11/20/502719871/energized-by-trumps-win-white-nationalists-gather-to-change-the-world.
94. "Trump Disavows Alt-Right in *New York Times* Interview," *The New York Times*, November 22, 2016, https://www.pbs.org/newshour/politics/inside-donald-trumps-meeting-new-york-times.
95. Quoted in Green, *Devil's Bargain*, p. 208.
96. "Steve Bannon: 'Racist is a Badge of Honor,'" *Daily Beast*, March 10, 2018, https://www.thedailybeast.com/steve-bannon-racist-label-is-a-badge-of-honor.

Chapter 8

Trump, Bigotry, and the 2020 Election

At the start of the 2020 election year, Donald Trump appeared in a solid position to win. True, his standing in the polls wasn't great, but other mitigating factors seemed to more than offset that problem. The American economy was humming: The U.S. unemployment rate was 3.5 percent, near a record low, and the Democrats were without a prominent presidential candidate of note. Sure, Trump was divisive, but he looked to have more people on his side than against.

Then, there was the issue of running his presidential reelection campaign. Trump had a war chest exceeding 100 million dollars, the absence of any serious Republican Party challenger, and a cast of Democratic wannabes in disarray.[1] Before the campaign's end, his team raised more than one billion dollars.[2] Not bad for a president who had been mired in one controversy after another highlighted by a failed impeachment effort, and with public disapproval mired north of 50 percent. If nothing else, it was an odd time for an incumbent, but then again, Trump was hardly the typical office holder seeking another term.

Trump began his reelection effort with the same strategy that secured his first victory: it's "us" versus "them," with the "thems" alternating between other nations, immigrants, or most often, racial and ethnic minorities at home. All of these topics were spokes under the umbrella of defending "our culture," the refrain offered by Trump again and again, that separated the "unwanteds"—racial, ethnic, and religious minorities—from the rest of us. Surely, that would be a winning theme, he thought. After all, he beat the odds with the same harsh confrontational approach in 2016, and now would be campaigning as an incumbent, including the myriad benefits that came with the title.

Slowly, what seemed to be a sure thing began to unravel. Trump was at a loss as to how to deal with COVID-19, alternately blaming China, the FDA, vaccine producers, the press, and incompetent governors, to name a few. Additionally, as the pandemic took root, the nation's economy fell apart. Meanwhile, the once-seemingly hapless Democrats were somehow getting their act together, ultimately nominating former vice president Joe Biden, who Trump initially viewed as little more than a worn-out political punching bag. But as time went on, Biden and the Democrats picked up steam, ultimately securing a stunning election victory.

As surprised as Trump was with his presidential win in 2016, he was even more flabbergasted with the imploding of his 2020 election campaign. No matter, he said, for the only way he could lose would be if the election was rigged, a refrain that had become a centerpiece of Trump's campaign shtick in 2016. Repeatedly at his rallies, he warned of the election threat to "our culture" that would occur with a Biden victory.

But this time, the forewarning didn't work, at least with enough voters, anyway. By the time the election was over, Trump lost the all-important electoral vote 306 to 232, and the popular contest by almost 7,000,000 votes. Predictably, he explained away the loss as the result of widespread voter fraud stemming from a rash of last-minute mailed in ballots that were not counted until well after the polls had closed. Of course, just about every state had offered or extended existing mailed in ballots to encourage voter participation in the midst of the COVID-19 pandemic, but that didn't matter to the imperiled incumbent. And so began the effort by Trump and his allies to reverse the outcome of the 2020 presidential election by any means possible, an extraordinary activity that had never occurred in an American presidential election.

The authoritarian tendencies exhibited by Trump during his four years in power boiled over menacingly as he showed his willingness to do anything to stay in power. Still, although most Americans fretted over Trump's malicious attempt to keep his job, a sizable minority of American society wanted him to succeed, whatever the cost. Even more important than Trump's unfathomable actions was the ease with which so many sycophants were willing to sacrifice the nation's long-standing democratic norms and constitutional procedures to keep a would-be person with clearly undemocratic objectives in office. More about that in chapter 9.

This chapter chronicles Trump's descent from the pinnacle of power to the near-bottom of political relevance. His presidency began well enough. A robust tax cut passed by the Republican-dominated Congress in 2017 framed the first two years, working in tandem with a consistent Trump barrage of comments against immigrants, minorities and countries challenging "our way of life." The one-two punch was on the way to scoring a knock-out over the opposition en route to a successive four-year term. Surely, he thought, if the voters were with him (barely) in 2016, they would be with him now.

Then came change. The first hint of trouble actually began in 2019 after Democrats captured majorities in both legislative chambers, which allowed investigations of Trump's questionable actions to begin in earnest. But that was just the beginning of Trump's problems. An embarrassing impeachment trial, the incredibly dark shroud of COVID-19, and a sudden soured economy combined to seriously threaten Trump's reelection chances. The closer it came to November 3, 2020, the more desperate Trump became both in his overreach of presidential authority and turn to racist alt-right groups, which he embraced as legitimate stakeholders of a changing political base. Suddenly, the concerns from his opponents that stemmed from Trump's surprising 2016 triumph paled next to the fear brought about by his outrageous behavior during and after the 2020 election campaign. A reelection once thought to be a sure thing became a toss-up, and ultimately defeat.

CONDITIONS LEADING UP TO THE 2020 PRESIDENTIAL CAMPAIGN

Republican congressional majorities in the Senate and House during his first two years in power provided Donald Trump with a firewall of sorts that shielded his presidency from serious political and legal problems. As the minority in both chambers, Democrats had little clout and less visibility. But things changed with the 2018 midterm elections, after which the Democrats gained a majority in the House. Now, they had majorities in every House committee, the power to investigate, and the ability to gain attention.

Actually, potential problems for Trump had begun in early 2017, when he fired FBI Director James Comey without cause due to Comey's refusal to grant Trump "absolute loyalty." A bipartisan uproar in Congress led to recusal of any investigation efforts by then-Attorney General Jeff Sessions and subsequent appointment by Deputy Attorney General Ron Rosenstein of former FBI Director and Republican Robert Mueller as special counsel to investigate the firing of Comey and any related issues to the 2020 presidential election.[3] Mueller had an impeccable reputation with both Democrats and Republicans and was known for his thoroughness. Twenty-two months later, the 448-page Mueller Report, as it was informally known, chronicled a series of questionable meetings between Russian lawyers and Trump campaign officials during the 2016 presidential election as well as several possible domestic illegalities, including Trump's abrupt firing of Comey.[4] Later on, nine Americans connected with the Trump campaign were convicted as a result of the Mueller investigation, with indictments handed out to another 12 Russians.

Meanwhile, Trump fired a record number of independent agency and cabinet watchdogs known as inspectors general, repeatedly refused to allow key Executive Branch personnel to testify before Mueller's investigation as well as congressional committees, and filled key executive positions with "acting" heads so that he could replace them quickly if necessary without any U.S. Senate interference. Repeatedly, he demanded loyalty to himself rather than to the United States Constitution and the rule of law. Trump's appointees revolved around him, not the Constitution or the offices to which they were asked to serve. For example, he referred to his judicial appointments as "my judges," fully expecting them to issue decisions favorable to his views and needs.[5] Describing the military brass as "my generals," Trump once asked his Chief of Staff John Kelly, a former general, why they couldn't be totally loyal to him as his generals were to Hitler.[6] Oh, Trump thought, how things would be so different if he had complete control. That outlook would remain throughout his presidency.

Ill-Fated Impeachment Effort

The 2018 congressional elections gave Democrats new life and power. Now, with a majority in the House of Representatives came those coveted committee chairmanships and the ability to investigate, and investigate they did. Within months, various House committees found serious problems with Trump's presidency. The most serious concerns came out of investigations by the House Intelligence (foreign policy and national security) and Judiciary Committees (application of justice). Throughout 2019, the two committees examined many of the questionable areas of presidential activity that Trump and his Republican House colleagues had blocked during the first two years of Trump's presidency. Release of the Mueller Report[7] in March 2019 confirmed many of the trepidations expressed by members of Congress, particularly Democrats.

By December 2019, House Speaker Nancy Pelosi and her senior colleagues made the decision to impeach Trump on two counts: abuse of power and obstruction of justice, marking only the third time for such a trial. The vote took place along party lines, in itself an early indication of the difficulties Democrats would have persuading members of the Senate Republican majority to join with them to provide the two-thirds vote necessary to convict Trump of the charges. The first article of impeachment, "Abuse of Power," centered on Trump's threats to deny foreign aid to Ukrainian President Volodymyr Zelenskyy unless he provided negative (and untrue) information on Hunter Biden, son of the former vice president. The second article of impeachment, "Obstruction of Congress," focused on Trump's persistent defiance of Congressional subpoenas for testimony and information from various officials in the executive Branch on matters of concern to the Democratic majority.

With conviction requiring a two-thirds vote in the Senate, the upper chamber acquitted Trump of the charges after a short five-day trial. The result was not surprising, given a solid Republican Senate majority and loyalty to the President by many Republican members. Still, Democrats hoped that impeachment would not only expose Trump for his illegal behavior but lead to his reelection defeat the following November. They were only partly correct. While Trump would lose reelection, it would not be because of impeachment per se. A Morning Consult poll in December 2019 found the nation almost equally divided over whether Trump should be impeached.[8] In fact, there may have been a temporary upside for Trump from the entire episode. A Gallup Poll in January 2000, just before the trial, had Trump's popularity at 44 percent; one month later, after the trial, Trump's popularity was at 49 percent, an increase of five points.[9] Thus, for most Americans, it turned out that impeachment carried precious little sway in turning the electorate against Trump. Meanwhile, Trump viewed his acquittal as a sign of political rebound. Having dodged the impeachment bullet, Trump's 2020 reelection campaign continued almost as if the historic event had never occurred.

Given the failure of impeachment to move the voters, what remained? Of the issues drifting in and out of the 2020 presidential contest, two stood out: a fickle economy and the onset of COVID-19. Trump was able to deflect the first two concerns. Management of COVID-19, however, cost him more than he anticipated.

COVID-19

Perhaps the best test of a president lies with his or her ability to manage a crisis, which takes us to COVID-19. Donald Trump was not responsible for COVID-19 reaching American shores. Chances are that in today's interdependent global environment, an outbreak in one corner of the world would reach all others in a matter of days, anyway. The larger question is whether the United States could have been more capable of managing the pandemic than in the manner handled by the Trump administration. On that, there is a debate to this day.

We do know this: The Trump administration's battle against COVID-19 began with one hand tied behind its back—and the knot that had been secured by the Trump administration itself in the name of doing away with government waste.[10] In 2014, The Obama administration and Congress created the Global Health Security and Biodefense Unit in the Centers for Disease Control

(CDC) to fight (successfully) the Ebola outbreak in Africa and similar future events. After quickly quelling the epidemic, the unit developed a 69-page "Playbook" for responding to disease outbreaks worldwide within days and passed the book to Trump officials during the presidential transition. The Trump administration rejected the book and proposed reducing $277 million in pandemic preparedness funding from the 2017 national budget. That was just the beginning. In 2018, more than one billion dollars in pandemic-related funding was cut from the federal budget by the Republican Congress with Trump's approval.[11] As a result, the CDC was forced to reduce its pandemic research focus to ten countries from 59, one of which had been China.[12] That change prevented American scientists from learning about the COVID-19 events in China until the deadly virus had made its presence known abroad.

Fast forward to early 2020, and the facts were not flattering to President Trump. On January 22, he described the U.S. response to the suddenly fast-moving disease as "totally under control."[13] But the virus was anything but "under control," with infections in the United States growing at exponential rates. In February 2000, the President predicted without any knowledge that the virus would be gone by April 2000 "when it gets warm." He also accused the Democrats of politicizing the pandemic.[14] On March 17th, Trump reversed himself when he said about COVID-19, "I felt it (COVID-19) was a pandemic long before it was called a pandemic." Matters deteriorated from there. An investigative report in *The Washington Post* on March 20, 2020 recounted that U.S. intelligence agencies had been warned about the pandemic as early as January.[15] By the end of the month, Trump was blaming China for the pandemic.[16] Just imagine what might have happened if the United States had been able to continue its research in China per the Obama administration program.

Over time, Trump's characterizations of China assumed an increasingly racist tone. At first, he replaced the term "Corona Virus" with the term "Chinese Virus." Later on, he also described COVID-19 as the "Kung Flu." Criticisms of Trump's derogatory descriptions of China quickly emerged, only for the president to offer that he was simply describing the geographical origin of the pandemic. Nevertheless, Trump's reconstruction of public opinion was done. In fact, it was a pretty fast redirection, and hardly in a positive way. A study of the public pulse in the first two weeks after Trump's "Chinese virus" remarks showed the number of Anti-Asian hashtags on Twitter increasing by a whopping 797 percent.[17] One assessment of Trump's action reasoned he was "throwing his Asian-American citizens as well as residents of Chinese and Asian descent 'under the bus' by ignoring the consequences of the language he uses."[18]

As damaging as that assessment was, it ignored two critical points: First, given his long background in racist trope, Trump knew exactly what he was doing, namely placing responsibility for the ruination of the American economy and health on non-White people, in this case, the Chinese. Second, as discussed throughout this volume, Americans have a long history of anti-Asian bigotry. In light of that existing precondition, many Americans were all too willing to accept Trump's account as gospel.

With respect to dealing with the pandemic, the response revealed several weaknesses in the Trump administration's organization. Medical equipment was in short supply, a reliable test for the disease was slow in development and distribution, and national coordination was all but nonexistent. Instead of working with the CDC, Trump, with no medical expertise whatsoever, repeatedly challenged the CDC, diminishing public faith in the internationally respected government institution. At one point during a nationally televised pandemic update, Trump mused with CDC representatives about the possibility of individuals self-injecting or ingesting bleach to combat the virus![19] Disinfectant companies immediately issued warnings that such efforts could cause death. Tragically, bleach poisonings in the United States soared 77 percent within one month of Trump's thoughtless suggestion, including some deaths.[20]

On April 16, 2020, Trump basically washed his hands of any presidential interest in the pandemic. Essentially announcing a departure from any directly coordinated federal response, he announced to the nation's 50 governors, "you're going to call your own shots."[21] Of course, there can be no shots without ammunition, of which the governors had precious little. On that date, 33,000 Americans had died from COVID-19; by November 3, 2020, election day, 225,000 Americans had perished from the disease.[22]

As the nation neared the election, a *YouGov* poll asked voters to choose the candidate who would do the better job managing COVID-19. Fifty-two percent sided with Joe Biden, compared with 33 percent choosing Donald Trump.[23] Now, having missed his opportunity to save the nation, Trump had to find a way to save himself and his reelection campaign. And given his passive attitude to the deadly virus notwithstanding, it wouldn't be easy.

FIRING UP THE BIGOTED CYLINDERS

As he plunged into his 2020 presidential reelection campaign, incumbency had not worn well on Donald Trump. Yes, he had beaten back impeachment with even a small gain in public support that might even have been viewed as sympathy. But otherwise, things weren't going so well courtesy of a one-two punch. First, the economy began to slow down, which is never a good sign during a presidential election year inasmuch as people often tend to vote their wallets more than their hearts. Second, the COVID-19 pandemic was discouraging everyone, even Trump, who refused to engage in any serious way on the problem after April 16, 2020. Some in his inner circle had warned him of running from COVID-19, even his wife, Melania, who, according to one account, pointedly told him, "you're blowing this. This (the COVID-19 pandemic) is serious."[24]

But for Trump, COVID-19 was a temporary nuisance and little else, something that temporarily got in the way of his reelection campaign. The problem just didn't fit in with the way that he did political business. The fact is, Trump has always succeeded by tapping into anger more than compassion, and it's from energized resentment that his hate-filled grievances motivated rally attendees and his voters.[25] That was Trump's special connection with his minions. This time, however, more of the campaign recipe that he used in 2016 wouldn't be enough.

The Problem of Demography

Beyond the pandemic and slumping economy, two demographic problems plagued Trump as he set his sights on reelection. The first obstacle centered on the likelihood of fewer working-class White voters than four years earlier. In a comprehensive study, demographers projected that this cohort, a major and particularly potent portion of the Trump electorate, would decrease nationally by 2.3 percent in 2020. The drop could be especially devastating for Trump in six key states that he won narrowly in 2016: Michigan, minus 2.0 percent; Pennsylvania, minus 2.3 percent; Wisconsin, minus 2.3 percent; Arizona, minus 2.8 percent; Florida, minus 2.1 percent, and North Carolina, minus 2.2 percent. Because of Trump's narrow 2016 victories in most of those states, the shifts to Biden even in small numbers could make a huge difference in the 2020 outcome. Additionally, the percentages of White college graduates, African-Americans, Hispanics, and Asian-American voters—all disproportionately in the Democratic fold, were expected to increase their numbers in those same states.[26] "Trump has a certain hill to climb, and this (data) suggests that the hill gets a little steeper," said a co-author of "States of Change," the report.[27] In fact, the demographic hill for Trump became an unconquerable mountain.

The second demographic problem for Trump concerned the evangelicals, another previously key support group. Despite trepidations over his character in 2016, evangelicals were almost evenly divided over Trump at the beginning of his presidency with 43 percent viewing him as very favorable/mostly favorable, compared with 52 percent who regarded him as mostly unfavorable/very unfavorable. By June 2020, however, the overall evangelical view of Trump had changed dramatically. Only 35 percent described Trump as very favorable/mostly favorable, compared with 63 percent who described him as mostly unfavorable/very unfavorable. The same study showed Biden with 54 percent mostly unfavorable/very unfavorable evaluations, in other words a lower "unfavorable" rating than Trump.[28] Bottom line: Trump lost the political advantage of a group that had been previously critical to his 2016 electoral success.

Return to Familiar Tactics

The issues cited above notwithstanding, the 2020 campaign began with emphasis on the same "us" versus "them" hot-button issues that had brought him success in 2016: immigration and the threat to "American" culture from minorities inserting themselves into the country.

Immigration

Throughout his presidency, Trump had portrayed runaway immigration as a menace to the wellbeing of American culture. Of course, we need to parse his words. By "immigration," Trump meant non-White newcomers; White people were never a problem. By "American culture," he meant the loose set of values purportedly enjoyed by White Christians of European heritage, which were different than the poverty, filth, and dependence upon government by immigrants of color. Trump's disdain was particularly palpable at campaign rallies, where his minions cheered the President's every warning about the threat of outsiders changing the hallowed American political landscape.

Trump's devoted followers had reason to cheer. During his administration Trump issued an unprecedented 472 executive actions affecting U.S. immigration policy. They ranged from an overhaul of the Department of Homeland Security (DHS) to unbearably lengthened time periods for asylum seekers and temporary immigrants seeking work permits. Not every effort succeeded, notably Trump's proposed 2,000-mile wall separating the United States from Mexico, which made little headway construction-wise; but other immigration changes were nothing less than profound. In the first three years of his administration alone, Trump policies reduced student visas by two percent and permanent residency visas by 13 percent. Refugee admissions to the United States fell by 65 percent. With respect to Trump's promise to deny Muslims entry, admissions to Muslim applicants from Iraq, Iran, and Syria had plunged to almost zero. Matters at the Mexican border weren't so good, however. Detentions of would-be immigrants at the border swelled from 300,000 in 2017 to more than 800,000 by late 2019, leaving DHS leaders well short of their objective. Rather than wait many months for an appointment across the border, sizable numbers of migrants returned to their countries of origin or went elsewhere.[29] Trump also ordered the removal of 333,000 people living in the United States under the Temporary Protected

Status program, which had granted applicants short-term residence because of humanitarian issues in their home countries.[30]

Other than his ill-fated 2,000-mile border wall, the most ambitious Trump effort to alter immigration patterns transpired with his effort to end the Deferred Action on Childhood Arrivals (DACA) program. Created via executive order by President Barack Obama in 2012, the program basically awarded temporary immigrant status to the children of undocumented parents who immigrated to the United States between 1981 and 2012. Approximately 800,000 children were enrolled in the program, which was designed as a placeholder until Congress passed immigration reform legislation, which is yet to happen. Executive orders can be fleeting under several circumstances; they can be changed at any time by Congress through a new law, the federal courts, or future presidents. That's exactly what happened in September 2017, when President Trump issued an executive order ending the program. Lawsuits followed, and in June 2020, the U.S. Supreme Court held 5-to-4 that while the constitutionality of DACA could face scrutiny in the future, the Trump administration had ended the program in an unfair, capricious manner.[31] Thus, Trump lost a battle on DACA, but the war is far from over.

While Trump continued to denigrate immigration, the issue no longer carried the same resonance with the voters in 2020 as it did in 2016. Republican strategists fretted that Trump should focus on the weakened economy and the perils of COVID-19 rather than immigration. As one Republican campaign analyst noted, "If he's (Trump) not talking about the pandemic or the economy, he's not talking about what most Americans are most concerned about."[32] Added another, "His (Trump's) message today is almost exactly what it was in 2016. The country has changed, but the president's message has not."[33] There was truth to such concerns. A Gallup Poll taken in June 2020 found that 34 percent of Americans favored increased immigration, compared with 28 percent who wanted decreased immigration. Four years earlier, only 21 percent approved of more immigration, versus 38 percent who supported less immigration. Clearly, immigration did not present the same uneasiness in 2020 as it did in 2016. Thus, while Trump remained riveted on immigration, a sizable portion of the country had moved on.[34] But that didn't matter to Trump's minions and neither did it matter to him.

Minorities

Beyond immigration, race remained a focal point for Trump, and he wasn't shy about his complaints. His frequent rallies included attacks on "the Chinese virus" (COVID-19), sports teams reconsidering their names because of their insensitivity to Native Americans, crime rates in the inner cities, and sanctuary cities. Some concerns were more prevalent than others, among them the failings of Black leaders, support for police in confrontations such as Black Lives Matter, defending Confederate statues as valued parts of American history, and even the necessity of teaching children "patriotic education" in place of information about racism.

Decrying Black Leaders

Trump had set the stage for demeaning Black leaders years earlier with his infatuation over birtherism and his baseless questions about Barack Obama's heritage and U.S. citizenship. As president, he had hired few Black Americans for any authoritative positions, compared to his predecessors. Members of the Congressional Black Caucus viewed meetings with Trump as little more than symbolic photo ops. Said Representative James Clyburn of South Carolina, the highest ranking Black member of the House after one meeting, "I know his (Trump's) type. He has been as caustic as he can be. Trump insults in public and then makes a private call to you to say that is really not what he meant. I have been around those kind of white people all my life."[35]

Trump's disparagement of Black leaders went beyond Congress. During the 2020 presidential campaign, he questioned future Vice President Kamala Harris's eligibility for political office given that her parents were immigrants;[36] Harris, of course, was born in the United States. After the Vice Presidential debate between Harris and then-Vice President Mike Pence, Trump described Harris as a "monster" and "totally unlikeable."[37] It's difficult to imagine such characterizations coming from a president, but harsh descriptions from Trump occurred with regularity. It also underscored his ongoing contempt for women.

If Trump thought he was fooling African-Americans or moderate White people hoping for some positive outreach, he was gravely mistaken. One review of his approach described it as "split screen approach: The president talks up his friendships with Black Americans (often famous ones like Kanye West) while running a campaign whose objective is to frighten white suburban voters into thinking a Biden presidency will bring problems from inner-city America to their front lawns."[38] Whether White people saw through Trump's veneer is uncertain; his African-American vote edged up slightly to eight percent, statistically insignificant from 2016.

Criticizing Black Lives Matter

Trump connected his disdain for Black people to the turmoil in inner cities. Throughout the spring and summer of 2020, much of Trump's campaign attention fixated on several killings of unarmed Black people by mostly White police officers. In many cases, protests emerged after the event, demanding that police be held accountable. Such episodes have occurred with regularity, but the video of a police officer's slow motion-like killing of George Floyd, an unarmed Black man, in May 2020 was especially brutal and widely seen throughout the nation.

In the wake of the Floyd murder, the Black Lives Matter movement, long an effort to draw attention to the indignities suffered by Black people from police brutality, gained renewed notoriety and some success. In fact, their existence actually brought a bit of calm and restraint to police behavior. One study found that the presence of Black Lives Matter protesters reduced police homicides by between 15 and 20 percent, largely due to the attention the activists brought to police behavior.[39] Nevertheless, Trump repeatedly blamed the movement for inner-city violence, calling them "thugs."[40] He often pointed to Antifa, a nonviolent, anti-racist loose collection of far-left and anarchist groups, as the cause of urban terrorism with zero evidence, but then conspiracy theories don't rely on evidence.[41] Over and over again, Trump's description of the protest movement and reality were far apart. Declaring himself the "law and order president," he often urged police to crack down on anti-racism protesters and threatened to send in national troops to quell disturbances.[42] Yet, a detailed *USA Today* study of cities with police killings of unarmed African Americans found that protests were overwhelmingly peaceful.[43]

Trump's harangues did produce some results, however. Despite studies and reports indicating otherwise, polls showed many Americans buying into Trump's depiction of protesters. A USA/Ipsos poll in September 2020 found that 64 percent of Americans believed that protesters and counter-protesters had placed cities under siege.[44] Of interest was the split: 83 percent of Republicans answering in the affirmative compared with 48 percent of Democrats.

Defending Confederate Statues

Symbolism has long been a big part of American politics. The issue of Confederate statues and monuments has a historic bane for Americans who have viewed them as shrines to the slavery era representing, if not revering, a dark past of inequality. Most statues and monuments honoring Southern Civil War heroes were built between 1880 and 1925, a period that honored not only the heroes but also the slavery period during which they gained their fame. Some local governments and universities removed Confederate sculptures during the civil rights unrest during the 1960s, but thousands have remained throughout the South.

Following a mass killing of Black Church worshippers in Charleston, South Carolina, by a White man in 2015, a renewed movement to remove more than 2,000 Confederate statues and monuments mostly in the South took route. Some local and state governments took notice and removed them, but most remained. The tragedy in Charlottesville, Virginia, in 2017 stemmed from a protest against a Confederate statue of Robert E. Lee at the University of Virginia and the violent racist anti-protest throng that attacked the protesters. Over the next few years, White male individuals pledged to racism and antisemitism and murdered members of African-American and Jewish groups. Given these continuous events, protests against Confederate statues and monuments increased across much of the country.

For Donald Trump, no symbol was more important to his political well-being than Confederate statues and monuments. The political value of his attachment lay not so much in the shrines *per se* as the connection with anti-Black White people who were endeared to the structures for their representation of the pre-Civil War South and slavery. In the South, Black people and White people differed greatly on the condition of society, and that differentiation was amplified on issues such as Confederate statues. A 2018 Winthrop University poll of residents in 11 southern states about statues found that only 20 percent of White people wanted them placed in museums or removed, compared to 55 percent of Black people who called for removal or museum placement.[45] Trump won all of these states except Virginia in 2016. It's no secret that White southerners were central to Trump's support. Given their attachment to Confederate symbols, Trump appreciated the benefit from nurturing the relationship.

Trump repeatedly paid homage to Confederate statues, often characterizing them on the same level of the honors bestowed on historic American revolutionaries or Constitutional framers. But statues were only part of his connection with racist symbols. Confederate flags and other images praising White southern heritage were often at Trump rallies in sizable numbers, another sign of the connection. At an Independence Day rally at Mount Rushmore, South Dakota in 2020, he attacked Democrats and protesters as representatives of "a new far-left fascism" intended to "overthrow the American Revolution"[46]—this from someone who had little allegiance to the Constitution emanating from the American Revolution.

Calling Teaching of Racism in America "Hateful"

Trump's penchant for racist values, statements, and action went beyond political rallies and voting. Vowing to eliminate efforts to discuss or act on racism wherever possible, he went so far as to attack the teaching about the topic at public schools, referring to such efforts as "systemic racism." He complained that teaching themes such as slavery and racial discrimination reframe the nation's true history with "toxic propaganda" and "ideological poison." Condemning *The 1619 Project*, a Pulitzer Prize-winning study that examined American history by tracing slavery and its consequences, Trump said he would create a "1776 Commission" to support true "patriotic education."[47] Several Republican-controlled state legislatures responded by passing new laws that limited the ways teachers could approach slavery and other civil rights issues. Serious book banning on race-related works at public libraries also took place mostly in southern and rural states.

But Trump went beyond the schools. In September 2020, he issued an Executive order designed to combat the "misrepresentation" of American history. In it, he directed all federal agencies, military organizations, and government contractors to refrain from promoting race or sex stereotyping, blame, and any scapegoating that suggested the superiority of any race or gender over others. Themes such as inclusion and diversity would be banned, the order also stated.[48]

Upon taking office on January 20, 2021, President Joe Biden revoked the Trump Executive Order.[49] Nevertheless, Trump made his point. His persistent racist comments about Black, Hispanic, and Muslim elements of American society gave comfort to his followers who believed that the country wouldn't be safe until Trump was president once again. For many, their job was to make that happen.

SHORING UP SUPPORT FROM THE ALT-RIGHT

As the 2020 presidential election neared, Donald Trump doubled down his relationship with the alt-right. During the 2016 campaign, Trump willingly accepted alt-right support especially at his rallies. Then, however, he parsed words carefully, keeping his approval of alt-right themes and organizations at a politically correct distance. Now, however, Trump realized he needed to bring alt-right groups and their votes into his orbit.

Some of his remarks, such as creation of a "1776 Commission" to praise patriotism and offset historically praised treatments such as the 1619 Project and ending racial sensitivity training, remained officially removed from any direct connection to the alt-right, although they clearly pointed to alt-right themes.[50] Other remarks were pointed, such as when Trump criticized Democratic Senator Kamala Harris upon her selection by Democratic nominee Joe Biden as his vice presidential running mate as "extraordinarily nasty" and "so angry," he touched on an age-old racist description of Black women.[51] On occasion, Trump was less opaque, such when he retweeted videos focusing on "White power."[52]

Then there were the times with explicit ties between Trump and his alt-right allies. For example, lest there be any doubt of where the Proud Boys fit in with Trump's values, the answer emerged on September 30, 2020, during an election debate between Trump and Democratic opponent Joe Biden, when moderator Chris Wallace asked whether Trump would denounce White supremacists. After Trump gave a vague response, Biden asked him to denounce the Proud Boys, to which Trump said, "Proud Boys stand back, and stand by." Trump then went on to say, "But I'll tell you what, somebody's got to do something about Antifa and the left."[53] Those words, "stand by," were all the Proud Boys needed to feel totally validated and a welcome part of the Trump orbit. Within minutes of Trump's words, Proud Boys members shared the news on private social media channels, calling Trump's remarks "a tacit endorsement of their violent tactics."[54] The next day, Trump commented that he didn't know anything about the Proud Boys, a denial strategy he used after sensing an unanticipated negative reaction to his remarks at the debate.[55] Nevertheless, the Proud Boys believed otherwise. Between the 2020 presidential election and the end of the year, the Proud Boys leadership estimated that the organization added more than 20,000 new members.[56] So offensive were the Proud Boys with their calls for violence on social media platforms that Facebook, Twitter, Instagram, and YouTube all banned the organization's presence in 2020.

A similar tie existed between Trump and the Oath Keepers, which routinely provided security at Trump rallies and other events such as 2017 confrontation at Charlottesville, Virginia. Routinely, when vocal opposition arose at Trump's events, Oath Keeper members stepped in and quickly removed the "troublemakers," often with little gentleness. The partnership may have been silent, but it was real and consistent. How close was the relationship between the Oath Keepers and Donald Trump? During the 2020 presidential campaign, leader Stewart Rhodes had a front row seat in the VIP section of a Donald Trump rally in San Antonio, Texas. That should not have been surprising. Later that year, Trump tweeted that if he was removed from office via impeachment, "it will cause a Civil War like fracture in this Nation from which our Country will never heal." To that Rhodes tweeted, "Here's the money from that (Trump's) thread. This is the truth. This is where we are. We ARE on the verge of a HOT civil war."[57] The relationship was tight and continues to be so. In 2021, Trump endorsed Oath Keepers member Mark Finchem in his 2022 campaign to be elected Arizona's Secretary of State.[58]

Finally, we turn to the budding relationship between Trump and QAnon, whose dedication to Trump appeared increasingly during his 2020 presidential reelection rallies. Q supporters began attending Trump rallies in droves, wearing Q-shirts, carrying Q-flags, and tweeting their total devotion to Trump. It's difficult to know how many people subscribe to QAnon beliefs because of the secretive way in which the movement operates, but the numbers available are somewhat stunning. In 2020, Twitter shut down 150,000 QAnon-affiliated sites; in the same year, Facebook also removed 200,000 QAnon-related groups.[59] Nevertheless, one respected national survey in 2022 found that one in six Americans are QAnon believers. Among Republicans, 25 percent pledged loyalty to QAnon, compared with nine percent of

Democrats.⁶⁰ Meanwhile, Trump returned the favor of QAnon support with gratitude. When told that the group was dedicated to saving the nation from a satanic cult of child sex traffickers, Trump replied, "Is that such a bad thing? I heard that these are people that love our country."⁶¹

Trump wasn't alone in his affection for QAnon. Nearly two dozen Republican candidates for the House of Representatives and two Republican candidates for the U.S. Senate identified with QAnon in the 2020 November elections; two congressional candidates actually won office. Said Marjorie Taylor Greene, a House member and Trump supporter just before the election, "Q is a patriot, we know that for sure. There's a once-in-a-lifetime opportunity to take this global cabal of Satan-worshipping pedophiles out, and I think we have the President (Trump) to do it."⁶² By the end of the 2020 presidential campaign, QAnon and the mainstream Republican Party had become political soulmates.⁶³

Put it all together and we see something analogous to distant relatives suddenly finding themselves participating in an intimate family gathering, only there was nothing sudden about the new arrangement. Indeed, it had been building for years, perhaps out of the public eye, but building nonetheless.

OLD ENEMIES AND NEW ALLIANCES

History shows the extent to which Donald Trump has pointed accusatory fingers for his problems at everyone but himself. A major key to his success has been his racist behavior. We've learned that for much of his political career, Trump has deftly divided White people from non-White people, with enough White support from the division to survive. But he has had help. Throughout this country's existence, sizable swaths of American society have demonstrated racist behavior, something that Trump has been able to seize and use racism as ammunition for his own objective, power. During his presidency, again and again Trump relied on grievance and racial fears as justification for his disregard for laws, institutions and customs, attempting instead to insert his own loyalty-based laws and norms. His Republican Party colleagues did little to stop Trump, or even question him, for his abuse of power. The same goes with racism, where few Republicans have dared to challenge Trump on his behavior.

Whatever goodwill Trump had with voters in 2016 soured by 2020, or at least enough to provide for his defeat at the polls. Impeachment over Trump's attempt to deny foreign aid to Ukrainian President Volodymyr Zelenskyy for bogus reasons, his inability to manage a sagging economy, and most of all, his callous disregard for the COVID-19 pandemic, combined to cost Trump reelection.

Still, Trump's behavior prior to and during his presidency brought radical racist allies historically on the periphery of society closer to the mainstream. Just how close and for how long remain to be seen. Nevertheless, by 2020 alt-right groups replaced much of Trump's lost support and energy, moving the nation's politics to a dark place not seen since McCarthyism. Throughout his presidency, alt-right groups stoked the racist flames of Americans already unhappy with their lives and looking for someone to blame, growing bolder and bolder with the approach of the 2020 presidential election. Now, together, the alt-right groups and Trump could provide that villain—non-White people, immigrants, Jews, and Muslims—and dispense of them with the authority of law, or at least their interpretation of the law.

Thus, out of Trump's 2020 election loss emerged the hope of him somehow remaining in office through the assistance of reenergized allies. Viewing Trump as the key to ridding American society of the "thems," alt-right forces found renewed purpose to violently work their will. After all, they had worked too hard and for too long to miss this opportunity to cleanse the nation once and for all. They labored to keep Trump in power so that their objective of a purged society might move forward. It was time for less talk and more action. For that moment in American political history, we turn to chapter 9.

NOTES

1. "Trump's Campaign War Chest Tops $100 Million Heading Into Election Year," *The Wall Street Journal*, January 2, 2020, https://www.wsj.com/articles/trump-campaignraised-46-million-infourth-quarter-11577970640.

2. "How Trump's Billion Dollar Campaign Lost Its Cash Advantage," *The New York Times*, September 7, 2020, https://www.nytimes.com/2020/09/07/us/politics/trump-election-campaign-fundraising.html.

3. Order 3915-2017, Office of the Deputy Attorney General, "Appointment of Special Counsel to Investigate Russian Interference with the 2016 Presidential Election and Related Matters," May 17, 2017, https://www.justice.gov/archives/opa/press-release/file/967231/download.

4. "Report on the Investigation Into Russian Interference in the 2016 Presidential Election," March 22, 2019.

5. "Inside Trump's Closed-Door Meeting, Held To Reassure 'The Evangelicals,'" *NPR*, June 15, 2016, https://www.npr.org/2016/06/21/483018976/inside-trumps-closed-door-meeting-held-to-reassures-the-evangelicals.

6. Susan B. Glasser and Peter Baker, "Inside the War between Trump and His Generals," *The New Yorker*, August 8, 2022, https://www.newyorker.com/magazine/2022/08/15/inside-the-war-between-trump-and-his-generals.

7. The report was officially called "Report on The Investigation Into Russian Interference In The 2016 Presidential Election."

8. "'Poll' Majority Approves of Trump's Impeachment," *Politico*, December 12, 2019, https://www.politico.com/news/2019/12/20/poll-trump-impeachment-088812.

9. "Presidential Approval Ratings—Donald Trump," *The Gallup Poll*, January 2017 through January 2021, https://news.gallup.com/poll/203198/presidential-approval-ratings-donald-trump.aspx.

10. Beth Cameron, "I Ran the White House Pandemic Office. Trump Closed It," *The Washington Post*, March 13, 2020, https://www.washingtonpost.com/outlook/nsc-pandemic-office-trump-closed/2020/03/13/a70de09c-6491-11ea-acca-80c22bbee96f_story.html.

11. "Timeline of the Coronavirus Pandemic and the U.S. Response," *Just Security*, November 30, 2020, https://www.justsecurity.org/69650/timeline-of-the-coronavirus-pandemic-and-u-s-response/.

12. "CDC to Cut by 80 Percent Efforts to Prevent Global Disease Outbreak," *The Washington Post*, February 1, 2018, https://www.washingtonpost.com/news/to-your-health/wp/2018/02/01/cdc-to-cut-by-80-percent-efforts-to-prevent-global-disease-outbreak/.

13. The remaining observations and dates in this paragraph are found in "The President vs. the Experts: How Trump Downplayed the Coronavirus," *The New York Times,* March 20, 2020, https://www.nytimes.com/interactive/2020/03/18/us/trump-coronavirus-statements-timeline.html.

14. "Trump Claims Coronavirus Will 'Miraculously' Go Away By April," *Vanity Fair*, February 11, 2020, https://www.vanityfair.com/news/2020/02/donald-trump-coronavirus-warm-weather.

15. "U.S. Intelligence Reports from January and February Warned about a Likely Pandemic," *The Washington Post*, March 20, 2020, https://www.washingtonpost.com/national-security/us-intelligence-reports-from-january-and-february-warned-about-a-likely-pandemic/2020/03/20/299d8cda-6ad5-11ea-b5f1-a5.

16. "Trump Says China 'Should Have Told Us' about the Coronavirus. He Removed the Official Meant to do that," *Vox*, March 23, 2020, https://www.vox.com/policy-and-politics/2020/3/23/21190713/coronavirus-trump-china-cdc-embed-quick.

17. Yulin Hswen, Xiang Xu, Anna Hing, Jared B. Hawkins, John S. Brownstein, and Gilbert Gee, "Association of '#covid19' Versus '#chinesevirus' with Anti-Asian Sentiments on Twitter: March 9-23, 2020," *American Journal of Public Health*, May 2021, https://ajph.aphapublications.org/doi/10.2105/AJPH.2021.306154.

18. Quoted in "Trump has no Qualms about Calling Coronavirus the 'Chinese Virus.' That's a Dangerous Attitude, Experts Say," *The Washington Post*, March 20, 2020, https://www.washingtonpost.com/nation/2020/03/20/coronavirus-trump-chinese-virus/.

19. "Trump's Suggestion That Disinfectant s Could Be Used to Treat Coronavirus Prompts Aggressive Pushback," *The New York Times*, April 20, 2020, https://www.nytimes.com/2020/04/24/us/politics/trump-inject-disinfectant-bleach-coronavirus.html.

20. "Accidental Poisonings Increased after President Trump's Disinfectant Comment," *Time*, May 12, 2020, https://time.com/5835244/accidental-poisonings-trump/.

21. "Inside Trump's Failure: The Rush to Abandon Leadership Role on the Virus," *The New York Times*, September 9, 2020, https://www.nytimes.com/2020/07/18/us/politics/trump-coronavirus-response-failure-leadership.html.

22. "National Data: Deaths, The COVID Tracking Project," https://covidtracking.com/data/national/deaths.

23. "Voters Increasingly Confident that Biden would Handle COVID-19 Better than Trump," *YouGov*, October 10, 2020, https://today.yougov.com/topics/politics/articles-reports/2020/10/20/biden-trump-handle-covid-better-poll.

24. Peter Baker and Susan Glasser, *The Divider* (New York, NY: Doubleday, 2022), p. 437.

25. See Thomas B. Edsall, "The Audacity of Hate," *The New York Times*, February 19, 2020, https://www.nytimes.com/2020/02/19/opinion/trump-anger-fear.html.

26. These data come from Rob Griffin, William H. Frey, and Ruy Teixeira, "States of Change," June 27, 2019, https://www.americanprogress.org/series/states-of-change/.

27. Quoted in "Demographic Shift Poised to Test Trump's 2020 Strategy," *The Wall Street Journal*, https://www.wsj.com/articles/demographic-shift-poised-to-test-trumps-2020-strategy-11578047402. Trump actually narrowly lost four of the six states in question (Michigan, Pennsylvania, Wisconsin, and Arizona) with 57 electoral votes.

28. PRRI 2020 Race Survey, *Public Religion Research Institute*, June 26–29, 2020, https://prri.parc.us.com/client/index.html#/search.

29. These data come from "U.S. Election in 2020: Trump's Impact on Immigration—in Seven Charts," *BBC*, October 22, 2020, https://www.bbc.com/news/election-us-2020-54638643.

30. President Biden suspended Trump's order in October 2021.

31. The case was *Department of Homeland Security v. Regents of the University of California*.

32. "Trump Pushes Anti-immigrant Message Even as Coronavirus Dominates Campaign," *Reuters*, August 14, 2020, https://www.reuters.com/article/us-usa-election-immigration-insight/trump-pushes-anti-immigrant-message-even-as-coronavirus-dominates-campaign-idUSKCN25A18W.

33. Ibid.

34. See "Immigration," *Gallup Poll*, https://news.gallup.com/poll/1660/immigration.aspx.

35. "In Encounters with Black Leaders, Trump Has Chosen Photo Ops over Substance," *The New York Times*, September 11, 2020, https://www.nytimes.com/2020/09/10/us/politics/trump-black-leaders.html.

36. "Trump Encourages Racist Conspiracy Theory about Kamala Harris," *The New York Tomes*, August 14, 2020, https://news.gallup.com/poll/1660/immigration.aspx.

37. "Trump Calls Harris a 'Monster,' Reviving a Pattern if Attacking Women of Color," *NPR*, October 9, 2022, https://www.npr.org/2020/10/09/921884531/trump-calls-harris-a-monster-reviving-a-pattern-of-attacking-women-of-color.

38. "In Encounters with Black Leaders, Trump Has Chosen Photo Ops over Substance."

39. See Travis Campbell, "Black Lives Matter's Effect on Police Lethal Use-of-Force," *Social Science Research Network*, May 13, 2021, https://papers.ssrn.com/sol3/papers.cfm?abstract_id=3767097.

40. "Trump Called BLM Protesters 'Thugs' But Capitol-Storming Supporters 'Very Special,'" *Forbes*, April 14, 2022, https://www.forbes.com/sites/tommybeer/2021/01/06/trump-called-blm-protesters-thugs-but-capitol-storming-supporters-very-special/?sh=136c10f03465.

41. "How 'Antifa' became a Trump Catch-All," *Politico*, June 2, 2020, https://www.politico.com/news/2020/06/02/how-antifa-became-a-trump-catch-all-297921.

42. "Trump to Send Federal Forces to More 'Democrat' Cities," *Reuters*, July 20, 2020, https://www.reuters.com/article/us-global-race-protests-portland/trump-to-send-federal-forces-to-more-democrat-cities-idUSKCN24L1I1.

43. "'A Fanciful Reality': Trump claims Black Lives Matter Protests Are Violent, but the Majority Are Peaceful," *USA Today*, October 25, 2020, https://www.usatoday.com/in-depth/news/nation/2020/10/24/trump-claims-blm-protests-violent-but-majority-peaceful/3640564001/.

44. "USA Today/Ipsos Poll: A majority of Americans Say Cities under Siege by Protesters," *USA Today*, September 23, 2020, https://www.usatoday.com/story/news/politics/2020/09/22/usa-today-ipsos-poll-majority-americans-say-cities-under-siege/3483172001/.

45. "Winthrop Poll Southern Focus Survey," Winthrop University, December 2018, https://www.winthrop.edu/uploadedFiles/wupoll/november-2018-results.pdf. The states were Alabama, Arkansas, Florida, Georgia, Louisiana, Mississippi, North Carolina, South Carolina, Tennessee, Texas, and Virginia.

46. "At Mt. Rushmore, Trump uses Fourth of July Celebration to Stoke a Culture War," *Los Angeles Times*, July 3, 2020, https://www.latimes.com/politics/story/2020-07-03/trump-july-4-culture-war.

47. "Trump Claims Teaching Kids about Racism Is 'Child Abuse,' Wants it Abolished from Schools and Replaced with a 'Patriotic Education,'" *Vanity Fair*, September 9, 2020, https://www.vanityfair.com/news/2020/09/donald-trump-1776-commission.

48. See "Executive Order on Combating Race and Sex Stereotyping," September 22, 2020, https://trumpwhitehouse.archives.gov/presidential-actions/executive-order-combating-race-sex-stereotyping/.

49. Executive Order 13,985.

50. "Trump Claims Teaching Kids about Racism Is 'Child Abuse,' Wants it Abolished from Schools and Replaced with a 'Patriotic Education,'" *Vanity Fair*, September 17, 2020, https://www.vanityfair.com/news/2020/09/donald-trump-1776-commission.

51. "When Trump Calls a Black Woman 'Angry,' He Feeds This Racist Trope," *The New York Times*, August 15, 2020, https://www.nytimes.com/2020/08/14/arts/trump-black-women-stereotypes.html.

52. "Trump Adds to Playbook of Stoking White Fear and Resentment," *The New York Times*, July 6, 2020, https://www.nytimes.com/2020/07/06/us/politics/trump-bubba-wallace-nascar.html.

53. "Trump's Debate Comments give an Online Boost to a Group Social Media Companies have Long Struggled Against," *The Washington Post*, September 30, 2020, https://www.washingtonpost.com/technology/2020/09/30/trump-debate-rightwing-celebration/.

54. "Proud Boys Celebrate Trump's 'Stand By' Remarks about them at the Debate," *The New York Times*, September 29, 2020, https://www.nytimes.com/2020/09/29/us/trump-proud-boys-biden.html.

55. "Trump Now Tells Far Right to 'Stand Down' Amid White Supremacy Row," *BBC News*, October 1, 2020, https://www.bbc.com/news/election-us-2020-54359993.

56. "New Details Suggest Senior Trump Aides Knew Jan. 6 Rally Could Get Chaotic," *ProPublica*, June 25, 2021, https://www.propublica.org/article/new-details-suggest-senior-trump-aides-knew-jan-6-rally-could-get-chaotic.

57. "Armed Militias Are Taking Trump's Civil War Tweets Seriously," *Lawfare*, October 2, 2019, https://www.lawfareblog.com/armed-militias-are-taking-trumps-civil-war-tweets-seriously.

58. "Trump Endorses Arizona SoS Candidate Mark Finchem, a Self-Proclaimed Member of Oath Keepers," *Newsweek*, September 13, 2021, https://www.newsweek.com/trump-endorses-arizona-sos-candidate-mark-finchem-self-proclaimed-member-oath-keepers-1628715.

59. "QAnon Explained: The Antisemitic Conspiracy Theory Gaining Traction around the World," *The Guardian*, August 25, 2020, https://www.theguardian.com/us-news/2020/aug/25/qanon-conspiracy-theory-explained-trump-what-is.

60. "New PPRI Report Reveals Nearly One in Five Americans and One in Four Republicans Still Believe in QAnon Conspiracy Theories," *PPRI*, February 24, 2022, https://www.prri.org/press-release/new-prri-report-reveals-nearly-one-in-five-americans-and-one-in-four-republicans-still-believe-in-qanon-conspiracy-theories/.

61. "Trump Praises QAnon Conspiracists, Appreciates Support," *AP News*, August 19, 2020, https://apnews.com/article/election-2020-ap-top-news-religion-racial-injustice-535e145ee67dd757660157be39d05d3f.

62. "The Congressional Candidates Who have Engaged with the QAnon Conspiracy Theory," *CNN Politics*, October 30, 2020, https://www.cnn.com/interactive/2020/10/politics/qanon-cong-candidates/.

63. Mike Rothchild, *The Storm Is Upon Us* (Brooklyn, NY: Melville Press, 2021), pp. 45–47.

Chapter 9

The January Sixth Insurrection
Before, During, and After

January 6, 2021 (also referred to as 1/6) was both the temporary political high point for President Donald Trump and low point for the nation. The ecstatic moment for Trump emerged as thousands of Americans violently attacked the national Capitol with the sole intent of preserving Trump's presidential power as the members of Congress voted to confirm the results of the 2020 election. In effect, his followers were willing to abandon the rule of law in favor of a lawless ruler.

The low point for the nation emerged through exactly the same event, one that revealed American democracy under the greatest threat since the Civil War, and a threat that many in the nation were slow to appreciate for its potentially long-lasting devastating effects. For supporters of democracy, however, the insurgency was more than an attack; it was an indication of just how easy it was for a democracy to fall apart.

By the end of that emotionally and physically draining day, the assault on the Capitol was quelled, the November 3, 2020, presidential election outcome was officially confirmed, and our democratic institutions remained in place—at least for the moment. But January 6 didn't occur in a political vacuum. Well before the quadrennial election event, Trump and his minions had begun considering ways, legal and mostly otherwise, to keep his presidency, whatever the cost. Their efforts were intentional, devious and, worst of all, with total disregard for the Constitution and the rule of law. Meanwhile, step by step, a few individuals both in and out of government dedicated to preserving the nation's core values and election outcome struggled to prevent Trump from turning the world's oldest modern democracy into an authoritarian state.

Numerous accounts by journalists and political scientists have provided insight into Trump's presidential behavior and deeply flawed governance during his presidency. Much analysis emerged from the investigation conducted by the United States House Select Committee on the January 6, 2021, attack.[1] The task here, however, is different from in-depth election analyses. Our work at hand has reached the point where we will focus our discussion of Trump, racism, and Trump's reliance upon a substantially bigoted mob dedicated to using force for restoring their sense of the good society to be led by a leader with similar values.

What follows is discussion of the unprecedented political revolt that almost destroyed American democracy. We will explore this dangerous event by reviewing the end of Trump's presidency in the context of his reliance on racist tools and organizations to keep American politics in a state of anger and near revolt in his effort to preserve, and later return, to the presidency for another term. Next, we will examine the January 6 insurrection against Congress (and the electorate) in the context of racist and authoritarian participants. Following the insurrection event, we will review the various machinations conducted by Trump and his minions to keep control of the presidency.

It's important to note that these events were not spontaneous instances of citizen indignation over an election outcome. Rather, virtually every major aspect of the January 6 debacle was planned by insurrection leaders, and in some cases in great detail. That Donald Trump may have coordinated, or at a minimum condoned, so much of the activity with sizable numbers of committed participants who knew better is both breathtaking and frightening. It's equally important to understand that while Trump may have been derailed on January 6, the elements that allowed him to almost succeed are largely still in place. American democracy continues to remain at a political tipping point.

TRUMP'S REACTION TO THE 2020 PRESIDENTIAL ELECTION

Donald Trump's worst fears came to fruition on November 3, 2020, with the loss of his bid for reelection. With 74,000,000 votes, Trump exceeded his 2016 popular vote total by about 11,000,000 votes. But Trump's total wasn't nearly enough to beat Joe Biden, who amassed more than 81,000,000 votes. Insult to injury was added with Biden's electoral vote victory over Trump by 306 to 232, ironically the exact opposite numbers from the 2016 presidential election outcome, which led to Trump's unexpected victory over Democrat Hillary Clinton. Both in raw numbers and electoral votes, this was not a particularly close election, although the outcomes in a half dozen states were tight, as is often the case in presidential elections. Given such a one-sided outcome, however, one would expect the loser to admit defeat, but Donald Trump has never taken well to losing. The election was stolen, he claimed over and over again, and he would prove it.

Predictably, Trump offered a seemingly endless list of causes for his debacle. Among them, inaccurate voting machines; mysterious late ballots that appeared from nowhere; state laws that suppressed his voters' abilities to cast ballots; large numbers of Biden supporters who voted more than once; dead people whose "votes" were recorded in the ballot totals; out of state residents who flooded battleground states to alter the outcome; corrupt election workers who were all too willing to throw the election for Biden; and even election interference from the Chinese government!

Several Republican leaders in and out of elected office claimed "foul" about the 2020 election results. Over time, however, their numbers dwindled. The results of post-election audits in several states, clearly showed well-run elections, with nothing close to any illegalities or questionable activity. Still, we know from the congressional reaction at the confirmation occasion on January 6, 2021, after the insurrection, many Republican members voted to overturn the election despite the results, investigations, and judicial responses. All this over what is typically little more than a ceremonial event.

ROLE OF THE RIGHT-WING MEDIA

Negative reaction to the election extended well beyond Congress. Right-wing media was among the parties unwilling to admit defeat. Resistance from alt-right social media sites was predictable enough, given their ongoing conspiratorial attitude about election fraud long before the balloting occurred, along with continued protests after the fact.[2]

More surprising were the persistent claims by key talk show hosts at Fox, a Trump-friendly cable news channel, who continued their rejections of the outcome through and after the January 6, 2021, insurrection. They were preaching to the choir. In a 2021 national poll, more than 80 percent of Fox News Channel viewers believed that the 2020 election was stolen.[3] Given that Fox viewership was larger than cable competitors CNN and MSNBC combined, the remarks from its pundits carried great sway, thereby contributing significantly to public doubt and giving much-needed political oxygen to Trump's never-ending allegations of election fraud.

More than a year later, the sinister intentions of Fox commentators became clear. As part of the network's effort to delegitimize the election outcome, they claimed that Dominion Voting Systems, a vote-counting company used entirely or in part by 28 states, had falsified returns. Dominion sued Fox for defamation and ultimately accepted a settlement of $787.5 million just before going to trial—the largest disbursement of its kind on record. In the process of gathering documentation, Dominion uncovered conversations between Fox television anchors clearly showing that they knew all along that Trump had lost, but publicly insisted otherwise as a way of keeping their large audience share.[4] Of course, this revelation came long after the contentious climate leading up to January 6, some of which was shaped by the Fox false portrayals of the election. Still, it shows the extent to which election denial was planted in the minds of millions of Trump loyalists.

The persistent "rigged election" complaints notwithstanding, numerous rigorous and impartial post-election investigations of the voting procedures and outcomes in several states—in some cases, more than once—showed that none of the claims related to widespread election fraud, abuse, or vote tabulation procedures were true. Such conclusions offered little solace to Trump or his dedicated minions, who remained steadfast in their beliefs of a rigged election. Given these unacceptable results, Trump and his supporters set about to change the outcome of the election by whatever means necessary, legal or otherwise.

TRUMP'S ATTEMPTS TO CO-OP FEDERAL AND STATE LEADERS

In the frenetic days after the November 3, 2020 presidential election, Donald Trump attempted to coerce key individuals in government institutions and agencies for electoral resurrection. Such efforts shouldn't have been surprising, given Trump's expansive and often unconstitutional view of the presidency and presidential powers. After all, it was at his 2016 Republican presidential nomination acceptance speech that in describing America's disarray, Trump declared that "I alone can fix it." Later, as chief executive during the COVID-19 pandemic, Trump advised that "when somebody's president of the United States, the authority [of the president] is total." Thus, he concluded, the nation's chief executive could re-open commerce during COVID-19 and send children back to school as he viewed necessary, despite the 10th Amendment of the U.S. Constitution that awards such powers to the states.[5] On another occasion, he contended that the president had the power to adjourn Congress whenever he wished, a "power" seriously doubted by most constitutional experts.[6] In short, Trump dismissed the thought of virtually any constraints on the president's power irrespective of more than two centuries of American law and tradition.

Trump had a pattern of using government agencies for his own political purposes. John Kelly, Trump's second Chief of Staff between July 2017 and December 2018, noted Trump's frequent interest in using the Department of Justice and Internal Revenue Service against his critics. According to Kelly, a former four-star general and Secretary of Homeland Security, Trump was particularly interested in pressuring the IRS to investigate former (and Trump-fired) FBI Director James Comey and his chief deputy, Andrew McCabe. Upon questioning, Trump stated he had no memory of such a request. Yet, during the time that a Trump appointee headed the IRS, both men were investigated. The IRS claimed the events were "random." Yet, when Comey was investigated in 2019, only 5,000 of 153 million tax returned were audited. Similarly, when McCabe was audited in 2021, only 8,000 of 154 million returns were audited.[7] To say that the investigations of both leaders were random defies the boundaries of mathematical probabilities.

Then there was the time when Trump attempted to pressure Ukrainian President Volodymyr Zelenskyy to dig up misdeeds by Hunter Biden as Zelenskyy waited for badly needed American foreign aid, a package that had already been awarded by the Trump administration although not yet delivered.[8] So much did Trump's demand appear like the makings of a transactional *quid pro quo* that his behavior became the focal point of his first impeachment trial in 2019. Trump claimed no such exchange during the trial, but a military aide present at the time specifically indicated otherwise. The point is simply this: Trump operated under his own rules without regard or care about the boundaries of his office.

Below are the key individuals in government institutions and agencies approached by Trump and allies in his unsuccessful attempt to reverse the 2020 presidential election results.

Judges

There is little doubt that Trump played a major role in reshaping the federal courts. Throughout his term of office, he was outraged by any decisions that prevented the implementation of his policies and often attacked judges for their rulings.[9] At times, he even demanded (without success) that judges recuse themselves in cases where they might decide against the president's policies. At one point, an incensed Trump actually sought to eliminate the U.S. Ninth Circuit Court of Appeals because of its decision that prevented him from immediately deporting asylum seekers without hearings, according to one account.[10] Never mind that the federal courts represent an independent co-equal branch of government established in the U.S. Constitution; Trump wouldn't tolerate what he perceived as political opposition, no matter its constitutional legitimacy or authority.

In his four years of office, Trump appointed 226 federal district court and appeals court judges, a smaller number than the 320 chosen by Barack Obama and 322 by George W. Bush. But two factors stand out. First, Trump's appointees were nominated over a four-year period, while Obama and Bush spread their appointees over eight years. Second, of his total number of federal judicial nominations, Trump was able to fill 54 appeals court vacancies, just a few less than Obama and Bush; that's important because appeals courts in effect decide about 85 percent of all federal cases.[11] Regardless of the federal court levels, a large majority of Trump's judicial appointees were conservative, White and young. The last descriptor is particularly important; as appointees with life-long tenure conferred upon all federal jurists, they would impact countless decisions by the federal judiciary for decades.[12]

Referring to his judicial appointees as "my judges," Trump fully expected them to rule in concert with his wishes. To a great degree, the judges appointed by Trump did behave as the president and his conservative allies hoped on a variety of constitutional questions including voting rights, immigration, gerrymandering, religion in the schools, abortion, as well as a host of regulatory issues from previous administrations which the new judges often viewed as governmental overreach. But that's where the common bond ended.

In terms of untangling a 2020 presidential election "gone wrong," Trump fully expected the courts to rule for him on his assorted claims focusing on election fraud; after all, in his eyes, they "owed" him. He felt a particular kinship with the U.S. Supreme Court, the nation's highest judicial body, where he had the rare opportunity to appoint three of the nine members. But the judicial system doesn't work that way. To begin with, only a handful of Trump's bogus election fraud claims reached the nation's highest court and they were quickly dismissed. In fact, of the ten federal judges and justices appointed by Trump, all ruled against his claims every time a case or motion appeared before them. Their findings were in line with the decisions of other state and federal judges who ruled against Trump in 61 of 62 cases.[13] As one Trump-appointed federal judge who later ruled on a Trump lawsuit clarified, "My boss is not my appointing president, my boss is the Constitution and the laws."[14] And how did Trump explain the unwillingness of *his* judges to rule favorably on his various cases? "They don't have the courage," he said.[15] But they did. In terms of their responses to Trump-initiated lawsuits, the federal judiciary remained an independent institution.

Department of Justice

William Barr, President Trump's Attorney General for the second half of his term, had been a crucial asset to the president during his residence in the nation's highest law enforcement post. Once the attorney general under former president George H.W. Bush, Barr was a big supporter of the "unitary executive theory" of governance, which places the president clearly above the other branches of government.[16] Given Trump's belief that he was the singular source of governing, that suited the president just fine.

Barr had been brought on in early 2019 after writing to Trump about the investigation conducted by Robert Mueller, a special council, some aspects of which Barr considered unreasonable. Mueller had been appointed by Acting Attorney General Ron Rosenstein, himself a Trump appointee, to examine allegations that Trump had committed various crimes before assuming and during his tenure as President. In April 2019, after Mueller completed his report on the investigation but before it was released to the public, Barr redacted key portions of the document and publicly offered an inaccurate interpretation of Mueller's work. Mueller was furious about Barr's "interpretation" which exonerated Trump of several wrong doing allegations[17] and, as such, promoted the public face of the report in a much more benign direction than Mueller had intended. Trump was thrilled with his Attorney General's analysis.

Barr's usefulness to Trump waned after the 2020 election. On several occasions immediately afterward, Trump demanded that Barr act on several unproven allegations of voter fraud and other misdoings related to the election vote, yet Barr didn't take any action. In early December 2020, an angry Trump publicly declared that the Department of Justice was "missing in action"[18] with respect to examining the disputed 2020 election outcome. Within days of Trump's outburst, Barr resigned not in protest of Trump, he wrote, but rather because the timing of his departure coincided with the impending transition of power to a new administration. Only during the subsequent January 6 Select Committee hearings did Barr reveal his strong belief that Trump had lost the election, not exactly a timely divulgence.

Undeterred, Trump pressured the Department of Justice for relief. At one point, he ordered department executives to seize voting machines from the states on the basis that they had been tampered; they refused on the basis that the Department of Homeland Security (the federal agency charged with responsibility for overseeing the use of the machines) had found no reason to take such action.[19] When key Justice officials told Trump that their own research had found no evidence of widespread election fraud, Trump dismissed their conclusion and said, "Just say the election is corrupt and leave the rest to me."[20] The Justice personnel in the meeting told Trump that his demand was illegal, to which one high-ranking official recalled Trump responding, "What do I have to lose?"[21]

Trump continued pressuring the Department of Justice to overturn the 2020 election results. Seeing little action, he sought to replace Acting Attorney General Jeffrey Rosen, Barr's temporary successor, with Jeffrey Clark, a Trump D.O.J. protégé all too willing to do Trump's bidding.[22] Only after the highest-ranking personnel in Justice threatened mass resignations of the intended appointment did Trump stop his replacement plan.[23] Their resistance revealed an increasingly isolated and panicked president now forced to look in other directions for his redemption.

Fake State Electors

In addition to trying to move the Department of Justice to reverse a "stolen election," Trump had another angle: undermine the Electoral College. A little explanation is in order. The electoral college, with its 538 votes, officially decides the winner of a presidential election. Per the U.S. Constitution, every state has a given number of electoral votes. They include two votes in every state for its U.S. Senators plus one or more electoral votes determined by the states' populations, with those having larger numbers of residents receiving more electoral votes than less populated states. The District of Columbia has three electoral votes, courtesy of the 23rd Amendment. That brings the total to 538 electors (100 for the two U.S. senators), 435 for the number of Representatives in the House, and three for the residents of DC.

Prior to the presidential election, each state's political leaders construct a list of individuals who will serve as the electors in what traditionally has been a largely symbolic task. Thus, the states won by Trump would officially send their Republican elector list of votes to the National Archives, the receiving agency of record; ditto for states won by Biden. But Trump, attorneys John Eastman, Rudy Giuliani, and additional allies had another idea: provide their own Republican delegates in seven selected states won by Democrat Joe Biden but challenged by Trump.[24] In an effort to gather "evidence," they dispatched lawyers to challenged states, where they would check voting machines for their accuracy. No irregularities were found anywhere, although subsequent examinations discovered that some local election officials had breached security through availing data and access to voting machines to the unofficial examiners.[25]

Nevertheless, in the seven states where Trump lost, yet claimed victory, fake Republican elector lists were sent to the National Archives along with the official Democratic lists on the unproven "grounds" that Trump was victimized by widespread voter fraud. Dubbed "alternative delegates," Trump hoped that if these lists were accepted as legitimate at the January 6, 2021, certification by Congress, he would have enough electoral votes to win the election. Even if the dispute created confusion for the January 6, 2021, official confirmation in Congress, there was the possibility that the House of Representatives would settle the case. Under such highly unusual circumstances, every state delegation would be allowed one vote per the Constitution, a situation that might also help Trump. At the time of the 2020 election, there were two more states with Republican member majorities of Congress (25) than states dominated by Democrats (23); two states had evenly divided delegations. There was also the possibility that a confused Congress might even send the election back to the states for additional analysis, which also suited Trump just fine. Any confusion, Trump thought, would only be an asset and potentially an off-ramp for a new election. And with his allies in many of the states that he officially lost, this time they would assure his victory.

In early December 2020, the White House Counsel's Office, headed by Pat Cippolone (the official attorney for the presidency), warned Trump Chief of Staff Mark Meadows and others that the fake delegate plan was not legally sound. Pushing the concept, Cippolone wrote, would be nothing less than a "murder-suicide pact."[26] Even though plan architects and allies John Eastman and Rudy Giuliani acknowledged the likelihood of unconstitutionality, they and Trump allies went ahead with the fake electors plan.

On December 14, 2020, representatives of 84 fake delegates from seven states attempted to deliver copies of the fraudulent signed documents attesting to a Trump victory to Vice President Mike Pence, who would preside in the House of Representatives over the election outcome on January 6. Some of the effort actually originated in Congress. In at least one case, according to a top aide of Republican U.S. Senator Ron Johnson of Wisconsin, Johnson sought to hand over fake lists from Wisconsin and Michigan to Pence, but the Vice President instructed his legislative aide to reject delegate records, and the issue ended there.[27]

Of note is that many on the fake delegate lists were seasoned politicians who had decided to reject the vote outcomes in their states. They included six current state and local officeholders, the party chairs or former chairs in all seven of the disputed states, and several candidates for elective office.[28] In other words, these were not political neophytes; they knew better and chose to trample the law for their leader, Donald Trump.

The fake elector event served as one more example of the extent of Trump's efforts to keep the presidency. Moreover, according to one federal judge handling a case on the fake elector issue, Trump was "explicitly tied" to implementing the fake elector idea through his efforts to facilitate at least two meetings on the plan.[29] Ironically, Trump had attempted to rely on fake documents to prove his claim of widespread fraud!

Trump Takes Matters into His Own Hands

In the examples cited above, Donald Trump relied on others to preserve his defeated presidency. However, Trump was not beyond exerting direct pressure, himself. On December 19, 2020, Trump posted a message on Twitter, asking supporters to be in Washington on January 6 to protest the Biden victory, ending his pleas with "It will be wild." But as the time for certification in the House of Representatives neared, Trump became increasingly direct. Three examples particularly stand out: Trump personally soliciting nonexistent votes, Trump pressuring Vice President Mike Pence to overturn the election result, and Trump ultimately exhorting his followers at the rally on

January 6, 2021 to help him reach his destiny. Each of these action steps show Trump willing to take election matters into his own hands, regardless of the illegalities connected with his efforts.

Tampering with the Election Outcome

In most states, the secretary of state has constitutional responsibility for confirming the election outcome. In previous elections, this activity had been rather routine, benign, and inconsequential. But with rampant accusations of voter fraud in states lost by the Republicans, the secretary of states' offices became something of a political football. Fully aware of the secretary of state's role at a contentious moment, President Trump took it upon himself to call upon some state election officials for assistance. The most prominent example was his effort to persuade Georgia Secretary of State Brad Raffensperger, a Republican who voted for the president, to "find" enough votes necessary for Trump to prevail over Joe Biden, who had won the state by 11,779 votes.

In a taped phone conversation later publicly released by Raffensperger, Trump claimed without any evidence that as many as 300,000 votes in Georgia were fraudulent. He explained that Raffensperger could correct the voter fraud problem by adding 11,780 votes to Trump's total, which would be one more than the number of votes that defeated him. When Raffensperger refused and defended Georgia's results as accurate, Trump threatened the Secretary of State with prosecution for knowingly confirming a fraud-filled election! He also told Raffensperger that because of his unwillingness to adjust the outcome, Georgia voters would never again elect Raffensperger to office. (Raffensberger had easily won reelection in 2022.) The Secretary of State remained convinced of his position and the conversation ended without any alteration of votes.[30] Clearly, Trump had illegally attempted to tamper with the election outcome.

The Georgia episode was the most egregious example of Trump's interference with the states, but not the only instance. Shortly after the election, Trump separately invited Republican leaders from Michigan and Pennsylvania, two other states with narrow Biden victories, to visit the White House. The discussion topics were not disclosed, but given Trump's claims of widespread voter fraud in both states, it doesn't take much imagination to guess the topic. In an even bolder move, on November 11, 2020, and again on January 3, 2021, Trump called Republican legislators in the seven contested states, asking them to overturn the will of the voters on the grounds of widespread voter fraud and other unsubstantiated election irregularities.[31] He didn't receive any cooperation, but not for any lack of trying.

Pressuring Vice President Mike Pence

As the January 6 confirmation date approached, a desperate Donald Trump turned to his vice president, who would preside over what is typically a largely ceremonial vote confirming the presidential election results. For weeks prior to the final certification date, Trump had privately urged Pence to deny the election result in his role as convener.

On January 5, after being noncommittal for a period of time and consulting constitutional experts, Pence finally told Trump that he, Pence, had no such power to impact the election other than to acknowledge the Electoral College results as certified individually by the states. In a statement issued on the morning of January 6, 2021, Pence wrote, "It is my considered judgment that my oath to support and defend the Constitution constrains me from claiming unilateral authority to determine which electoral votes should be counted and which should not." Pence based his decision on The Electoral Count Act, an 1887 law that established the official procedure for counting the electoral votes once submitted to Congress. According to Pence's account, Trump then admonished the Vice President that he would "go down as a wimp" for not protecting our country, to which Pence replied that "We both took an oath to support and defend the Constitution."[32] Still, Trump would not be deterred. Instead, he upped the ante.

Shortly before the Congressional gathering, Trump went public with his demand. At a Georgia rally two days before the meeting, Trump stated to the crowd, "I hope our great vice president comes through for us. He's a great guy. Of course, if he doesn't come through, I won't like him very much."[33] More intimation. The attendees roared with approval in response to Trump's demand. In a last-ditch effort on the morning of January 6, Trump addressed Pence via Twitter, where he told the vice president it was time to "show extreme courage" by overturning the 2020 presidential election results.[34] Pence did not respond.

January 6 Rally

Motivating crowds was nothing new to Trump. Of course, given that so many at his rallies bordered on "true believer" religious revivals, his throngs were politically charged even before the rallies began. So, from Trump's standpoint, it made perfect sense to assemble his followers at a January 6 meeting shortly before Congress met to take the last step in confirming the 2020 election result. Emphasizing the critical juncture of his effort to stay in office, on January 5, 2021, Trump tweeted to his followers about the rally, "I will be speaking at the SAVE AMERICA RALLY tomorrow at the Ellipse. Arrive early. Doors open at 7 AM Eastern. BIG

CROWDS." Inasmuch as many pro-Trump groups had been preparing for the gathering—and some for the insurrection, a huge attendance at the January 6 rally was a given.

On the day of the rally, as he was waiting backstage for his turn to speak, Trump learned that Secret Service-installed magnetometers, standard at presidential events, had prevented entry of his supporters with weapons, which is exactly what they were supposed to do. According to testimony by White House staffer Cassidy Hutchison, who later appeared before the House Select Committee on January 6, Trump said to the Secret Service officers, "I don't f—ing care if they (the crowd) have weapons. Take the f—ing mags away. Let my people in. They can march to the Capitol from here."[35] The Secret Service officers rejected Trump's demand, but they were in no position to monitor the growing crowd outside the Capitol a short distance away, where weapons flowed freely.

During his rambling 70-minute speech to the huge crowd, Trump again went through his grievances. The crowd had to stop the steal, he said, because the election had been taken from him and them. They needed to convince reluctant Republicans to go along with allies already prepared to proceed, he said. Showing his disregard for law and the Constitution, Trump told the crowd, "When you catch somebody in a fraud, you're allowed to go by very different rules." At one point during the frenzied rally, a frustrated Trump, for a final time, exhorted to Vice President Mike Pence to reject the outcome and send the results back to the states: "Do it Mike, this is a time for extreme courage,"[36] Trump pleaded. If Pence wasn't about to act, the crowd would convince him otherwise, Trump added. As he neared the end of his speech and the now-frenzied crowd prepared to head to the Capitol, Trump said, "We fight. We fight like hell and if you don't fight like hell, you're not going to have a country anymore." And off they marched into battle.

Endless Pressure

Whether through intimidation of judges, key cabinet departments, state electors, or by his own volition, Donald Trump's efforts to reverse the 2020 presidential election outcome was stunning in scope and detail. Never in the nation's modern history had a president acted in such a brazen fashion to retain power after defeat in the polls. And Trump understood the stakes. Commenting on Pence's potential role a year after the insurrection, Trump said that he believed that Pence "could have overturned the election"[37] by sending the results back to the states. We'll never know what kind of chaos might have happened had Pence complied with Trump's demand. But we do know this: Trump's attempt to keep his presidency through so many political conduits in a patently illegal manner revealed a person who would stop at nothing to stay in office, even if it meant doing so at the expense of core democratic values which obviously held no importance for him.

THE JANUARY 6, 2021, INSURRECTION

The Trump-inspired effort to eradicate the 2020 presidential election results immediately preceded the violent assault on the Capitol by thousands of Trump supporters on January 6, 2021. The attack was planned well in advance of the day and facilitated by numerous meetings and events. Alt-right groups brought weapons, some of which were confiscated by authorities before the march began. As evidence of a coordinated effort, a few alt-right groups worked out alliances ahead of time.[38] Shockingly to some, as many as a dozen Republican members of the House of Representatives were part of the group planning the rally preceding the insurrection, although it remains unclear the extent to which any participated beyond the rally.[39] The organizers were joined by right wing television and radio personalities, along with social media and racist groups ready to tear apart the legislative branch of national government whose members were tasked with carrying out the sacred constitutional duty of peacefully transferring political power from one elected leader to another.

Right-Wing Cable Media and Social Media

The prelude to the January 6 calamity actually began with right-wing denouncements of the 2020 election results. At Fox television, program hosts initially focused more on the general election outcome than the forthcoming January 6 assault. Mark Levin called the election a "mail-in ballot hoax." Newt Gingrich described Joe Biden and the Democrats as "thieves." Lou Dobbs blamed the Trump loss on "the radical Dems and corporate-owned left-wing national media."[40] Talk show host Laura Ingraham blamed Democrats for their attempt to "destroy the integrity of our election process with this mail-in day of registration effort."[41] Tucker Carlson, the most-watched cable television host, added, "the election outcome was seized from the hands of voters."[42] All this, of course, was later proven to be subterfuge inasmuch as many of the Fox commentators later admitted they knew otherwise.[43] Nevertheless, continuous bombardments such as these were the backdrop for even more pointed and dangerous language appearing on social media platforms.

Regarding social media, Trump issued 1,500 messages on Twitter between November 4 and January 8, 2021, alone, the date when Twitter permanently suspended him for continuous language with the likely potential to incite violence.⁴⁴ During that nine-week period, 60 percent of Trump's tweets condemned the election outcome, using such terms as "rigged," "stolen," and "fraud."⁴⁵ On January 5, 2021, the day before Trump's rally followed by the assault on the Capitol, Trump tweeted, "Washington is being inundated with people who don't want to see an election victory stolen by emboldened Radical Left Democrats. Our Country has had enough, they won't take it anymore." More than 88,000,000 people followed Trump on the social media platform. Many of them believed him and heeded his repeated calls to come to Washington.

Other social media platforms were less traveled but even more potent with their messages. For example, Gab, which bills itself as a platform for free speech and a "censorship-free" alternative, became a haven for extremist ideologies and 2020 election deniers.⁴⁶ After traditional platforms like Twitter and Facebook began to shut down violent political discussions about the forthcoming January 6 rally, individuals and groups angered by the election outcome migrated to Gab and other alt-right friendly entities. There, insurrection chatter continued unabated.

Over the internet, supporters on pro-Trump websites discussed bringing military body armor, handcuffs, and various assault weapons to the rally and march. Enrique Tarrio, leader of the Proud Boys, promised in a communique that "The Proud Boys will turn out in record numbers on Jan. 6," incognito and in small teams.⁴⁷ The alt-right group provided attendees a 23-page planning booklet describing everything from a pre-rally walk-through to a post-event debriefing.⁴⁸ Stewart Rhodes, leader of the Oath Keepers, texted his members two days before the rally that "We aren't getting through this (the protest) without a civil war."⁴⁹ Nick Fuentes, a 24-year old leader of America First Forum and live streamer who quickly gained notoriety as an antisemite and White supremacist, urged his followers to keep Trump in power "so that he could take every last illegal alien and throw them back over the border."⁵⁰ Ironically, neither Tarrio, Rhodes, nor Fuentes joined the insurrection on scene, although they communicated with their members from outside the rebellion throughout the event.

Then, there was the podcast space. For months prior to the January 6 assault, Steve Bannon, Trump's former chief strategist, urged resistance to the 2020 election loss, saying at one point "he's (Trump) not going out easy." On his January 5, 2021 *War Room* podcast, Bannon pointedly declared "All hell is going to break loose tomorrow. It's all converging now, and we're on, as they say, the point of attack." Bannon's podcast had millions of listeners. Bannon was not alone in the podcast space. On January 1, 2021, during his podcast *Infowars*, Texas-based conspiracy theorist Alex Jones called for one million marchers to descend on the Capitol "to resist the globalists." Added

Jones, "I don't know how all this is going to end, but if they (law enforcement) want to fight, they better believe they've got one."[51]

All told, there was no shortage of information flow from numerous prominent alt-right sources in the aftermath of the 2020 general election. They continued their anger over the election result on November 3, 2020, until January 6, 2021, without any pause or caution. Their goal is to fight to regain control of their country. And there is little question that the chief beneficiary of their endless grievances would be Donald Trump.

Participants in the Insurrection

Once the insurrection began in full force, the major alt-right groups discussed above descended upon the Capitol *en masse*. They weren't alone. Others included the Three Percenters, white supremacists, antisemites, Nazis, and anarchists.[52] They were joined by members of lesser-known groups including, but not limited to Texas-based Cowboys for Trump; The Boogaloo Bois; No White Guilt; America First; the Michigan Home Guard Militia; the Woodland Wild Dogs; The Texas Freemen Force; and NSC 131 (short for Nationalist Social Club), a New England-based White supremacist, Neo-Nazi organization. Confederate flags appeared throughout the area outside the Capitol, while a man in odd attire professing to be QShaman (an individual allegedly with special access to the mysterious "Q.") was prominent among a large contingent of QAnon followers.[53] To that point, large numbers of QAnon adherents were also present as noted by their apparel and flags displaying the "Q" logo. Then, of course, there were the thousands of Trump conspiracy theory loyalists who traveled to Washington, they insisted, at the President's call. Together, these Trump-committed foot soldiers believed they would save the country for the President.

Among the throng, there were those participants whose very presence at the insurrection violated all boundaries of integrity and credibility. Among them were firefighters, current and former military personnel, and at least two former 2020 presidential election poll workers, along with several current and retired law enforcement individuals.[54] How these people whose very responsibilities revolved around protecting society from chaos and law-breaking criminals could become willing insurgent members defied the imagination. Yet, they were present at the scene, fully engaged in violent physical altercations with fellow stewards of defending the Capitol.

Another unexpected category of participants was present on the Capitol grounds—many on the Capitol steps—in the midst of the mayhem. Post-riot investigations determined that several elected local and state government officials as well as gubernatorial and Congressional candidates had contributed to the mayhem outside the Capitol, although it's unclear as to the number who actually entered the building. Yet, they also were there, and from their statements not as innocent witnesses of history but rather participants.[55]

With respect to demographic characteristics, a study of the first 716 individuals charged with various crimes found that 93 percent were non-Hispanic White; among the others, most were Hispanic. Regarding gender, 85 percent were male. The average age of the group was 39; 25 percent had graduated college, while less than 1 percent were high school dropouts. Other data of interest: 15 percent of the insurrectionists had some military service, and 33 percent had criminal records. As for their places of origins, the highest turnouts included 10 percent from Florida, 9 percent from Pennsylvania, and 8 percent from Texas.[56] Male, White and largely high school graduates—these were key characteristics of the Capitol insurrectionists.

Of the thousands on the Capitol grounds and inside the building that day, more than one thousand individuals ultimately were charged with crimes ranging from disorderly conduct to conspiracy. Slightly less than 100 of the rioters were members of major alt-right racist groups, including 22 members of the Oath Keepers. But beyond the organized racist groups, the gathering had a distinct collective tenor of anger, hate, and revenge for a "stolen" election and anyone defending it. One account of the overwhelmingly White male mob reported a "striking array of far-right iconography . . ., such as a Confederate flag, Crusader crosses, an Auschwitz-themed hoodie and 'white power' hand gestures."[57] From there, it was only a matter of time before more than two thousand rioters overpowered a woefully understaffed Capitol police contingent. All of this occurred in the name of "Stopping the Steal" and restoring the presidency to Donald Trump.

As the incensed crowd grew outside the Capitol, some insurrectionists constructed gallows on the Capitol grounds with the intent of hanging Vice President Mike Pence for his unwillingness to stop the congressional confirmation of the 2020 presidential election. Hangman's nooses were in abundant presence throughout the grounds, underscoring the gravity of the moment. For some observers, this scene had a particular reference to the treatment of African-Americans in the days of segregation. Yet, whatever the shock from the gallows, the unabated anger and hatred in the crowd quickly transformed into a huge violent force that could not be stopped as it bashed its way into the Capitol. Many had harmful weapons including firearms, bats, Molotov cocktails, fire extinguishers, sledgehammers, batons, knives, and pipe bombs. Handcuffs and heavy-duty zip ties were also part of the rioters' supplies. In a particularly troubling setting seen all too often, insurrectionists carrying Trump flags thrust the tips of the metal flagpoles into Capitol police, or in some cases, windows for their brazen entry into the building. It was a bloodbath of unprecedented proportions. Clearly, the insurrection was anything but spontaneous.

For their part, the Capitol police were simply overpowered. As the rioters broke through the barriers, the calls went out to the District of Columbia Metropolitan Police for assistance. They came, although even their numbers weren't sufficient to repel the determined insurrectionists. Only hours later, when the National Guard finally arrived, was order in the Capitol restored. That it took so long for the Guard to arrive was, in itself, a story that suggested either confusion within or intentional refusal by the Trump administration to respond.[58] Given the findings by the House Select Committee, the latter seemed much more likely than the former.

After the insurrectionists pierced the walls of the Capitol, frightened members of Congress increasingly looked for help. Clearly, the relatively few Capitol police were inadequate in numbers to protect the occupants. Calls and texts to Trump from high ranking White House employees asking him for a message telling the insurrectionists to stop went without any reply. Tellingly, attempts for help from Republican members of Congress, even those well within the Trump orbit, also went without reply. Most astonishing was a frantic call from House Republican Minority Leader and close Trump ally Kevin McCarthy to the President that left even those advisers closest to Trump dumbfounded. Fellow House Republican Jaime Herrera Butler recalled McCarthy's description of a telephone conversation between McCarthy and Trump where the Minority Leader begged for relief, relating the extent to which the insurrectionists were by then ravaging the innards of the building and searching for Congressional leaders. After hearing McCarthy's plea, Trump callously replied, "Well, Kevin, I guess these people are more upset about the election than you are." "More upset?" McCarthy screamed. "They're trying to f—ing kill me."[59]

Another hour or so later, Trump issued a benign tweet gently asking protesters to be peaceful. The fighting continued. Finally, after more than three hours of combat, Trump appeared in a video where he asked the insurrectionists to leave the Capitol and go home. Toward the end, Trump said "we love you" to his followers. Given Trump's tepid response to the insurgents, it's hard to escape the conclusion that his inaction was anything but tacit approval of the tragedy. Confirmation came with a tweet issued by Trump later that evening, where he wrote, "These (the insurrection) are the things and events that happen when a sacred landslide election victory is so unceremoniously & viciously stripped away from great patriots. . . . Remember this day forever." Trump's messages made his feelings perfectly clear: the insurrection was a necessity to save his presidency.

THE AFTERMATH

The January 6 insurrection was quelled by the end of the day after the belated arrival of the National Guard, whose delayed appearance remains a mystery.[60] We know this much: Trump was in no hurry to end the Capitol horror spectacle. Once order was restored, Congress reconvened, Vice President Pence resumed his ceremonial task, and the electoral votes division between Biden and Trump yielded the exact result everyone knew before the horrific day began. However, a politically stench residue from the event has lingered, and worse yet, festered additional anti-democratic activity.

Republican reaction to the insurrection was swift, yet ever changing. To begin with, when the Congress reassembled on the evening of January 6, the vote to confirm the 2020 election was hardly resounding. With the insurrectionist-caused destruction all about them, 139 House Republicans, accounting for two-thirds of the House Republican membership, and eight Republican Senators nevertheless voted in unprecedented numbers to overturn the will of American voters. Their votes fell considerably short from causing any change in the outcome. Still, in a moment of irony that could not be overlooked, a substantial number of the same Republicans who had hidden after the insurrectionists breached the Capitol voted to overturn the election and send it back to state legislatures. Their loyalty to Trump was clear then, and continued through the 2022 midterm election campaigns.

Republican Leaders

With respect to Republican leaders, their responses to the insurrection were accentuated by their differences. Days after the attack, Republican Senate Minority Leader Mitch McConnell bluntly stated "the (insurrection) mob was fed lies. They were provoked by the president and other powerful people, and they tried to use fear and violence to stop a specific proceeding of the first branch of the federal government which they did not like."[61] Seven of his Republican colleagues may have voted to overturn the results, but McConnell's conclusion of Trump's culpability in the disaster and belief in the 2020 presidential election results never changed.

Most House Republicans charted a different post-insurrection course than their Senate counterparts. Shortly after the insurrection, then-House Republican Leader Kevin McCarthy on the House floor clearly placed blame for the insurrection on President Trump: "The President bears responsibility for Wednesday's attack on Congress by mob rioters," McCarthy said. In a meeting with his caucus, McCarthy added that "Trump should be censured and that (Republican) members should accept the fact that Joe Biden was the legitimately elected president."[62] A few days later, McCarthy went further and declared in a telephone call with House Republican leaders that Trump should resign from office.[63] McCarthy later denied the conversation, but an audio tape distinctly proved otherwise. Some facts are not disputable regardless of what might be said in their wake.

What made McCarthy's remarks all the more incredible was that within two weeks of the insurrection, he was at Trump's side at Mar-a-Lago. After their meeting and a published picture of the two, Trump aides released a statement saying that McCarthy's "endorsement means more than perhaps any endorsement at any time." For his part, McCarthy released a statement praising Trump for his commitment to a "united conservative movement."[64] It was as if the January 6 attack never happened.

About a year later, the National Republican Committee completed its revisionist account of the January 6 event at its winter meeting in Salt Lake City. Delegates passed a resolution condemning Republican House members Liz Cheney and Adam Kitzinger for criticizing Trump and taking part in the House Select Committee on the January 6 Attack. Further, the resolution described the event as nothing more than "legitimate political discourse."[65] Simply put, the official Republican description of the insurrection officially evaporated in the eyes of party leaders and most elected officials. By 2023, several Republican members of the House had rewritten the insurrection altogether. Georgia Republican House member Andrew Clyde typified the revisionism, saying, "Watching the TV coverage of those who entered the Capitol and walked through Statuary Hall showed people in an orderly fashion staying between the stanchions and ropes taking videos and pictures."[66]

The sentiment wasn't unanimous. In a rare display of contempt for the 2022 proceedings in Salt Lake City, Republican Senate Minority leader Mitch McConnell forcefully pushed back on the resolution, saying the riot "was a violent insurrection for the purpose of trying to prevent the peaceful transfer of power after a legitimately certified election, from one administration to the next. That's what it was."[67] The Republican National Committee, the same committee that at the 2020 Republican National Convention had basically described the party platform as whatever Trump said, ignored McConnell's protest.

Republican Voters

Republican leaders weren't alone in their reassessment of the January 6 insurrection. A national poll undertaken by Monmouth University revealed that a substantial percentage of Republican voters had rendered the insurrection a nonevent. Two years after the sordid event, a July 2022 survey found 61 percent of Republicans viewing the attack on the U.S. Capitol as a "legitimate" protest, up from 47 percent a year earlier. Meanwhile, 33 percent of political independents considered the incident an innocent event; however, their numbers had decreased by six percent. Among Democrats, only 14 percent described the insurrection as "legitimate," identical to their feelings in June 2021.[68] Why are these comparative data important? Because they show the extent that Republicans as a whole minimized the seriousness of the Capitol attack, otherwise considered by several political historians as the most significant assault on American democracy since the Civil War.[69]

Republican feelings about widespread fraud in the 2020 presidential election benefiting Joe Biden changed little after the campaign's end. A Monmouth University poll taken days after the 2020 election found that 70 percent of Republicans declared Biden's victory as a result of voter fraud, compared with 23 percent of Independents and four percent of Democrats.[70] Eighteen months after the 2020 presidential election, most Republicans still hadn't accepted Joe Biden's presidential victory as "fair and square"; 58 percent of Republicans agreed with the statement that Biden won due to "voter fraud," compared with 29 percent of Independents and three percent of Democrats.[71] These sentiments came despite the conclusions of the 18-month investigation of the 2020 election and January 6, 2021, insurrection by the United States House Select Committee on the January 6 Attack, which interviewed more than 1,000 witnesses and collected thousands of documents.

IMPEACHMENT (AGAIN!) AND THE JANUARY 6 HOUSE SELECT COMMITTEE

If Harry Houdini was the world's premier escape artist for his uncanny ability to free himself from challenging physical restraints, Donald Trump seemed his political equivalent for his ability to elude accountability for his continuous wrongdoings, including the incitement of insurrectionism. Even a second impeachment vote didn't stop Trump from continuing to dispute an obvious election result, thanks to help from allies in and out of government, Republican voters who refused to accept the facts, and a rabid assortment of racists, anarchists, and true believers who served as Trump's willing army.

The Second Impeachment

Try as they might to make talk of the insurrection go away, Republicans faced two repercussions from the attack on the Capitol: an unprecedented second impeachment and subsequent bipartisan investigation by a select House committee. The first consequence was an extraordinary rebuke of Trump. The country had endured only three presidential impeachments in history: Andrew Johnson (1868), Bill Clinton (1998), and Trump (2019).

That Trump would be the only president in history to be impeached twice underscored the serious nature of the insurrection. Yet, with only seven days remaining in his presidency, all House Democrats and ten House Republicans voted to impeach Trump for inciting the insurrection. The act was a necessary "constitutional remedy that will ensure that the republic will be safe from this man (Trump) who is so resolutely determined to tear down the things that we hold dear and that hold us together,"[72] said Democratic Speaker Nancy Pelosi.

After a short trial in the U.S. Senate, House impeachment managers were unable to secure the necessary two-thirds vote for conviction. Seven Republican Senators did join all 50 Democrats in the effort, not nearly enough to prevail, but at least a small sign of condemnation. Nevertheless, that so few Republicans joined the Democrats revealed their general unwillingness to rebuke Trump's abuse of power. Mitch McConnell explained away his disinterest in conviction by saying that Trump was on his way out, so a vote didn't matter.[73] McConnell's refusal to join the majority and bring along as many as perhaps members of his party once again showed the extent that Republicans were disinclined to take Trump to task for his actions. Their lack of commitment to convict gave Trump an incredible amount of political oxygen to pursue his thoroughly invalidated stolen election claim without any serious opposition from party leaders.

The January 6 Committee

While Trump avoided impeachment conviction, a new effort to shine light on the truth emerged with creation of the Select Committee to Investigate the January 6th Attack on the United States Capitol. On June 30, 2021, all 222 House Democrats and two Republicans (Liz Cheney and Adam Kitzinger) voted to create a select committee to investigate all of the elements before, during, and after the January 6 insurrection to better understand the tragic event in its totality. The Democrats had wanted the committee to be a bipartisan unit but House Republicans refused because of Speaker Nancy Pelosi's unwillingness to seat two election deniers offered to the committee by then-House Minority Leader Kevin McCarthy.[74] Given no alternative, House Democrats created a nine-person committee with seven Democrats and Republicans Cheney and Kitzinger.

Over time, the committee interviewed more than 1,000 individuals, including some who were extraordinarily close to President Trump during times surrounding the insurrection. Ultimately, their investigative efforts produced eight televised sessions where key individuals were interviewed publicly and the most significant findings revealed. The committee's conclusions were that Donald Trump had been instrumental in planning and inciting the January 6 insurrection. Further, Trump had done nothing to stop the assault, knowing full well of its threat to democratic rule.

Perhaps the most important takeaway from the January 6 hearings was the polarized response over the Committee's findings. In a July 2022 national poll taken near the conclusion of the Committee's findings, respondents were asked "How much do you think former President is to blame for what happened at the U.S. Capitol on January 6. A great deal, a good amount, not very much, or not at all?" The overall response showed 57 percent agreement by the respondents to "a great deal/a good amount," with 37 percent at "not very much/or not at all." But the most important data lay with the division by political party affiliation. Ninety-two percent of the Democrats polled agreed with the "a great deal/a good amount," categories, whereas as 79 percent of Republicans sided with the "not very much/or not at all" categories.[75] Clearly, regardless of the information learned by the Committee, few Republicans were moved by the evidence.

THE JANUARY 6 INSURRECTION IN PERSPECTIVE

The events related to the January 6, 2021, insurrection were hardly spontaneous or without considerable thought. The incident itself was well-planned, coordinated, and sanctioned by participants inside and outside of the federal government. With an understaffed Capitol police force and the delayed arrival of reinforcements, the rioters achieved their immediate goal of breaking into the building. Their "success"—if such a term could be given to describe an effort to overturn the government—ended after a relatively brief occupation of the building. At that, tremendous damage was done physically, to those who died or were harmed, and perhaps even more significantly, to the reputation of a nation with an impressive history for the peaceful transfer of power.

Analysts and academics will debate the extent to which President Donald Trump managed the entire sad affair, although investigation by Special Counsel Jack Smith, appointed by Attorney General Merrick Garland, may offer clarity. Nevertheless, Trump's fingerprints were on enough parts of the multifaceted operation to confirm his substantial involvement. Moreover, beyond his own direct efforts, Trump had considerable cooperation and assistance from allies in and out of government in executing the insurrection—lots of help from lots of people in different places.

The insurrection was a response as much to political conditions as it was AN attempt at change, although patently illegal and a profound threat to our democracy. Much like a slowly disappearing glacier, a gradual shift in the nation's demography threatened the status of a sizable swath of White citizens over their once dominant position in American society. Continuous immigration of non-White people and non-Christians continued to alter the nation's demographic composition without any sign of slowing down. Those who felt particularly endangered rebelled from time to time by replacing elected officials felt ignored and left behind, but such activities never seemed to provide any relief.

Then, along came Donald Trump. He wasn't the first to hear the cries of those who viewed themselves as "oppressed Whites," but he reacted in ways that other politicians hadn't. Most elected officials didn't listen, or that's how it seemed, anyway. But Trump did. He not only complained about the changing demography as the offended White people did, but Trump campaigned for change—*real* change. He would put a stop to "different" people flooding our country and threatening "our culture." He would leave it to other nations to solve their own problems. Trump would put America first, especially White America. Just elect him President, he said, and he would follow through.

Dispossessed White people joined with fiscal conservatives, evangelicals, and others in the Republican orbit to elect him and Trump went about changing America. But when he ran for reelection to continue his make-over, Trump lost according to official vote counts. But official results didn't matter to Trump, who had even warned ahead of time how powerful forces would "rig" the outcome. Sure enough, large numbers of votes appeared at key vote tabulation centers long after the polls had closed, the "fix" was in, and Trump's disciples were the losers for it just like they'd been in suffering the brunt from the country's evolution. So, when Trump called for an insurrection after the 2020 election, his minions were ready to oblige not only him, but their call for rebirth. They revolted not only in response to the election, but because of their perceived loss of dignity and potential slippage to second-class citizenship in American society. They meant business.

Meanwhile, most Republican leaders and elected officials had gravitated into Trump's circle, not always because they agreed with him, but because they won with him, at least in the early going. And when the insurrection occurred, most Republicans in the House of Representatives and a handful of Republican U.S. Senators actually voted against confirming the outcome. They were silent co-conspirators in beliefs, if not action.

In the end, order was restored and the insurrection had failed. But what about Trump? And Trumpism? And Republicans? We will discuss these topics in the next chapter.

NOTES

1. The Committee's eighteen-month findings are reported in *The January 6th Report* (Random House, New York, NY, 2023).

2. "Post-election, Extremists Use Fringe Social Networks to Push Fraud Claims, Violence," *Politico*, November 13, 2020, https://www.politico.com/news/2020/11/13/extremists-fringe-social-media-election-fraud-436369.

3. "82% of Fox News Viewers Believe the Election Was Stolen: New Poll," *Mediate*, November 1, 2021, https://www.mediaite.com/politics/82-of-fox-news-viewers-believe-the-election-was-stolen-new-poll/.

4. "Off the Air. Fox News Stars Blasted the Election Fraud Scheme they Peddled," *NPR*, February 16, 2023, https://www.npr.org/2023/02/16/1157558299/fox-news-stars-false-claims-trump-election-2020.

5. "Trump's Unconstitutional View of Presidential Power," *Expert Forum*, American Constitutional Society, April 16, 2020, https://www.acslaw.org/expertforum/trumps-unconstitutional-view-presidential-power/.

6. See "Trump Threatens to Adjourn Congress to Get His Nominees but likely would be Impeded by Senate Rules," *The Washington Post*, April 16, 2020, https://www.washingtonpost.com/politics/trump-threatens-to-adjourn-congress-to-get-his-nominees-through/2020/04/15/e3bfc4c6-7f6a-11ea-9040-68981f488eed_story.html and "Trump Threatens to Adjourn Congress to Get His Nominees Through," *Courthouse News Service*, April 15, 2020, https://www.courthousenews.com/trump-threatens-to-adjourn-congress-to-get-his-nominees-through/.

7. "Trump Wanted I.R.S. Investigations of Foes, Top Aide Says," *The New York Times*, November 14, 2022, https://www.nytimes.com/2022/11/13/us/politics/trump-irs-investigations.html/.

8. "Trump Repeatedly Pressed Ikraine President to Investigate Biden's Son," *The Wall Street Journal,* September 21, 2019, https://www.wsj.com/articles/trump-defends-conversation-with-ukraine-leader-11568993176.

9. "In His Own Words: The President's Attacks on the Courts," The Brennan Center for Justice, June 5, 2020, https://www.brennancenter.org/our-work/research-reports/his-own-words-presidents-attacks-courts.

10. Peter Baker and Susan Glasser, *The Divider: Trump in the White House, 2017-2021* (New York, NY: Doubleday Publishers, 2022), p. 285.

11. Henry J. Abraham, *The Judicial Process*, 6th ed. (New York, NY: Oxford University Press, 1993), p. 166.

12. "How Trump Compares with Other Recent Presidents in Appointing Federal Judges," Pew Research Center, January 13, 2021, https://www.pewresearch.org/fact-tank/2021/01/13/how-trump-compares-with-other-recent-presidents-in-appointing-federal-judges/.

13. The only "victory" by the Trump team occurred when a Pennsylvania judge reduced the amount of time for a small number of voters to fix errors in their mail-in ballots.

14. U.S. 3rd Circuit Court Appeals Judge Stephanos Bibas, quoted in "Take it from the 'Trump' Judges: There was No Election Fraud," *Westlaw Today*, January 5, 2021, https://today.westlaw.com/Document/I97e9ff804fb211eb8404f825ce3db5c8/View/FullText.html?transitionType=Default&contextData=(sc.Default)&firstPage=true.

15. Quoted in Bob Woodward and Robert Costa, *Peril* (New York, NY: Simon & Schuster, 2021), p. 180.

16. Barr discusses this theory at length in the *Harvard Journal of Law and Public Policy*. See his "The Role of the Executive," 3, no. 3 (Summer 2020), https://www.nbcbayarea.com/news/politics/reviewing-nancy-pelosis-leadership/3083544/.

17. "Mueller Complained that Barr's Letter did not Capture the 'Context' of Trump Probe," *The Washington Post*, April 19, 2019, https://www.washingtonpost.com/world/national-security/mueller-complained-that-barrs-letter-did-not-capture-context-of-trump-probe/2019/04/30/d3c8fdb6-6b7b-11e9-a66d-a82d3f3d96d5_story.html.

18. Quoted in "77 Days: Trump's Campaign to Subvert the Election," *The New York Times*, February 1, 2021, https://www.nytimes.com/2021/01/31/us/trump-election-lie.html.

19. "WATCH: Trump Pressured Justice Department to Seize States' Voting Machines, Former DOJ Officials Say," *PBS News Hour*, June 23, 2022, https://www.pbs.org/newshour/politics/watch-trump-pressured-justice-department-to-seize-states-voting-machines-former-doj-officials-say.

20. "Jan. 6 Panel Outlines Trump's Bid to Coerce Justice Dept. Officials," *The New York Times*, June 23, 2022, https://www.nytimes.com/2022/06/23/us/politics/jan-6-hearing-trump-justice-department.html.

21. Ibid.

22. "Report: Trump Wanted to Fire Acting AG Rosen Because He Wouldn't Help Overturn the Election," *Forbes*, January 22, 2021, https://www.forbes.com/sites/rachelsandler/2021/01/22/report-trump-wanted-to-fire-acting-ag-rosen-because-he-wouldnt-help-overturn-the-election/?sh=4d07510460a5.

23. "Trump and Justice Dept. Lawyer Said to Have Plotted to Oust Acting Attorney," *The New York Times*, October 13, 2022, https://www.nytimes.com/2021/01/22/us/politics/jeffrey-clark-trump-justice-department-election.html.

24. The seven states were Arizona, Georgia, Michigan, Nevada, New Mexico, Pennsylvania, and Wisconsin.

25. "Trump-Allied Lawyers Pursued Voting Machine Data in Multiple States, Records Reveal," *The Washington Post*, August 15, 2022, https://www.washingtonpost.com/investigations/2022/08/15/sidney-powell-coffee-county-sullivan-strickler/.

26. Quoted in "Timeline: False Alternative Slate of Electors Scheme, Donald Trump and His Close Associates," *Just Security*, July 18, 2022, www.Justsecurity.org.

27. "Ron Johnson Tried to Hand Fake info to Mike Pence on Jan.6, Panel Reveals," *Politico*, June 21, 2022, https://www.politico.com/news/2022/06/21/jan-6-panel-trump-overturn-2020-election-00040816.

28. "UPDATED Trump's Fake Electors: Here's the Full List," *AZ Mirror*, June 29, 2022, https://www.azmirror.com/2022/06/29/updated-trumps-fake-electors-heres-the-full-list/.

29. "The Fake Electors Scheme, Explained," *The New York Times*, August 3, 2022, https://www.google.com/search?q=the+fake+electors+scheme%2C+explained&rlz=1C5CHFA_enUS773US773&oq=the+fake+electors+scheme%2C+explained&aqs=chrome..69i57.13225j0j7&sourceid=chrome&ie=UTF-8.

30. For a full transcript of the conversation, see "I Just Want To Find 11,780 votes': In Extraordinary Hour-Long Call, Trump Pressures Georgia Secretary of State to Recalculate the Vote in His Favor," *The Washington Post*, January 3, 2021, https://www.washingtonpost.com/politics/trump-raffensperger-call-transcript-georgia-vote/2021/01/03/2768e0cc-4ddd-11eb-83e3-322644d82356_story.html.

31. "Trump Calls on GOP State Legislators to Overturn Election Results," *Politico*, November 21, 2020, https://www.politico.com/news/2020/11/21/trump-state-legislatures-overturn-election-results-439031, and "Exclusive: Trump Urges State Legislators to Reject Electoral Votes, 'You Are the Real Power,'" *Washington Examiner*, January 2, 2021, https://www.washingtonexaminer.com/washington-secrets/exclusive-trump-urges-state-legislators-to-reject-electoral-votes-you-are-the-real-power.

32. Mike Pence, *So Help Me God* (New York, NY: Simon & Schuster, 2022), p. 460.

33. "Trump Presses Pence to 'Come Through' and Overturn Electoral College Results at Georgia Rally," *Independent*, January 5, 2021, https://www.independent.co.uk/news/world/americas/us-election-2020/trump-pence-electoral-college-georgia-rally-b1782330.html.

34. Quoted in "Trump Tells Pence to Show 'Extreme Courage' and Overturn Results," *NPR*, January 6, 2021 https://www.npr.org/sections/congress-electoral-college-tally-live-updates/2021/01/06/953907019/trump-tells-pence-to-show-extreme-courage-and-overturn-results.

35. "Trump Wanted Armed Supporters Allowed into Jan. 6 Rally and to Lead Capitol Charge, Aid Says," *Roll Call*, June 28, 2022, https://rollcall.com/2022/06/28/trump-wanted-armed-supporters-allowed-into-jan-6-rally-and-to-lead-capitol-charge/.

36. Ibid.

37. Quoted in "Trumps Words, and Deeds, Reveal Depths of His Drive to Keep Power," *The New York Times*, February 1, 2022, https://www.nytimes.com/2022/02/01/us/politics/trump-election-jan-6-voting-machines.html.

38. "New Evidence Suggests 'Alliance' between Oath Keepers, Proud Boys Ahead of Jan. 6," *Politico*, March 25, 2021, https://www.politico.com/news/2021/03/24/oath-keepers-proud-boys-alliance-capitol-riot-477741.

39. "GOP Lawmakers were 'Intimately Involved' in Jan. 6 Protest Planning, New Report Shows," *PBS News Hour*, October 25, 2021, https://www.pbs.org/newshour/show/gop-lawmakers-were-intimately-involved-in-jan-6-protest-planning-new-report-shows.

40. "Of Course Fox News Is Fueling Election Denialism," *Vanity Fair*, November 9, 2020, https://issueone.org/articles/60-of-president-donald-trumps-post-election-tweets-sought-to-undermine-legitimacy-of-presidential-race/.

41. Megan Garber, "Fox Hits a Dangerous New Low," *The Atlantic*, December 6, 2020, https://www.theatlantic.com/culture/archive/2020/11/fox-news-trump-election-dangerous-new-low/617019. /

42. "Fox News Hosts Sow Distrust in Legitimacy of Election," *CNN*, November 5, 2020, https://www.cnn.com/2020/11/05/media/fox-news-prime-time-election/index.html.

43. "Off the Air. Fox News Stars Blasted the Election Fraud Claims they Peddled."

44. "Permanent Suspension of @realDonaldTrump," *Twitter*, January 8, 2021, https://blog.twitter.com/en_us/topics/company/2020/suspension.

45. "60% of President Donald Trump's Post-election Tweets Sought to Undermine Legitimacy of Presidential Race," *Issue One*, February 9, 2021, https://issueone.org/articles/60-of-president-donald-trumps-post-election-tweets-sought-to-undermine-legitimacy-of-presidential-race/.

46. Ryan-Kor-Sins, "The Alt-Right Digital Migration: A Heterogeneous Engineering Approach to Social Media Platform Branding," *New Media and Society*, 2021, https://journals.sagepub.com/doi/10.1177/14614448211038810.

47. "Members of Several Well-Known Hate Groups Identified at Capitol Riot," *Propublica*, January 9, 2021, https://www.propublica.org/article/several-well-known-hate-groups-identified-at-capitol-riot.

48. "Proud Boys Memo Reveals Meticulous Planning for 'Street-Level Violence,'" *The Guardian*, September 19, 2022, https://www.theguardian.com/world/2022/sep/19/proud-boys-document-jan-6-violence.

49. Quoted in "'We must Defeat Them': New Evidence Details Oath Keepers' 'Civil War' Timeline," *The Guardian*, https://www.theguardian.com/us-news/2022/oct/08/oath-keepers-trial-evidence-civil-war.

50. Quoted in "We Have to Push the Envelope," Political Research Associates, January 5, 2022, https://politicalresearch.org/2022/01/05/we-have-push-envelope.

51. Quoted in "U.S. Investigating Possible Ties between Roger Stone, Alex Jones, and Capitol Rioters," *The Washington Post*, February 20, 2021, https://www.washingtonpost.com/local/legal-issues/stone-jones-capitol-riot-investigation-radicalization/2021/02/19/97d6e6ee-6cad-11eb-9ead-673168d5.

52. "Members of Right-Wing Militias, Extremist Groups Are Charged in Capitol Siege," *NPR*, January 19, 2021, https://www.npr.org/sections/insurrection-at-the-capitol/2021/01/19/958240531/members-of-right-wing-militias-extremist-groups-are-latest-charged-in-capitol-si.

53. Abigail Blender, "In Pictures: Insurrection and Anti-Semitism at the Capitol Riots," *Moment*, January 8, 2021, https://momentmag.com/pictures-anti-semitism-at-the-capitol-riots/.

54. "Why Veterans of the Military and Law Enforcement Joined the Capitol Insurrection," *Los Angeles Times*, January 15, 2021, https://www.latimes.com/world-nation/story/2021-01-15/capitol-riot-police-veterans-extremists.

55. "How Many Newly Elected Officials and Congressional Candidates were 'involved' in the Capitol Riot," *Politifact*, December 2, 2021, https://www.nytimes.com/2022/09/06/us/politics/jan-6-griffin-insurrection.html.

56. "American Face of Insurrection," Chicago Project on Security and Threats, University of Chicago, Chicago, IL, https://d3qi0qp55mx5f5.cloudfront.net/cpost/i/docs/Pape_-_American_Face_of_Insurrection_(2022-01-05).pdf?mtime=1654548769.

57. "'So the Traitors Know the Stakes:' The Meaning of the Jan.6 Gallows," *The New York Times*, June 16, 2022, https://www.nytimes.com/2022/06/16/us/politics/jan-6-gallows.html.

58. "A Jan. 6 Mystery: Why Did It Take So Long to Deploy the National Guard?" *The New York Times*, July 7, 2021, https://www.nytimes.com/2022/07/21/us/politics/national-guard-january-6-riot.html.

59. Quoted in "McCarthy Told Trump that Jan. 6 Rioters 'were trying to f...... Kill Me': Book," *The Hill*, October 11, 2022, https://thehill.com/homenews/house/3682571-mccarthy-told-trump-that-jan-6-rioters-were-trying-to-ing-kill-me-book/.

60. One examination of the delay lists a minimum of three possibilities. However, none takes issue with Trump's desire to see the event happen. See Ryan Goodman and Justin Hendrix, "Crisis of Command: The Pentagon, the President, and January 6," *Just Security*, December 21, 21, 2021, https://thehill.com/homenews/house/3682571-mccarthy-told-trump-that-jan-6-rioters-were-trying-to-ing-kill-me-book/.

61. "McConnell Blames Trump, Others in Power for Provoking Capitol Riot: 'The Mob was Fed Lies,'" *Chicago Tribune*, January 19, 2021, https://www.chicagotribune.com/nation-world/ct-nw-mitch-mcconnell-trump-capitol-riots-20210119-wcvfpibhjrhohimy3y4wckdfbq-story.html.

62. "McCarthy Says Trump 'Bears Responsibility' for Capitol Riot," *Politico*, January 13, 2021, https://www.politico.com/news/2021/01/13/mccarthy-trump-responsibility-capitol-riot-458975.

63. This conversation is discussed at length in Jonathan Martin and Alexander Burns, *This Will Not Pass* (New York, NY: Simon & Schuster, 2022), 222-223.

64. "McCarthy Joins List of Top Republicans Trying to Mend Fences With Trump," *The New York Times*, January 29, 2021, https://www.google.com/search?q=McCarthy+Joins+List+of+Top+Republicans+Trying+to+Mend+Fences+With+Trump&rlz=1C5CHFA_enUS773US773&oq=McCarthy+Joins+List+of+Top+Republicans+Trying+to+Mend+Fences+With+Trump&aqs=chrome..69i57.30151j0j7&sourceid=chrome&ie=UTF-8.

65. "G.O.P Declares Jan. 6 Attack 'Legitimate Political Discourse,'" *The New York Times*, February 4, 2022, https://www.google.com/search?q=McCarthy+Joins+List+of+Top+Republicans+Trying+to+Mend+Fences+With+Trump&rlz=1C5CHFA_enUS773US773&oq=McCarthy+Joins+List+of+Top+Republicans+Trying+to+Mend+Fences+With+Trump&aqs=chrome..69i57.30151j0j7&sourceid=chrome&ie=UTF-8.

66. Quoted in "A Republican House Member just Described January 6 as a 'Normal Tourist Visit,'" *CNN*, May 13, 2013, https://www.nbcbayarea.com/news/politics/why-is-california-a-key-state-for-republicans/3269582/.

67. "McConnell Denounces R.N.C. Censure of Jan. 6 Panel Members," *The New York Times*, February 8, 2022, https://www.nytimes.com/2022/02/08/us/politics/republicans-censure-mcconnell.html.

68. "National: Faith in American System Drops," Monmouth University Poll, July 7, 2022, https://www.monmouth.edu/polling-institute/documents/monmouthpoll_us_070722.pdf/.

69. See Lindsay Chervinsky, "The U.S. Has Weathered Crises Before. Here's Why Jan. 6 Was Different," *Governing*, January 6, 2022, https://www.governing.com/context/the-u-s-has-weathered-crises-before-heres-why-jan-6-was-different.

70. "National: More Americans Happy about Trump Loss than Biden Win," Monmouth University Poll, November 18, 2020, https://www.monmouth.edu/polling-institute/documents/monmouthpoll_us_111820.pdf/.

71. "National: Faith in American System Drops."

72. "Trump Impeached for Inciting Insurrection," *The New York Times*, January 13, 2021, https://www.nytimes.com/2021/01/13/us/politics/trump-impeached.html.

73. "4 Final Takeaways from Trump's Impeachment Trial," *The Washington Post*, February 13, 2021, https://www.washingtonpost.com/politics/2021/02/13/takeaways-trump-impeachment-trial-final/.

74. See "Bipartisan House Probe of Jan. 6 Insurrection Falls Apart after Pelosi Blocks Two GOP Members," *The Washington Post*, July 21, 2021, https://www.washingtonpost.com/politics/pelosi-mccarthy-jan6-committee/2021/07/21/21722d44-ea41-11eb-84a2-d93bc0b50294_story.html.

75. These data come from "The January 6th Hearings, July 2022," *NPR/Marist Poll*, July 21, 2022, https://maristpoll.marist.edu/polls/npr-pbs-newshour-marist-national-poll-the-january-6th-hearings-july-2022/.

Chapter 10

Trump on the Wane?

No longer in office after January 20, 2021, former president Donald Trump found himself in the middle of a half dozen investigations ranging from a seemingly never-ending defamation and sexual assault accusation to possible federal charges concerning his unsuccessful efforts to continue in office. Civil cases could be dealt with relatively easily since the penalties usually came in the form of monetary penalties. Criminal cases were another matter, however. Questions about top secret government documents found at his Mar-a-Lago residence and other properties, misuse of his powers while in office, and the extent to which Trump may have been involved in the now infamous January 6, 2021, insurrection at the Capitol were serious and not about to disappear. Allegations that he attempted to reverse the outcome of the presidential election in Georgia by demanding that the Georgia Secretary of State illegally add enough votes to secure victory in the Peach State also haunted Trump. Being president would have protected Trump from most, but not all, of the dicey criminal questions, or at a minimum extended a shield from prosecution until the end of another four-year term. But with his departure from office, that legal wall no longer safeguarded him. Legally, he was vulnerable as he had never been before.

Initially, Trump may have been comforted knowing that no former president had ever been indicted on any state or federal crime, much less convicted. Given that history, perhaps he could with his seemingly endless collection of attorneys, somehow navigate his way through these troubled political waters one more time. But that wasn't to be the case. Increasingly, the question seemed to be not whether Trump would suffer political damage but how much.

Still, Trump remained the titular head of the Republican Party, courtesy of his recent presidency. Much of the Republican base, *his* people, remained steadfastly in his corner. Throughout 2021, between 65 and 75 percent of Republicans believed that the 2020 election had been stolen from Trump, and that core belief was his most important asset.[1] Similar Republican percentages were quick to endorse him for another presidential election run well in advance of the 2024 campaign. In an October 2021 Quinnipiac Poll, a whopping 78 percent of his political party members wanted Trump to run for the presidency in 2024.[2] Even in March 2023, on the verge of his Manhattan indictment for money laundering, another Quinnipiac Poll found that 93 percent of Republicans viewed the charges as "motivated by politics;" the same poll counted 72 percent of Republicans saying that the former president had "mainly a positive impact on their political party."[3] With so much encouraging political wind at his back, Trump felt as if he had free rein and behaved as if he were untouchable. Indictments, he said, would not keep him from seeking a second term to the presidency. Nothing would.

As for those who opposed Trump, more times than not they paid a price, especially if they were Republicans. Trump had no room for what he considered treason, and he deemed those Republicans who voted to impeach him perpetrators of that crime. And they would pay for their disloyalty. Of the ten Republican incumbents in the House of Representatives who voted to impeach Trump for inciting the January 6 insurrection, only two were re-elected in 2022. The balance of the anti-Trumpers either retired because of unfavorable redistricting courtesy of the 2020 census, the threat of a well-financed Trump-backed primary election opponent, or by losing to a Trump-backed candidate in their primary, which was potentially the most humiliating price of all.[4] Most of the other elected Republicans quietly kept their negative thoughts about Trump to themselves, not exactly a badge of courage but at least a way of maintaining political survival.

Beyond his Republican base, Trump had other arrows in his political quiver. The collection of alt-right racist groups that had supported his failed 2020 re-election bid remained unwaveringly loyal in 2021 and thereafter. Trump had been good to them through his frequent public condemnations about immigrants, non-White racial and ethnic groups, and religious minorities. Several times during and after the 2020 campaign, Trump also had tweeted and retweeted comments supportive of racist leaders and organizations.[5] At last, the radical right-wing extremists thought, someone with power is really looking out for us.

There were blips for Trump, to be sure. The 2022 midterms were admittedly a blow to his seemingly omnipotent stature, as many of his anointed candidates who won their primaries suffered defeat in the general election. Of importance, however, was that the essence of his message was digested and echoed by other leaders and would-be leaders in his political party. Simply put, the alt-right racist messages of so many White Republicans wasn't about to go away, Trump or no Trump. Moreover, they came in greater numbers than many had anticipated.

Nevertheless, legal problems surrounded Trump in a circle-like fashion that seemed to become smaller over time. Between a series of bad 2022 election results attributed to his questionable candidate endorsements and mounting woes from state and federal investigations, Trump no longer appeared so invincible. For some, the magic he seemed to possess in the 2016 presidential race seemed to be losing its potency.

This chapter begins with a discussion of Donald Trump's post-election legal problems. Their outcomes had the potential to impact Trump's future, perhaps even derail it. Beyond Trump's uncertain prospects in electoral politics, we focus on the authoritarian themes of leaders in and out of the Republican Party, and political candidates that enabled the continuation of Trumpism. As discussed earlier in this volume, American history has long been filled with persistent racist and potential authoritarian patterns, although in the past, they eventually were checked by combinations of leaders, norms, laws, and even an awakened public. Maybe, not this time, however. Through his own words, Trump had conferred a huge validation to bigots who sought meaningful action beyond symbolic rhetoric. In their eyes, he gave them legitimacy on the political stage and they would take advantage of it. In return, Trump would seek advantage from their loyalty when he sought presidential renewal in 2024.

WINNING THE PRIMARY BATTLES, LOSING THE GENERAL ELECTION WAR

Trump's problems with his candidate endorsements that originally appeared in 2018 continued with the 2020 elections. Along with Trump campaigning for a second term, all 435 districts of the House of Representatives and 35 seats in the U.S. Senate were at stake. Heading into the 2020 campaign, a Democratic majority controlled the House of Representatives, while Republicans held sway over the Senate. At the election's end, House Democrats continued their majority, albeit in smaller numbers.

But the real surprise came in the U.S. Senate. At the end of the November 3, 2020, election, the candidates for two seats held by Republicans in Georgia were forced into a January 5, 2021, runoff because neither candidate in each race had received 50 percent plus one of the votes as required by state law. In the full six-year term primary, favored Republican incumbent David Perdue edged Democratic challenger Jon Ossoff 49.7 percent to 47.9 percent. In the other Georgia Senatorial election for the final two years of a vacated seat temporarily occupied by gubernatorial appointee Republican Kelly Loeffler,[6]

Democrat challenger Raphael Warnock with 32.9 percent bested Loeffler's 25.9 percent and Republican challenger Doug Collins with 20.0 percent. For Senate Republicans, winning at least one of the two runoffs was critical to keeping their majority in the upper chamber because at the end of the November 3 elections, there were 50 Senate Republicans and 48 Democrats. Given the state's conservative political history, Georgia Republicans felt good about their chances in the January runoff, but the races didn't end that way.

Trump, wildly popular among Georgia Republicans, campaigned in the Georgia runoffs. Yet, rather than urge voters to come out for the two Republicans on the January 5th runoff date, Trump spent the bulk of his time revisiting grievances associated with his 2020 presidential defeat. His criticisms also focused on Governor Brian Kemp and fellow Republican Secretary of State Brad Raffensberger for allowing a "rigged" election to take place in Georgia, helping to prevent a Trump victory. Trump went so far as to tell the crowd at a rally the night before the runoff election, "I'll be here (in Georgia) in about a year and a half campaigning against your governor, I guarantee you."[7]

The result was that, astonishingly, the two Democrats prevailed. Ossoff squeaked by Perdue 50.6 percent to 49.4 percent, while Warnock narrowly defeated Loeffler 50.5 percent to 49.5 percent. Those two victories evened Senate Democrats with Republicans at 50 members each, but Democrats gained the majority with Democratic Vice President Kamala Harris in the chamber to cast any tie-breaking votes. Now, the presidency, House of Representatives, and the Senate all were under Democratic control, a nightmare for Republicans.

How could such an election outcome have happened? Most Republican strategists blamed Trump for focusing on himself and his issues instead of the critically important Republican Senatorial campaigns.[8] Angered by Trump's insistence of a "stolen" November presidential election, Republicans, at least enough of them, didn't bother to vote.

Matters didn't improve for Trump in the 2022 elections. In his position as former president, Trump continued to present himself as the gatekeeper for aspiring candidates as well as many of those already in office. During the winter and spring of 2022, countless would-be Republican candidates for various offices trekked to Mar-a-Lago, where they made their case for a Trump endorsement. In advance of their meetings, some would-be candidates hired Trump advisers to help them win the former president's endorsement. Others hoped to win Trump's blessing by holding fundraisers at his properties which, according to one account, collectively deposited $1.4 million into Trump-owned businesses.[9] During on-site interviews, Trump would inquire about the candidates' portfolios containing poll results, fundraising data, local endorsements, media exposure, and the candidates' chances against the opposition for winning the party nomination. Shortly thereafter, Trump would announce his endorsement intentions. Of course, he was particularly interested in supporting candidates with interests in "primarying" Republican adversaries who had not subscribed to Trump's claim of election fraud in the 2020 presidential election.[10]

It turned out that most of Trump's endorsements were perfunctory, but necessary to give him the appearance of a high success rate at the election's end. He loaded up supporting Republican incumbents and Republican candidates in open Republican-favored congressional districts and state contests, most of whom emerged victorious in November, where they would have won, anyway. Beyond the superficial numbers, however, Trump's candidates in competitive states fared poorly, and those were the races that could make a difference. With respect to governors' elections in open states (no incumbents), Democrats flipped three (Arizona, Massachusetts, Maryland), while Republicans flipped one (Nevada).

But the real damage occurred at the federal level. In four Senate seats considered toss-ups (Georgia, Ohio, Pennsylvania, Wisconsin), Trump candidates won only one state. Also, in five of the most competitive House races, all of Trump's candidates lost. As a result, House Republicans wound up with a slim four-seat majority instead of the 40–50 seats that nonpartisan experts had predicted during the summer.

Most of the Republican candidates in those defeats had secured their nominations with Trump support, particularly for their claims that the 2020 presidential election had been laced with fraud. But the voters weren't buying it. According to Charlie Cook, a well-respected nonpartisan political analyst, "candidate quality and the toxicity of former president Trump and the MAGA movement hurt certain Republicans where it (the vote) mattered most."[11] Senate Minority Leader Mitch McConnell was less gracious, concluding that "Our (Republican) ability to control the primary (elections) outcome was quite limited in '22 because the support of the former president proved to be very decisive in these primaries. . . . We tended to having a candidate quality test."[12] Translation: Trumpendorsed candidates more for their loyalty to him than their qualities as contenders for elected office, and in many cases, the voters weren't impressed.

It didn't help Trump's cause that during the 2022 campaign, he doubled down on accusations of voter fraud and racist associations. He had been barred from major social media platforms, Facebook and Twitter, in 2021 for repeatedly breaking their rules related to messages inciting violence. So, Trump and a few supporters created his own social media platform, Truth Social. In short order, he endorsed a rash of unsupported conspiracy claims ranging from accusations that the FBI was "a campaign arm of the Democratic Party" to QAnon posts about the Satan-worshipping Democratic pedophiles.[13]

Looking back at previous Trump candidate endorsements, there is some evidence suggesting that Trump's Republican 2022 candidate primary election successes may have been more elusive than real. According to one study of Trump-endorsed Republican nominees in the 2018 Congressional elections, Republicans actually would have captured 11 more House races and four more Senate races had Trump refrained from involvement in the contests. The authors concluded that Trump's endorsements did "little to elicit engagement from voters on the Republican side, all the while creating a rallying effect around opposing candidates and increasing engagement among Democratic voters."[14] So, perhaps there were limits after all.

TROUBLE FROM ALL SIDES

Donald Trump enjoyed a long history of avoiding, or at least minimizing, trouble with governmental entities. Early in his career, when indicted by the federal government for discriminatory practices relating to rents, he settled with a fine. He had even fewer problems with the private sector, where he often clashed with opponents, commonly emerging unscathed. According to a study by *USA Today*, Trump and his businesses had been involved in more than 3,500 legal actions at the federal and state court levels during the last three decades preceding his 2016 presidential election victory.[15] When accused of violating contractual agreements, Trump protected himself with a collection of lawyers who, thanks to Trump's deep pockets, usually wore out the underfunded opposition.[16] Yet, over time, Trump's questionable, if not illegal, activities caught up with him.

State and Local Government Levels

Throughout 2021, 2022, and into 2023, former president Donald Trump found himself under the legal microscopes of several governmental jurisdictions. In Fulton County, Georgia, District Attorney Fani Willis led an investigation of Trump's possible obstruction of justice related to the 2020 presidential election. Specifically, the issue concerned his possible role in recruiting fake electoral college Republican delegates instead of the Democratic delegates chosen in the election. There was also a focus on Trump's previous demand that Georgia Secretary of State Brad Raffensberger "find" 11,780 votes for his candidacy, enough for Trump to win the election in Georgia and therefore the state's 16 electoral delegates. Indictments looked likely, although the central question was whether they would focus on Trump alone, include Georgia elected officials, or both. Either way, the optics were not good.

In December 2022, a New York City jury found the Trump organization guilty of a tax-fraud scheme where the company knowingly provided valuable benefits to two high-ranking employees that were not reported by the organization to the IRS.[17] Trump described the incident as income tax evasion by employees who failed to report the payments. Nevertheless, as the result of a guilty verdict on 17 counts of tax fraud, Trump's company was fined $1.62 million.[18] It marked the first time that a Trump company had actually been found at fault by a court.

A much more serious problem for Trump unfolded at about the same time at the state level. New York State Attorney General Leticia James alleged in a 220-page document that Trump's companies repeatedly underreported the values of properties for tax purposes while overvaluing the same properties when applying for bank loans. As a result, James argued, the organization profited illegally to the tune of $250 million, an amount the state demanded in its lawsuit.[19] In this case, Trump and three of his adult children Donald, Jr., Eric, and Ivanka were all cited as defendants. Trump characterized the case as "another Witch Hunt by a racist Attorney General, Leticia James,"[20] who was Black. The case was scheduled for trial in October 2023. Predictably, Trump immediately criticized the presiding judge, calling him "a vicious, biased, and mean 'rubber stamp' for the Communist takeover of the great & prosperous American company that I have built over a long period of years."[21] Meanwhile, in response to a petition by the attorney general, the judge in the case assigned an independent monitor to make sure that Trump refrained from moving his organization's resources elsewhere.

Then there was the E. Jean Carroll trial, which ended with a unanimous verdict and the Manhattan hush money charges. On May 9, 2023, Trump was found liable in a civil suit for sexually abusing and defaming writer E. Jean Carroll over her allegations of rape years earlier. The jurors voted unanimously to assess Trump a fine of just under $5 million as compensation. Trump called the verdict "a disgrace," blamed the judge and media for prejudiced behavior, and he appealed.[22]

There was more. On March 30, 2023, Trump was indicted by a Manhattan Grand Jury on 34 charges for illegally transferring hush money payments prior to the 2016 election as part of an effort to prevent the voters from knowing about two previous affairs. The judge in the case set a firm trial date for March 25, 2024, smack in the middle of the Republican presidential primary season. Whether that helped or hurt Trump remained to be seen.

Federal Level

Trump's problems at the state level paled compared to his problems with federal authorities. At the end of his presidency in January 2021, Trump found himself in trouble with the federal government on two fronts: unlawful possession of government documents at his Mar-a-Lago residence and involvement with the January 6, 2021, insurrection against the Capitol in an attempt to overturn the 2020 presidential election results. In light of the potential gravity of both issues, in November 2022, Attorney General Merrick Garland appointed career Department of Justice prosecutor Jack Smith Special Counsel to oversee the ongoing investigations to assure "both independence and accountability."[23] The circumstances of these highly unusual events are explained below.

Disappearing Government Documents

When he left Washington, DC, the day before the inauguration of President Joe Biden, Donald Trump took numerous government documents along with his personal effects, even though prior to his departure, he had informed the National Archives that he had no such documents. It should be noted that by law a former president has no right to possess any material that appeared in his office during his stay other than personal gifts. But Trump's haul consisted of much more than gifts, including "confidential," "secret," and "top secret" documents, some of which could only be viewed in the most guarded setting. They included defense and national security secrets, information on U.S. allies and enemies, and the names and locations of irreplaceable undercover agents working for the United States who could lose their lives if discovered by enemy personnel.[24]

Shortly thereafter in early May 2021, the National Archives Office informed Trump that he still possessed several important official records, only to be told by Trump that there were no more records at Mar-a-Lago; between then and the end of the year, National Archives made several requests for return of the materials which were ignored. Finally, in January 2022, Archives representatives retrieved 15 boxes of government documents, some of which were torn into pieces. Several of the boxes included sensitive information not meant for public eyes. But the issue was hardly settled.

In June 2022, the FBI obtained a search warrant to pursue additional government documents that Trump had failed to send, even though his attorneys wrote that there were no more in Trump's residence. In August, armed with yet another search warrant, this time the FBI found 33 boxes at Mar-a-Lago, including more than 100 with classification markings. Several dozen were out of their jackets and scattered about in plain sight, all of which was contrary to federal government policy for sensitive documents.[25]

Upon losing custody of the documents, Trump sued to keep government agencies from examining the contents of the materials, but those efforts were rejected by the courts. There's more: In August 2022, Trump claimed he had declassified the materials through a "standing presidential order." Declassification is an intentionally cumbersome effort, however, which takes place only when the agency originally in charge of the documents—for example, Defense or the CIA—is formally made aware of the president's intention.[26] In other words, there is no way by which a president can declassify anything without bringing in appropriate government officials as part of the official process. Moreover, the Espionage Act of 1917 makes no allowance for a president alone to declassify defense-related information.

In a second effort to deflect concerns about his possession of government documents, Trump said that the president could declassify instantly or whenever he wanted. In Trump's words to Fox television host Sean Hannity, "If you're president of the United States, you can declassify just by saying it's declassified." Later in the conversation, Trump upped the ante, claiming without foundation that the president can declassify "even by thinking about it."[27] In an effort to justify his actions, Trump was literally creating new rules to explain away the potential crime.

It remains a mystery as to why Trump insisted on keeping government documents that were not his to retain. In interviews with the press, at least three of Trump's senior advisers stated that Trump claimed the documents were his property. He simply said, "they're (the documents) mine." Later on, Trump accused the FBI of "planting" the papers at his residence as part of a plot that would give the government justification for arresting him.[28] Trump's sense of entitlement notwithstanding, his possession of such valuable information caused a major investigation by the department of Justice. More to the point, he disregarded laws in favor of his own set of rules. The documents were his, he reasoned, just like *his* generals and *his* judges.

Trump caught a bit of a break on the documents issues temporarily when, shortly after the Mar-a-Lago disaster, classified documents were found at the outside office and home of President Joe Biden as well as the home of former vice president Mike Pence. Trump tried to explain the problem as universal to the three officeholders. In fact, there was a major difference: While Trump hid the documents from federal authorities, fought their repossession, and claimed personal ownership, Biden and Pence both cooperated fully about their presence and notified authorities as soon as they became aware of the problem.

On June 13, 2023, Trump was indicted by a federal Grand Jury on several federal charges in a 49-page meticulously organized and detailed document.[29] The grave charges included withholding and concealing dozens of several highly sensitive government documents, conspiring to obstruct justice, and making false statements to federal agents.[30] The news stunned the nation, although many savvy political observers saw it coming. Even more stunning, however, were the reactions of most Republicans seeking the party's presidential nomination. Florida's governor Ron DeSantis, Trump's closest competitor at the time, called the indictment "the weaponization of federal law enforcement." Former South Carolina governor Nikki Haley characterized the indictment as "prosecutorial overreach" and "vendetta politics," while U.S. Senator Tim Scott described the event as an example of "a justice system where the scales are weighted."[31] In the House of Representatives, Republican Speaker Kevin McCarthy tweeted "It is unconscionable for a President (Biden) to indict the leading candidate opposing him" and that the action step was a "grave injustice."[32] (As president, Biden had nothing whatsoever with the investigation.) Arizona Representative Andy Biggs, a defender of the January 6 insurrection, implied future violence, when se said "We have now reached a war phase . . . eye for eye."[33] Fox commentator Mark Levin joined the fray, citing the indictment as war on Trump and the Republican Party. Levin went on to proclaim the indictment "war on the Republic."[34]

It's important to note that none of the rebukes of the Trump indictment dealt with any of the merits of the allegations against the former president; instead, they focused on government institutions gone amuck. Their collective responses once again revealed that while Trump may have been the most prominent individual in disregarding U.S. law and traditions, he had plenty of company willing to accept, and perhaps even undertake such behavior in the context of "legitimate activities."

On June 13, 2023, the day of Trump's arraignment, the judge set a trial date. Given Trump's proclivity for stalling court dates through endless appeals—almost always rejected after lengthy reviews, it remained to be seen whether the trial would take place before the November 2024 presidential election.

January 6, 2021, Insurrection Fallout

As noted in chapter 9, the January 6 insurrection against Congress precipitated two investigations of the event: one by the House Select Committee and the other by Attorney General Merrick Garland, who ultimately offloaded the Department's investigation to a Special Council, long-time Department of Justice prosecutor Jack Smith. Most prominent of the many issues surrounding the unprecedented insurgency was the possible role of Trump, himself, in the activity.

Central to Trump's role in the January 6 insurrection was the "Be there, will be wild" tweet he issued on December 19, 2020, where he summoned his minions to attend a rally prior to confirmation of the November 2020 presidential election by Congress. In a chain reaction-like fashion, the leaders of several extremist and paramilitary groups repeated Trump's message to their members.

According to the final 845-page report issued by the Select Committee to Investigate the January Attack on the United States Capitol, Trump played a major role in "a multipart plan to overturn the 2020 presidential election."[35] He did so fully aware that he lost the election, not wondering or believing that he won. Star witness Cassidy Hutchinson, General Mark Milley, Chairman of the Joint Chiefs of Staff, and others heard both directly from Trump and his staff of Trump's awareness of his election defeat and his intent to reverse the result through any means possible, legally or otherwise.[36]

Trump's call for action to protest what he repeatedly described as a "stolen election" attracted his minions by the thousands. As discussed in chapter 9, the major players were the Oath Keepers, Proud Boys, and Three Percenters, along with several fringe groups as well as angry individuals all too eager to answer Trump's call at the rally. Trump's additional tweet on January 5 reminding his followers to show up the next day was a final prompt for the deadly violence to follow; then again, the would-be insurgents no longer needed any encouragement. Thousands were already in Washington, DC, many with firearms and other dangerous weapons.

As the insurrection unfolded, abundant evidence revealed that in addition to Trump's role in planning the attack, he did nothing to stop it. He showed absolutely no remorse or responsibility for bloodshed. The violence went on for 187 minutes before Trump politely requested the insurrectionists to leave. Even then, to the rioters Trump said "we love you," seemingly in gratitude for their violent action. After interviewing more than 1,000 witnesses and reviewing more than one million pages of documents, the Committee concluded that Trump was most responsible for the insurrection.[37]

The Select Committee had little power beyond its investigative authority. The members could recommend federal prosecution of those involved with the insurrection, but such suggestions carried no clout or route to action. The Committee could only hope that their mounds of information might persuade the Attorney General and Department of Justice to take action. For its part, Justice had been investigating Trump and the other January 6 protesters for months, although the secrecy with which it operates produced more speculation than actual knowledge. DOJ had to work that way to protect those who might be innocent as well as individuals who would only disclose information privately. There was also the matter of safeguarding evidence gathered until such time that it could be made public without compromising sources not yet fully mined. The delicacy of it all left some people fearful that the government's top prosecutorial body might have been intimated by the targets of its investigation, particularly former president Donald Trump.

It's not as if the DOJ had been idle. On the two-year anniversary of the January 6 attack, the Department announced that more than 1,000 individuals had been arrested in all 50 states. Many declared that they had been called to the insurrection by President Trump and were "only following instructions."³⁸ Those identified as leaders were treated quite differently, however. Nearly 300 had been charged with assault, resisting arrest, or impeding police officers; about 100 had been charged with the use of deadly or dangerous weapons; and 50 defendants had been charged with conspiracy. Another 465 rioters had pleaded guilty and accepted plea bargain arrangements. Of the 335 rioters completing the judicial process, 185 had been sentenced to prison and another 150 to local jails. At the two-year mark, 45 cases had been resolved at trial, with convictions obtained in all but one instance.

While many sentences had been relatively light to accommodate plea bargaining, some substantial convictions emerged. In one case, Oath Keeper leader Stewart Rhodes was convicted of several charges, including seditious conspiracy, and was sentenced to 18 years in prison. At the time of sentencing, the presiding judge said to Rhodes, "You, sir, present an ongoing threat and a peril to this country and to the republic and to the very fabric of this democracy."³⁹ Other prison sentences included 10 years to a former New York Police Department policeman for attacking a Capitol police officer with a flagpole, and five years to a man clothed in QAnon garb for chasing a police officer.⁴⁰

Donald Trump felt differently about the insurrection, the participants, and the outcomes. Six months after the event, in an interview on Fox News. He described the rioters as "patriots" and "great people."⁴¹ Trump extended his remarks about the insurrectionists in a televised Town Hall with CNN's Kaitlan Collins on May 11, 2023. When asked how he would treat the convicted insurrectionists, the former president responded that if re-elected, "I am inclined to pardon many of them (the insurrectionists) . . . a great portion."⁴² Given the federal investigation of Trump's potential role in the January 6 insurrection, those remarks would not be helpful to the former president. Meanwhile, Trump and the nation awaited the outcome of Special Council Jack Smith's investigation of any laws that Trump may have broken around the time of the January 6 tragedy.

On August 1, 2023, Smith presented a new indictment against the former president by the federal Grand Jury in Washington, DC. Referring to the events leading up to January 6, 2021, insurrection, the indictment focused on accusations that Trump attempted to defraud the United States with unproven claims that he won the 2020 election, that he conspired to obstruct the results of the election, and that he conspired to overturn the election outcome.⁴³ Ironically, the day before, the *New York Times* released a public opinion survey of Republicans showing that 71 percent believed that Trump had done nothing wrong during the turbulent post-2020 election period, versus 17 percent who believed that Trump's actions threatened American democracy.⁴⁴ Trump's base remained strong.

Comparing Federal and State Charges

There's little doubt that, for the most part, the federal charges against Trump are far more serious than those issued in the states. However, if upon conviction of the charges in either New York or Georgia, Trump would have great difficulty erasing the outcome, even if elected president. That's because the only time a state court outcome can be overturned at the federal level is when a federal court finds that the state trial has violated a federal constitutional guarantee of the accused individual.[45]

The federal charges were another matter for two reasons. First, as president, there is little doubt that Trump might seek to make any futured federal indictments disappear simply by instructing his Attorney General to dismiss the charges. Similarly, Trump might well have the power to pardon himself for any conviction or perhaps wipe any such convictions off the books. We say "might" because no such circumstances have ever occurred in American presidential history. The second concern centers on the timing of trials stemming from any federal charges. Given Trump's uncanny ability to use various motions as means to delay trials and the federal government's long-standing practice of keeping politically-related trials far from election times, there is every expectation that any federal trial date during the 2024 election year would be delayed until 2025. Given the two trial outcome possibilities—conviction or acquittal, Trump had much to gain from delay.

TRUMP DECLARES FOR THE 2024 PRESIDENTIAL NOMINATION

Astonishingly to some, none of the allegations, investigations, and court cases interfered with Donald Trump's future plans. On November 15, 2022, one week after the disappointing midterm elections, the twice-impeached former president announced his candidacy for a second term of office. He claimed credit for the new slim Republican majority in the House of Representatives. At the same time, he ignored the losses of several hand-picked Senate candidates, which allowed the Democrats to maintain control of the upper chamber of the Congress, as well as the Trump-endorsed House candidates who also were defeated for election. Incredibly, Trump placed himself in a win-win situation. Speaking on *NewsNation* on election day, he said, "I think if they (Republicans) win, I should get all the credit. And if they lose, I should not be blamed at all."[46]

Reaction to Trump's Announcement

For some Republican loyalists, the idea of Trump's return to office was just what the doctor ordered to deal with the lingering immigration problem, high inflation, and an economy thought to be edging closer to recession. South Carolina U.S. Senator Lindsey Graham, who at the time harshly condemned Trump for his role in the January 6 insurrection, was back on the Trump team shortly thereafter. Republican House Minority Leader Kevin McCarthy went through a similar reincarnation when, after publicly berating Trump immediately after the insurrection, days later, he had a "kiss and make up" meeting in Mar-a-Lago. Elise Stefanik, now a Trump convert and number three in the House Republican leadership after McCarthy dumped conservative Liz Cheney for her constant criticism of Trump, was also among Trump's cheerleaders. She was joined with outspoken House members Jim Jordan, Marjorie Taylor Greene, and Paul Gosar, all of whom who saw no reason to condemn Trump or the January 6 insurrection.

Beginning in early 2023, Trump drew candidacy opposition for re-nomination from several Republicans who had been former allies. Most, however, focused on the "Trump is unelectable" theme, rather than the significance of the serious indictments about his behavior. Former United Nations Ambassador Nikki Haley, former Arkansas governor, and former vice president, and for the most part, Florida governor Ron DeSantis all fell into this category. Only former New Jersey governor and ex-Trump ally Chris Christie criticized Trump on the merits. At one point during a CNN Town Hall in June 2023, Christie focused on the federal charges against Trump for withholding and concealing sensitive defense information, saying, "This is vanity run amok. . . . He's (Trump) saying, I'm more important than the country . . . he took the documents he wasn't supposed to take."[47] Few Republicans spoke out with such clarity, which Christie did repeatedly.

Beyond the Republican leadership, some potential problems emerged in Trump world. The post–2022 era seemed to present new challenges as the Trump base appeared to be shrinking rather than expanding. Given the results from Trump's 2020 failed re-election effort, and the 2022 disappointing election results, the Rupert Murdoch-owned *Wall Street Journal* and *New York Post* pulled away from Trump. The writing was on the wall when, on the day after the election, a *Wall Street Journal* editorial wrote that during the 2022 campaign, Trump unnecessarily "led Republicans into one political fiasco after another."[48] On the same day, the well-respected conservative *The National Review* commented, "It is painfully evident that Republicans would have had a far easier time winning Senate seats in Pennsylvania, Arizona, Nevada, New Hampshire and elsewhere if they had not chosen the Trump-endorsed candidate in the primary."[49] For many traditional conservative Republicans who were never excited with Trump to begin with, Trump's time had run its course.

Then there was the evangelical vote, a key portion of the Trump vote in 2016 and 2020. It will be remembered that Trump courted the evangelical vote, promising to appoint federal justices and judges supportive of the anti-abortion, pro-life movement. Nearly four out of five White evangelicals voted for Trump on both occasions, resulting in a win-win for both sides. The relationship changed markedly; however, as Trump began his 2024 campaign, Trump blamed the abortion issue as the reason for making it harder for him to secure moderate support. Now, many evangelicals were spooked. Scott Walker, a former Wisconsin governor and key evangelical leader, commented that many evangelicals wondered "if in some way he'd (Trump) gone back to some of the sentiments he had long before becoming a Republican candidate."[50] Had they done their research, evangelicals would have realized that Trump has been on both sides of virtually every social and economic issue during his entire public life.[51] That's the essence of his transactional politics.

Some party leaders publicly stated their belief that a new day had come for the GOP. Republican U.S. Senator from Wyoming Cynthia Lummis went so far as to declare DeSantis the "leader of the Republican Party."[52] Other Senate Republicans weren't necessarily ready to endorse any particular but nonetheless expressed their desire to move on, absent the former president.[53] The growing discontent included major Republican financial benefactors. Americans for Prosperity, a conservative organization that spent $500 million for Republican candidates during the 2020 election cycle, announced about Trump at a 2023 conference of likeminded donors, that it was "turning a page on the past."[54] Also in 2023, The Club for Growth, a conservative anti-tax group that spent $150 million on candidates in 2020 and 2022, invited a half dozen potential Republican candidates to its annual meeting, excluding Donald Trump. In their announcement, the group declared that "the [Republican] party should be open to another [presidential] candidate."[55] Clearly, major Republican contributors were casting about for an alternative to Trump, but would they find one?

The "New" Trump

As Trump positioned himself for the 2024 campaign, he gradually realized that he had to make adjustments. Never known for having a set of core values, Trump set out to find voting block replacements for possible losses from traditional Republican conservatives and evangelicals. He moved to strengthen his relations with the most racist flank of the electorate. Most of the dozen or so other Republican candidates stayed away for one of two reasons: either because they considered the racist connection toxic or because their own political values as candidates were incompatible with that group. Thus, among the possible major presidential candidates, Trump believed that he had racist-minded supporters largely to himself.

A potentially large field of candidates would also be helpful to Trump's new campaign approach. If the 2024 nomination contest emerged with as many candidates as the 2016 collection, Trump's loyal base, even if different than his 2016 collection, could be enough to win him the nomination. Inasmuch as a large number of states utilizing winner-take-all primaries for awarding most of the delegates to the candidate with the largest number of votes, in other words a plurality, Trump hoped that gaining more votes than any other candidate might be enough to win the Republican nomination. After all, that approach worked in 2016.

Slamming Old Enemies and Adding New Ones

Trump began his quest for 2024 by lashing out at his foes with references that became increasingly bold and direct. He began by attacking Elaine Chao, his former Secretary of Transportation (and wife of enemy and Senator Minority Leader Mitch McConnell), whom he called Coco Chao, also described by Trump as McConnell's "China loving wife." His remarks fit in well with the spike in anti-Asian rhetoric and hate crimes. In an interview, Trump took a swipe at Asian Americans and popular governor and potential 2024 rival newly elected Virginia governor Glenn Youngkin by mocking him by pronouncing Youngkin's name as "Young Kin," following up his description with "Sounds Chinese, doesn't it?" He added that Youngkin couldn't have won his race without Trump's support.[56]

With respect to antisemitism, another area of growing hostile public sentiments, Trump described American Jews in October 2022 as ungrateful to him for his Israeli policy that included a controversial move of the American embassy to Jerusalem from Tel Aviv, and that American Jews needed to "get their act together . . . before it is too late."[57] Many Jewish organizations took Trump's statement as a threat.[58] They were also offended by Trump's assumption that his support for Israel should dictate automatic support from Jewish voters, many of whom were concerned with countless issues besides U.S. relations with Israel. Inasmuch as Trump operated in a transactional world, the trade made perfect sense.

Trump's lashing out at Jews was nothing new, but condemning evangelicals did turn heads. Nevertheless, Trump did precisely that after learning that key evangelical leaders remained on the sidelines in the early endorsement period. In a January 17, 2023, podcast interview with conservative journalist David Brody, Trump reminded the audience that "Nobody has ever done more for the Right to Life than Donald Trump," referring to himself in the third person. Yet, he continued about evangelicals, "There's a great disloyalty in the world of politics and that's (the lack of evangelical support) the sign of disloyalty."[59] For Trump, of course, anything less than total deference represented "disloyalty."

Trump's contempt for African Americans, established early in his adulthood, continued throughout his administration and after. As the Fulton County investigation of Trump's infamous call regarding missing votes ramped up, Trump referred to African-American Fani Willis, the district attorney, as "radical, vicious, racist."[60] He offered a similar assessment of African-Americans Letitia James, the New York Attorney General, and Manhattan District Attorney Alvin Bragg, as they pursued their lawsuits against the former president.

Regarding Hispanics, Trump threaded the needle between groups. Recognizing the clout of Cuban Americans in Florida, a state he needed badly for election victories, he discussed their helpful role in living the American Dream. Nevertheless, the bulk of his criticism originated and remained with Hispanics coming to the United States at the southern border, many without the proper documentation for legal entry. By the end of his presidency in January 2021, his famous wall covered about 452 miles or 23 percent of the border between the United States and Mexico, of which 80 miles were new construction.[61] On a trip to the southern border in 2021, Trump criticized Biden for opening up the border, even though the Biden administration had largely maintained Trump's policy.[62] Still, Trump's words were an important reminder to his anti-immigrant supporters.

Upping the Ante with White Racists

Along with being more vocal with racist statements, Trump moved to openly cultivate White supremacist individuals and groups. In November 2022, Trump dined at his Mar-a-Lago residence with Ye, formerly known as Kanye West, who had been denounced for blatant antisemitic rhetoric and pro-Hitler statements. His comments were so outrageous that several companies with whom Ye had relationships severed their contractual involvement with him. Ye brought with him Nick Fuentes, a 24-year-old prominent white supremacist leader of America First Political Action Committee and Holocaust denier. Trump later said that Ye was seeking business advice and that Trump had no idea of Fuentes' reputation.[63] His pretense of ignorance about Fuentes was no different than other after-the-fact expressions of unfamiliarity with White supremacists and antisemites David Duke, Richard Spencer, and others of their ilk. Similar to his behavior in previous controversial endorsements of racists, upon receiving criticism of the meeting, Trump denied ever knowing anything about the individuals' racist values.[64]

Increasingly, Trump became more connected to QAnon, the group that described Democrats as Satan-worshipping pedophiles.[65] When Trump first commented about QAnon, he said, "I don't know very much about the movement (QAnon) other than I understand they like me very much. . . . [T]hese are people that love our country very much."⁶⁶ Apparently, he liked them, too. During Fall 2022, he reposted an image of himself with a Q label pin stating, "The Storm is Coming," a quote of sorts implying that Trump's return to office was imminent. He posted dozens of other Q-related stories and messages during September 2022 alone.⁶⁷ At a Toledo, Ohio, rally in October, Trump went so far as to walk out to the gathering to the accompaniment of a QAnon theme song.⁶⁸ Many in the crowd roared in approval, raising their arms in a QAnon salute.

The bottom line is that if anything, Trump amped up his racist rhetoric after he left the presidency. None of this was much of a surprise to Maggie Haberman, a *New York Times* reporter who published a book on Trump after his 2020 defeat. With respect to Trump's increasing racist comments, Haberman observed that Trump was "leaning into racist statements" and expected such behavior to continue.⁶⁹ "Bulldozing," rather than "leaning" might have been a better description.

What can be said of the "New" Trump? Little more other than that he is an outsized version of the "Old" Trump. In short, he is the Trump of old, only more focused on conspiracy theories and racism as the basis for getting enough votes to regain the presidency.

Dismissing the Constitution

Since the day Joe Biden's presidential election victory was made clear, Donald Trump has claimed a rigged election. That's not news. However, Trump did attract attention in December 2022 with his demand that as the result of voter fraud, all the laws governing the United States, including the Constitution, should be thrown out. Trump wrote on his *Truth Social* media site on December 3, "Do you throw the Presidential Election Results of 2020 OUT and declare the RIGHTFUL WINNER, or do you have a NEW ELECTION? A Massive Fraud of this type and magnitude allows for the termination of all rules, regulations, and articles, even those found in the Constitution." Clearly, rules, laws and even the Constitution were meant for anyone except Donald Trump.

Remarkably, few Republican leaders took issue with Trump, in itself testament to the extent that they were afraid, unwilling, or perhaps in agreement with him. In a rare rebuke, U.S. Senator Lisa Murkowski tweeted, "Suggesting the termination of the Constitution is not only a betrayal of our Oath of Office, it's an affront to our Republic."⁷⁰ Four days after Trump's shocking statement, Republican Senate Minority Leader Mitch McConnell offered tepidly, "Anyone seeking the presidency who thinks the Constitution could somehow be suspended, it seems to me, would have a very hard time being sworn in as president of the United States." McConnell didn't include

Trump's name in his criticism.[71] Virtually every other major Republican leader remained eerily silent.

A larger group, while critical, dismissed the thought that Trump's remark did not necessarily disqualify him from serving as president again. Republican U.S. Representative David Joyce, chair of the centrist Republican Governance Group, dismissed negative reaction, declaring to ABC's George Stephanopoulos, "He (Trump) says a lot of things, but that doesn't mean that it's ever going to happen."[72] Joyce continued that he would support any Republican who won the nomination for the presidency, including Donald Trump. Arizona U.S. Representative Paul Gosar tweeted support of Trump's desire to terminate the Constitution, only to delete it two days later.

Perhaps the biggest surprise about Trump's statement was the lack of response from Republican Speaker of the House Kevin McCarthy. It will be remembered that the soon-to-be Speaker of the House pleaded with Trump during the January 6 insurrection, to which Trump is alleged to have responded, "Well Kevin, I guess these people (the insurrectionists) are more upset about the election than you are."[73] A shouting match between the two continued, yet McCarthy emerged days later as a born again Trumper. On Trump's anti-Constitution remarks, McCarthy offered no voice. Simply put, the collective Republican leadership reaction to Trump's recommendation for ditching the Constitution was all but absent.

HAS TRUMP'S TIME PASSED?

Trump's first 2024 rally occurred on March 25, 2023, in Waco, Texas, on the 30th anniversary of a standoff between an anti-government sect and government agents seeking to serve search warrants for sexual abuse charges and illegal weapons possession. The area has a long history of advocating White power, rightwing extremism, and militia-organizing.[74] Trump representatives characterized the choice of the site as coincidental; others saw the location as a way for Trump to tap into the anti-government theme increasingly emblematic of his "deep state" oriented campaigns.[75] In this spirit Waco was an ideal place for Trump to air his grievances. Others that followed have taken place in rural areas of the nation.

Life has been different for Trump in his third run for the presidency. Social media outlets Twitter and Facebook had been great outlets for Trump during the 2020 campaign, but both had placed him off-limits by January 2021 because of what they viewed as persistent inflammatory remarks surrounding the January 6 insurrection. By 2023, both had shown a willingness to welcome back Trump under vaguely constructed conditions that he shy away from provocation, but instead, he relied on *Truth Social*, his own site where he has total control. Meanwhile, Fox News, which was something of a *de facto* Trump outlet until the 2022 Republican election outcomes, pulled away from the former president. Yes, there was OAN (One America News Network), a small conservative cable channel, but like the limitations of Trump's Truth Social media site, its audience paled next to Fox. For the moment, Trump's social media outreach remains a work in progress. Then, again, given that Trump is a well-known commodity, he doesn't require the exposure necessary for a less established political figure.

Given the myriad investigations and lawsuits hounding Donald Trump, many Republican leaders have viewed him as doing more harm than good and, as such, have been willing to write him off via the "it's time to turn a page" route. Some have abandoned Trump because of their outright contempt for his attitudes, behavior, and/or abuse of office that, cumulatively, have harmed the Republican brand. However, most former supporters have taken leave via the "can't win" route, rather than condemn Trump for his behavior. Such an approach is likely a safer offramp that offers some protection from any Trump vendetta. However, it basically gives a pass to Trump for his unconscionable action. So much for leadership.

Trump has been written off so many times before, such as the October 2016 Hollywood bus scandal, the Mueller investigation, two impeachment trials, illegally possessing confidential documents after leaving, and, of course, his role in the January 6, 2021, insurrection against Congress and the American people. With each potentially fatal disgrace, Trump has seemed to do the impossible by maintaining a powerful presence despite the odds. As an illustration, his campaign claimed $15 million in new contributions over the first two weeks after his Manhattan indictment.[76] Clearly, he remains a force.

The end of Trump's current chapter in American politics is yet to be written, but it's of little consequence, given the many elements of Trumpism that have been embraced by others seeking power and who have it. That discussion takes place next.

NOTES

1. See "One year on, Republicans Still don't Consider Biden the Rightful Winner," Poll, University of Rochester, December 21, 2021, https://www.rochester.edu/newscenter/one-year-on-republicans-still-dont-consider-biden-the-rightful-winner-506702/.

2. "78% Of Republicans Want To See Trump Run For President In 2024, Quinnipiac University National Poll Finds; Americans Now Split On Border Wall As Opposition Softens," Quinnipiac Poll, October 19, 2021, https://poll.qu.edu/poll-release?releaseid=3825.

3. "Mixed Signals on Trump: Majority Says Criminal Charges Should Disqualify '24 Run, Popularity is Unchanged, Leads DeSantis by Double Digits, Quinnipiac Poll Finds," Quinnipiac Poll, March 29, 2023, https://poll.qu.edu/poll-release?releaseid=3870.

4. "What Happened to the 10 Republicans Who Voted to Impeach Trump?" *The Washington Post,* November 23, 2022, https://www.washingtonpost.com/politics/2022/11/23/gop-trump-impeachment-house/.

5. See "Trump Promotes Video of a Supporter Saying 'White Power,'" *The Washington Post,* June 28, 2020, https://www.washingtonpost.com/politics/2020/06/28/trump-promotes-video-supporter-saying-white-power/ and "Trump Isn't Secretly Winking at QAnon. He's Retweeting its Followers," *Politico,* July 12, 2020, https://www.politico.com/news/2020/07/12/trump-tweeting-qanon-followers-357238.

6. In 2019, per Georgia law, Governor Brian Kemp appointed Kelly Loeffler to fill the vacated seat held by Johnny Isakson, who retired because of health reasons.

7. "Trump's Last Rally as President was Supposed to be about the Georgia Runoffs. It wasn't," *Vox,* January 4, 2021, https://www.vox.com/2021/1/4/22214512/trump-dalton-georgia-rally-runoffs-perdue-loeffler.

8. See "'A Hostage Situation Every Day': Strategists Blame Trump for Georgia Senate Losses," *NPR,* January 21, 2021, https://www.npr.org/2021/01/29/961837774/a-hostage-situation-every-day-strategists-blame-trump-for-georgia-senate-losses.

9. "Trump-Endorsed Candidates Have Funneled At Least $1.4 million Into His Businesses," *Forbes,* https://www.forbes.com/sites/zacheverson/2022/06/23/trump-endorsed-candidates-have-funneled-at-least-14-million-into-his-businesses/?sh=28a29f295c36.

10. "The Mar-a-Lago Machine: Trump as a Modern-Day Party Boss," *The New York Times,* April 18, 2022, https://www.nytimes.com/2022/04/17/us/politics/trump-mar-a-lago.html.

11. "GOP Won the Votes, but Not the Seats," *The Cook Political Report,* November 15, 2022, https://www.cookpolitical.com/analysis/national/national-politics/gop-won-votes-not-seats.

12. "Mitch McConnell to Republicans on Midterms: I Told You These Weirdos would Lose," *Vanity Fair,* December 14, 2022, https://www.vanityfair.com/news/2022/12/mitch-mcconnell-laments-gop-candidate-quality-2022-midterms.

13. "Trump Embraces Conspiracy Theories He Only Winked at Before," *The New York Times,* September 2, 2022, https://www.nytimes.com/2022/09/02/technology/trump-conspiracy-theories-truth-social.html.

14. Andrew O. Ballard, Hans J. G. Hassell, and Michael Heseltine, "Be Careful What You Wish For: The Impacts of president Trump's Midterm Endorsements," *Legislative Studies Quarterly,* May 19, 2020, https://doi.org/10.1111/lsq/12284.

15. "Exclusive: Trump's 3,500 Lawsuits Unprecedented for a Presidential Nominee," *USA Today,* October 23, 2017, https://www.usatoday.com/story/news/politics/elections/2016/06/01/donald-trump-lawsuits-legal-battles/84995854/.

16. Michael Kranish and Marc Fisher chronicle one such example in their *Trump Revealed* (New York, NY: Simon and Schuster, 2016), pp. 253–254.

17. "Trump Organization Found Guilty in Tax Fraud Scheme," *The New York Times*, December 6, 2022, https://www.nytimes.com/live/2022/12/06/nyregion/trump-organization-trial-verdict.

18. "Former President Donald Trump's Company is Found Guilty of Criminal Tax Fraud," *NPR*, December 6, 2022, https://www.npr.org/2022/12/06/1140756394/former-president-donald-trumps-company-found-guilty-criminal-tax-fraud.

19. "New York Sues Trump, Citing Decade of 'Staggering' Fraud," *The New York Times*, September 22, 2022, https://www.nytimes.com/2022/09/21/nyregion/trump-fraud-lawsuit-ny.html.

20. Ibid.

21. "'Vicious, Biased': Trump Assails Judge in NY Fraud Case," *AP News*, October 28, 2022, https://apnews.com/article/business-new-york-social-media-8947607e8dad62cecba6c6de6ab4d302.

22. "Jury Finds Trump Liable for Sexual Abuse and Defamation," *The New York Times*, May 9, 2023, https://www.nytimes.com/live/2023/05/09/nyregion/trump-carroll-rape-trial-verdict.

23. "Appointment of a Special Counsel," Department of Justice, November 18, 2022, https://www.justice.gov/opa/pr/appointment-special-counsel-0.

24. "Mar-a-Lago Classified Papers Held U.S. Secrets about Iran and China," *The Washington Post*, October 21, 2022, https://www.washingtonpost.com/national-security/2022/10/21/trump-documents-mar-a-lago-iran-china/.

25. The information in this paragraph comes from "Timeline: The Government's Effort to get Sensitive Documents Back from Trump's Mar-a-Lago," *CBS News*, September 22, 2022, https://www.cbsnews.com/news/trump-search-timeline-mar-a-lago-justice-department/.

26. "Presidential Power to Declassify Information, Explained," *Indiana Express*, August 15, 2022, https://indianexpress.com/article/explained/explained-global/presidential-power-declassify-information-explained-8090991/.

27. "Trump Says Presidents can Declassify Docs 'Even by Thinking about It,'" *The Washington Post*, September 22, 2022, https://www.washingtonpost.com/national-security/2022/09/22/trump-hannity-declassify-documents/.

28. "Trump gave Conflicting Defenses about the Mar-a-Lago Raid, Claiming that all the Documents Are 'Mine,' and that Some Were Planted," *Business Insider*, October 22, 2022, https://www.businessinsider.com/trump-mar-a-lago-docs-mine-but-also-planted-conflicting-2022-10.

29. United States of America v. Donald J. Trump and Waltine Nauta, https://www.justice.gov/storage/US_v_Trump-Nauta_23-80101.pdf.

30. "Trump Put National Secrets at Risk, Prosecutors Say in Historic Indictment," *The New York Times*, https://www.nytimes.com/2023/06/09/us/politics/trump-indictment-charges-classified-documents.html.

31. "How Other Candidates Are Reacting to Trump's Federal Indictment," fivethirtyeight.com, June 9, 2023, https://fivethirtyeight.com/features/trump-indictment-republican-primary-candidates-reaction.

32. Quoted in "Kevin McCarthy's Tweet is either a Bluff or Really Dangerous," Editorial, *The Fresno Bee*, June 9, 2023, https://www.fresnobee.com/opinion/editorials/article276258706.html.

33. "Trump Allies in Congress Leap to Defend Former President after Federal Indictment," *PBS News Hour*, June 10, 2023, https://www.pbs.org/newshour/politics/trump-allies-in-congress-leap-to-defend-former-president-after-federal-indictment.

34. "Trump Indictment: Mark Levin Rails against Biden's hand in Document Case, Calls 'An Insurrection,'" *Washington Examiner*, June 12, 2023, https://www.washingtonexaminer.com/news/justice/trump-indictment-mark-levin-rails-against-biden-doj-insurrection.

35. "Landmark Jan. 6 Report Concludes Trump Intentionally Misled and Provoked Insurrectionists," *Los Angeles Times*, December 22, 2022, https://www.latimes.com/politics/story/2022-12-22/jan-6-committee-final-report-explained. See *Final Report of the Select Committee to Investigate the January 6th Attack on the United States Capitol*, U.S. Government Publishing Office, December 2022.

36. See "New Insights Into Trump's State of Mind on Jan. 6 Chip Away at Doubts," *The New York Times*, July 3, 2022, https://www.nytimes.com/2022/07/03/us/politics/new-insights-into-trumps-state-of-mind-on-jan-6-chip-away-at-doubts.html and "Trying to Trademark 'Rigged Election' and Other Revelations From the Jan. 6 Transcripts," *The New York Times,* January 2, 2023, https://www.nytimes.com/2023/01/02/us/politics/jan-6-committee-transcripts.html.

37. See "Jan. 6 Panel Issues Final Report, Placing Blame for Capitol Riot on 'One Man,'" *The New York Times*, December 22, 2022, https://www.nytimes.com/2022/03/29/us/politics/trump-tweet-jan-6.html.

38. "'I Answered the Call of My President': Rioters Say Trump Urged Them On," *The New York Times,* January 22, 2021, https://www.nytimes.com/2021/01/17/nyregion/protesters-blaming-trump-pardon.html.

39. "Oath Keepers Founder Sentenced to 18 years in Jan. 6 Seditious Conspiracy Case," *NBC News*, May 25, 2023, https://www.nbcnews.com/politics/justice-department/oath-keepers-founder-sentenced-18-years-jan-6-seditious-conspiracy-cas-rcna85852.

40. "Two Years Later, Prosecutions of Jan. 6 Rioters Continue to Grow," *The New York Times*, January 6, 2023, https://www.nytimes.com/2023/01/06/us/politics/jan-6-capitol-riots-prosecutions.html.

41. "Trump on Jan. 6 Insurrection: 'These were Great People'," *Politico*, July 11, 2021, https://www.politico.com/news/2021/07/11/trump-jan-6-insurrection-these-were-great-people-499165.

42. "Trump again Refuses to Concede 2020 Election While Taking Questions from New Hampshire GOP Primary Voters," *CNN*, May 10, 2023, https://www.cnn.com/2023/05/10/politics/cnn-town-hall-trump/index.html.

43. https://www.justice.gov/storage/US_v_Trump_23_cr_257.pdf.

44. "Top Lines: July 2023 Times/Sienna Poll of Likely Republican Primary Electorate," *The New York Times,* July 31, 2023, https://www.nytimes.com/interactive/2023/07/31/us/elections/times-siena-poll-republican-primary-toplines.html.

45. Under the auspices of federalism, an aspect of American governance, state and federal courts have different jurisdictions. For a deeper explanation, see Larry N. Gerston, *American Federalism: A Concise Introduction* (Armonk, NY: M.E. Sharpe Publisher, 2007).

46. Quoted in "Trump Says He 'Should Get All the Credit' if Republicans Win Midterm Elections," *Washington Examiner*, November 8, 2022, https://www.washingtonexaminer.com/news/campaigns/trump-credit-republicans-win-midterms.

47. "Christie Attacks Trump, Calling Conduct Detailed in Indictment 'Awful,'" *The New York Times*, June 12, 2023, https://www.nytimes.com/2023/06/12/us/politics/chris-christie-trump-cnn-town-hall.html.

48. "Trump is the Republican Party's Biggest Loser," *The Wall Street Journal*, November 9, 2022, https://www.wsj.com/articles/donald-trump-is-the-gops-biggest-loser-midterm-elections-senate-house-congress-republicans-11668034869.

49. "The Message of the Midterms," *National Review*, November 9, 2022, https://www.nationalreview.com/corner/the-message-of-the-midterms/.

50. Quoted in Tim Alberta, "Donald Trump Is on the Wrong Side of the Religious Right," *The Atlantic*, May 24, 2023, https://www.theatlantic.com/politics/archive/2023/03/trump-religious-right-evangelical-vote-pence-desantis-support/673475/.

51. "On Trump, Pro-Life Opportunity, and Transactional Politics," *National Review*, January 4, 2023, https://www.nationalreview.com/corner/on-trump-pro-life-opportunism-and-transactional-politics/.

52. "Republicans Cringe as Trump 2024 Approaches," *Politico*, November 14, 2022, https://www.politico.com/news/2022/11/14/republicans-trump-2024-00066874.

53. "Trump Angst Grips Republicans (Again) as 2024 Announcement Looms," *The New York Times*, https://www.nytimes.com/2022/11/12/us/politics/trump-2024-republicans.html.

54. "Taking Aim at Trump, Koch Network Wil Back G.O.P. Primary Candidates," *The New York Times*, https://www.nytimes.com/2023/02/05/us/politics/koch-donors-trump-campaign-finance.html.

55. "Club for Growth Distances Itself further from Trump," *The New York Times*, https://www.nytimes.com/2023/02/06/us/politics/club-for-growth-trump-desantis.html.

56. "Trump Calls Out Youngkin Amid 2024 Chatter," *CNN*, November 11, 2022, https://thehill.com/homenews/campaign/3730886-trump-calls-out-youngkin-amid-2024-chatter/.

57. Bess Levin, "Donald Trump, Who Reportedly Praised Hitler in Private, Gives Antisemites the Greenlight to Go after Jews," *Vanity Fair*, October 17, 2022, https://www.vanityfair.com/news/2022/10/donald-trump-jews-israel-truth-social.

58. See "ADL Chief: Trump Post on American Jews 'Sounds like a Threat,'" *The Hill*, December 17, 2022, https://thehill.com/policy/international/3692763-adl-chief-trump-post-on-american-jews-sounds-like-a-threat/.

59. Quoted in "Trump Criticizes Evangelical Leaders for not Backing His Presidential Bid," *CNN*, January 18, 2023, https://www.cnn.com/2023/01/18/politics/donald-trump-evangelicals-2024/index.html.

60. "Trump Calls Black Prosecutors Investigating Him 'Racist,' Suggests Protests In Retaliation," *Forbes*, February 1, 2022, https://www.forbes.com/sites/dereksaul/2022/01/30/trump-calls-black-prosecutors-investigating-him-racist-suggests-protests-in-retaliation/?sh=2da5374551bf.

61. "Trump's Wall: How much has been Built during His Term?" *BBC News*, January 12, 2021, https://www.bbc.com/news/world-us-canada-46748492.

62. "Trump, at US-Mexico Border, Slams Biden for 'Open, Really Dangerous Border'," *Fox News*, July 1, 2021, https://www.foxnews.com/politics/trump-at-u-s-mexico-border-slams-biden-for-open-really-dangerous-border.

63. "Trump's Latest Dinner Guest: Nick Fuentes, White Supremacist," *The New York Times*, https://www.nytimes.com/2022/11/25/us/politics/trump-nick-fuentes-dinner.html.

64. "Trump Confirms He had Dinner with Ye, White Supremacist Nick Fuentes," *NY1*, November 25, 2022, https://www.ny1.com/nyc/all-boroughs/politics/2022/11/25/trump-confirms-he-had-dinner-with-ye--white-nationalist-fuentes.

65. "Trump Embraces Conspiracy Theories," op. cit.

66. Quoted in "Trump Praises QAnon Supporters: 'I Understand they like Me Very Much,'" *Axios*, August 19, 2020, https://www.axios.com/2020/08/19/trump-praises-qanon-supporters-i-understand-they-like-me-very-much.

67. "Trump Begins Openly Embracing and Amplifying False Fringe QAnon Conspiracy Theory," *PBS News Hour*, September 16, 2022, https://www.pbs.org/newshour/politics/trump-begins-openly-embracing-and-amplifying-false-fringe-qanon-conspiracy-theory.

68. "Trump's Embrace of QAnon Realizes the Dream of the Religious Right," *The Nation*, September 23, 2022, https://www.thenation.com/article/politics/trump-qanon/.

69. "Haberman: Trump 'Seems to be Leaning into Racist Statements'," *The Hill*, October 6, 2022, https://thehill.com/homenews/media/3676186-haberman-trump-seems-to-be-leaning-into-racist-statements/.

70. Quoted in "GOP Lawmakers Largely Silent after Trump Suggests 'Termination' of Constitution," *The Washington Post*, December 5, 2022, https://www.washingtonpost.com/national-security/2022/12/04/trump-constitution-republicans/.

71. "McConnell Criticizes Trump's Calls to Terminate the Constitution," *NPR*, December 6, 2022, https://www.npr.org/2022/12/06/1141096473/mcconnell-trump-terminate-constitution.

72. "'Centrist' Republican Still Willing to Support Trump after He Calls to Terminate the Constitution," *Salon*, December 5, 2022, https://www.salon.com/2022/12/05/centrist-still-willing-to-support-after-he-calls-to-terminate-the-constitution/.

73. "New Details about Trump-McCarthy Shouting Match Show Trump Refused to Call Off the Rioters," *CNN*, February 12, 2021, https://www.cnn.com/2021/02/12/politics/trump-mccarthy-shouting-match-details/index.html.

74. "The Violent History of Waco, the Infamous Site of Trump's Next Rally," *Time*, March 22, 2023, https://time.com/6265218/waco-texas-history-trump-rally/.

75. "Why Is Donald Trump Kicking Off His 2024 Campaign in Waco?" *The Texas Monthly*, March 22, 2023, https://www.texasmonthly.com/news-politics/why-is-trump-kicking-off-2024-campaign-in-waco/.

76. "Trump's Indictment Sparked $15.4 Million Fundraising Bonanza," *Bloomberg*, April 15, 2023, https://www.bloomberg.com/news/articles/2023-04-15/trump-s-indictment-sparked-15-4-million-fundraising-bonanza#xj4y7vzkg.

Part IV

TRUMPISM, BIGOTRY, AND THE THREAT TO AMERICAN DEMOCRACY

After the 2022 midterm elections, many political pundits felt that the threat to American Democracy had abated, if not disappeared altogether. Most of the Trump-endorsed candidates for major offices lost their races, few defeated Trump-endorsed candidates claimed rigged election outcomes, and organized violent threats against major public institutions were nowhere to be found. Coupled with Trump's 2020 presidential defeat, some optimistic pundits believed that the consecutive defeats of authoritarian-friendly candidates restored political stability in the United States. Michael Waldman of the Brennan Center for Justice summarized the sense of renewal when he wrote, "In 2022, the forces of American democracy rallied. . . . [T]he midterm elections were smoothly, fair and calm—dare I say, *normal*."[1] There were and would be major differences of opinion on political issues of the day, Waldman continued, but outside of a few political hotheads, the system was restored to absorb and deal with disagreements in a largely civil manner.

There is room for debating Waldman's claim. An election is just that—a single, momentary determination by the will of the voters and, as such, an episode of political behavior in the ongoing episodes of society's existence. To evaluate the significance of an isolated event outside of the larger behavioral context ignores the political ecosystem and conditions before the voters in advance and likely after the election. That's the problem with considering the value of any single election removed from the issues and activities surrounding it. Yes, Trump and his aspirations had been severely weakened. And, yes, some of Trump's followers had deserted him, perhaps because of exhaustion from his endless deafening claims of rigged elections, his inability to "come through" with victories for many Republican candidates particularly in 2020 and 2022, or disgust with Trump's increasing public comfort with bigots and other would-be disrupters of democracy. That said, any conclusions about

Trump as the primary source of America's problems are overly simplistic, and as such inadequate and incomplete.

While Trump may have been relegated by some analysts to political outlier status, we need to ask, what about Trumpism? What about racism? Has the blend of racism and intended authoritarianism so masterfully orchestrated by Donald Trump been cleansed from American politics? Maybe. Or perhaps the elements of Trumpism that have long floated in and out of the imperfect American political tapestry remain prominent in an altered form, and are now the fodder for other radical leaders. Should the latter be the case, then American society may well continue vulnerable to the next surge of despotism. This discussion is the centerpiece of chapter 11, followed by a warning about the future in chapter 12.

NOTE

1. Michael Waldman, "2022: Democracy Rises," Brennan Center for Justice, December 27, 2022, https://www.brennancenter.org/our-work/analysis-opinion/2022-democracy-rises.

Chapter 11

Understanding the Threat to American Democracy

In this volume, we have focused on the interaction among three characteristics of American politics: democracy, bigotry, and Trumpism. This combination has served as a possible foundation for authoritarianism, which would be inimical to historic American political values and tradition. To repeat what should now be the obvious, democracy is an incredibly fragile form of political organization, difficult to achieve and easy to lose. Somehow, despite major cracks in principles and behavior throughout the nation's history, we have been able to avoid demise of the world's oldest democracy. Until now.

Regarding racism and other elements of bigotry in the United States, this long-standing, pernicious practice by some members of society has a 400-year history here which has, at times, fundamentally threatened the well-being of our democracy. The slavery era might be the most glaring, clear-cut example, but the fact remains that, in numerous ways, xenophobia has been and remains a cruel centerpiece of American political behavior. Moreover, rarely has its ugliness been as pronounced in American politics as in the period from 2015 to the present.

This leads us to authoritarianism, an undemocratic means of governing employed by a leader or leaders who rely on power often generated outside the laws and norms of society. Under such rule, those in control thrive on undermining major institutions and core values, leaving alienated constituents looking to the leader for rescue from chaos and misery. Unwittingly, perhaps, the disaffected portions of society are willing to trade uncertainty for a false sense of security. Donald Trump adroitly saw such disarray and used racism as the political cudgel to enlarge and intensify society's preexisting divisions. That manipulation helped Trump achieve election to the presidency. Once in power, he consistently relied UPON this open cultural wound as the foundation for wielding power in an authoritarian manner unmatched in American history.

The most heinous example of Trump's undemocratic behavior occurred during and after November 3, 2020, when he clearly was defeated for reelection by Democratic opponent Joe Biden. Soon thereafter, the January 6 Committee concluded that Trump "disregarded the rulings of the courts and rejected the findings and conclusions and advice from his Justice Department, his campaign experts, and his White House and Cabinet advisors. He chose instead to overturn the election on January 6 (2021) and took a series of very specific attempts to attempt to achieve that result."[1] The insurrection unfolded under Trump's guidance and watch, with the future of American democracy in peril.

But the story doesn't end there. The fact remains that Trump didn't act alone; he had countless numbers of enablers up and down the authoritarian food chain en route to his failed attempt to continue in the nation's highest elective office. That support included 147 Republican members of Congress who voted to reject the 2020 presidential election results—even *after* the attempted coup.

There were other conspirators. Trump had active, participatory support from anti-democratic groups through their mobilization for action and manipulative use of social media. He also had post-election backing from key on-air allies at Fox television and other right-wing media outlets over election fraud claims they absolutely knew not to be true. Except for a few brave individuals in and near Trump's inner circle, he might well have been enabled to unconstitutionally remain in power. However, Trump's unsuccessful struggle to stay in office is only part of the story.

Although Trump was thwarted from illegally continuing in the presidency, Trumpism persists in the hearts and minds of millions of Americans. Examples of efforts by those committed to undemocratic rule abound in ways small and large and will be illustrated in the pages that follow. That noted, the principal argument here is that the United States remains but a small step away from the next authoritarian disrupter in Trump-like political clothing, making their case to a frustrated society for undemocratic control. Our remaining challenge is to understand the circumstances and depth of the despotic threat to American society that remains in play.

THE CONTINUING IMPACT OF BIGOTRY UPON AMERICAN SOCIETY

There's nothing new about bigotry in the United States; it's a despicable characteristic of America's political and cultural DNA. Chapter 5 of this volume chronicles the role of racism in Donald Trump's life. What's important here, however, is the extent of devotion by Trump to racism, his use of the concept to win election to the presidency, and how it has affected society since his election. Equally important are the racist views of so many Trump supporters that have connected them with him.

Trump's Ongoing Rhetoric

In the United States, virtually all non-White and/or non-Protestant religious groups have been victimized throughout by racism, antisemitism, and Islamophobia. More has been written about the chasm between White people and Black people than any other comparisons, which is a good starting point for this discussion. The literature shows that both groups believe that race relations in the United States are generally bad. That said, White people and Black people approach race relations from two distinctly different points of view. On whether Black people will ever achieve equality with White people, 7 percent of White people believe such an outcome is not likely, compared with 50 percent of Black people. With respect to Donald Trump's impact on racism, 49 percent of White people and 73 percent of Black people believe that since his arrival in the presidency, Trump "made race relations worse."[2] Particularly among Trump supporters, anti-Black attitudes by White people hardened from the onset of Trump's 2016 candidacy and during his presidency.[3]

Much of the difference between the races centers on how the two groups view each other. According to one study, most White people see racism as a "zero-sum" game where Black gains in society come at the expense of White losses.[4] If true, Black advances in education, employment, politics, or any endeavor would be harmful to White individuals in the same areas, perhaps giving White people reason to worry. Yet a detailed longitudinal study of voters in 2020 finds that movements toward equality provide social benefits for all without taking any away from those who are privileged.[5] According to this research, minority gains in general would not account for any social or financial loss for those who are more affluent.

Clearly, the second viewpoint offers more hope for peaceful coexistence than the first. However, it differs from the approach taken by Donald Trump and others of his ilk, who portray minority gains as a zero-sum condition where White losses are in inverse proportion to Black gains. Trump said as much rather pointedly at a 2022 political rally when he warned the gathering about the discriminatory administering of COVID-19 vaccinations: "The left is now rationing life-saving therapeutics based on race, discriminating and denigrating, just denigrating white people to determine who lives and who dies. . . .You get it (the vaccine) based on race."[6] Such fear-based comments have perpetuated Trump's infamous "us versus them" approach to politics, thereby discouraging any thoughts of expanding opportunities for all.

In addition to African Americans, other groups have suffered from the harm of racism and other elements of bigotry as a consequence of Trump's rise to power. Consider examples of the growth of hate behavior toward various groups since the Trump presidency:

- Asian Americans: In addition to Trump's general contempt for African Americans, his description of COVID-19 as the "Chinese virus" may well have contributed to the huge spike in anti-Asian hate in the United States. Between 2019 and 2021, anti-Asian hate crimes increased to 13,021 from 8,517. The most critical period came during 2020, when President Trump repeatedly spoke of the "Chinese virus," inspiring huge issues in hate language on social media.[7] Prior to Trump's remarks, during 2017 through 2019, anti-Asian hate crimes went up but at smaller pace, 8,517 from 5,197.[8]
- Latinos: Hate crimes against Hispanics increased by 70 percent between 2015, the year Trump declared his presidential candidacy, and 2020, his final year of office.[9] Observers have correlated the spike in anti-Latino behavior to Trump's negative comments about the threat of migrants from largely Spanish-speaking nations[10] and nearby "shithole" countries, to use Trump's language.[11]
- Jews: A national survey of Jews in 2022 found that 89 percent considered antisemitism a problem; 82 percent believed that antisemitism had increased over the past five years. They have a reason for concern.[12] National incidents including vandalism, harassment, and violent physical assault against Jews in the United States soared from 1,267 in 2016 to 3,717 in 2022.[13] By comparison, incidents between 2010 and 2016, a similar period, grew from 1,239 to 1,267.[14]

It's important to note that the numbers of reported hate crimes against various minorities are likely to be relatively small fractions of the actual number of events. Of the slightly more than 15,000 police agencies in the United States, only about 2,000 regularly provide data on hate crime incidents. Sometimes, victims are afraid or intimated to report racist incidents; in other instances, law enforcement personnel either don't recognize hate crimes as such or don't want to risk sullying the reputation of their city with hate crime disclosures.[15]

Current Instruments for Sustaining Bigotry in the United States

A point made throughout this book merits reinforcement at this time. Trump alone is not responsible for hate crimes in the United States. We must remember that intolerance and the wrongdoings related to it are part of this country's history. However, judging from all that has been produced here and elsewhere, it's fair to say that Trump seized upon the longstanding animus of some White people toward non-White and non-Christian groups as a basic political strategy. Moreover, he showed a new generation of would-be despots the power of racist tropes as stepping stones to political power and election victories. Accordingly, in concert with Trump's expressed warnings about the loss of White dominance, many racist leaders in state and local governments have taken steps to assure that equality does not occur. Some of these tools existed before Trump, while others are relatively new. Below are the major historical and contemporary instruments used to perpetuate racism since Trump's departure from the White House.

Racial Gerrymandering

One of the best-known methods of minimizing the voter influence of non-White people has come through utilization of racial gerrymandering. Every ten years, as required by the census, states reapportion legislative and congressional districts so that each has approximately the same number of residents. In 33 states, this process is carried out by the legislature; the remaining 17 states use nonpartisan independent commissions. In those states where the legislature divides the population into districts with approximately the same populations, gerrymandering is a means through which minority populations lose their voting clout by being shoved into a small number of districts disproportionately to their overall percentage of the state population. Meanwhile, White people have disproportionate influence in more districts than their overall population would suggest. There is nothing new about gerrymandering. The concept is fairly simple, yet historically successful. It extends all the way back to the 1890s, when White people imposed racial gerrymandering as a means of minimizing African-American political influence.[16]

The Voting Rights Act of 1965 was designed in part to prevent racial gerrymandering. Section 5 of the Act specifically forbade states with a history of racial discrimination from altering voting arrangements without preapproval from the U.S. Attorney General. But in *Shelby County v. Holder* (2013), the U.S. Supreme Court held that the persistent voter discrimination leading to the Voting Rights Act no longer existed, and eliminated Section 5 as a means to prevent racial bias.[17] Thus, data from the 2020 census provided states with the first opportunity in more than a half-century to redistrict their populations without the fear of federal oversight or reprisal. So, what happened?

At least a half dozen states with Republican legislative majorities in 2022 redistricted their congressional seats with maps initially rejected by federal judges at the district court level but ultimately overturned by the U.S. Supreme Court. In four states alone—Alabama, Georgia, Louisiana and

Ohio—Republican majorities drew lines that packed Black populations into districts that minimized their strength. In Alabama, Black voters accounted for 27 percent of the electorate. At the end of the state's redistricting process for its seven congressional seats, however, only a single congressional district contained a Black majority, with the rest of the Black population spread out among the other districts as distinct minorities. The map was tested in the U.S. Supreme Court, as were the others, with the justices initially denying the plaintiffs' claims of discrimination on the basis that such claims should be managed by the states. One election expert estimated that as a result of the gerrymandering in these four states alone, Republicans were likely to win "five to seven seats that they otherwise would not have won."[18] Surprisingly to some, in June 2023, the U.S. Supreme Court declared 5-to-4 that Alabama's redistricting effort was unconstitutional.[19] Shortly thereafter, the justices struck down a Louisiana reapportionment plan that had assured White victories in five out of the state's six congressional districts, even though Black people composed about one-third of the Louisiana's population.[20]

Still, there have been other examples of modern racial gerrymandering. In Florida, the Republican-dominated state legislature created a new set of congressional districts based upon maps drawn by Republican Governor Ron DeSantis. As a result, two of the four seats with previous Black majorities were eliminated and replaced with White majorities. As with Alabama, Black people were squeezed into fewer districts, thereby reducing their representation in Congress.[21]

In Texas, at the time of redistricting in 2021, the political parties were almost evenly divided at 40 percent Republican and 39 percent Democratic. However, Republicans controlled the state legislature and governor's office. With respect to racial lines, non-Hispanic White people accounted for 39.3 percent of the population, with Hispanics (40.2 percent), Black people (11.6 percent), and others amounting to 60 percent of the state's residents. During the 2011–2020 decade, non-White people constituted 95 percent of the state's growth of 4,000,000 new residents. Yet, at the end of the redistricting process, 22 of the state's 36 congressional districts had non-Hispanic White majorities, eight had Hispanic majorities, one had a Black majority, and the rest had no racial majority.[22] That's the power of racial gerrymandering.

It's worth noting that post-2020 census gerrymandering capabilities existed in 26 states with 226 House members. Republicans controlled 177 seats in 19 of those states, whereas Democrats managed 49 seats in 7 states. Given the artificially created racial imbalances, most experts expected to see a Republican margin of victory in approximately two dozen seats in the 2022 congressional elections.[23] But in the end, Republicans won a small four-seat majority in the U.S. House of Representatives. It's not much of a stretch of the imagination to assume that without the gerrymandering, House

Democrats may well have easily carried the day. Moreover, these changes offer signs of the political manipulations that can be expected in the 2024 presidential elections. Gerrymandering has had the disproportionate effect of limiting the value of minority voters and lessening equality.

Voter Suppression Laws

With *Shelby County v. Holder* and other U.S. Supreme Court decisions placing voter legislation squarely in the hands of the states, hundreds of new bills in state legislatures were proposed during 2021 and 2022. According to the Brennan Center for Justice, in the 18 months after the 2020 election alone, more than 400 restrictive bills were proposed in every state except Vermont. Dozens became law. Race was prominent in voter restriction legislation proposals, inasmuch as "representatives from whiter districts in racially diverse states were the most likely to sponsor restrictive legislation."[24]

By April 2022, 19 states had enacted legislation to prevent "voter fraud" that allegedly occurred in the 2020 presidential election.[25] Ironically, numerous rigorous examinations revealed no widespread voter fraud in 2020, despite repeated claims by President Donald Trump and his allies who actually knew better.[26] So, you may ask, why did so many states enact laws that really weren't needed? One answer has to do with manipulating voter turnout by minorities whose full participation otherwise could produce outcomes undesirable for racist elements. Defenders of the post-2020 election "reforms" argued they would make it easier for voters to participate in elections. In fact, the number of voters nationwide fell to 104 million in the 2022 congressional elections, compared with 114 million in 2018. More to the point, evidence indicated that the changes affected racial minorities more than the White majority.

These conclusions are not merely theoretical propositions—they are based on voter results after suppression laws were enacted, despite the absence of any widespread voter fraud. Texas is a good place to start. The results were palpable. In 2021, the legislature in the Lone Star state passed a law making it more difficult to vote by absentee ballot. In the 2022 party primary election, new rules led to the rejection of 13 percent of the mail-in ballots; in contrast, the 2020 presidential election had a rejection rate of 1 percent. Among those rejected, Asian American, Latino, and African American absentee ballot applicants were all disallowed at rates considerably higher than non-Hispanic White people.[27] The results were even worse in Harris County, the home of Houston, the nation's fourth-largest city. There, where two-thirds of the population is non-White, 19 percent of the mail-in ballots were rejected, compared with a 0.3 percent rejection rate in 2018.[28]

In Louisiana, the state legislature passed a spate of voter reform laws in 2021. Some actually extended voting opportunity conditions. Others discouraged voter turnout, particularly among African Americans. Two such laws toughened the rules for absentee ballots and made it easier for the Secretary of State to remove voters from registration rolls 30 days after the election. Between 2018 and 2022, the African-American vote fell from 46.9 percent to 37.9 percent. Meanwhile, the White vote remained virtually the same, dipping slightly from 53.7 percent in 2018 to 52.6 percent in 2022.[29]

Another example of the uneven impact from legislation occurred in South Carolina, where new laws in 2021 tightened qualifications for mail-in ballots, which were now due earlier than previous years. Additional state legislation established requirements for more voter identification than previous years to avoid alleged voter fraud. As with Texas and elsewhere, there had been no examples of widespread voter fraud in 2020. With respect to turnout, the same numbers of White Republicans voted in 2022 as in 2018, the last gubernatorial election year. However, the overwhelmingly African-American Democratic turnout decreased by 25 percent.[30]

Other "reforms" occurred in Georgia, where the state legislature enacted several voting laws, including one that allowed partisan election commissioners to choose election supervisors. That change produced the dismissal of several Black officials."[31] The overall result from Georgia's new laws produced skewed results. While the number of voters in 2022 approximated the turnout in 2018, the participation gap between White and Black voters increased from 3.9 percent in 2018 to 7.3 percent in 2022.[32] At the end of the "reforms," the percentage of participating White voters grew much more than Black voters, thus reducing the power of minority voters.

Great Replacement Theory

If nothing else, conservative commentator Patrick Buchanan has a history of being clear about race. In his *Suicide of a Super Power*, the two-time Reform Party presidential candidate wrote that growing percentages of racial minorities in the United States "is not a formula for social peace. . . . Racially, culturally, ethnically, politically, America is disintegrating." Instead of racial pluralism, Buchanan argued, "We need to reform our immigration laws to give preference to those from countries that have historically been most of our immigrants, who share our values, speak English, have college or advanced degrees, and can be easily assimilated."[33] In other words, Buchanan suggests, White Christian Europeans are the key to America's glory past, present, and future.

These days, most American White supremacists are not as overt in their behavior as Buchanan, choosing instead to offer more nuanced accusations about non-White people, non-Christians taking control of the United States.

As in the past, they also tend to be disproportionately Republican and Protestant evangelicals, and all too willing to blame Democrats for allowing racial demographic changes in American society. During his 2022 U.S. Senatorial campaign in Ohio, Republican nominee J.D. Vance warned that "Democrats have decided that they can't win reelection in 2022 unless they bring in a large number of new voters to replace the voters already here."[34] Echoed Republican U.S. Senator Ron Johnson of Wisconsin rhetorically, "This [Biden] administration wants complete open borders. And you have to ask yourself, why? Is it really [that] they want to remake the demographics of America to [ensure] that they stay in power forever?"[35] House of Representatives leader Elise Stefanik, chair of the House Republican Conference and third-ranking House Republican member, answered Johnson's rhetorical question directly, claiming that the "Radical Democrats . . . plan to grant amnesty to 11 MILLION illegal immigrants who will overthrow our current electorate and create a permanent liberal majority in Washington."[36] These not-so-subtle remarks underscore the prominence of Great Replacement Theory, an unsubstantiated racist ideology that non-White people are conspiring to replace White culture and power with immigrants from non-White, non-English speaking, non-Protestant countries.[37]

The racial replacement accusations by national Republican leaders correlate directly with the views of most Republicans. In April 2022, the Southern Poverty Law Center sponsored a nationwide poll about Great Replacement Theory. When asked "whether the changing demographics of America pose a threat to white Americans and their culture and values, or not," 53 percent of Republicans replied "yes," compared to 22 percent of Democrats and 31 percent of Independents.[38] The 53 percent number is not an outlier. A survey carried out by *YouGov* in June 2022 found that 54 percent of Republicans agreed that "a group of people is trying to replace white Americans with immigrants and people of color," compared with 13 percent of Democrats and 26 percent of Independents.[39] Simply put, Great Replacement Theory is now a cornerstone of Republican political values; it has become acceptable in anti-immigrant circles for explaining how to protect "our culture" of keeping America White. By its definition and application, Great Replacement Theory is undemocratic.

Critical Race Theory

White parents and state legislators already angry with increasing numbers of racial minorities have been drawn to Critical Race Theory (CRT) as a means of shaping K-12 public education in a manner that plays down or even ignores the nation's racial history. In fact, CRT is not intended as a K-12 educational tool or instruction methodology for driving minority discrimination. Rather, it is a province of academic theorists that addresses the historical relationship between racism and other social, economic, psychological, and political aspects of life, and far from the pedagogy of K-12 public education.[40] But that simple fact hasn't stopped CRT critics who aren't concerned with the theory as much as finding a rationalization for controlling education content that avoids any honest discussion of race and the history of discrimination in America.

CRT critics have reconstructed the meaning of the term as the teaching of any topic that reflects inequality in America from the time of slavery to the present day.[41] As of the beginning of 2023, at least 16 states had banned instruction of CRT even though no educators had taught the concept.[42] In their attempt to rewrite history, CRT opponents have provided penalties in instances when the new rules were not applied to classroom pedagogy. An English teacher in Missouri was fired for assigning a worksheet titled "How Racially Privileged Are You"?[43] In Tennessee, a teacher was dismissed for telling his class that White privilege is a fact.[44] In Texas, a principal was reprimanded for writing a letter in the wake of the George Floyd tragedy that asked the community to work together to defeat systemic racism.[45]

In some states, a broadened version of CRT has gone beyond racism to gender issues. For example, in Florida, the state legislature passed a bill prohibiting "classroom instruction and discussion about sexual orientation and gender identity." Remarked Governor Ron DeSantis as he signed the bill into law, "We will make sure that parents can send their kids to school to get an education, not an indoctrination."[46] In other words, discussions about sexual orientation and identity are out of bounds. Another Florida law about gender and race, the Stop Woke Act, bars university professors from discussing anything in the classroom that "espouses, promotes, [or] advances" anything that might lead students to feel guilty about history.[47] In short, the reconstructed interpretation of CRT has become the means through which K-12 educators and university professors have been kept from focusing on race, racism, and other controversial issues in American society. Such an approach is nothing less than a purposive reframing of America's provocative issues. Moreover, laws dealing with interpretations of students feelings are likely to produce endless lawsuits.

Elected and appointed officials concerned with CRT have taken their concern about the issue of books in the classrooms. PEN America, a 100+-year-old nonpartisan organization of journalists, essayists, and publishers, cataloged the growing school book ban movement between July 2021 and March 2022. During that brief nine-month period, PEN America discovered more than 1,600 books in 17 states had been banned from classrooms and instruction, more than double the number from 2020. Seventy-one percent of the prohibited books centered on race, racism, and activism. More than 40 percent addressed LGBTQ themes. Texas led the pack with 801 bans, followed by Florida's 566 and Pennsylvania with 457. The banned authors included winners of the Nobel Prize in Literature, the National Book Award for Young People's Literature, the NAACP Image Award, and the GLAAD Award for Media Representation.[48]

Racist revisionism hasn't stopped with public education. In some states, the concerns of residents and policymakers have extended the ban to local libraries over material they see as pornographic, hateful, or unkind to White people. Some have challenged books that they find objectionable and insisted on their removal. Often, all that's needed is for a single member of the community to object, followed by months of wait until a decision is made. Until then, the book is unavailable. When librarians have resisted demands as intrusions on First Amendment guarantees, activists have gone so far as to try to fire uncooperative personnel or dissolve resistant library governing bodies. That's exactly what happened in Texas when a librarian was fired for not removing *How to Be an Antiracist* by Ibram X. Kendi, a dismissal that has occurred in several other states.[49]

Such efforts are nothing less than political censorship.[50] In 2023, seven states passed legislation, often vague, enabling challenges to books on racial abuse, sexual discussions, and other "community standards," with substantial fines and imprisonment for librarians that violate the rules. Another dozen states were expected to pass similar legislation in 2024.[51] In most cases, books are removed upon the challenge and are not returned until the veracity of the dispute is settled, which can take months or longer.

The outcome from these assaults on knowledge has been predictable enough. Afraid of the consequences from violating new laws and regulations, many teachers have abandoned or severely diluted treatment of traditional topics like Black History Month, slavery, racism, and sexism. Others have quit the profession because of limitations that they feel undermine a complete education.[52] A few teachers in the affected states have found the rules sufficiently vague that they have continued teaching threatened topics because they believe in their educational value, yet they continue their work in fear. With respect to libraries, fierce First Amendment debates have occurred with unusual interpretations of the Constitution leading to rewritten rules or even dismissal of personnel not respectful of "community standards."

Whether in public schools or public libraries, book-banning advocates are clear in their desire to control subject matter, particularly regarding race and sexuality. No Left Turn, a national organization dedicated to opposing "aggressive, radical totalitarian ideology in the schools," puts it this way: the goal of *The 1619 Project* (A documented and well-received history of race and racism in America) and CRT is "to overturn [American society] by sowing divisiveness and hate."[53] Yet, by virtue of their intent to rid schools and libraries of literature that confronts longstanding social, ethical and political values in American society, book ban activists are sweeping any discussion and knowledge of important themes under a racist rug.

Practices at Odds with Democracy

What can be said about racism in the third decade of the twenty-first century? All one has to do is review racial gerrymandering, voter suppression, Great Replacement Theory, and CRT to realize that for many people, racism remains a tragic cornerstone of American society. We're reminded that this persistent unfortunate behavior in America existed long before Donald Trump's rise to power in 2016 and remains after his removal from power by the voters in 2020. Nevertheless, one fact is crystal clear, namely that the continued racial and antisemitic discrimination by anti-democrats to reduce the worth of others through denial of their value guarantees a society mired in inequality, and where there is inequality, there cannot be democracy.

THE PERPETUATION OF TRUMPISM IN AMERICAN SOCIETY

Regardless of Donald Trump's future in politics, Trumpism remains a political fixture in American society. Trump's sinister brilliance in seizing and thriving on society's vulnerabilities and insecurities have not been put to rest as much as it has become a road map for would be authoritarians to follow in his footsteps. Such rhetoric has become a cornerstone of several Republican candidate campaigns in search of support for the 2024 Republican presidential nomination. Moreover, dozens of Republican members in Congress now embrace the basic tenets of Trumpism in areas ranging from opposition to gender- and race-related policies to attacks on key institutions such as the FBI, IRS, Department of Homeland Security and even the Department of Defense. In other words, they are attacking the very institutions designed to protect society.

Authoritarian Appeals—Thriving on Divisiveness

Looking to the 2024 presidential election and beyond, the politics of division remains a central focus for would-be authoritarians. Building on traditional explosive concepts in some cases, and exploring new wrinkles in others, anti-democrats have continued to foment hate and distrust in American society. One such longstanding issue, illegal immigration, remains a consistent tool for racial discord. Another authoritarian weapon, wokeness, is a relatively new, or at least reconstructed, topic serving as an umbrella of sorts for attacking the litany of efforts by White liberals and minorities to reverse the long-standing foundation of discrimination and inequality in the United States.

Immigration

Much of this volume reviews the perils of attacks on immigration, viewed by detractors as a historically demographic disrupting agent that threatens the status quo. Under Trumpism, illegal immigration has been given as the primary reason for threatening White people already here with a soon-to-be non-White majority. This feeling is most pronounced among Republicans and White evangelical Protestants, whose numbers tend to overlap extensively. According to the findings of a major national poll released in 2023, 40 percent of all Americans "believe the growing number of newcomers from other countries threatens traditional American customs and values." When broken down by political parties, 69 percent of Republicans felt in jeopardy, compared to 17 percent of Democrats. This correlates with the attitudes of religious denominations. Sixty-five percent of White evangelical Protestants feared losing traditional American values, compared to 40 percent of other Christians and 27 percent of those with non-Christian religions.[54] So, to what extent do these figures mesh with Trumpism? In a national poll taken by *The Hill* 18 months after the 2020 election, 69 percent of Trump voters expressed concern that U.S.-born citizens "are losing economic, political and cultural influence in the country to immigrants," compared to 30 percent of Biden voters.[55] The connection between evangelical Republican Trump voters and racist attitudes seems indisputable.

In a bizarre way, all of this correlates with the consistent inability of national political leaders to reach agreement on a new immigration policy. Particularly, Republicans have been singled out as the party using the perils of the immigration issue as a means to draw voter support. During Donald Trump's presidency, conservative Fox television commentator Juan Williams noted that "Trump plays politics with immigrants. . . . The facts show the (border) wall is all about politics because most illegal immigrants overstay visas, and most illegal drugs come through legal points of entry."[56] Williams is right. U.S. Government data shows that more than half of the illegal immigrants in the United States are people who have overstayed their visas.[57] They hardly fit the typical anti-immigrant description of poor, nomadic, criminal families trying to crash through America's border. And regarding Trump's claim that almost all illegal drug smuggling takes place through illegal border crossings, official government estimates are that as much as 90 percent actually arrive through legal ports of entry.[58] The facts are light years away from the perceptions of bigots.

But why deal with the facts when you can characterize life in the United States as a nation overwhelmed in terms of illegal border crossings by criminals full of drugs? The answer, according to a 2022 Pew Research Poll, is that 72 percent of Republicans say they are "very concerned" about U.S. security along the U.S.-Mexican border, compared with 22 percent of Democrats. Fear, even manufactured fear, sells especially when it comes to race. Therefore, there is little incentive for Republicans in Congress to come to the immigration reform table when the issue is so charged with Republican followers.

Shipping migrants to northern cities is a recent twist carried out by Republican governors. Three state chief executives in the post-Trump era—Ron DeSantis (Florida), Greg Abbott (Texas), and Doug Ducey (Arizona)—have bused migrants awaiting processing by federal authorities to cities far from the southern border and less impacted by the immigration issue, costing several millions of state taxpayer dollars in the process. Their migrant removal efforts have been predicated on the claim that large numbers of migrants have negatively impacted their local economies and health conditions. One particularly controversial shipment occurred when Florida Governor Ron DeSantis used state funds to send a planeload of migrants in Texas to affluent Martha's Vineyard in Massachusetts. DeSantis defended his actions as an effort "to protect Florida,"[59] but he moved migrants from Texas! Moreover, an investigation of the scheme showed that the agents transporting the migrants falsely told them that jobs and other opportunities would be available upon their arrival.[60] Clearly, immigration remains an issue worthy of exploitation for Trumpists preying on public anxieties.

Wokeness

Much of the racism-based discussion in the post-Trump presidency era centers on what anti-race leaders call the "woke" mentality. The term "woke" emerged in 2014 as part of the Black Lives Matter movement after a police shooting of Michael Brown, an unarmed teenager in Ferguson, Missouri.[61] "Stay woke," slang for "awake," refers to African Americans keeping aware of police brutality and racial injustice. By the 2020 election, "woke" was bantered about by leading Republican conservatives not as a warning against abuse and injustice, but rather as a short-cut pejorative term to the evils of Black and liberal White activism focusing on police brutality and policies viewed as harmful to racial minorities. Like so many other race-related issues, Americans are divided over the term "woke." A March 2023 *USA Today/Ipsos* survey found that 56 percent of respondents agreed with the description of woke as "being informed about social injustices," whereas 39 percent of the respondents chose "overly politically correct." When examined by political party, 78 percent of Democrats agreed with the first definition, while 56 percent of Republicans chose the latter.[62]

Trumpist Republican leaders have wrapped their anger with modern civil rights and civil liberties issues into anti-woke strategies. Among their woke criticisms are complaints against public school course work on the history of slavery and other events reflective of Black history; police reforms that allow violent demonstrations; corporate sensitivities to civil rights; and separation of religion and the state. Additional concerns about woke behavior have expanded to abortion; homosexuality; transgender issues; climate change; gun control; and even the FDA's management of the COVID-19 pandemic.[63] Some anti-woke adherents have gone so far as to adopt the QAnon perspective of connecting woke with pedophilia.

One recent account describes anti-woke as "a modern-day mixture of McCarthyism and white grievance."[64] It's that and more. In essence, being anti-woke means opposition to any reflection on or concern with conditions smacking of inequality or, in a broader sense, denial of individual's right to self-determination and full participation in society. More to the point, it's Trumpism wrapped in a new name.

Woke opponents bear much of the same anti-government, conspiratorial beliefs exploited by Donald Trump in his 2016 presidential campaign. They blame the "deep state" and its allies for the loss of "American values" on such issues as abortion, LGBTQ rights, and book bans, otherwise the "culture war."[65] As noted earlier, these issues have been particularly important to Republican party primary voters and remain so to this day. And, of course, primary elections provide delegates for the presidential nominations.

With the approach to the 2024 presidential election, many Republican leaders, including candidates for the Republican nomination, continued to jump on the anti-woke movement. Florida Governor Ron DeSantis has been among the most outspoken critics against wokeness. In 2022, he signed into law the WOKE law, short for "Stop the Wrongs to Our Kids and Employees Act," which prevents public schools and employers from racial sensitivity instruction training. He has also come out against vaccine mandates, protection for journalists from frivolous lawsuits, and math books, which he erroneously claimed relied upon CRT.[66] In 2023, DeSantis signed a bill defunding diversity programs in Florida colleges and universities.[67] Also in 2023, the DeSantis-appointed Florida Board of Education rejected a new A.P. African-American history course on the basis that it "lacked educational value."[68] The course had been successfully piloted in 60 classes and contained sections on civil rights, politics, literature, the arts, and geography, and was totally unrelated to CRT. That was of little concern, however, to the Florida governor who in all probability saw a benefit in pitting White people against Black people.

DeSantis has learned much from Trump with respect to using the power of his office to push around opponents and frustrate potential critics. He suspended a twice-elected local state attorney for Hillsborough County (and a Democrat) who pledged not to prosecute anyone who provides or undergoes an abortion, saying that he disobeyed state law. As he neared the moment of a presidential candidacy announcement, DeSantis took control of the state bureaucratic machinery that could be utilized to provide impartial assessments of him and his administration. With respect to state public records requests, he made it very difficult for those requesting the documents to obtain them.[69] In 2023, DeSantis all but shut down any exchanges with national media other than occasional exceptions for Fox television.[70] In an authoritarian world, control of the media goes a long way toward silencing voices of the opposition. DeSantis has planted himself as the Trump heir-apparent in terms of using race to divide American society. For example, in the book he produced as an introduction to his presidential candidacy, DeSantis described Black Lives Matter-inspired protests as "riots."[71] On the issue of race, little difference exists between DeSantis and Donald Trump.

Wokeness and its implications emerged as a centerpiece in the Republican response by Arkansas Governor Sarah Huckabee Sanders to President Biden's State of the Union Address on February 7, 2023. Focusing on social policies at one point, the former press secretary to President Trump accused Democrats of forcing Americans "to partake in their rituals, salute their flags, and worship their false idols" and that "the Biden administration seems more interested in the woke fantasies than the hard reality Americans face every day." Like DeSantis, Governor Sanders seemed to insert "woke" as a description of virtually any socio-economic program undertaken by Democrats.

A softer approach to the race issue was offered by former South Carolina Governor Nikki Haley, United Nations Ambassador under Donald Trump, in her presidential candidacy announcement on February 14, 2023. Haley noted that there is "too much self-loathing in the United States" and proudly claimed that "America is not a racist country." What she failed to mention is that South Carolina ranked 30th among states making racial progress.[72]

In a still less direct way that nonetheless made the point, then-Governor of Arkansas, Asa Hutchinson, allowed a bill to become law that prohibited state agencies from teaching employees and contractors "divisive concepts" and topics concerning race or sex. Hutchinson declared for the Republican presidential nomination in May 2023 with the intent to" bring the country together" and "not create chaos."[73]

The latest twist involving the "us" versus "them" discrimination pattern has focused on anti-transgender legislation. State legislatures with large conservative majorities have passed laws forbidding classroom discussions about transgender issues, the availability of bathrooms to accommodate transgender populations, and even medical care for children transitioning to a different gender. So disconcerting was the transgender xenophobia in Montana in 2023 that the state legislature exiled the only transgender member from the chamber while the members debated—and later passed—a series of bills that restricted transition-related care. The legislation paralleled similar laws recently passed in a dozen other states.⁷⁴ Shortly thereafter, Republican U.S. Senator Steve Daines of Montana commended the state lawmakers for the removal of its legitimately elected transgender member from debate.⁷⁵

Viewed in their totality, the actions and statements by key national and state Republican figures in the post-Trump presidency period share one vital characteristic: the divisive culture war approach led by Donald Trump has a litany of would-be successors ready to seize the "us" versus "them" mantle. And while it's true that not all Trump supporters subscribe to these themes, the data show that a sizable number do. Racism and newer forms of exclusion remain a powerful dynamic in the United States and many Republican leaders are not about to address it.

Domestic Terrorism

The Federal Bureau of Investigation defines "domestic terrorism" as "acts dangerous to human life that are a violation of the criminal laws of the United States or of a State, Intended to: intimidate or coerce a civilian population; Influence the policy of government by intimidation or coercion; or Affect the conduct of a government by mass destruction, assassination or kidnapping."⁷⁶ In its 2022 annual report, the FBI reported that acts of domestic terrorism nearly doubled to 2,700 in 2021 from 1,400 in 2020. Attacks against elected public officials, once thought outlier events, have become part of routine political discussions and no longer carry any shock value. When five men were accused of plotting to kidnap Michigan Governor Gretchen Whitmer for "tyrannical COVID-19 policies" in 2020, a Michigan jury acquitted two and deadlocked on charges for the others. Only a second trial in a federal court did a jury find all five guilty of several charges.⁷⁷

Defenders of Trumpism have minimized the significance of attacks on public officials. Just before the 2022 midterm elections, a man broke into the San Francisco home of then-Democratic Speaker of the House Nancy Pelosi, with the intent to take her hostage for the lies she told as the "leader of the (Democratic) pack." The House leader was in Washington, but the intruder fractured the skull of her husband, Paul Pelosi, who was at home.⁷⁸ Shortly after the assault, Donald Trump suggested the attack was staged. Fox television host Tucker Carlson accused the police of falsifying the attack (body cams showed much of the attack as police entered the building), and new Twitter owner Elon Musk irresponsibly linked his 112 million followers to a discredited allegation that Pelosi was harmed by a male prostitute.⁷⁹ That Musk retracted his tweet shortly thereafter did little to dampen the discussion.

Attacks against members of Congress have skyrocketed in recent years, and some observers connect the increase with the skyrocketing tensions brought about by the Trump administration.⁸⁰ According to U.S. Capitol

Police, the agency responsible for protecting the Capitol, in 2016, the last year before Trump assumed office, there were 902 attacks against members of Congress. The numbers of attacks jumped every year so much that by 2020, 8,813 events were recorded.[81] They reached a high of 9,625 in 2021 before subsiding in 2022, when they still remained above 7,000.[82] The evidence is clear: when one is elected to Congress these days, he or she serves at their own risk. That Trumpists and their allies ignore or minimize the value of attacks on public officials only invites more disruption downstream by those with little concern for democratic institutions.

Domestic terrorism goes far beyond Washington, DC. In his remarks before the U.S. Senate in September 2021, FBI Director Christopher Wray stated that "homegrown violent extremists posed the greatest, most immediate IT (information technology) threat to the homeland." During an eighteen-month period between March 2020 and September 2021, Wray noted that the number of domestic investigations doubled to more than 2,700.[83] Adds a report from the ADL, White supremacists have become involved with destroying institutions such as the nation's electric grid to hasten the collapse of society.[84]

A significant amount of domestic terrorism has surfaced with efforts to destroy the nation's infrastructure, particularly the electricity grid. Through the first eight months of 2022, one examination of the Department of Energy data found more than one hundred such intentional events. The number of cyberattacks conducted during the same period also went up relative to previous years. Many of these activities connect with efforts to destroy the nation's social fabric in favor of an authoritarian regime. And while authorities have not uncovered the motivation of all attacks, a number have been undertaken by self-admitted White supremacists and neo-Nazis committing to causing a race war.[85] Testimony before the January 6 Select Committee by members of violent rightwing groups clearly linked their disruptive activities leading up to, during and following the insurrection with Donald Trump as well as key political allies supportive of undemocratic efforts to overturn the 2020 presidential election.[86]

Public Opinion

What have we learned from exploding divisiveness detonated during the Donald Trump presidency and the violent insurrection against Congress that unconstitutionally sought to keep Trump in power? Maybe not as much as we might have expected. Not for a sizable segment of American society, anyway. The polling site *YouGov* asked Americans about the January 6, 2021, insurrection right after the event, one year later, and then again in January 2023, with remarkable findings over time. When questioned whether they approved or disapproved of the insurrection, overall disapproval in 2023 stood at 64 percent, down from 81 percent in 2021. Among Democrats, disapproval remained high in 2023 at 80 percent, down slightly from 94 percent in 2021. The greatest decline, however, came from Republicans, where disapproval of the insurrection in 2023 stood at 49 percent, down sharply from 74 percent in 2021.[87] In the most significant rebellion against American government since the Civil War, only half of Republicans disapproved of the attack. That piece of data is hard to overlook.

Two years after the disturbingly dark January 6 insurrection event, the ongoing chasm between Democrats and Republicans remains deeper than ever. And while each side may look to the other as the source of America's problems, there is agreement that the future of our system of government is at a dangerous tipping point. When asked in a 2022 Quinnipiac national poll about whether American democracy was threatened more from other countries or from within, three-quarters of the respondents answered from within. There was a sizable difference between the political parties with 66 percent of Republicans citing instability within compared to 83 percent of Democrats.[88]

Another poll by *Ipsos* in early 2022 drilled down to responsibility for the January 6 political earthquake at the nation's Capital. Thirty percent of Republicans blamed Antifa (a Black consciousness movement) and the federal government, compared with seven percent of Democrats. It's worth noting that post-insurrection analyses by experts found no presence of Antifa at the tragic event. Similar to the Quinnipiac data, 70 percent of the respondents agreed that with the statement that "American government is in crisis and failing" regardless of political party.[89] The point is, most people now see American government in crisis, although predictably the two sides don't agree on the cause.

It doesn't take rocket science to realize that Americans are deeply concerned about the future of the nation. However, reaching consensus on the causes and solutions seem a near impossibility. A sizable minority either refuses or is unable to recognize the pressing underlying problems that place the nation in political peril.

NOTES

1. *The January 6th Report: Findings from the Select Committee to Investigate the January 6th Attack on the United States of America* (New York, NY: Random House Books, 2023), p. 29.

2. These data come from "Race in America 2019," Pew Research Center, April 9, 2019, https://www.pewresearch.org/social-trends/2019/04/09/race-in-america-2019/.

3. Benjamin C. Ruisch and Melissa J. Ferguson, "Did Donald Trump's Presidency Reshape Americans' Prejudices," *Trends in Cognitive Sciences*, 27, no. 3 (March 2023), https://www.sciencedirect.com/journal/trends-in-cognitive-sciences/vol/27/issue/3.

4. Michael I. Norton and Samuel R. Sommers, "Whites See Racism as a Zero-Sum Game That They Are Now Losing," *Perspectives on Psychological Science*, 6, no. 3 (2011): 215–218, https://www.hbs.edu/ris/Publication%20Files/norton%20sommers%20whites%20see%20racism_ca92b4be-cab9-491d-8a87-cf1c6ff244ad.pdf.

5. N. Derek Brown, Drew S. Jacoby-Senghor, and Isaac Raymundo, "If You Rise, I Fall: Equality is Prevented by the Misperception that it Harms Advantaged Groups," *Science Advances*, 8, no. 18 (May 6, 2022), https://www.science.org/doi/10.1126/sciadv.abm2385.

6. "Trump Claims White People 'at the Back of the Line' for COVID Vaccines, Treatments," *Newsweek*, January 16, 2022, https://www.newsweek.com/trump-claims-white-people-back-line-covid-vaccines-treatments-1669884.

7. Andy Cao, Jason M. Lindo, and Jiee Zhong, "Can Social Media Rhetoric Incite Hate Incidents? Evidence from Trump's 'Chinese Virus' Tweets," National Bureau of Economic Research Working Paper 30588, Washington, DC, October 2022, https://www.nber.org/papers/w30588.

8. "Federal Bureau of Investigation: Crime Data Explorer," Washington, DC, 2022, https://cde.ucr.cjis.gov/LATEST/webapp/#/pages/home.

9. "2014 Hate Crime Statistics," Federal Bureau of Investigation, Washington, DC, https://ucr.fbi.gov/hate-crime/2014/tables/table-1, and "2020 Hate Crime Statistics," Federal Bureau of Investigation, Washington, DC, https://www.justice.gov/crs/highlights/2020-hate-crimes-statistics. For the years between 2015 and 2020, FBI figures are 449. 2016; 427, 2017; 485, 2018; and 527, 2019.

10. Monica Verea, "Anti-Immigrant and Anti-Mexican Attacks during the First 18 Months of the Trump Administration," *Norteamerica*, 13, no. 2 (2018), https://www.revistanorteamerica.unam.mx/index.php/nam/article/view/335.

11. See "Trump Derides Protections for Immigrants from 'Shithole Countries,'" *AP News*, January 11, 2018, https://apnews.com/article/immigration-north-america-donald-trump-ap-top-news-international-news-fdda2ff0b877416c8ae1c1a77a3cc425.

12. "The State of Antisemitism in America, 2022: AJC's Survey of American Jews," American Jewish Committee, New York, NY, 2023, https://www.ajc.org/news/the-state-of-antisemitism-in-america-ajc-advocacy-anywhere-0.

13. "With Watchful Eyes, a Nationwide Network Tracks Antisemitic Threats," *The New York Times,* May 29, 2023, https://www.nytimes.com/2023/05/29/us/anti-semitic-attacks-jewish-secure-community-network.html.

14. "Audit of Antisemitic Incidents 2010, ADL, October 2011," https://www.jewishvirtuallibrary.org/2010-adl-audit-of-anti-semitic-incidents-in-u-s .

15. See "Millions Are Victims of Hate Crimes though Many Never Report Them," The Center for Public Integrity, August 16, 2016, https://publicintegrity.org/politics/millions-are-victims-of-hate-crimes-though-many-never-report-them/ and "Why Hate Crimes Are Underreported—and What Police Departments have to do with

it," *Northeastern Global News*, May 23, 2021, https://news.northeastern.edu/2021/08/23/why-hate-crimes-are-underreported-and-what-police-departments-have-to-do-with-it/.

16. V.O. Key, Jr., *Politics, Parties & Pressure Groups*, fifth edition (New York, NY: Thomas Y. Crowell Company, 1964), p. 603.

17. "Supreme Court Invalidates Key Part of the Voting Rights Act," *The New York Times*, June 25, 2013, https://www.nytimes.com/2013/06/26/us/supreme-court-ruling.html#:~:text=WASHINGTON%20%E2%80%94%20The%20Supreme%20Court%20on,laws%20without%20advance%20federal%20approval..

18. "Maps in Four States Were Ruled Illegal Gerrymanders. They're being Used Anyway," *The New York Times*, August 8, 2022, https://www.nytimes.com/2022/08/08/us/elections/gerrymandering-maps-elections-republicans.html.

19. "Supreme Court Rejects Voting Map That Diluted Black Voters' Power," *The New York Times*, June 8, 2023, https://www.nytimes.com/2023/06/08/us/supreme-court-voting-rights-act-alabama.html.

20. "Supreme Court Clears Way for Louisiana to Redo Congressional Map," *The Hill*, June 26, 2023, https://thehill.com/homenews/4067876-supreme-court-clears-way-for-louisiana-to-redo-congressional-map/.

21. "Florida Republicans Pass Congressional Map Severely Limiting Black Voter Power," *Reuters*, April 7, 2022, https://www.reuters.com/world/us/us-supreme-court-lets-alabama-use-electoral-map-faulted-racial-bias-2022-02-07/.

22. "Texas Reduces Black and Hispanic Majority Congressional Districts in Proposed Map, Despite People of Color Fueling Population Growth," *The Texas Tribune*, September 27, 2021, https://www.texastribune.org/2021/09/24/texas-congressional-redistricting/.

23. "Who Controlled Redistricting in Every State," The Brennan Center for Justice, October 5, 2022, https://www.brennancenter.org/our-work/research-reports/who-controlled-redistricting-every-state.

24. "Patterns in the Introduction and Passage of Restrictive Voting Bills are Best Explained by Race," The Brennan for Justice, August 3, 2022, https://www.brennancenter.org/our-work/research-reports/patterns-introduction-and-passage-restrictive-voting-bills-are-best.

25. For a list of states and the specifics of their legislation see "Checking in with the Major Voter Suppression Laws," Democracy Docket, April 12, 2022, https://www.democracydocket.com/news/checking-in-with-the-major-voter-suppression-laws/.

26. See Andrew C. Eggers, Haritz Garro, and Justin Grimmer, "No Evidence for Systematic Voter Fraud: A Guide to Statistical Claims about the 2020 Election," *Proceedings of the National Academy of Sciences*, November 2, 2021, and https://www.pnas.org/doi/abs/10.1073/pnas.2103619118, and "AP Finds Fewer than 475 Cases of Potential Voter Fraud in Six 2020 Battleground States," *The Hill*, December 15, 2021, https://thehill.com/homenews/presidential-campaign/585901-ap-finds-fewer-than-475-cases-of-potential-voter-fraud-in-six/.

27. See "Records Show Massive Disenfranchisement and Racial Disparities in 2022 Texas Primary," Brennan Center for Justice, January 17, 2023, https://www

.brennancenter.org/our-work/research-reports/records-show-massive-disenfranchise-ment-and-racial-disparities-2022-texas and "19% of Harris County Mail-in Ballots in the 2022 Primary were Rejected due to SB1, according to Elections Administrator," *Houston Public Media*, March 11, 2022, https://www.houstonpublicmedia.org/articles/news/politics/2022/03/11/420985/the-states-new-election-law-led-to-19-of-harris-county-mail-ballots-in-the-primary-to-be-rejected/.

28. "Analysis: When 1 in 8 Texas Mail Ballots Gets Trashed, that's Vote Suppression," *The Texas Tribune*, March 3, 2022, https://www.texastribune.org/2022/03/18/texas-rejected-election-ballots/.

29. See Louisiana Secretary of State Election Report, 2018 and 2022 General Elections, https://electionstatistics.sos.la.gov/Data/Post_Election_Statistics/statewide/2018_1106_sta.pdf and https://electionstatistics.sos.la.gov/Data/Post_Election_Statistics/statewide/2022_1108_sta.pdf.

30. "Blacks Represent 78 Percent of Registered Democrats in South Carolina." See "Party Affiliation among Adults in South Carolina by Race/Ethnicity," Pew Research Center, May 30, 2014, https://www.pewresearch.org/religion/religious-landscape-study/compare/party-affiliation/by/racial-and-ethnic-composition/among/state/south-carolina/.

31. "Voting Laws Roundup: May 2022," The Brennan Center for Justice, May 26, 2022, https://www.brennancenter.org/our-work/research-reports/voting-laws-roundup-may-2022.

32. "Georgia's Racial Turnout Gap Grew in 2022," The Brennan Center for Justice, December 16, 2022, https://www.brennancenter.org/our-work/analysis-opinion/georgias-racial-turnout-gap-grew-2022.

33. Patrick J. Buchanan, *Suicide of a Super Power* (New York, NY: St Martin's Press, 2011), pp. 156, 402, and 421–422.

34. "From Embrace to 'Replace,'" *U.S. News*, May 20, 2022, https://www.usnews.com/news/the-report/articles/2022-05-20/the-republican-embrace-of-the-great-replacement-theory.

35. *Media Matters*, April 15, 2021, https://www.mediamatters.org/white-nationalism/fox-business-larry-kudlow-allows-sen-ron-johnson-push-racist-replacement-theory.

36. Facebook post, September 14, 2021–October 4, 2021.

37. "What is 'Great Replacement Theory' and How Does It Fuel Racist Victims," *PBS*, May 16, 2022, https://www.pbs.org/newshour/politics/what-is-great-replacement-theory-and-how-does-it-fuel-racist-violence.

38. "SPLC Poll Finds Substantial Support for 'Great Replacement' Theory and Other Hard-Right Ideas," Southern Poverty Law Center, June 1, 2022, https://www.splcenter.org/news/2022/06/01/poll-finds-support-great-replacement-hard-right-ideas.

39. "Views on Great Replacement Theory," *YouGov Poll*, June 1–5, 2022, https://today.yougov.com/topics/politics/articles-reports/2022/06/07/views-great-replacement-theory-yougov-poll-june-1-.

40. See Monita Mungo, "The Real Problem with Critical Race Theory," *The Hill*, May 26, 2021, https://thehill.com/opinion/civil-rights/555351-the-real-problem-with-critical-race-theory/.

41. "New Critical Race Theory Laws have Teachers Scared, Confused and self-censoring," *The Washington Post*, February 14, 2022, https://www.washingtonpost.com/education/2022/02/14/critical-race-theory-teachers-fear-laws/.

42. Most of the information in this paragraph comes from Theodore R. Johnson, Emelia Gold, and Ashley Zhao, "How Anti-Critical Race Theory Bills Are Taking Aim at Teachers," *fivethirtyeight.com*, May 9, 2022, https://fivethirtyeight.com/features/how-anti-critical-race-theory-bills-are-taking-aim-at-teachers/.

43. "Missouri Teacher Accused of Teaching Critical Race Theory Loses Job," *Springfield News-Leader*, April 7, 2022, https://www.news-leader.com/story/news/education/2022/04/07/greenfield-missouri-teacher-kim-morrison-accused-teaching-critical-race-theory-crt-loses-job/.

44. "A White Teacher Taught White Students about White Privilege. It Cost Him His Job," *The Washington Post*, December 6, 2021, https://www.washingtonpost.com/education/2021/12/06/tennessee-teacher-fired-critical-race-theory/.

45. "School Board Member Says Black Principal's Activism 'Got Him Fired' From School," *HuffPost*, July 18, 2022, https://www.huffpost.com/entry/school-board-black-principal-texas-activism_n_62d3be34e4b0e6fc1a97dfeb.

46. "DeSantis Signs Florida Bill that Opponents Call 'Don't Say Gay,'" *The New York Times*, March 28, 2022, https://www.nytimes.com/2022/03/28/us/desantis-florida-dont-say-gay-bill.html.

47. Quoted in Michael R. Bloomberg, "Republican Censors Go for Woke," *The Wall Street Journal*, August 16, 2022, https://www.wsj.com/articles/republican-censors-go-for-woke-florida-ron-desantis-critical-race-theory-ban-gender-universities-businesses-training-dei-free-expression-11660595313.

48. See "Banned in the USA: The Growing Movement to Censor Books in the Schools," Pen America, 2022, https://pen.org/report/banned-usa-growing-movement-to-censor-books-in-schools/#. Percentages exceed 100 because some banned books carried more than theme. The numbers of banned books exceed 1.600 because some books were banned by more than one state.

49. "With Rising Book Bans, Librarians Have Come under Attack," *The New York Times*, July 7, 2022, https://www.nytimes.com/2022/07/06/books/book-ban-librarians.html.

50. "Censorship Battles' New Frontier: Your Public Library," *The Washington Post*, April 17, 2022, https://www.washingtonpost.com/nation/2022/04/17/public-libraries-books-censorship/.

51. See "School Librarians Face a New Penalty in the Banned-Book War: Prison," *The Washington Post*, https://www.washingtonpost.com/education/2023/05/18/school-librarians-jailed-banned-books/ and "Presidential Hopeful DeSantis Inspires Push to Make Book Bans Easier in Republican-Controlled States," *San Francisco Chronicle*, May 26, 2023, https://www.sfchronicle.com/news/politics/article/latest-gop-2024-hopeful-desantis-blazing-a-18121208.php.

52. "Caught in the Culture Wars, Teachers Are being Forced from their Jobs," *The Washington Post*, June 16, 2022, https://www.washingtonpost.com/education/2022/06/16/teacher-resignations-firings-culture-wars/.

53. "Mission, Goals & Objectives," No Left Turn, https://www.noleftturn.us/mission-goals-objectives/.

54. "Are Immigrants a Threat? Most Americans Don't Think So, but Those Receptive to the 'Threat' Narrative Are Predictably More Anti-immigrant," Public Research Religion Institute, January 17, 2023, https://www.prri.org/research/are-immigrants-a-threat-most-americans-dont-think-so-but-those-receptive-to-the-threat-narrative-are-predictably-more-anti-immigrant/.

55. "6 in 10 Trump Voters Agree with Core Tenet of Great Replacement Theory: Survey," *The Hill*, May 24, 2022, https://thehill.com/homenews/state-watch/3499877-6-in-10-trump-voters-agree-with-core-tenet-of-great-replacement-theory-survey/.

56. "Juan Williams: My Immigrant Story," *The Hill*, June 25, 2018, https://thehill.com/opinion/immigration/393887-juan-williams-my-immigrant-story/.

57. "AP Fact Check: Visa Overstays Outpace Border Crossings," *Associated Press*, January 3, 2019, https://apnews.com/article/north-america-donald-trump-az-state-wire-ca-state-wire-immigration-48d0ad46f143478d9384410f5ae3d38b.

58. "How Do Illegal Drugs Cross the U.S.-Mexico Border," *NPR*, April 6, 2019, https://www.npr.org/2019/04/06/710712195/how-do-illegal-drugs-cross-the-u-s-mexico-border.

59. "DeSantis defends Martha's Vineyard Migrant Flights, Suggests More to Come," *Reuters*, September 16, 2022, https://www.reuters.com/world/us/tears-uncertainty-migrants-depart-marthas-vineyard-amid-political-standoff-2022-09-16/.

60. "The Story behind DeSantis's Migrant Flights to Martha's Vineyard," *The New York Times*, October 4, 2022, https://www.nytimes.com/2022/10/02/us/migrants-marthas-vineyard-desantis-texas.html.

61. For a detailed history of woke, see "How 'Woke' went from a Social Justice Term to a Pejorative Favored by Some Conservatives," *CNN*, July 10, 2022, https://www.cnn.com/2022/07/10/us/woke-race-deconstructed-newsletter-reaj/index.html.

62. "Americans Are Divided on whether 'Woke' is a Compliment or an Insult," *USA Today*, March 8, 2023, https://www.ipsos.com/en-us/americans-divided-whether-woke-compliment-or-insult.

63. For a list of issues and state actions, see Jonathan Chait, "Indoctrination Nation," *New York Magazine*, May 8–21, 2023, https://nymag.com/intelligencer/article/desantis-florida-trump-education-politics.html.

64. Michael Harriot, "War on Wokeness: The Year the Right around a Made-Up Menace," *The Guardian*, December 21, 2022, https://www.theguardian.com/us-news/2022/dec/20/anti-woke-race-america-history.

65. Ibid.

66. See "DeSantis, Aiming at a Favorite Foil, Wants to Roll Back Press Freedom," *The New York Times*, February 10, 2023, https://www.nytimes.com/2023/02/10/us/politics/ron-desantis-news-media.html and "The Race Politics of Ron DeSantis," *The Washington Post*, February 1, 2023, https://www.washingtonpost.com/politics/2023/02/01/desantis-race-politics/.

67. "DeSantis Signs Bill to Defund DEI Programs at Fla. Colleges," *The Washington Post,* May 15, 2023, https://www.washingtonpost.com/education/2023/05/15/desantis-defunds-dei-programs-florida-colleges/.

68. "Florida Rejects A.P. African American Studies Class," *The New York Times,* January 19, 2023, https://www.nytimes.com/2023/01/19/us/desantis-florida-ap-african-american-studies.html.

69. "DeSantis 'Review' of Public Records can Add Months of Delays, Newly Uncovered Log Reveals," www.Clickorlando.com, February 28, 2023, https://www.clickorlando.com/news/politics/2023/02/28/desantis-review-of-public-records-can-add-months-of-delays-newly-uncovered-log-reveals/.

70. "DeSantis Usually Avoids the Press. For Murdoch, He'll Make an Exception," *The New York Times,* March 3, 2023, https://www.nytimes.com/2023/03/02/business/media/ron-desantis-murdoch-media.html and "DeSantis Spokeswoman Christina Pushaw makes Sure Reporters Feel the Burn," *The Washington Post,* July 27, 2022, https://www.washingtonpost.com/media/2022/07/27/christina-pushaw-desantis/.

71. Ron DeSantis, *The Courage to Be Free* (New York, NY: Broadside Press, 2023), p. 125.

72. "2023's States with the Most Racial Progress," *WalletNews,* January 20, 2023, https://wallethub.com/edu/states-with-the-most-and-least-racial-progress/18428.

73. "Former Arkansas Gov. Asa Hutchinson Pushes Optimistic White House Bod, not a Candidate that 'Creates Chaos,'" *Killeen Daily Herald,* May 23, 2023, https://kdhnews.com/news/politics/former-arkansas-gov-asa-hutchinson-pushes-optimistic-white-house-bid-not-a-candidate-that-creates/article_06bf7c44-ec18-5ae5-b3c8-ea749907ed96.html.

74. "Montana Governor Signs Law Banning Transition Care for Minors," *The New York Times,* April 28, 2023, https://www.nytimes.com/2023/04/28/us/montana-trans-gianforte.html.

75. "A Transgender Lawmaker Is Exiled as Montana G.O.P. Flexes New Power," *The New York Times,* April 27, 2023, https://www.nytimes.com/2023/04/28/us/montana-trans-gianforte.html

76. "Strategic Intelligence Assessment and Data on Domestic Terrorism," Federal Bureau of Investigation and Department of Homeland Security, Washington, DC, October 2022, https://www.dhs.gov/sites/default/files/2022-10/22_1025_strategic-intelligence-assessment-data-domestic-terrorism.pdf.

77. See "Two Men Convicted in Plot to Kidnap Michigan's Governor," *The New York Times,* August 23, 2022, https://www.nytimes.com/2022/08/23/us/verdict-trial-gretchen-whitmer-kidnap.html and "Jury Convicts Men of Supporting Plot to Kidnap Michigan Governor," *The New York Times,* https://www.nytimes.com/2022/10/26/us/michigan-wolverine-watchmen-trial.html.

78. "Intruder Wanted to Break Speaker Pelosi's Kneecaps, Federal Complaint Says," *The New York Times,* October 31, 2022, https://www.nytimes.com/2022/10/31/us/pelosi-home-attack-suspect-charged.html.

79. Robert Reich, "Elon Musk's Paul Pelosi Tweet Proves He has no Business Running Twitter," *The Guardian,* October 31, 2022, https://www.theguardian.com/commentisfree/2022/oct/31/elon-musk-paul-pelosi-tweet-twitter.

80. "Mounting Intimidation against Members of Congress Threatens Us All," *The Washington Post*, October 3, 2022, https://www.washingtonpost.com/opinions/2022/10/03/threats-violence-members-congress-intimidation/ and "Donald Trump is the Accelerant," *Vox,* January 9, 2021, https://www.vox.com/21506029/trump-violence-tweets-racist-hate-speech.

81. "Threats against Members of Congress Are Skyrocketing. It's Changing the Job," *Los Angeles Times*, September 20, 2021, https://www.latimes.com/politics/story/2021-09-20/threats-members-of-congress.

82. "Threats to Congress Decreased after Record High in 2021, but Are Still Concerning: Police," *ABC News*, January 17, 2023, https://abcnews.go.com/Politics/threats-congress-decreased-after-record-high-2021-police/story?id=96492983.

83. Christopher Wray, "Threats to the Homeland: Evaluating the Landscape 20 Years After 9/11," Testimony before the U.S. Senate, September 21, 2021, https://abcnews.go.com/Politics/threats-congress-decreased-after-record-high-2021-police/story?id=96492983.

84. "White Supremacists Embrace 'Accelerationism,'" *ADL*, April 4, 2019, https://www.adl.org/resources/blog/white-supremacists-embrace-accelerationism/

85. "Physical Attacks on Power Grid Surge to New Peak," *Politico*, December 26, 2022, https://www.politico.com/news/2022/12/26/physical-attacks-electrical-grid-peak-00075216.

86. Mary B. McCord and Jacob Glick, "January 6th Report Exposes Ongoing, Converging Threat of Anti-democracy Schemes and Paramilitary Violence," *Just Security*, January 6, 2023, https://www.justsecurity.org/84669/the-january-6th-report-exposes-the-ongoing-converging-threat-of-anti-democracy-schemes-and-paramilitary-violence/.

87. "Most Americans—but Fewer than in 2021—Disapprove of the January 6 Capitol Takeover," *YouGov*, January 2023, https://today.yougov.com/topics/politics/articles-reports/2023/01/04/most-americans-disapprove-january-6-capitol-attack.

88. "Political Instability not U.S. Adversaries, Seen as Bigger Threat, Quinnipiac National Poll Finds; Nearly 6 in 20 Think Democracy is in Danger of Collapse," Quinnipiac Poll, January 12, 2022, https://poll.qu.edu/poll-release?releaseid=3831.

89. "Seven in Ten Americans Say the Country is in Crisis, at Risk of Failing," *NPR/Ipsos Poll*, January 3, 2022, https://www.ipsos.com/sites/default/files/ct/news/documents/2022-01/Topline-NPR-Ipsos-poll.pdf.

Chapter 12

Saving the American Experiment

Just underneath the masthead of *The Washington Post* lies the slogan, "Democracy Dies in Darkness." Adopted by the paper in 2017, it reflects the concern for transparency and the belief that information helps the public maneuver its way to truth in a democratic society. The *Post* wasn't the first place for the slogan to appear,[1] but there is little doubt that the catchphrase has received more exposure in that publication than anywhere previously because of its emergence as an internationally respected newspaper.

Despite what some might believe in current times, the message wasn't implemented as a warning about Trumpism *per se*. In fact, the idea of a tagline for the *Post* had been debated among the newspaper's management long before Trump's presence on the political stage. Nevertheless, with the growing acceptance by many of bigotry by many Americans as just another part of the political landscape, the horrific events surrounding the January 6, 2021, insurrection, and the political manipulation by Donald Trump and others, the slogan's appearance has presented a certain unpredicted timeliness. The power of the *Post's* tagline notwithstanding, it may well be that the fragility of democracy doesn't necessarily owe its vulnerability to darkness or even the political sleight of hand by Trump or anyone else.

If we've learned nothing else during these turbulent times, it's that the once-great American democratic experiment now sputters in the light of day for us all to clearly witness. From openly racist outbursts in public meetings, to election outcome deniers, to growing numbers of threats to public officials, and to those who would slam the door of truth and knowledge shut, the increasingly precarious foundation of American democracy has become a troubled open book with an uncertain ending.

Combined, authoritarian appeals, embedded racism and xenophobia, and domestic terrorism form a frightening foundation for unconstitutional regime change by an undemocratic element in American politics. The amalgamation presents a potentially terrifying crisis for American society. Far from exaggeration, the issues are real, with a new wave of insurrectionists ready to continue Trumpism in its next iteration.

THE THREAT TO DEMOCRACY CONTINUES

No one has demonstrated the possibility of would-be-authoritarian rule more than Donald Trump, a major sponsor if not ring leader of the January 6, 2021, insurrection. Moreover, he and his supporters are far from finished in their effort to remake America as an autocracy. The former president and announced 2024 Republican nomination candidate reminded us of the still-existent threat in 2023. In his address to the annual Conservative Political Action Conference (CPAC) in National Harbor, Maryland, on March 4, Trump bluntly said, "In 2016, I declared 'I am your voice.' Today, I add: I am your warrior. I am your justice. And for those who have been wronged and betrayed, I am your retribution."[2] In those four sentences, Trump reminded allies and opponents alike of his demagogic approach to governance: Take sole control of power and use it to punish those who resist you, with all the various activities carried out in the name of saving the public from calamitous disarray.

Blatantly and forcefully, in 2023 Trump presented himself ready to resume his authoritarian behavior in another presidential term as the disrupter-in-chief. In the wake of one criminal indictment after another, he repeatedly pronounced his innocence while foisting blame on President Biden, Attorney General Merrick Garland and the Department of Justice, the FBI, and the various state and federal judges who presided over his criminal trials. They, their institutions, and thousands of civil servants in the "deep state" had conspired against him, Trump would say, with the American public suffering as a consequence. He doubled down on hate with increased reliance on bigot-driven organizations for support, hoping that animus toward minorities would energize White voters to provide just enough of a margin to win again.

In the short term, Trump's strategy seemed to pay off, at least among his core supporters. During the first half of 2023, Trump's popularity as a potential Republican nominee increased with each indictment, trial, and conviction. Supporters viewed each state and criminal indictment as an insult to their culture. Meanwhile, opponents wondered whether any of the current and forthcoming criminal charges would ever be enough to discourage Trump's upward trajectory toward another Republican presidential nomination and possible election.

Donald Trump's approach to politics is a threat to our wellbeing. But worse, much worse, is Trump's presence as a symbol of a larger would be-despotic movement in American society that would forsake democratic rules for dictatorial dominance. Recall the 147 Republican members of Congress who voted to overturn the 2020 election results, upending the Constitution in the process; fake electors from at least seven states attempting to present false election outcomes; numerous Republican candidates for the 2024 presidential nomination who have refused to condemn Trump's outrageous behavior and who have been all too willing to rewrite history; several rightwing groups dedicated to chaos and anarchy at any cost; increased intolerance and violence against minorities; dangerous and irresponsible social media websites; and even some mischievous elements of the mainstream press. In all of these sectors of society, support for authoritarian rule has emerged through their actions and statements. For these elements, truth, logic, and decency are the enemies the undemocratic exercise of power necessary to regain their lost positions in American society.

Those holding or seeking office with would-be authoritarian attitudes are the most dangerous of the anti-democratic class because of their proximity to power and, in many cases, their knowledge of the government process. They don't present themselves as authoritarians *per se*, but their disdain for open political and social discourse, narrowly defined cultural values, and criticism of American institutions would suggest otherwise. Without a doubt, Trumpism is thriving beyond its namesake.

There is more. Some anti-democratic antagonists who would transform our democracy to repressive authoritarian rule operate out of the public eye in their positions of provocateurs, especially those who donate millions of dollars to malevolent independent expenditure groups and other organizations supportive of Trumpism. Their financial assistance has underwritten efforts to prescribe violence as normal public discourse, ban school books that discuss racism, and gerrymander their state legislative and congressional districts with the intention to intentionally minimize minority power.

All of this raises the question of just how invested we are as a society to fend off a slow but steady slippage into authoritarianism. Or simply put, how important is it for us to keep our democracy, where treasured institutions and values are threatened by power-hungry bigots and would be despots? Given that polls consistently reveal a sizable minority willing to embrace Trumpism over democracy, the answer may not be as encouraging as we might think.

In a strange way, Donald Trump and his minions may have done us a favor. They have given us a vision about the future they would have. The door is open for anti-democratic provocateurs to criticize journalists for their "biases"; condemn long-revered institutions, and undermine public schools for their submission to "woke" values. Most of all, these saboteurs of democracy will continue to argue unproven conspiratorial themes, often in conjunction with accusations against minorities as the sources of our problems. Growing disillusion with our institutions; permanently subjecting some groups to the dominance of others; turning away from a truly free press; placing strict limits on public discourse; promoting the private hijacking of public authority; and demonstrating the willingness to accept violence as normal in the marketplace of ideas are among the many warning signs already in place. They are all around us and are found in various shapes and forms virtually every day. If we as a society fail to see these developments for the threats they represent, we will fall into a decline that may be beyond reversing.

The disastrous events during and around the January 6 insurrection have provided a crude prototype of sorts to serve as the groundwork for a future effort. And given that so many Americans view the United States as vulnerable to losing its democratic moorings from internal struggles, it would seem that the next insurrection, should it occur, would not even be that surprising. Perhaps that might be the most significant takeaway of all: we know it's coming. The question is, what can be done to prevent it? Serious thought about who and what we are as a nation must begin now.

If our democracy degenerates into a twenty-first-century version of authoritarian rule, such a change in American governance likely will not occur overnight or through a quick secret militia strike. It will come in erratic fits and starts with seemingly random, subtle alterations at first along the edges of our democratic values, ultimately followed by events of greater intensity and significance. The persistent demonizing of institutions and reference to historic values as "outdated" have already become part of the nation's political discussions.

GLIMMERS OF HOPE

The winds of bigotry blow hard these days across the United States; they also augur a grave prognosis for our future. Still, there are glimmers of hope. In the 2020 presidential election, the greatest increase in voter turnout came from members of the 18–29 age group. Polls show members of this group were particularly concerned about the consequences from a Trump re-election, and as such, were strongly committed to racial and ethnic inclusion in a pluralist society.[3] Yet, their emergence didn't occur without notice. In response to the growing numbers of young voters and non-White people, legislators in several states attempted to further restrict their participation barriers. In many cases, they were thwarted by student-friendly "get out the vote" political coalitions.[4] Regardless, a new base of Trumpism opponents would still require more than energized young voters to be assured of victories in the coming elections.

In another sign of hope, post-2020 election studies have shown that fewer numbers of Americans have visited disingenuous political websites with misinformation in preparing for their vote than in the past.[5] Some misinformation experts, in fact, are "increasingly resilient that the majority of the population is increasingly resilient to misinformation on the web."[6] These data may reveal the potential for Americans to stand up to false narratives. Nevertheless, such observations, while promising, pale compared to a barrage of hateful language, funding, action and policies promoted by those preaching bigoted rhetoric to audiences all too willing to listen and react. Still, much more needs to be done.

On the constitutional front, the U.S. Supreme Court has emerged partially as a potential protector of democratic rule. Recall that in the midst of the January 6 insurrection, then President Trump and some self-professed Republican constitutional "experts" opined that state legislatures could overturn election votes without state judicial interference. Their "independent state legislature" theory was based on a section of Article I, Section 4 of the U.S. Constitution that provides state legislators with the right to determine "the Times, Places, and Manner of holding an election." If true, complete control of the election process by state legislatures would prevent the state courts from overturning or rejecting legislative manipulation.

Perhaps anticipating the revisit of such a claim, or worse yet action in the 2024 presidential election, the U.S. Supreme Court declared by a 6-to-3 vote in June 2023 that election-related activities of state legislatures were subjected to independent judicial review as part of the checks and balances concept provided in the Constitution.[7] At the same time, the justices have allowed most state gerrymandering and voter suppression laws to continue, jeopardizing the voting rights of millions of Americans of color.

The stakes regarding America's future are huge, perhaps the most significant since the Civil War. Our challenge is to face and reject the impinging signs of Trumpism and related authoritarian dangers now rather than wait for others to save us when it may be too late. Otherwise, our democracy with all of its imperfections will decline into a likely irreversible dictatorship for which we will all bear responsibility. Beyond losing our way, we no longer will serve as the counterbalance to undemocratic nations elsewhere.

Given the events of recent years, Americans are now at the proverbial fork in the road that offers undemocratic rule down one path and democratic renewal down the other. Which path we take as a nation remains to be seen.

NOTES

1. "The Washington Post's New Slogan Turns Out to be an Old Saying," *The Washington Post*, February 24, 2017, https://www.washingtonpost.com/lifestyle

/style/the-washington-posts-new-slogan-turns-out-to-be-an-old-saying/2017/02/23/cb199cda-fa02-11e6-be05-1a3817ac21a5_story.html.

2. "Trump, Vowing 'Retribution,' Foretells a Second Term of Spite," *The New York Times*, March 7, 2023, https://www.nytimes.com/2023/03/07/us/politics/trump-2024-president.html.

3. Morley Winograd, Michael Hais, and Doug Rose, "How Younger Voters will Impact Elections: Younger Voters Are Poised to Upend American Politics," Brookings Institution, February 27, 2023, https://www.brookings.edu/articles/younger-voters-are-poised-to-upend-american-politics/.

4. "Republicans Face Setbacks in Push to Tighten Voting Laws on College Campuses," *The New York Times*, March 30, 2023, https://www.nytimes.com/2023/03/29/us/politics/republicans-young-voters-college.html.

5. For example, see Ryan C. Moore, Ross Dahike, and Jeffrey T. Hancock, "Exposure to Untrustworthy Websites in the 2020 US Election," *Nature Human Behavior*, April 13, 2023, file:///Users/gerstondocs/Downloads/s41562-023-01564-2.pdf.

6. "Misinformation Defense Worked in 2020, Up to a Point, Study Finds," *The New York Times*, April 14, 2023, https://www.nytimes.com/2023/04/13/business/media/misinformation-2020-election-study.html.

7. "Supreme Court Rejects Theory That Would Have Transformed American Elections," *The New York Times*, June 27, 2023, https://www.nytimes.com/2023/06/27/us/politics/supreme-court-state-legislature-elections.html#:~:text=The%20Supreme%20Court%20on%20Tuesday,maps%20warped%20by%20partisan%20gerrymandering.

Bibliography

"2014 Hate Crime Statistics," Federal Bureau of Investigation, Washington, DC, https://ucr.fbi.gov/hate-crime/2014/tables/table-1, and "2020 Hate Crime Statistics," Federal Bureau of Investigation, Washington, DC, https://www.justice.gov/crs/highlights/2020-hate-crimes-statistics.

"2016 Post-election Jewish Surveys Summary Findings," Report by GBA Strategies, Presented to J Street, November 9, 2016, https://jstreet.org/wp-content/uploads/2016/11/J-Street-Election-Night-Survey-Analysis-110916.pdf.

"68% Say Discrimination against Black Americans a 'Serious Problem,' Quinnipiac University National Poll Finds; Slight Majority Supports Removing Confederate Statues," Quinnipiac Poll, June 17, 2020, https://poll.qu.edu/Poll-Release?releaseid=3786.

"78% Of Republicans Want To See Trump Run For President In 2024, Quinnipiac University National Poll Finds; Americans Now Split On Border Wall As Opposition Softens," Quinnipiac Poll, October 19, 2021, https://poll.qu.edu/poll-release?releaseid=3825.

"Alt Right: A Primer on the New White Supremacy," ADL.org, February 10, 2016, https://www.adl.org/resources/backgrounders/alt-right-a-primer-on-the-new-white-supremacy.

"American Face of Insurrection," Chicago Project on Security and Threats, University of Chicago, Chicago, IL, https://d3qi0qp55mx5f5.cloudfront.net/cpost/i/docs/Pape_-_American_Face_of_Insurrection_2022-01-05).pdf?mtime=1654548769.

"Annual Risk of Coup Report," One Earth Future, April 2019, Broomfield, CO, https://oneearthfuture.org/publication/annual-risk-coup-report-2019.

"Anti-Asian Hate Crime Reported to Police in America's 16 Largest Cities," Center for the Study of Hate and Extremism, California State University, San Bernardino, March 21, 2021, https://www.csusb.edu/sites/default/files/FACT%20SHEET-%20Anti-Asian%20Hate%202020%20rev%203.21.21.pdf.

"Anticorruption in Transition: A Contribution to the Policy Debate," The World Bank, Washington, DC, 2000, p. 40, http://web.worldbank.org/archive/website00504/WEB/PDF/TOC-7.PDF.

Bibliography

"Appointment of a Special Counsel," Department of Justice, November 18, 2022, https://www.justice.gov/opa/pr/appointment-special-counsel-0.

"Are Immigrants a Threat? Most Americans Don't Think So, but Those Receptive to the 'Threat' Narrative Are Predictably More Anti-immigrant," Public Research Religion Institute, January 17, 2023, https://www.prri.org/research/are-immigrants-a-threat-most-americans-dont-think-so-but-those-receptive-to-the-threat-narrative-are-predictably-more-anti-immigrant/.

"Asian American Access to Democracy in the 2008 Elections," Asian American Legal Defense Fund, 2008, https://www.aaldef.org/uploads/pdf/AALDEF_Election_2008_Report.pdf.

"Audit of Antisemitic Incidents 2010, ADL, October 2011," https://www.jewishvirtuallibrary.org/2010-adl-audit-of-anti-semitic-incidents-in-u-s .

"Banned in the USA: The Growing Movement to Censor Books in the Schools," Pen America, 2022, https://pen.org/report/banned-usa-growing-movement-to-censor-books-in-schools/#.

"Black History Month 2022: History of Jamaica," https://www.blackhistorymonth.org.uk/article/section/jamaica/history-of-jamaica/.

Bloomberg, "Trump's Indictment Sparked 15.4 Million Fundraising," April 15, 2023, https://www.bloomberg.com/news/articles/2023-04-15/trump-s-indictment-sparked-15-4-million-fundraising-bonanza#xj4y7vzkg.

"Checking in With the Major Voter Suppression Laws," Democracy Docket, April 12, 2022, https://www.democracydocket.com/news/checking-in-with-the-major-voter-suppression-laws/.

"Chinese Persecution of the Uyghurs," United States Holocaust Muscum, https://www.ushmm.org/genocide-prevention/countries/china/case-study/current-risks/chinese-persecution-of-the-uyghurs.

"Colombia: Situation of Afro-Colombians, Including Treatment by Society and Authorities; State Protection and Support Services Available 2017-May 2020," Research Directorate, Immigration and Refugee Board of Canada, https://www.justice.gov/eoir/page/file/1277501/downloa.

"Estimates of the Unauthorized Immigrant Population Residing in the United States January 2015-January 2018," Department of Homeland Security, January 2021, https://www.dhs.gov/sites/default/files/publications/immigration-statistics/Pop_Estimate/UnauthImmigrant/unauthorized_immigrant_population_estimates_2015_-_2018.pdf.

"Executive Order on Combating Race and Sex Stereotyping," September 22, 2020, https://trumpwhitehouse.archives.gov/presidential-actions/executive-order-combating-race-sex-stereotyping/.

"Family-Based Immigration Backlogs: 5 Things to Know," fwd.us, San Francisco and Washington, DC, February 10, 2022, https://www.fwd.us/news/family-based-immigration-backlogs/.

"Federal Bureau of Investigation: Crime Data Explorer," Washington, DC, 2022, https://cde.ucr.cjis.gov/LATEST/webapp/#/pages/home.

"Four Years of Profound Change: Immigration Policy during the Trump Presidency," Migration Policy Institute, Washington, DC, February 2022, https://www

.migrationpolicy.org/sites/default/files/publications/mpi-trump-at-4-report-final.pdf.

"Gallup Poll, Huckabee, Trump, Romney Set Pace for 2012 GOP Field," April 22, 2012, https://news.gallup.com/poll/147233/huckabee-trump-romney-pace-gop-field-2012.aspx.

"Global Freedom Scores: Countries and Territories," Freedom House, Washington, DC, 2021, https://freedomhouse.org/countries/freedom-world/scores.

"Going for Broke: The 442nd Regimental Combat Team," The National World War II Museum, New Orleans, September 24, 2020, https://www.nationalww2museum.org/war/articles/442nd-regimental-combat-team.

"GOP Lawmakers Largely Silent after Trump Suggests 'Termination' of Constitution," *The Washington Post*, December 5, 2022, https://www.washingtonpost.com/national-security/2022/12/04/trump-constitution-republicans/.

"Haberman: Trump 'Seems to be Leaning into Racist Statements'," *The Hill*, October 6, 2022, https://thehill.com/homenews/media/3676186-haberman-trump-seems-to-be-leaning-into-racist-statements/.

"Harvard Youth Poll," Cambridge, MA, Fall 2021, https://iop.harvard.edu/youth-poll/fall-2021-harvard-youth-poll.

"Hate Crime Homicides," Report to the Nation: Illustrated Almanac, Center for the Study of Hate and Extremism, California State University, San Bernardino, November 22, 2020, https://www.csusb.edu/sites/default/files/Special%20Status%20Report%20Nov%202020%2011.22.20%20combined.pdf.

"Hate Speech against Christians in Erdogan's Turkey," Stockholm for Freedom, August 2017, https://usercontent.one/wp/stockholmcf.org/wp-content/uploads/2017/08/Hate-Speech-Against-Christians-in-Erdog%CC%86an%E2%80%99s-Turkey_21.08.2017.pdf?media=1647703225.

"How Other Candidates Are Reacting to Trump's Federal Indictment," fivethirtyeight.com, June 9, 2023, https://fivethirtyeight.com/features/trump-indictment-republican-primary-candidates-reaction.

"Immigration Facts: The Positive Economic Impact of Immigration," Fwd.US, 2020, https://www.fwd.us/wp-content/uploads/2020/09/Immigration-Facts-The-Positive-Impact-of-Immigration-2020-Fact-Sheet.pdf.

"In His Own Words: The President's Attacks on the Courts," The Brennan Center for Justice, June 5, 2020, https://www.brennancenter.org/our-work/research-reports/his-own-words-presidents-attacks-courts.

"Jamaica Population 2022, World Population Review," https://worldpopulationreview.com/countries/jamaica-population.

"Jamaica," Washington, DC, https://freedomhouse.org/country/jamaica/freedom-world/2021 and "United States," Freedom House, Washington, DC, 2021, https://freedomhouse.org/country/united-states/freedom-world/2021.

Mike Pence, *So Help Me God*, New York, NY: Simon & Schuster, 2022, p. 460.

"Millions Are Victims of Hate Crimes though Many Never Report Them," The Center for Public Integrity, August 16, 2016, https://publicintegrity.org/politics/millions-are-victims-of-hate-crimes-though-many-never-report-them/ and "Why Hate Crimes Are Underreported—What Police Departments have to do with it,"

Northeastern Global News, May 23, 2021, https://news.northeastern.edu/2021/08/23/why-hate-crimes-are-underreported-and-what-police-departments-have-to-do-with-it/.

"Mission, Goals & Objectives," No Left Turn, https://www.noleftturn.us/mission-goals-objectives/.

"Mixed Signals on Trump: Majority Says Criminal Charges Should Disqualify '24 Run, Popularity is Unchanged, Leads DeSantis by Double Digits, Quinnipiac Poll Finds," Quinnipiac Poll, March 29, 2023, https://poll.qu.edu/poll-release?releaseid=3870.

"More than 1 in 3 Americans Believe that the 'Deep State' is Working to Undermine Trump," *Ipsos*, December 30, 2020, https://www.ipsos.com/sites/default/files/ct/news/documents/2020-12/topline_npr_misinformation_poll_123020.pdf.

"National: Faith in American System Drops," Monmouth University Poll, July 7, 2022, https://www.monmouth.edu/polling-institute/documents/monmouthpoll_us_070722.pdf/.

"National: More Americans Happy about Trump Loss than Biden Win," Monmouth University Poll, November 18, 2020.

"National Data: Deaths, The COVID Tracking Project," https://covidtracking.com/data/national/deaths.

"New from ADL: Leaked Oath Keepers' Membership List Reveals Hundreds of Current & Former Law Enforcement Officers, Members of Military, and Elected Officials," September 6, 2022, https://www.theatlantic.com/magazine/archive/2020/11/right-wing-militias-civil-war/616473/.

"Number of Mass Shootings in the United States between 1982 and July 2022. By Shooter's Race or Ethnicity," statista.com, https://www.statista.com/statistics/476456/mass-shootings-in-the-us-by-shooter-s-race/.

"Oath Keepers," Southern Poverty Law Center, 2017, https://www.splcenter.org/fighting-hate/extremist-files/group/oath-keepers.

"One year on, Republicans Still don't Consider Biden the Rightful Winner," Poll, University of Rochester, December 21, 2021, https://www.rochester.edu/newscenter/one-year-on-republicans-still-dont-consider-biden-the-rightful-winner-506702/.

"One-Third of Innovators in U.S. Are Immigrants," VOA Learning English, Washington, DC, https://learningenglish.voanews.com/a/more-than-one-third-of-inventors-discoverers-in-us-are-foreign-born/3242494.html.

"Patterns in the Introduction and Passage of Restrictive Voting Bills are Best Explained by Race," The Brennan for Justice, August 3, 2022, https://www.brennancenter.org/our-work/research-reports/patterns-introduction-and-passage-restrictive-voting-bills-are-best.

"Political Instability Not U.S. Adversaries, Seen As Bigger Threat, Quinnipiac National Poll Finds; Nearly 6 in 20 Think Democracy Is In Danger of Collapse," Quinnipiac Poll, January 12, 2022, https://poll.qu.edu/poll-release?releaseid=3831.

"Seven in Ten Americans Say the Country is in Crisis, at Risk of Failing," NPR/Ipsos Poll, January 3, 2022, https://www.ipsos.com/sites/default/files/ct/news/documents/2022-01/Topline-NPR-Ipsos-poll.pdf.

"'Poll' Majority Approves of Trump's Impeachment," *Politico*, December 12, 2019, https://www.politico.com/news/2019/12/20/poll-trump-impeachment-088812.

"President Trump Celebrates the Body-Slam of a Reporter in Montana," *The Washington Post*, September 17, 2018, https://www.washingtonpost.com/blogs/erik-wemple/wp/2018/09/07/president-trump-celebrates-the-body-slam-of-a-reporter-in-montana/.

"Projecting Majority-Minority," U.S. Census Bureau, Washington, DC, 2014, https://www.census.gov/content/dam/Census/newsroom/releases/2015/cb15-tps16_graphic.pdf.

"Racist and Xenophobic Hate Crimes," Office for Democratic Institutions and Human Rights: Organization for Democratic Institutions, Warsaw, Poland, 2022, https://hatecrime.osce.org/racist-and-xenophobic-hate-crime.

"Records Show Massive Disenfranchisement and Racial Disparities in 2022 Texas Primary," Brennan Center for Justice, January 17, 2023, https://www.brennancenter.org/our-work/research-reports/records-show-massive-disenfranchisement-and-racial-disparities-2022-texas

"Slavery's Roots: War and Economic Domination," https://www.freetheslaves.net/slavery-today-2/slavery-in-history/.

"Special Report 2021, From Crisis to Reform: A Call to Strengthen America's Battered Democracy," Freedom House, 2021, p. 3, https://freedomhouse.org/report/special-report/2021/crisis-reform-call-strengthen-americas-battered-democracy.

"SPLC Poll Finds Substantial Support for 'Great Replacement' Theory and Other Hard-Right Ideas," Southern Poverty Law Center, June 1, 2022, https://www.splcenter.org/news/2022/06/01/poll-finds-support-great-replacement-hard-right-ideas.

"Strategic Intelligence Assessment and Data on Domestic Terrorism," Federal Bureau of Investigation and Department of Homeland Security, Washington, DC, October 2022, https://www.dhs.gov/sites/default/files/2022-10/22_1025_strategic-intelligence-assessment-data-domestic-terrorism.pdf.

"Take it from the 'Trump' Judges: There was No Election Fraud," *Westlaw Today*, January 5, 2021, https://today.westlaw.com/Document/I97e9ff804fb211eb8404f825ce3db5c8/View/FullText.html?transitionType=Default&contextData=sc.Default)&firstPage=true.

"The Empire and Ego of Donald Trump," *The New York Times*, August 7, 1983, https://www.nytimes.com/1983/08/07/business/the-empire-and-ego-of-donald-trump.html.

"The EU-Turkey Deal, Five Years On: A Frayed and Controversial but Enduring Blueprint," The Migration Policy Institute, April 8, 2021, https://www.migrationpolicy.org/article/eu-turkey-deal-five-years-on.

"The Hate Report: Get to know the Three Percenters," *RevealNews*, March 18, 2018, https://revealnews.org/blog/hate-report-get-to-know-the-three-percenters/.

"The Impact of International Scientists, Engineers, and Students on Research Outputs and Global Competitiveness," *MIT Science Policy Review*, August 30, 2021, https://sciencepolicyreview.org/2021/08/impact-international-scientists-engineers

-students-us-research-output/#:~:text=International%20scientists%20and%20engineers%20f.

"The Impact of Voter Suppression on Communities of Color," The Brennan Center, January 10, 2022, https://www.brennancenter.org/our-work/research-reports/impact-voter-suppression-communities-color.

"The Islamophobic Administration," Brennan Center for Justice, April 19, 2017, https://www.brennancenter.org/our-work/research-reports/islamophobic-administration.

"The Rise and Fall of Liberal Democracy in Turkey: Implications for the West," The Brookings Institution, Washington, DC, February 2019, https://www.brookings.edu/research/the-rise-and-fall-of-liberal-democracy-in-turkey-implications-for-the-west/.

"The State of Antisemitism in America, 2022: AJC's Survey of American Jews," American Jewish Committee, New York, NY, 2023.

"The U.S. will become 'Minority White' in 2045, Census Projects," Brookings, March 14, 2018, https://www.brookings.edu/blog/the-avenue/2018/03/14/the-us-will-become-minority-white-in-2045-census-projects/.

The Washington Post, "School Librarians Face a New Penalty in the Banned-Book War: Prison," https://www.washingtonpost.com/education/2023/05/18/school-librarians-jailed-banned-books/. San Francisco Chronicle, "Presidential Hopeful DeSantis Inspires Push to Make Book Bans Easier in Republican-Controlled States," May 26, 2023, https://www.sfchronicle.com/news/politics/article/latest-gop-2024-hopeful-desantis-blazing-a-18121208.php.

"Threats against Members of Congress Are Skyrocketing. It's Changing the Job," *Los Angeles Times*, September 20, 2021, https://www.latimes.com/politics/story/2021-09-20/threats-members-of-congress.

"Trump Threatens to Adjourn Congress to Get His Nominees Through," *Courthouse News Service*, April 15, 2020, https://www.courthousenews.com/trump-threatens-to-adjourn-congress-to-get-his-nominees-through/.

"Trump's Unconstitutional View of Presidential Power," *Expert Forum*, American Constitutional Society, April 16, 2020, https://www.acslaw.org/expertforum/trumps-unconstitutional-view-presidential-power/.

"Turkey is Committing War Crimes and Crimes against Humanity in Syria," *Genocide Watch*, June 9, 2020, https://www.genocidewatch.com/single-post/2020/06/08/turkey-is-committing-war-crimes-and-crimes-against-humanity-in-syria.

"Voters Increasingly Confident that Biden would Handle COVID-19 Better than Trump," *YouGov*, October 10, 2020, https://today.yougov.com/topics/politics/articles-reports/2020/10/20/biden-trump-handle-covid-better-poll.

"Voting Laws Roundup: May 2022," The Brennan Center for Justice, May 26, 2022.

"We Have to Push the Envelope," Political Research Associates, January 5, 2022, https://politicalresearch.org/2022/01/05/we-have-push-envelope.

"'We Must Defeat Them': New Evidence Details Oath Keepers' 'Civil War' Timeline," *The Guardian*, https://www.theguardian.com/us-news/2022/oct/08/oath-keepers-trial-evidence-civil-war.

"What is 'Great Replacement Theory' and How Does It Fuel Racist Victims," *PBS*, May 16, 2022, https://www.pbs.org/newshour/politics/what-is-great-replacement-theory-and-how-does-it-fuel-racist-violence.

"White Supremacists Embrace 'Accelerationism,'" *ADL*, April 4, 2019.

"Who Controlled Redistricting in Every State," The Brennan Center for Justice, October 5, 2022, https://www.brennancenter.org/our-work/research-reports/who-controlled-redistricting-every-state.

"Why Scholars and Activists Increasingly Fear a Uyghur Genocide in Xinjiang," *Journal of Genocide Research*, Volume 23, Issue 3, 2021, https://www.tandfonline.com/doi/full/10.1080/14623528.2020.1848109?scroll=top&needAccess=true.

"Winthrop Poll Southern Focus Survey," Winthrop University, December 2018, https-swww.winthrop.edu/uploadedFiles/wupoll/november-2018-results.pdf.

ABC News, "Donald Trump Runs Second in Poll: Can He Win Republican Nomination," April 7, 2011, https://abcnews.go.com/Politics/poll-donald-trump-catapults-place-2012-gop-field/story?id=13318814.

ABC News, "Federal Judge Rules Children, Parents Separated at Border must be Reunited within 30 Days," https://abcnews.go.com/Politics/federal-judge-rules-children-parents-separated-border-reunited/story?id=56192051.

ABC News, "President Trump's 'Dysfunctional' Upbringing Created 'Dangerous Situation' for America, Niece Claims," July 15, 2020, https://abcnews.go.com/Politics/president-trumps-dysfunctional-upbringing-created-dangerous-situation-america/story?id=71788912.

ABC News, "Survey: 1 in 4 in U.S. Have Asian-American Bias," April 26, 2001, https://abcnews.go.com/US/story?id=93457.

ABC News, "Threats to Congress Decreased after Record High in 2021, but Are Still Concerning: Police," January 17, 2023, https://abcnews.go.com/Politics/threats-congress-decreased-after-record-high-2021-police/story?id=96492983.

Abraham, Henry J., *The Judicial Process*, 6th ed., New York, NY: Oxford University Press, 1993, p. 166.

Abrajano, Marisa, Zoltan L. Hajnal, Daron Acemoglu, and James A. Robinson, *Why Nations Fail: The Origins of Power, Prosperity, and Poverty*, New York, NY: Crown Publishers, 2012, p. 399.

Aceves, Paula, "Ilhan Tohti, Wants the Uyghurs to Be Free," *The New Yorker*, March 23, 2022, https://nymag.com/intelligencer/2022/03/ilham-tohti-wants-the-uyghurs-to-be-free.html.

Alberta, Tim, "Donald Trump Is on the Wrong Side of the Religious Right," *The Atlantic*, May 24, 2023, https://www.theatlantic.com/politics/archive/2023/03/trump-religious-right-evangelical-vote-pence-desantis-support/673475/.

Allen, John R., "Like Truman's Military Desegregation Order, Leadership against Racism begins at the Top," Brookings, July 26, 2019, https://www.brookings.edu/blog/up-front/2019/07/26/like-trumans-military-desegregation-order-leadership-against-racism-starts-at-the-top/.

Almond, Gabriel and G. Bingham Powell, Jr., *Comparative Politics: A Developmental Approach* Boston, MA: Little, Brown and Company, 1966, pp. 258–263.

Altink, Henrice, "Black Lives Matter in Jamaica: Debates about Colourism Follow Anger at Police Brutality," *The Conversation*, June 22, 2020, https://theconversation.com/black-lives-matter-in-jamaica-debates-about-colourism-follow-anger-at-police-brutality-140754.

Altink, Henrice, "Out of Place: Race and Color in Jamaican Hotels, 1962-2020," *New West Indian Guide*, Volume 95, Issue 3–4, 2021, file:///Users/gerstondocs/Downloads/[22134360%20-%20New%20West%20Indian%20Guide%20_%20Nieuwe%20West-Indische%20Gids]%20Out%20of%20Place%201.pdf.

Anderson, Terry H., "A History of Voter Suppression," National Low Income Housing Coalition, September 2020, https://nlihc.org/resource/history-voter-suppression.

Anderson, Terry H., *The Pursuit of Fairness: A History of Affirmative Action*, New York, NY: Oxford University Press, 2004, pp. 5, 82.

AP News, "Native American Votes Helped Secure Biden's Win in Arizona," November 19, 2020, https://apnews.com/article/election-2020-joe-biden-flagstaff-arizona-voting-rights-fa452fbd546fa00535679d78ac40b890.

AP News, "Trump Derides Protections for Immigrants from 'Shithole Countries,'" January 11, 2018, https://apnews.com/article/immigration-north-america-donald-trump-ap-top-news-international-news-fdda2ff0b877416c8ae1c1a77a3cc425.

AP News, "Trump Praises QAnon Conspiracists, Appreciates Support," August 19, 2020, https://apnews.com/article/election-2020-ap-top-news-religion-racial-injustice-535e145ee67dd757660157be39d05d3f.

AP News, "'Vicious, Biased': Trump Assails Judge in NY Fraud Case," October 28, 2022, https://apnews.com/article/business-new-york-social-media-8947607e8dad62cecba6c6de6ab4d302.

Applebaum, Anne, *Red Famine: Stalin's War on Ukraine*, New York, NY: Anchor Books, 2017.

Associated Press, "AP Fact Check: Visa Overstays Outpace Border Crossings," January 3, 2019, https://apnews.com/article/north-america-donald-trump-az-state-wire-ca-state-wire-immigration-48d0ad46f143478d9384410f5ae3d38b.

Associated Press, "Few in US Say Democracy is Working Well," February 8, 2021, https://apnews.com/article/ap-norc-poll-us-democracy-403434c2e728e42a955c72a652a59318.

Attack on the United States of America, New York, NY: Random House Books, 2023, p. 29.

Axios, "Trump Praises QAnon Supporters: 'I Understand they like Me Very Much,'" August 19, 2020, https://www.axios.com/2020/08/19/trump-praises-qanon-supporters-i-understand-they-like-me-very-much.

AZ Mirror, "UPDATED Trump's Fake Electors: Here's the Full List," June 29, 2022, https://www.azmirror.com/2022/06/29/updated-trumps-fake-electors-heres-the-full-list/.

Baker, Peter and Susan Glasser, *The Divider*, New York, NY: Doubleday, 2022, p. 437.

Ball, Andrew O., Hans J. G. Hassell, and Michael Heseltine, "Be Careful What You Wish For: The Impacts of President Trump's Midterm Endorsements," *Legislative Studies Quarterly*, May 19, 2020, https://doi.org/10.1111/lsq/12284.

Baptiste, H. Prentice and Blanca Araujo, "American Presidents and Their Attitudes, Beliefs, and Actions Surrounding Education and Multiculturalism," Multicultural Education, Spring, 2004, https://files.eric.ed.gov/fulltext/EJ783087.pdf.

Barber, James David, *The Presidential Character: Predicting Performance in the White House*, 4th ed., Englewood Cliffs, NJ: Prentice Hall, 1992, p. 82.

Barr discusses this theory at length in the *Harvard Journal of Law and Public Policy*. See his "The Role of the Executive," Volume 3, Number 3, Summer 2020, https://www.nbcbayarea.com/news/politics/reviewing-nancy-pelosis-leadership/3083544/.

Barrett, Wayne, *Trump: The Deals & The Downfall*, New York, NY: HarperCollins, 1992, pp. 74, 171–195.

BBC, "South Africa Elections: Who Controls the Country's Business Sector?" May 2019, https://www.bbc.com/news/world-africa-48123937.

BBC, "U.S. Election in 2020: Trump's Impact on Immigration—in Seven Charts," October 22, 2020, https://www.bbc.com/news/election-us-2020-54638643.

BBC News, "Trump Now Tells Far Right to 'Stand Down' Amid White Supremacy Row," October 1, 2020https://www.bbc.com/news/election-us-2020-54359993.

BBC News, "Trump's Wall: How much has been Built during His Term?" January 12, 2021, https://www.bbc.com/news/world-us-canada-46748492.

Bendix, Reinhard, *Nation-Building and Citizenship*, Garden City, NY: Double Day & Company, 1969, p. 135.

Bernhard, Michael, "Democratic Backsliding in Poland and Hungary," *Slavic Review*, Volume 80, Number 3, https://www.cambridge.org/core/journals/slavic-review/article/democratic-backsliding-in-poland-and-hungary/8B1C30919DC33C0BC2A66A26BFEE9553.

Bitecofer, Rachel, *The Unprecedented 2016 Presidential Election*, Cham, Switzerland: Palgrave Publisher, 2018, pp. 170–173.

Blankfield, Keren, "Donald Trump for President 2012? A Conversation with the Donald," *Forbes Magazine*, January 5, 2021, https://www.forbes.com/sites/kerenblankfeld/2011/01/05/donald-trump-for-president-2012-a-conversation-with-the-donald/?sh=5861f5e51e28.

Blender, Abigail, "In Pictures: Insurrection and Anti-Semitism at the Capitol Riots," *Moment*, January 8, 2021, https://momentmag.com/pictures-anti-semitism-at-the-capitol-riots/.

Bloomberg, "Trump's Indictment Sparked $15.4 Million Fundraising Bonanza

Bloomberg, Michael R., "Republican Censors Go for Woke," *The Wall Street Journal*, August 16, 2022.

Borjas, George J., "Yes, Immigration Hurts American Workers," *Politico Magazine*, September/October 2016, https://www.politico.com/magazine/story/2016/09/trump-clinton-immigration-economy-unemployment-jobs-214216/.

Bratspies, Rebecca, "'Territory is Everything': Afro-Colombian Communities, Human Rights and Illegal land Grabs," *Columbian Human Rights Law Review*,

May 27, 2020, https://hrlr.law.columbia.edu/hrlr-online/territory-is-everything-afro-colombian-communities-human-rights-and-illegal-land-grabs/.

Brooker, Russell and Todd Schaefer, *Public Opinion in the 21st Century: Let the People Speak*, Boston, MA: Houghton Mifflin Company, 2006, pp. 113–114.

Brown, N. Derek, Drew S. Jacoby-Senghor, and Isaac Raymundo, "If You Rise, I Fall: Equality is Prevented by the Misperception that it Harms Advantaged Groups," *Science Advances*, Volume 8, Number. 18, May 6, 2022, https://www.science.org/doi/10.1126/sciadv.abm2385.

Buchanan, Patrick J., *Suicide of a Super Power*, New York, NY: St Martin's Press, 2011, pp. 156, 402, and 421–422.

Budhos, Marina, "Donald Trump's Childhood in Queens can Explain His Obsession with Borders," *Quartz*, October 20, 2016, https://qz.com/814851/donald-trumps-childhood-in-queens-can-explain-his-obsession-with-borders/.

Burnham, Walter Dean, *Critical Elections and the Mainsprings of American Politics*, New York, NY: W.W. Norton Company.

Burns, James MacGregor, *Leadership*, New York, NY: Harper and Row, 1978, pp. 345–356.

Business Insider, "Trump Gave Conflicting Defenses about the Mar-a-Lago Raid, Claiming that all the Documents Are 'Mine,' and that Some Were Planted," October 22, 2022, https://www.businessinsider.com/trump-mar-a-lago-docs-mine-but-also-planted-conflicting-2022-10.

Butros, Marina, "Donald Trump's Childhood in Queens can Explain His Obsession with Borders," *Quartz*, October 20, 2016, https://qz.com/814851/donald-trumps-childhood-in-queens-can-explain-his-obsession-with-borders.

Buzzfeed, "Teen Beauty Queens Say Trump Walked in on Them Changing," October 12, 2016, https://www.buzzfeednews.com/article/kendalltaggart/teen-beauty-queens-say-trump-walked-in-on-them-changing.

Cameron, Beth, "I Ran the White House Pandemic Office. Trump Closed It," *The Washington Post*, March 13, 2020, https://www.washingtonpost.com/outlook/nsc-pandemic-office-trump-closed/2020/03/13/a70de09c-6491-11ea-acca-80c22bbee96f_story.html.

Campbell, Travis, "Black Lives Matter's Effect on Police Lethal Use-of-Force," *Social Science Research Network*, May 13, 2021, https://papers.ssrn.com/sol3/papers.cfm?abstract_id=3767097. "Trump Called BLM Protesters 'Thugs' But Capitol-Storming Supporters 'Very Special,' " *Forbes*, April 14, 2022, https://www.forbes.com/sites/tommybeer/2021/01/06/trump-called-blm-protesters-thugs-but-capitol-storming-supporters-very-special/?sh=136c10f03465.

Cao, Andy, Jason M. Lindo, and Jiee Zhong, "Can Social Media Rhetoric Incite Hate Incidents? Evidence from Trump's 'Chinese Virus' Tweets," National Bureau of Economic Research Working Paper 30588, Washington, DC, October 2022, https://www.nber.org/papers/w30588.

Carroll, Rory, "Hugo Chavez Revolution Mired by Claims of Corruption," *The Guardian*, April 18, 2010, https://www.theguardian.com/world/2010/apr/18/hugo-chavez-revolution-corruption-claims.

Caryl, Christian "Donald Trump's Talking Points on Crimea are the same as Vladimir Putin," *The Washington Post*, July 3, 2018, https://www.washingtonpost.com/news/democracy-post/wp/2018/07/03/donald-trumps-talking-points-on-crimea-are-the-same-as-vladimir-putins/.

CBS News, "Timeline: The Government's Effort to get Sensitive Documents Back from Trump's Mar-a-Lago," September 22, 2022, https://www.cbsnews.com/news/trump-search-timeline-mar-a-lago-justice-department/.

CBS News, "U.S. Sanctions Officials in China over Persecution of Uyghurs and Other Minorities," March 22, 2022, https://www.cbsnews.com/news/us-sanctions-china-genocide-persecution-uyghurs-other-religious-minorities/.

Chait, Jonathan, "Americans Are Divided on whether 'Woke' is a Compliment or an Insult," *USA Today*, March 8, 2023, https://www.ipsos.com/en-us/americans-divided-whether-woke-compliment-or-insult.

Chervinsky, Lindsay, "The U.S. Has Weathered Crises Before. Here's Why Jan. 6 Was Different," *Governing*, January 6, 2022, https://www.governing.com/context/the-u-s-has-weathered-crises-before-heres-why-jan-6-was-different.

Chicago Tribune, "Armed 'Three Percenters' Turn Protests toward Muslim Americans," December 11, 2015, https://www.chicagotribune.com/nation-world/ct-protests-toward-muslim-americans-20151211-story.html.

Chicago Tribune, "Descendants if Black Slaves in some Native American Tribes—Know as Freedmen—Struggle for Recognition as Tribal Citizens," May 1, 2021, https://www.chicagotribune.com/nation-world/ct-aud-nw-freedmen-native-american-tribes-20210501-zxsby5vrmbgmpo37a7x6y4cvpe-story.html. https://theconversation.com/the-right-to-vote-is-not-in-the-constitution-144531.

Chicago Tribune, "McConnell Blames Trump, others in Power for Provoking Capitol Riot: 'The Mob was Fed Lies,'" January 19, 2021, https://www.chicagotribune.com/nation-world/ct-nw-mitch-mcconnell-trump-capitol-riots-20210119-wcvfpibhjrhohimy3y4wckdfbq-story.html.

Childress, Sarah, "The Battle over Bunkerville: The Bundys, the Federal Government, and the New Militia Movement," *Frontline*, May 16, 2017, https://www.pbs.org/wgbh/frontline/article/the-battle-over-bunkerville/.

Cineas, Fabiola, "Donald Trump is the Accelerant," *Vox*, January 9, 2021, https://www.vox.com/21506029/trump-violence-tweets-racist-hate-speech.

Civicus, "Mexico: Recall Referendum Ruse Leaves No One Satisfied," April 22, 2022, https://lens.civicus.org/mexico-recall-referendum-ruse-leaves-no-one-satisfied/.

CNN, "15 Times Donald Trump Praised Authoritarian Rulers," https://www.cnn.com/2019/07/02/politics/donald-trump-dictators-kim-jong-un-vladimir-putin/index.html.

CNN, "A Republican House Member just Described January 6 as a 'Normal Tourist Visit,'" May 13, 2013, https://www.nbcbayarea.com/news/politics/why-is-california-a-key-state-for-republicans/3269582/.

CNN, "Fox News Hosts Sow Distrust in Legitimacy of Election," November 5, 2020, https://www.cnn.com/2020/11/05/media/fox-news-prime-time-election/index.html.

CNN, "How 'Woke' went from a Social Justice Term to a Pejorative Favored by Some Conservatives," July 10, 2022, https://www.cnn.com/2022/07/10/us/woke-race-deconstructed-newsletter-reaj/index.html.

CNN, "New Details about Trump-McCarthy Shouting Match Show Trump Refused to Call Off the Rioters," February 12, 2021, https://www.cnn.com/2021/02/12/politics/trump-mccarthy-shouting-match-details/index.html.

CNN, "The Congressional Candidates Who have Engaged with the QAnon Conspiracy Theory," October 30, 2020, https://www.cnn.com/interactive/2020/10/politics/qanon-cong-candidates/.

CNN, "The Long List of Trump Administration Officials Turned Critics," June 5, 2020, https://www.cnn.com/2020/06/04/politics/officials-who-criticized-donald-trump/index.html.

CNN, "Trump Abruptly Ends Press Conference after Contentious Exchange," May 12, 2020, https://www.cnn.com/2020/05/11/media/trump-press-briefing-weijia-jian-kaitlan-collins/index.html.

CNN, "Trump again Refuses to Concede 2020 Election While Taking Questions from New Hampshire GOP Primary Voters," May 10, 2023, https://www.cnn.com/2023/05/10/politics/cnn-town-hall-trump/index.html.

CNN, "Trump Calls Out Youngkin Amid 2024 Chatter," November 11, 2022, https://thehill.com/homenews/campaign/3730886-trump-calls-out-youngkin-amid-2024-chatter/.

CNN, "Trump Criticizes Evangelical Leaders for not Backing His Presidential Bid," January 18, 2023, https://www.cnn.com/2023/01/18/politics/donald-trump-evangelicals-2024/index.html.

CNN, "Trump has been on Putin's Side in Ukraine's Long Struggle against Russian Aggression," March 6, 2022, https://www.cnn.com/2022/03/06/politics/trump-putin-ukraine/index.html.

CNN, Trump post-2020 news conference, video displayed in Chris Cillizza, "Donald Trump just Accidentally Told the Truth about His Disinformation," July 5, 2022, https://www.cnn.com/2021/07/05/politics/trump-disinformation-strategy/index.html.

CNN, "Trump Says He 'Essentially' Fired Mattis Who Actually Resigned in Protest," January 2, 2019, https://www.usatoday.com/story/news/politics/2018/12/07/rex-tillerson-donald-trump-remarks/2237327002/.

CNN, "Under Pressure, Trump Slaps long-Overdue Sanctions on Russia over Weapons Use," August 2, 2019, https://www.cnn.com/2019/08/02/politics/trump-russia-sanctions-chemical-weapons-spy-poisoning/index.html.

Coats, Ta-Nehisi, "The First White President," *The Atlantic*, October 2017, https://www.theatlantic.com/magazine/archive/2017/10/the-first-white-president-ta-nehisi-coates/537909/.

Comey, James, *A Higher Loyalty: Truth, Lies, and Leadership*, New York, NY: Flatiron Books, 2018, p. 237.

Coppedge, Michael, "Venezuela: Popular Sovereignty Versus Liberal Democracy," Working Paper #294, April 2002, The Kellogg Institute, University of Notre Dame, Notre Dame, Indiana, https://kellogg.nd.edu/documents/1587.

Corn, David and Michael Isikoff, "What Happened in Moscow: The Inside Story of How Mother Jones, Trump's Obsession with Putin Began," March 8, 2018, https://www.motherjones.com/politics/2018/03/russian-connection-what-happened-moscow-inside-story-trump-obsession-putin-david-corn-michael-isikoff/.

Coronel, Gustavo, "The Corruption of Democracy in Venezuela," Cato Institute, Washington, DC, March 4, 2008, https://www.cato.org/commentary/corruption-democracy-venezuela.

Cutlip, Kimbra, "In 1868, Two Nations Made a Treaty, the U.S. Broke It and Plains Indians Tribes are Still Seeking Justice," *The Smithsonian*, November 7, 2018, https://www.smithsonianmag.com/smithsonian-institution/1868-two-nations-made-treaty-us-broke-it-and-plains-indian-tribes-are-still-seeking-justice-180970741/.

Daily Beast, "Breibart News Helped Trump Win. Under Steve Bannon, It Might Also Help Him Lose," December 20, 2017, https://www.thedailybeast.com/breitbart-news-helped-trump-win-under-steve-bannon-it-might-also-help-him-lose.

Daily Beast, "Steve Bannon: 'Racist is a Badge of Honor,'" March 10, 2018, https://www.thedailybeast.com/steve-bannon-racist-label-is-a-badge-of-honor

Daily Kos, "'Civil War Is Here, Right Now': Patriots' Urge Trump to Empower Militias to Fight Antifa in Streets," August 31, 2020, https://www.dailykos.com/stories/2020/8/31/1974015/-Oath-Keepers-to-Trump-Send-out-the-militias-to-stop-antifascists-Marxist-takeover-of-America.

Dasche, John, "Land Reform in South Africa: How Can the U.S. Respond?" The Wilson Center, November 23, 2021.

"Deferred Action for Childhood Arrivals DACA Immigration Equality," August 30, 2020, https://immigrationequality.org/legal/legal-help/other-paths-to-status/deferred-action-for-childhood-arrivals-daca/.

Department of State, United States, Government, "2020 Report on International Religious Freedom: Turkey," https://www.state.gov/reports/2020-report-on-international-religious-freedom/turkey/.

DeSantis, Ron, *The Courage to Be Free*, New York, NY: Broadside Press, 2023, p. 125.

Diamond, Jeremy, "Donald Trump's 'Star of David' Tweet Controversy, Explained," *CNN*, July 5, 2016, https://www.cnn.com/2016/07/04/politics/donald-trump-star-of-david-tweet-explained.

Diamond, Larry, "Empowering the Poor: What Does Democracy Have to Do with It?," in Deepa Narayan (ed.), *Measuring Empowerment: Cross-Disciplinary Perspectives*, Washington, DC: The World Bank, 2005, p. 411, https://openknowledge.worldbank.org/entities/publication/847bc88a-b2db-5e7e-b271-cb587bb2bebe.

Dias, Elizabeth, "How Evangelicals Helped Donald Trump Win," *Time*, November 9, 2017, https://time.com/4565010/donald-trump-evangelicals-win/.

Du, Martin "Georgia's Democracy Still in Peril," *E-International Relations*, October 9, 2021, and Nino Lejava, "Georgia's Unfinished Search for Its Place in Europe," Brussels, Belgium, Carnegie Europe, April 6, 2021, https://www.e-ir.info/2021/10/09/opinion-georgias-democracy-still-in-peril/.

Edsall, Thomas B., "The Audacity of Hate," *The New York Times*, February 19, 2020, https://www.nytimes.com/2020/02/19/opinion/trump-anger-fear.html.

Edwards III, George C. and Stephen J. Wayne, *Presidential Leadership*, 8th ed., Boston, MA: Cengage, Wadsworth, 2010, p. 1.

Eggers, Andrew C., Haritz Garro, and Justin Grimmer, "No Evidence for Systematic Voter Fraud: A Guide to Statistical Claims about the 2020 Election," *Proceedings of the National Academy of Sciences*, November 2, 2021, and https://www.pnas.org/doi/abs/10.1073/pnas.2103619118, "AP Finds Fewer than 475 Cases of Potential Voter Fraud in Six 2020 Battleground States," *The Hill*, December 15, 2021, https://thehill.com/homenews/presidential-campaign/585901-ap-finds-fewer-than-475-cases-of-potential-voter-fraud-in-six/.

Farkash, Andrew Tzvi, "The Ghosts of Colonialism: Economic Inequality in Post-Apartheid South Africa," *Global Studies Journal*, 2015, https://escholarship.org/content/qt9p08t856/qt9p08t856.pdf?t=o1vgqz.

Felbab-Brown, Vanda, "The Ills and Cures of Mexico's Democracy," The Brookings Institution, Washington, DC, March 11, 2019, https://www.brookings.edu/wp-content/uploads/2019/03/FP_20190315_mexico_felbab_brown.pdf.

Fish, M. Steven and Matthew Kroenig, "Diversity, Conflict and Democracy: Some Evidence from Eurasia and East Europe," *Democratization*, Volume 13, Number 5, 2006, https://polisci.berkeley.edu/sites/default/files/people/u3833/DiversityConflictandDemocracy.pdf. FiveThirtyEight.com, "Barr's Summary of the Mueller Report Seems Good for Trump," March 24, 2019, https://fivethirtyeight.com/features/barrs-summary-of-the-mueller-report-seems-good-for-trump/.

FiveThirtyEight.com, "Why Donald Trump Isn't a Real Candidate, in One Chart," June 16, 2015, https://fivethirtyeight.com/features/why-donald-trump-isnt-a-real-candidate-in-one-chart/#fn-1.

For example, William Hudson offers four models of democracy: protective, developmental, pluralist, and participatory. See *American Democracy in Peril*, 9th ed., Thousand Oaks, CA: Sage Publications, 2021, pp. 8–24. Another approach is offered by John Anthony Maltese, Joseph A. Pika and W. Phillips Shively, where they divide democracy into two approaches: direct and indirect. See their *American Democracy in Context*, Thousand Oaks, CA: Sage Publicans, 2021, pp. 4–5. Alternatively, Suzanne Mettler and Robert Lieberman speak of democracy as "a system of government in which citizens are able to hold those in power accountable through elections," with those elected being responsible to citizens. See *Four Threats: The Recurring Crises of American Democracy*, New York, NY: St. Martin's Press, 2020, p. 11.

Forbes, "Report: Trump Wanted to Fire Acting AG Rosen Because He Wouldn't Help Overturn The Election," January 22, 2021, https://www.forbes.com/sites/rachelsandler/2021/01/22/report-trump-wanted-to-fire-acting-ag-rosen-because-he-wouldnt-help-overturn-the-election/?sh=4d07510460a5.

Forbes, "Trump Calls Black Prosecutors Investigating Him 'Racist,' Suggests Protests in Retaliation," February 1, 2022, https://www.forbes.com/sites/dereksaul/2022/01/30/trump-calls-black-prosecutors-investigating-him-racist-suggests-protests-in-retaliation/?sh=2da5374551bf.

Forbes, "Trump-Endorsed Candidates Have Funneled At Least $1.4 million Into His Businesses," https://www.forbes.com/sites/zacheverson/2022/06/23/trump-endorsed-candidates-have-funneled-at-least-14-million-into-his-businesses/?sh=28a29f295c36.

Fox News, "Trump, at US-Mexico Border, Slams Biden for 'Open, Really Dangerous Border'," July 1, 2021.

Freedlander, David, "An Oral History of Donald Trump's Almost-Run for President in 2000," *New York Magazine*, October 11, 2018, https://nymag.com/intelligencer/2018/10/trumps-almost-run-for-president-in-2000-an-oral-history.html.

"Freedom in the World 2021," Freedom House, Washington, DC, 2021, https://freedomhouse.org/country/colombia/freedom-world/2021.

Frej, Willa, "Here's a Running List of Racist Things That Have Happened at Trump Rallies," *HuffPost*, March 16, 2016, https://www.huffpost.com/entry/list-racist-things-trump-rallies_n_56d7019ae4b0871f60ed519f.

Friedman, Steven, *Prisoners of the Past*, Johannesburg: WITS University Press, 2021, p. 45.

Friedman, Thomas L., "We Have Never Been Here Before," *The New York Times*, February 27, 2022, https://www.nytimes.com/2022/02/25/opinion/putin-russia-ukraine.html.

Fukuyama, Francis, "The Long Arc of Historical Progress," *The Wall Street Journal*, April 30, 2022, https://www.wsj.com/articles/the-long-arc-of-historical-progress-11651244262.

Gallup Poll, "Obama's Birth Certificate Convinces Some, but Not All, Skeptics," May 13, 2011, https://news.gallup.com/poll/147530/obama-birth-certificate-convinces-not-skeptics.aspx.

Garber, Andrew, "Debunking False Claims About the John Lewis Voting Act," The Brennan Center for Justice, January 13, 2022, https://www.brennancenter.org/our-work/research-reports/debunking-false-claims-about-john-lewis-voting-rights-act.

Garber, Megan, "Fox Hits a Dangerous New Low," *The Atlantic*, December 6, 2020, https://www.theatlantic.com/culture/archive/2020/11/fox-news-trump-election-dangerous-new-low/617019. /

Gashaw, Tasew, "Colonial Borders in Africa: Improper Design and Its Impact on African Borderland Communities," Africa Up Close, Woodrow Wilson Center, https://africaupclose.wilsoncenter.org/colonial-borders-in-africa-improper-design-and-its-impact-on-african-borderland-communities/.

"Georgia's Racial Turnout Gap Grew in 2022," The Brennan Center for Justice, December 16, 2022, https://www.brennancenter.org/our-work/analysis-opinion/georgias-racial-turnout-gap-grew-2022.

Gerston, Larry N., *American Federalism: A Concise Introduction*, Armonk, NY: M.E. Sharpe Publisher, 2007.

Gest, Justin, "What the 'Majority Minority' Shift Really Means for America," *The New York Times*, August 24, 2021, https://www.nytimes.com/2021/08/24/opinion/us-census-majority-minority.html.

Giglio, Mike, "A Pro-Trump Group Has Recruited Thousands of Police, Soldiers, and Veterans," *The Atlantic*, November 2020, https://www.theatlantic.com/magazine/archive/2020/11/right-wing-militias-civil-war/616473/.

Glasser, Susan B. and Peter Baker, "Inside the War between Trump and His Generals," *The New Yorker*, August 8, 2022, https://www.newyorker.com/magazine/2022/08/15/inside-the-war-between-trump-and-his-generals.

Glazer, Nathan and Daniel Patrick Moynihan, *Beyond the Melting Pot*, Cambridge, MA: The M.I.T. Press, 1963, p. 12.

Glickman, Lawrence, "How White Backlash Controls American Progress," *The Atlantic*, May 21, 2020, https://www.theatlantic.com/ideas/archive/2020/05/white-backlash-nothing-new/611914/.

GlobalPost, "8 Reminders of How Horrible Syrian President Bashar al-Assad has been to His People," September 24, 2014, https://theworld.org/stories/2014-09-24/8-reminders-how-horrible-syrian-president-bashar-al-assad-has-been-his-people.

Goldman, Ralph M., "Party Chairmen and Party Faction, 1789-1900," Ph.D. dissertation. Stonecash, Jeffrey M., *Political Parties Matter: Realignment and the Return of Partisan*, Voting Boulder, CO: Lynne Rienner Publishers, 2006, p. 14.

Goldstone, Lawrence, *Inherently Unequal: The Betrayal of Equal Rights By the Supreme Court, 1865-1903*, 2011, p. 155.

Goodman, Ryan and Justin Hendrix, "Crisis of Command: The Pentagon, the President, and January 6," *The Hill*, December 21, 2021, https://thehill.com/homenews/house/3682571-mccarthy-told-trump-that-jan-6-rioters-were- trying-to-ing-kill-me-book/.

Gorchinskaya, Katya, "A Brief History of Corruption in Ukraine: The Yushchenko Era," *eurasianet*, May 28, 2020, https://eurasianet.org/a-brief-history-of-corruption-in-ukraine-the-yushchenko-era.

Graber, Doris, *Mass Media and American Politics*, 8th ed., Washington, DC: CQ Press, 2010, pp. 232–240.

Graham, David A., "The Lurking Menace of a Trump Rally," *The Atlantic*, March 10, 2016, https://www.theatlantic.com/politics/archive/2016/03/donald-trump-fayetteville/473169/.

Green, Joshua, *Devil's Bargain*, New York, NY: Penguin Press, 2017, pp. 146–147, 89, 170–171, 208.

Griffin, Rob, William H. Frey, and Ruy Teixeira, "States of Change," June 27, 2019, https://www.americanprogress.org/series/states-of-change/.

Guerrero, Jean, *Hatemonger: Stephen Miller, Donald Trump, and the White Nationalist Agenda*, New York, NY: William Morrow, 2022, pp. 9, 145, 148, 182, 192.

Haberman, Maggie, *Confidence Man*, New York, NY: Penguin Press, 2022, p. 63.

Haggard Stephan and Robert Kaufmann, *Backsliding*, New York, NY: Cambridge University Press, 2021, p. 1.

Hanchard, Michael G., *The Spectre of Race: How Discrimination Haunts Western Democracy*, Princeton, NJ: Princeton University Press, 2018, p. 105.

Haney-Lopez, Ian, "The Racism at the Heart of the Reagan Presidency," *Salon*, January 11, 2014, https://www.salon.com/2014/01/11/the_racism_at_the_heart_of_the_reagan_presidency/.

Harriot, Michael, "War on Wokeness: The Year the Right around a Made-Up Menace," *The Guardian*, December 21, 2022, https://www.theguardian.com/us-news/2022/dec/20/anti-woke-race-america-history.

Hassan, Miiad, "Ethnic Politics in Minority Dominant Regimes," *Ethnic Studies Review*, Volume 43, Number 1, Spring 2020, pp. 56–57, https://online.ucpress.edu/esr/article-abstract/43/1/43/107097/Ethnic-Politics-in-Minority-Dominant-RegimesThree?redirectedFrom=PDF.

Hawley, George, "The Demography of the Alt-Right," Institute for Family Studies, August 19, 2018, https://ifstudies.org/blog/the-demography-of-the-alt-right.

Heikkila, Niko, "Online Antagonism of the Alt-Right in the 2016 Election," *European Journal of American Studies*, Summer 2017, https://ifstudies.org/blog/the-demography-of-the-alt-right.

Helmond, Anne, "The Platformization of the Web: Making Web Data Platform Ready," *Social Media + Society*, July–December 2015, https://www.readcube.com/articles/10.1177%2F2056305115603080.

Hetherington, Marc J. and Jonathan D. Weiler, *Authoritarianism & Polarization of American Politics*, New York, NY: Cambridge University Press, 2009, p. 4.

Hockstader, Lee, "Jamaican Racial Harmony Challenged on Issue of Black Role in Economy," *The Washington Post*, July 4, 1990, https://www.washingtonpost.com/archive/politics/1990/07/04/jamaican-racial-harmony-challenged-on-issue-of-black-role-in-economy/e268b21e-f668-4051-831e-ad856de547e8/.

Holland, Alisha, "A Decade under Chavez: Political Intolerance and Lost Opportunities for Advancing Human Rights in Venezuela," Human Rights Watch, New York, NY, 2008, https://www.hrw.org/sites/default/files/reports/venezuela0908web.pdf.

Houston Public Media, "19% of Harris County Mail-in Ballots in the 2022 Primary were Rejected due to SB1, according to Elections Administrator," March 11, 2022, https://www.houstonpublicmedia.org/articles/news/politics/2022/03/11/420985/the-states-new-election-law-led-to-19-of-harris-county-mail-ballots-in-the-primary-to-be-rejected/.

"How Voter Suppression Laws Target Native Americans," The Brennan Center for Justice, May 23, 2022, https://www.brennancenter.org/our-work/research-reports/how-voter-suppression-laws-target-native-americans.

Hswen, Yulin, Xiang Xu, Anna Hing, Jared B. Hawkins, John S. Brownstein, and Gilbert Gee, "Association of '#covid19' Versus '#chinesevirus' with Anti-Asian Sentiments on Twitter: March 9-23, 2020," *American Journal of Public Health*, May 2021, https://ajph.aphapublications.org/doi/10.2105/AJPH.2021.306154.

HuffPost, "Here's a Running List of Racist Things That Have Occurred at Trump Campaigns," March 16, 2016, https://www.huffpost.com/entry/list-racist-things-trump-rallies_n_56d7019ae4b0871f60ed519f

HuffPost, "School Board Member Says Black Principal's Activism 'Got Him Fired' From School," July 18, 2022, https://www.huffpost.com/entry/school-board-black-principal-texas-activism_n_62d3be34e4b0e6fc1a97dfeb.

Human Rights Watch, "Global Condemnation of Chinese Government Abuse in Xinjianing," October 21, 2021, https://www.hrw.org/news/2021/10/21/global-condemnation-chinese-government-abuses-xinjiang.

Huntington, Samuel P., *The Clash of Civilizations and the Remaking of World Order*, New York, NY: Simon and Schuster, 1966, p. 252.

Huq, "Aziz, When Was Judicial Self-Restraint?" *California Law Review*, Volume 579, 2012, https://chicagounbound.uchicago.edu/cgi/viewcontent.cgi?article=2520&context=journal_articles.

Hyman, Zoe, Daniel Geary, Camilla Schofield, and Jennifer Sutton, "Transatlantic White Supremacy: American Segregationists and International Racism and Civil Rights," in *Global White Nationalism: From Apartheid to Trump*, Manchester, MI: Manchester University Press, 2020, p. 190.

Independent, "Trump Presses Pence to 'Come through' and Overturn Electoral College Results at Georgia Rally," January 5, 2021, https://www.independent.co.uk/news/world/americas/us-election-2020/trump-pence-electoral-college-georgia-rally-b1782330.html.

Indiana Express, "Presidential Power to Declassify Information, Explained," August 15, 2022, https://indianexpress.com/article/explained/explained-global/presidential-power-declassify-information-explained-8090991/.

Intelligence Report, "New Alt-Right 'Fight Club' Ready for Street Violence," Southern Poverty Law Center, Fall 2017, https://www.splcenter.org/fighting-hate/intelligence-report/2017/new-alt-right-%E2%80%9Cfight-club%E2%80%9D-ready-street-violence.

International Institute for Democracy and Electoral Assistance, "Summary: The Global State of Democracy 2019," https://www.idea.int/publications/catalogue/summary-global-state-of-democracy-2019?lang=en.

International Institute for Democracy and Electoral Assistance, "Summary: The Global State of Democracy 2021," Stockholm, Sweden, p. 6, https://static.poder360.com.br/2021/11/integra-the-global-state-of-democracy-2021_0.pdf.

Issue One, "60% of President Donald Trump's Post-election Tweets Sought to Undermine Legitimacy of Presidential Race," February 9, 2021, https://issueone.org/articles/60-of-president-donald-trumps-post-election-tweets-sought-to-undermine-legitimacy-of-presidential-race/.

Iyengar, Shanto, *Media Politics: A Citizen's Guide*, fourth edition, New York, NY: W.W. Norton and Company, 2019, p. 21.

Jimenez, Tomas R., *Replenished Ethnicity: Mexican Americans, Immigration, and Identity*, Berkeley, CA: University of California Press, 2010, p. 37, 40.

Johnson, Theodore R., Emelia Gold, and Ashley Zhao, "How Anti-Critical Race Theory Bills Are Taking Aim At Teachers," fivethirtyeight.com, May 9, 2022, https://fivethirtyeight.com/features/how-anti-critical-race-theory-bills-are-taking-aim-at-teachers/.

Jones, Stephen A. and Eric Freedman, *Presidents and Black America: A Documentary History*, Thousand Oaks, CA: Sage. Gross, Daniel A., "The U.S. Government Turned Away Thousands of Jewish Refugees, Fearing That They Were Nazi Spies," *Smithsonian Magazine*, November 18, 2015, https://www.smithsonianmag.com/history/us-government-turned-away-thousands-jewish-refugees-fearing-they-were-nazi-spies-180957324/.

Jones, Stephen A. and Eric Freedman, "Presidents have a Long History of Condescension, Indifference and Outright Racism toward Black Americans," *The Conversation*, August 26, 2020, https://theconversation.com/presidents-have-a-long-history-of-condescension-indifference-and-outright-racism-toward-black-americans-143166.

Just Security, "At Least 15 Trump Officials Do Not Hold Their Positions Lawfully," September 17, 2020, https://www.justsecurity.org/72456/at-least-15-trump-officials-do-not-hold-their-positions-lawfully/.

Just Security, "Timeline: False Alternative Slate of Electors Scheme, Donald Trump and His Close Associates," *Just Security*, July 18, 2022, www.Justsecurity.org.

Just Security, "Timeline of the Coronavirus Pandemic and the U.S. Response," November 30, 2020, https://www.justsecurity.org/69650/timeline-of-the-coronavirus-pandemic-and-u-s-response/.

Kalb, Marvin, *Enemy of the People: Trump's War on the Press, the New McCarthyism, and the Threat to American Democracy*, Washington, DC: The Brookings Institution, 2018, p. 7.

Kalb, Marvin, "Trump's Troubling Relationship with the Press," Brookings, February 21, 2017, https://www.brookings.edu/blog/up-front/2017/02/21/trumps-troubling-relationship-with-the-press/.

Kaufmann, Eric "Immigration and White Identity in the West: How to Deal with Declining Majorities," *Foreign Affairs*, September 8, 2017, https://www.foreignaffairs.com/articles/united-states/2017-09-08/immigration-and-white-identity-west. "The Global State of Democracy 2019," https:// www.idea.int/publications/catalogue/summary-global-state-of-democracy-2019?lang=en.

Kelly, Monique D.A., "Examining Race in Jamaica: How Racial Category and Skin Color Structure Social Inequality," *Race and Social Problems*, March 18, 2020, https://link.springer.com/article/10.1007/s12552-020-09287-z?utm_source=toc.

Kennedy, Randell, "Did Obama Fail Black America," *Politico Magazine*, July/August 2014, https://www.politico.com/magazine/story/2014/06/black-president-black-attorney-general-so-what-108017/.

Key, Jr., V.O., *Politics, Parties & Pressure Groups*, fifth edition, New York, NY: Thomas Y. Crowell Company, 1964, p. 603.

Killeen Daily Herald, "Former Arkansas Gov. Asa Hutchinson pushes optimistic White House Bod, not a Candidate that 'Creates Chaos,'" May 23, 2023, https://kdhnews.com/news/politics/former-arkansas-gov-asa-hutchinson-pushes-optimistic-white-house-bid-not-a-candidate-that-creates/article_06bf7c44-ec18-5ae5-b3c8-ea749907ed96.html.

Kirisci, Kemal and Amanda Sloat, "Global State of Democracy Report 2021," The International Institute for Democracy and Electoral Assistance, Stockholm, Sweden, https://www.idea.int/gsod/global-report.

Kirisci, Kemal and Amanda Sloat, "The Rise and Fall of Liberal Democracy in Turkey: Implications for the West," The Brookings Institution, Washington, DC, February 2019, https://www.brookings.edu/wp-content/uploads/2019/02/FP_20190226_turkey_kirisci_sloat.pdf.

Kor-Sins, Ryan, "The Alt-Right Digital Migration: A Heterogeneous Engineering Approach to Social Media Platform Branding," *New Media and Society*, 2021.

Kranish, Michael and Marc Fisher, *Trump Revealed*, New York, NY: Simon & Schuster, 2016, pp. 34–35 and pp. 37, 213, 253–254.

Kreko, Peter and Zsolt Enyedi, "Explaining Eastern Europe: Orban's Laboratory of Illiberalism," *Journal of Democracy*, Volume 29, Issue 3, July 2018, pp. 39–51, https://www.journalofdemocracy.org/articles/explaining-eastern-europe-orbans-laboratory-of-illiberalism/.

Kurashige, Lon, *Two Faces of Exclusion: The Untold History of Anti-Asian Racism in the United States*, Chapel Hill, NC: The University of North Carolina Press, 2016, p. 22 and pp. 171–183.

Kurtz, Lester, "Chile: Struggle against a Military Dictator 1985-1988," International Center of Nonviolent Conflict, Washington, DC, June 2009, https://www.nonviolent-conflict.org/chile-struggle-military-dictator-1985-1988/.

Lawfare, "Armed Militias Are Taking Trump's Civil War Tweets Seriously," October 2, 2019, https://www.lawfareblog.com/armed-militias-are-taking-trumps-civil-war-tweets-seriously.

Leighley, Jan E., *Mass Media and Politics: A Social Science Perspective*, Boston, MA: Houghton Mifflin Company, 2004, pp. 8, 206.

Levin, Bess, "Donald Trump, Who Reportedly Praised Hitler in Private, Gives Antisemites the Greenlight to Go after Jews," *Vanity Fair*, October 17, 2022, https://www.vanityfair.com/news/2022/10/donald-trump-jews-israel-truth-social.

Levitsky, Steven and Daniel Ziblatt, *How Democracies Die*, New York, NY: Random House, 2019, pp. 146–167.

Levy, Brian Alan Hirsch, Vinothan Naidoo, and Musa Nxele, "South Africa: When Strong Institutions and Massive Inequalities Collide," Carnegie Endowment for International Peace, Washington, DC, March 18, 2021, https://carnegieendowment.org/2021/03/18/south-africa-when-strong-institutions-and-massive-inequalities-collide-pub-84063.

Lew-Williams, Beth, *The Chinese Must Go*, Cambridge, MA: Harvard University Press, 2018, p. 234.

Lind, Dara, "How America's Rejection of Jews fleeing Nazi Germany Haunts Our Refugee Policy Today," *Vox*, January 27, 2017, https://www.vox.com/policy-and-politics/2017/1/27/14412082/refugees-history-holocaust.

Lipset, Seymour Martin, *The First New Nation*, New York, NY: Doubleday Books, 1967, p. 68.

Lipson, Leslie, *The Democratic Civilization*, New York: Oxford University Press, 1964, p. 578.

Los Angeles Times, "At Mt. Rushmore, Trump uses Fourth of July Celebration to Stoke a Culture War," July 3, 2020, https://www.latimes.com/politics/story/2020-07-03/trump-july-4-culture-war.

Los Angeles Times, "Central Park Five: Money was not the Issue in Settlement with NYC," *Los Angeles Times*, June 27, 2014, https://www.latimes.com/nation/nation-now/la-na-nn-central-park-five-jogger-20140627-story.html.

Los Angeles Times, "Landmark Jan. 6 Report Concludes Trump Intentionally Misled and Provoked Insurrectionists," December 22, 2022, https://www.latimes.com/politics/story/2022-12-22/jan-6-committee-final-report-explained. *See Final Report of* the Select Committee to Investigate the January 6th Attack on the United States Capitol, U.S. Government Publishing Office, December 2022.

Los Angeles Times, "QAnon Pushes Alarming Conspiracy Myths Targeting China and Jewish People," March 23, 2021, https://www.latimes.com/california/story/2021-03-23/qanon-conspiracy-evolves-new-world-order-china-jewish-people

Los Angeles Times, "We knew that QAnon is Anti-Semitic. Now we know it's Racist, Too," *Bulletin of the Atomic Scientists*, July 5, 2021, https://www.latimes.com/california/story/2021-03-23/qanon-conspiracy-evolves-new-world-order-china-jewish-people.

Los Angeles Times, "What Donald Trump has said through the Years about where President Obama was Born," September 16, 2016, https://www.latimes.com/politics/la-na-pol-trump-birther-timeline-20160916-snap-htmlstory.html.

Los Angeles Times, "Why Veterans of the Military and Law Enforcement Joined the Capitol Insurrection," January 15, 2021, https://www.latimes.com/world-nation/story/2021-01-15/capitol-riot-police-veterans-extremists.

Louisiana Secretary of State Election Report, 2018 and 2022 General Elections, https://electionstatistics.sos.la.gov/Data/Post_Election_Statistics/statewide/2018_1106_sta.pdf and https://electionstatistics.sos.la.gov/Data/Post_Election_Statistics/statewide/2022_1108_sta.pdf.

MacFarquhar, Neil, "Hafez al-Assad, Who Turned Syria into a Power in the Middle East, Dies at 69," *The New York Times*, https://www.nytimes.com/2000/06/11/world/hafez-al-assad-who-turned-syria-into-a-power-in-the-middle-east-dies-at-69.html.

Maizland, Lindsay, "Myanmar's Troubled History: Coups, Military Rule, and Ethnic Conflict," Council on Foreign Relations, Washington, DC, January 31, 2022, https://www.cfr.org/backgrounder/myanmar-history-coup-military-rule-ethnic-conflict-rohingya.

Martin, Jonathan and Alexander Burns, *Will Not Pass*, New York, NY: Simon & Schuster, 2022, pp. 222–223.

Martinez, Monica Munoz, "Oversight of the Trump Administration's Border Policies and the Relationship between Anti-Immigrant Rhetoric and Domestic Terrorism," Testimony before Congress, September 6, 2019.

McCord, Mary B. and Jacob Glock, "January 6 Report Exposes Ongoing, Converging Threat of, Anti-Democracy Schemes and Paramilitary Violence," *Just Security*, January 6, 2023, https://www.justsecurity.org/84669/the-january-6th-report-exposes-the-ongoing-converging-threat-of-anti-democracy-schemes-and-paramilitary-violence/.

McDougall, Gay, "Report of the Independent Expert on Minority Issues—Addendum," United Nations Human Rights Council, January 25, 2011, https://reliefweb.int/sites/reliefweb.int/files/resources/B7E1E403814947EA85257839005D82AA-Full_Report.pdf.

McKeever, Amy, "Voter Suppression has Haunted America since it was Founded," *National Geographic*, August 21, 2020, https://www.nationalgeographic.com/history/article/voter-suppression-haunted-united-states-since-founded.

Media Matters, April 15, 2021, https://www.mediamatters.org/white-nationalism/fox-business-larry-kudlow-allows-sen-ron-johnson-push-racist-replacement-theory.

Mediate, "82% of Fox News Viewers Believe the Election Was Stolen: New Poll," November 1, 2021, https://www.mediaite.com/politics/82-of-fox-news-viewers-believe-the-election-was-stolen-new-poll/.

Mediate, "Top of the Line! Trump Absolutely FAWNS Over Brutal Dictators Putin, Xi, and Kim Jung-Un to Tucker Carlson," April 12, 2023, https://www.mediaite.com/trump/top-of-the-line-trump-absolutely-fawns-over-brutal-dictators-putin-xi-and-kim-jong-un-to-tucker-carlson/.

Medium, "86 Times Donald Trump Displayed or Promoted Islamophobia," April 19, 2018, https://medium.com/nilc/86-times-donald-trump-displayed-or-promoted-islamophobia-49e67584ac10.

Mendelberg, Tali, The *Race Card: Campaign Strategy, Implicit Messages, and the Norm of Equality*, Princeton, NJ: Princeton University Press, 2001, pp. 269–276.

Mettler, Suzanne and Robert C. Lieberman, *Four Threats: The Recurring Crises of American Democracy*, New York, NY: St. Martin's Press, 2020, pp. 212–222.

Miller-Idriss, Cynthia, *Hate in the Homeland*, Princeton, NJ: Princeton University Press, 2020.

Moore, Ryan C., Ross Dahike, and Jeffrey T. Hancock, "Exposure to Untrustworthy Websites in the 2020 US Election," *Nature Human Behavior*, April 13, 2023

Morlino, Leonardo and Mario Quaranta, "What is the Impact of the Economic Crisis on Democracy?" *The American Political Science Review*, Volume 37, Number 5, November 2016, https://www.jstor.org/stable/26556876.

Morris, Alex, "False Idol—Why the Christian Right Worships Donald Trump," *Rolling Stone*, December 2, 2019, https://www.rollingstone.com/politics/politics-features/christian-right-worships-donald-trump-915381/.

Mounk, Yascha, *The Great Experiment: Why Diverse Democracies Fall Apart and How They Can Endure*, New York, NY: Penguin Press, 2022, p. 83.

Mungiu-Pippidi, Alina, "Corruption: Diagnosis and Treatment," *The Journal of Democracy*, Volume 17, Number 3, July 2006, pp. 86–99, https://muse.jhu.edu/pub/1/article/200112.

Mungo, Monita, "The Real Problem with Critical Race Theory," *The Hill*, May 26, 2021, https://thehill.com/opinion/civil-rights/555351-the-real-problem-with-critical-race-theory/.

Murray, Charles A. and Richard Hernnstein, *The Bell Curve: Intelligence and Class Structure in American Life*, New York, NY: Simon & Schuster, 1994.

Mutz, Diana C., "Status Threat, not Economic Hardship, Explains the 2016 Presidential Vote," *Proceedings of the National Academy of Sciences of the United States of America*, Volume 115, Number 19, 2018, https://www.pnas.org/doi/10.1073/pnas.1718155115.

Naftali, Tim, "Ronald Reagan's Long-Hidden Racist Conversation with Richard Nixon," *The Atlantic*, July 30, 2019, https://www.theatlantic.com/ideas/archive/2019/07/ronald-reagans-racist-conversation-richard-nixon/595102/.

National Review, "On Trump, Pro-Life Opportunity, and Transactional Politics," January 4, 2023, https://www.nationalreview.com/corner/on-trump-pro-life-opportunism-and-transactional-politics/.

National Review, "The Message of the Midterms," November 9, 2022, https://www.nationalreview.com/corner/the-message-of-the-midterms/.

NBC News, "Feds Concerned about Risk of Violence as Election Day Nears," October 26, 2016, https://www.nbcnews.com/news/us-news/feds-concerned-about-risk-violence-election-day-nears-n672821.

NBC News, "Oath Keepers Founder Sentenced to 18 years in Jan. 6 Seditious Conspiracy Case," May 25, 2023, https://www.nbcnews.com/politics/justice-department/oath-keepers-founder-sentenced-18-years-jan-6-seditious-conspiracy-cas-rcna85852.

Neustadt, Richard, *Presidential Power*, 2nd ed., New York, NY: John Wiley & Sons, 1980, pp. 195 and 213.

New Lines Institute for Strategy and Policy, "The Three Percenters: A Look Inside an Anti-Government Militia," February 2021, https://newlinesinstitute.org/wp-content/uploads/20210225-Three-Percenter-PR-NISAP-rev051021.pdf.

New York Magazine, "Indoctrination Nation," May 8–21, 2023, https://nymag.com/intelligencer/article/desantis-florida-trump-education-politics.html.

New York Post, "NBC gives Donald a Trump-Sized Raise to $160M," June 22, 2011, https://nypost.com/2011/06/22/nbc-gives-donald-a-trump-sized-raise-to-160m/#ixzz1Q08fudIS.

Newsweek, "Trump Claims White People 'at the Back of the Line' for COVID Vaccines, Treatments," January 16, 2022, https://www.newsweek.com/trump-claims-white-people-back-line-covid-vaccines-treatments-1669884.

Newsweek, "Trump Endorses Arizona SoS Candidate Mark Finchem, a Self-Proclaimed Member of Oath Keepers," September 13, 2021, https://www.newsweek.com/trump-endorses-arizona-sos-candidate-mark-finchem-self-proclaimed-member-oath-keepers-1628715.

Nguyen, Tina, "Donald Trump's Rallies Are becoming Increasingly Violent," *Vanity Fair*, March 16, 2016, https://www.vanityfair.com/news/2016/03/donald-trump-protesters-rally-violence.

Norton, Michael I. and Samuel R. Sommers, "Whites See Racism as a Zero-Sum Game That They Are Now Losing," *Perspectives on Psychological Science*, Volume 6, Number 3, 2011, pp. 215–218, https://www.hbs.edu/ris/Publication%20Files/norton%20sommers%20whites%20see%20racism_ca92b4be-cab9-491d-8a87-cf1c6ff244ad.pdf.

NPR, "6 in 10 Americans Say U.S. Democracy in Crisis as the 'Big Lie' Takes Root," January 3, 2022, https://www.wbur.org/npr/1069764164/american-democracy-poll-jan-6.

NPR, "30 Years Later, Photos Emerge From Killings in Syria," February 2, 2012, https://www.npr.org/2012/02/01/146235292/30-years-later-photos-emerge-from-killings-in-syria.

NPR, "'A Hostage Situation Every Day': Strategists Blame Trump for Georgia Senate Losses," January 21, 2021, https://www.npr.org/2021/01/29/961837774/a-hostage-situation-every-day-strategists-blame-trump-for-georgia-senate-losses.

NPR, "Energized By Trump's Win, White Nationalists Gather to 'Change The World'," November 2016, https://www.npr.org/2016/11/20/502719871/energized-by-trumps-win-white-nationalists-gather-to-change-the-world.

NPR, "Former President Donald Trump's Company is Found Guilty of Criminal Tax Fraud," December 6, 2022, https://www.npr.org/2022/12/06/1140756394/former-president-donald-trumps-company-found-guilty-criminal-tax-fraud.

NPR, "How Do Illegal Drugs Cross the U.S.-Mexico Border," April 6, 2019, https://www.npr.org/2019/04/06/710712195/how-do-illegal-drugs-cross-the-u-s-mexico-border.

NPR, "Inside Trump's Closed-Door Meeting, Held To Reassure 'The Evangelicals,'" June 15, 2016, https://www.npr.org/2016/06/21/483018976/inside-trumps-closed-door-meeting-held-to-reassures-the-evangelicals.

NPR, "McConnell Criticizes Trump's Calls to Terminate the Constitution," December 6, 2022, https://www.npr.org/2022/12/06/1141096473/mcconnell-trump-terminate-constitution.

NPR, "Off the Air. Fox News Stars Blasted the Election Fraud Claims they Peddled," February 16, 2023, https://www.npr.org/2023/02/16/1157558299/fox-news-stars-false-claims-trump-election-2020.

NPR, "Suspicious Timing and Convenient Reasoning for Trump's Firing of Comey," May 10, 2017, https://www.cnn.com/2020/06/04/politics/officials-who-criticized-donald-trump/index.html.

NPR, "Trump Calls for a 'Total and Complete Shutdown of Muslims Entering' U.S.," December 7, 2015, https://www.npr.org/2015/12/07/458836388/trump-calls-for-total-and-complete-shutdown-of-muslims-entering-u-s?utm_source=twitter.com&utm_campaign=politics&utm_medium=social&utm_term=nprnews.

NPR, "Trump Calls Harris a 'Monster,' Reviving a Pattern if Attacking Women of Color," October 9, 2022, https://www.npr.org/2020/10/09/921884531/trump-calls-harris-a-monster-reviving-a-pattern-of-attacking-women-of-color.

NPR, "Trump Downplays Police Violence, Deaths of Black Americans," July 14, 2020, https://www.npr.org/sections/live-updates-protests-for-racial-justice/2020/07/14/891144579/trump-says-more-white-people-killed-by-police-violence-than-blacks.

NPR, "Trump Tells Pence to Show 'Extreme Courage' and Overturn Results," January 6, 2021, https://www.npr.org/sections/congress-electoral-college-tally-live-updates/2021/01/06/953907019/trump-tells-pence-to-show-extreme-courage-and-overturn-results.

NPR, "Trump Wishes We Had More Immigration From Norway. Turns Out We Once Did," January 12, 2018, https://www.npr.org/sections/goatsandsoda/2018/01/12/577673191/trump-wishes-we-had-more-immigrants-from-norway-turns-out-we-once-did.

NPR/Marist Poll, "The January 6th Hearings, July 2022," July 21, 2022, https://maristpoll.marist.edu/polls/npr-pbs-newshour-marist-national-poll-the-january-6th-hearings-july-2022/.

NY1, "Trump Confirms he had Dinner with Ye, White Supremacist Nick Fuentes," November 25, 2022, https://www.ny1.com/nyc/all-boroughs/politics/2022/11/25/trump-confirms-he-had-dinner-with-ye--white-nationalist-fuentes.

O'Brien, Timothy L., "Trumpism is a Dish Republicans Can Serve without Trump," *Bloomberg Opinion*, November 9, 2022, https://www.bloomberg.com/opinion/articles/2022-11-09/midterm-elections-trumpism-doesn-t-need-trump.

O'Brien, Timothy L., *Trump Nation: The Art of Being the Donald*, New York, NY: Warner Business Books, 2005, p. 50.

O'Donnell, John and James Rutherford, *Trumped! The Inside Story of the Real Donald Trump—His Cunning Rise and Spectacular Fall*, New York, NY: Simon and Schuster, 1991, pp. 114–115.

O'Donnell, John R. with James Rutherford, *Trumped!* Hertford, NC: Crossroad Press, 1991, p. 3 and p. 115.

Obari, Chineyer, "Belgium: The Case of Flanders and Wallonia," *Harvard Political Review*, July 22, 2021, https://harvardpolitics.com/flanders-and-wallonia/.

Order 3915-2017, Office of the Deputy Attorney General, "Appointment of Special Counsel to Investigate Russian Interference with the 2016 Presidential Election and Related Matters," May 17, 2017, https://www.justice.gov/archives/opa/press-release/file/967231/download. "Report on the Investigation Into Russian Interference in the 2016 Presidential Election," Department of Justice, March 22, 2019.

Parker, Kunal M., *Making Foreigners: Immigration and Citizenship Law in America, 1600-2000*, New York, NY: Cambridge University Press, pp. 152, 174.

Paschel, Tianna S., *Becoming Black Political Subjects: Movements and Ethno-Rights in Colombia and Brazil*, Princeton, NJ: Princeton University Press, 2016, pp. 41–42.

Paumgarten, Nick, "The Death and Life of Atlantic City," *The New Yorker*, August 31, 2015, https://www.newyorker.com/magazine/2015/09/07/the-death-and-life-of-atlantic-city.

PBS, "Trump's Showdown," *Frontline*, PBS.org, May 23, 2018, https://www.pbs.org/wgbh/frontline/interview/elyse-goldweber/.

PBS News, "Trump Allies in Congress Leap to Defend Former President after Federal Indictment," *Hour*, June 10, 2023, https://www.pbs.org/newshour/politics/trump-allies-in-congress-leap-to-defend-former-president-after-federal-indictment.

PBS News Hour, "GOP Lawmakers were 'Intimately Involved' in Jan. 6 Protest Planning, New Report Shows," October 25, 2021, https://www.pbs.org/newshour/show/gop-lawmakers-were-intimately-involved-in-jan-6-protest-planning-new-report-shows.

PBS News Hour, "NBC Fires Donald Trump over 'Derogatory Statements about Immigrants'," June 29, 2015, https://www.pbs.org/newshour/politics/nbc-fires-donald-trump-moguls-derogatory-statements.

PBS News Hour, "Trump begins Openly Embracing and Amplifying False Fringe QAnon Conspiracy Theory, September 16, 2022, https://www.pbs.org/newshour/politics/trump-begins-openly-embracing-and-amplifying-false-fringe-qanon-conspiracy-theory.

PBS News Hour, "Trump Restricts Immigration Amid the Pandemic. Critics see it as an Excuse to Push His Own Agenda," July 28, 2020, https://www.pbs.org

/newshour/politics/trump-restricts-immigration-amid-the-pandemic-critics-see-it-as-an-excuse-to-push-his-own-agenda.

PBS News Hour, "WATCH: Trump Pressured Justice Department to Seize States' Voting Machines, Former DOJ Officials Say," June 23, 2022, https://www.pbs.org/newshour/politics/watch-trump-pressured-justice-department-to-seize-states-voting-machines-former-doj-officials-say.

PBS News Hour, "What Was George H.W. Bush's Record on Race?" December 4, 2018, https://www.pbs.org/newshour/politics/what-was-george-h-w-bushs-record-on-race.

PBS.org, "The Ku Klux Klan in the 1920s," American Experience, https://www.pbs.org/wgbh/americanexperience/films/klansville/. https://www.pbs.org/wgbh/americanexperience/features/flood-klan/.

Pearson, Amb. W. Robert, "What Caused the Turkish Coup Attempt," *Politico*, July 16, 2016, https://www.politico.com/magazine/story/2016/07/what-caused-the-turkish-coup-attempt-214057/.

Penn Medicine News, "Assaults Spiked on Trump Rally Days during 2016 Election," University of Pennsylvania, March 16, 2018, https://www.pennmedicine.org/news/news-releases/2018/march/assaults-spiked-on-trump-rally-days-during-2016-election.

Peters, Jeremy W., *Insurgency: How Republicans Lost Their Party and Got Everything They Ever Wanted*, New York, NY: Crown Books, 2021, p. 297.

Pew Research, "2016 Campaign: Strong Interest, Widespread Dissatisfaction," July 7, 2016, https://www.pewresearch.org/politics/2016/07/07/2016-campaign-strong-interest-widespread-dissatisfaction/.

Pew Research, "Behind Trump's Victory: Divisions by Race, Gender, Education," November 9, 2016, https://www.pewresearch.org/short-reads/2016/11/09/behind-trumps-victory-divisions-by-race-gender-education/.

Pew Research, "Blacks Represent 78 Percent of Registered Democrats in South Carolina." "Party Affiliation among Adults in South Carolina by Race/Ethnicity," May 30, 2014.

Pew Research, "Broad Public Support for Legal Status for Undocumented Immigrants," June 4, 2015, https://www.pewresearch.org/politics/2015/06/04/broad-public-support-for-legal-status-for-undocumented-immigrants/.

Pew Research, "How Trump Compares with other Recent Presidents in Appointing Federal Judges," January 13, 2021, https://www.pewresearch.org/fact-tank/2021/01/13/how-trump-compares-with-other-recent-presidents-in-appointing-federal-judges/.

Pew Research, "Partisan Divides on Media Trust Widen, Driven by a Decline among Republicans," August 31, 2021, https://www.pewresearch.org/fact-tank/2021/08/30/partisan-divides-in-media-trust-widen-driven-by-a-decline-among-republicans/.

Pew Research, "Many Black and Asian Americans Say They Have Experienced Discrimination Amid the COVID-19 Outbreak," https://www.pewresearch.org/social-trends/2020/07/01/many-black-and-asian-americans-say-they-have-experienced-discrimination-amid-the-covid-19-outbreak/.

Pew Research, "Modern Immigration Wave Brings 59 Million to U.S., Driving Population Growth and Change Through 2065," September 28, 1965, https://www.pewresearch.org/hispanic/2015/09/28/modern-immigration-wave-brings-59-million-to-u-s-driving-population-growth-and-change-through-2065/#:~:text=As%20a%20result%20of%20its,Americans%20were%20non%2DHispanic%20whites and "Most Americans Say the Declining Share of White People in the U.S. is Neither Good nor Bad for Society," Pew Research Center, August 23, 2021, https://www.pewresearch.org/fact-tank/2021/08/23/most-americans-say-the-declining-share-of-white-people-in-the-u-s-is-neither-good-nor-bad-for-society/.

Pew Research, "Race in America 2019," April 9, 2019, https://www.pewresearch.org/social-trends/2019/04/09/race-in-america-2019/.

Philadelphia Inquirer, "Questions Linger about Trump's Academic at Wharton," February 17, 2017, https://www.inquirer.com/philly/blogs/real-time/Questions-linger-Donald-Trump-academic-record-Wharton.html&outputType=app-web-view.

Pimcetl, Stephanie S., *Transforming California*, Baltimore, MD: The Johns Hopkins Press, 1999, p. 5.

Politico, "51% of Republican Voters: Obama Foreign," February 15, 2011, https://www.politico.com/story/2011/02/51-of-gop-voters-obama-foreign-049554.

Politico, "Biden Signed a New Hate Crimes Law—But there's a Big Flaw," May 20, 2021, https://www.politico.com/interactives/2021/state-hate-crime-laws/.

Politico, "Donald Trump 2016 RNC Draft Speech Transcript," July 21, 2016.

Politico, "How 'Antifa' became a Trump Catch-All," June 2, 2020, https://www.politico.com/news/2020/06/02/how-antifa-became-a-trump-catch-all-297921.

"Trump to Send Federal Forces to more 'Democrat' Cities," *Reuters*, July 20, 2020.

Politico, "McCain: Obama not an Arab, Crowd Boos," *Politico*, October 10, 2008, https://www.politico.com/story/2008/10/mccain-obama-not-an-arab-crowd-boos-014479.

Politico, "McCarthy Says Trump 'Bears Responsibility' for Capitol Riot," January 13, 2021, https://www.politico.com/news/2021/01/13/mccarthy-trump-responsibility-capitol-riot-458975.

Politico, "New Evidence Suggests 'Alliance' between Oath Keepers, Proud Boys Ahead of Jan. 6," March 25, 2021, https://www.politico.com/news/2021/03/24/oath-keepers-proud-boys-alliance-capitol-riot-477741.

Politico, "Physical Attacks on Power Grid Surge to New Peak," December 26, 2022, https://www.politico.com/news/2022/12/26/physical-attacks-electrical-grid-peak-00075216.

Politico, "Post-election, Extremists Use Fringe Social Networks to Push Fraud Claims, Violence," November 13, 2020, https://www.politico.com/news/2020/11/13/extremists-fringe-social-media-election-fraud-436369.

Politico, "President Trump's Enemies List," July 10, 2017, https://www.politico.com/story/2017/07/10/president-trump-enemies-list-240344.

Politico, "Republicans Cringe as Trump 2024 Approaches," November 14, 2022, https://www.politico.com/news/2022/11/14/republicans-trump-2024-00066874.

Politico, "Ron Johnson Tried to Hand Fake info to Mike Pence on Jan.6, Panel Reveals," June 21, 2022, https://www.politico.com/news/2022/06/21/jan-6-panel-trump-overturn-2020-election-00040816.

Politico, "Trump: Black Lives Matter is a 'Symbol of Hate,'" July 1, 2020, https://www.politico.com/news/2020/07/01/trump-black-lives-matter-347051.

Politico, "Trump Accuses John Kelly of 'Missing the Action' after Scathing Criticism," February 13, 2020, https://www.politico.com/news/2020/02/13/donald-trump-john-kelly-114861.

Politico, "Trump Calls on GOP State Legislators to Overturn Election Results," November 21, 2020, https://www.politico.com/news/2020/11/21/trump-state-legislatures-overturn-election-results-439031.

Politico, "Trump isn't Secretly Winking at QAnon. He's Retweeting its Followers," July 12, 2020, https://www.politico.com/news/2020/07/12/trump-tweeting-qanon-followers-357238.

Politico, "Trump on Jan. 6 Insurrection: 'These were Great People'," July 11, 2021, https://www.politico.com/news/2021/07/11/trump-jan-6-insurrection-these-were-great-people-499165.

Politico, "Trump Publicly Sides with Putin on Election Interference," July 16, 2018, https://www.politico.com/story/2018/07/16/trump-russia-putin-summit-722418.

Politico, "Trump's Media Relations Get Rocky Quickly," January 1, 2021, https://www.politico.com/story/2017/01/trump-media-relations-233981.

Politifact, "How Many Newly Elected Officials and Congressional Candidates were 'Involved' in the Capitol Riot," December 2, 2021, https://www.nytimes.com/2022/09/06/us/politics/jan-6-griffin-insurrection.html.

Potok, Mark, "The Radical Right's Reaction to the Election of Barak Obama," *Intelligence Report*, The Southern Poverty Law Center, November 30, 2008, https://www.splcenter.org/fighting-hate/intelligence-report/2008/radical-right%E2%80%99s-reaction-election-barack-obama.

Potter, David M., *The Impending Crisis, 1848-1861*, New York, NY: Harper and Row, 1976, pp. 90–120.

ProPublica, "Members of Several Well-Known Hate Groups Identified at Capitol Riot," January 9, 2021, https://www.propublica.org/article/several-well-known-hate-groups-identified-at-capitol-riot.

ProPublica, "New Details Suggest Senior Trump Aides Knew Jan. 6 Rally Could Get Chaotic," June 25, 2021, https://www.propublica.org/article/new-details-suggest-senior-trump-aides-knew-jan-6-rally-could-get-chaotic.

PRRI 2020 Race Survey, *Public Religion Research Institute*, June 26–29, 2020, https://prri.parc.us.com/client/index.html#/search.

Pye, Lucien, *Aspects of Political Development*, Boston, MA: Little, Brown and Company, 1970, pp. 6–8, 78–81 and 88.

Rathour, Amric Singh, "A Citizen Fights for His Civil Rights after 9/11," Advancing Justice, https://archive.advancingjustice-la.org/sites/default/files/UCRS%2013_Amric_Singh_Rathour_story%20r2.pdf.

Real Clear Politics, "Trump to Megyn Kelly: I Don't Have Time for Political Correctness and Neither Does the Country," August 6, 2015, https://www.realclearpolitics

.com/video/2015/08/06/trump_to_megyn_kelly_i_dont_have_time_for_political_correctness_and_neither_does_this_country.html.

Reich, Robert, "Elon Musk's Paul Pelosi Tweet Proves He has no Business Running Twitter," *The Guardian*, October 31, 2022, https://www.theguardian.com/commentisfree/2022/oct/31/elon-musk-paul-pelosi-tweet-twitter.

Reid, Shannon E. and Matthew Valasik, *Alt-Right Gangs*, Oakland, CA: University of California Press, 2020, p. 118.

Reilly, James A., *Fragile Nation, Shattered Land: The Modern History of Syria*, Boulder, CO: Lynne Reiner Publishers, 2019, p. 2.

Reny, Tyler T., Loren Collingwood, and Ali A. Valenzuela, "Vote Switching in the 2016 Election: How Racial and Immigration Attitudes, Not Economics, Explain Shifts in White Voting," *Public Opinion Quarterly*, Volume 83, Spring 2019, http://tylerreny.github.io/pdf/pubs/final_submission_reny_etal_poq_public.pdf.

Rettig, Charles, "No Ordinary Audit: Donald Trump Is Facing the IRS 'Wealth Squad,'" *Forbes*, February 28, 2016, https://www.forbes.com/sites/irswatch/2016/02/28/no-ordinary-audit-donald-trump-is-facing-the-irs-wealth-squad/#1658bd2c4d71.

Reuters, "DeSantis Defends Martha's Vineyard Migrant Flights, Suggests More to Come," September 16, 2022, https://www.reuters.com/world/us/tears-uncertainty-migrants-depart-marthas-vineyard-amid-political-standoff-2022-09-16/.

Reuters, "Fact Check: Trump had been Accused of Racism by Contemporaries Prior to Presidential Campaign," May 6, 2021, https://www.reuters.com/article/fact-check-trump-racism/fact-check-trump-had-been-accused-of-racism-by-contemporaries-prior-to-presidential-campaign-idUSL1N2MT312.

Reuters, "Florida Republicans Pass Congressional Map Severely Limiting Black Voter Power," April 7, 2022, https://www.reuters.com/world/us/us-supreme-court-lets-alabama-use-electoral-map-faulted-racial-bias-2022-02-07/.

Reuters, "Most American Voters Support Limited Travel Ban: Poll," July 5, 2017, https://www.reuters.com/article/us-usa-immigration-poll/most-american-voters-support-limited-travel-ban-poll-idUSKBN19Q2FW.

Reuters, "Trump Pushes Anti-immigrant Message Even as Coronavirus Dominates Campaign," August 14, 2020, https://www.reuters.com/article/us-usa-election-immigration-insight/trump-pushes-anti-immigrant-message-even-as-coronavirus-dominates-campaign-idUSKCN25A18W.

"RNC Autopsy," December 2012, https://www.documentcloud.org/documents/624581-rnc-autopsy.

Robertson, David Brian, *Federalism and the Making of America*, New York, NY: Routledge, 2012, pp. 62–63.

Roll Call, "Most of Pentagon Billions Moved to Border not Recoverable," May 7, 2021, https://rollcall.com/2021/05/07/most-of-pentagon-billions-moved-to-border-wall-not-recoverable/.

Roll Call, "Trump Wanted Armed Supporters Allowed into Jan. 6 Rally and to Lead Capitol Charge, Aid Says," June 28, 2022, https://rollcall.com/2022/06/28/trump-wanted-armed-supporters-allowed-into-jan-6-rally-and-to-lead-capitol-charge/.

Rothbart, Daniel and David Stebbins, "The Proud Boys Raging Righteously at the U.S. Capitol on January 6, 2021: A Hate Group in Action," *Peace and Conflict:*

Journal of Peace Psychology, advance online publication, 2022. https://doi.org/10.1037/pac0000634, https://psycnet.apa.org/doi/10.1037/pac0000634.

Rothchild, Mike, *The Storm Is Upon Us*, Brooklyn, NY: Melville Press, 2021, p. 50.

Rousseau, Jean-Jacques, *On the Social Contract*, originally published in 1762, republished by Garden City, NY: Classic Books International, 2010.

Ruisch, Benjamin C. and Melissa J. Ferguson, "Did Donald Trump's Presidency Reshape Americans' Prejudices," *Trends in Cognitive Sciences*, Volume 27, Number 3, March 2023, https://www.sciencedirect.com/journal/trends-in-cognitive-sciences/vol/27/issue/3.

Ruprecht, Daniel, "Executive Inaction: John F. Kennedy and the Civil Rights Crisis," January 1, 2016. https://ir.vanderbilt.edu/bitstream/handle/1803/8351/Executive-Inaction.pdf?sequence=1&isAllowed=y.

Sachs, Jeffrey D., *Commonwealth: Economics for a Crowded Planet*, New York, NY: Penguin Press, 2008, pp. 223–224.

Salon, "'Centrist' Republican Still Willing to Support Trump after He Calls to Terminate the Constitution," December 5, 2022, https://www.salon.com/2022/12/05/centrist-still-willing-to-support-after-he-calls-to-terminate-the-constitution/.

Salon, "Donald Trump's Big Debate Problem: Hillary Clinton Hit the Right Note on Race; Donald Trump Went off the Rails," September 27, 2-16, https://www.salon.com/2016/09/27/placeholder-for-simon-debate-cover/.

Salon, "How the Hillary Clinton Campaign Deliberately 'Elevated' Donald Trump with its 'Pied Piper' Strategy," November 9, 2016, https://www.salon.com/2016/11/09/the-hillary-clinton-campaign-intentionally-created-donald-trump-with-its-pied-piper-strategy/.

Sanandaji, Tino "The Cost of Sweden's Silent Consensus Culture," *Politico*, September 9, 2018, https://www.politico.eu/article/the-cost-of-swedens-silent-consensus-culture/.

Saramo, Samira, "The Meta-violence of Trumpism," *European Journal of American Studies*, Summer 2017, https://journals.openedition.org/ejas/12129.

Schudson, Michael "Why Democracies Need an Unlovable Press," in Doris A. Graber (ed.), *Media Power in Politics*, sixth edition, Washington, DC: CQ Press, 2011, p. 34.

Schumpeter, Joseph, *Capitalism, Socialism and Democracy*, third edition, New York, NY: Harper and Row Publishers, 1950, p. 294.

Serwer, Adam, "Birtherism of a Nation," *The Atlantic*, May 13, 2020, https://www.theatlantic.com/ideas/archive/2020/05/birtherism-and-trump/610978/.

Shuster, Simon, "The Road to War," *Time*, February 14–21, 2022, https://time.com/6144109/russia-ukraine-vladimir-putin-viktor-medvedchuk/.

Sides, John, Michael Tesler, and Lynn Vavreck, *Identity Crisis: The 2016 Presidential Campaign and the Battle for the Meaning of America*, Princeton, NJ: Princeton University Press, 2018, p. 35 and pp. 165–169.

Silva-Leander, Annika, "Exploring the Impact of COVID-19 on Democracies," Institute for Democracy and Electoral Assistance, April 4, 2020, https://www.idea.int/news/devastating-effects-covid-19-democracy-what-if-there-silver-lining

Sindelar, Daisy "1915: The Crumbling of an Empire, and the Massacre That Ensued," Radio Free Europe, August 23, 2015, https://www.rferl.org/a/crumbling-ottoman-empire-and-armenian-massacres/26974721.html.

Slate, "A Week on the Trail with 'Disgusting Reporters' Covering Trump," March 20, 2016, https://www.washingtonpost.com/blogs/erik-wemple/wp/2018/09/07/president-trump-celebrates-the-body-slam-of-a-reporter-in-montana/.

Smithsonian Magazine, "Is China Committing Genocide against the Uyghurs?, February 2, 2022," https://www.smithsonianmag.com/history/is-china-committing-genocide-against-the-uyghurs-180979490/.

Soldak, Katya "Two Steps Forward, One Step Backward: Georgia's Path from Soviet Republic to Free Market Democradcy," *Forbes*, November 23, 2021, https://www.forbes.com/sites/katyasoldak/2021/11/23/two-steps-forward-one-step-back-georgias-path-from-soviet-republic-to-free-market-democracy/.

Soyemi, Eniola Anuoluwapo, "Failures of a Weak State Are to Blame for Nigeria's Ethnicity problem," *The Conversation*, August 29, 2016, https://theconversation.com/failures-of-a-weak-state-are-to-blame-for-nigerias-ethnicity-problem-64186.

Spencer, Nekeisha Mikhail-Ann Orquhart, and Patrice Whitely, "Class Discrimination? Evidence from Jamaica: A Racially Homogeneous Labor Market," *Review of Radical Political Economics*, Volume 52 1, 2020, pp. 77–95, https://journals.sagepub.com/doi/full/10.1177/0486613419832674.

Springfield News-Leader, "Missouri Teacher Accused of Teaching Critical Race Theory Loses Job," April 7, 2022, https://www.news-leader.com/story/news/education/2022/04/07/greenfield-missouri-teacher-kim-morrison-accused-teaching-critical-race-theory-crt-loses-job/.

Stanford, Duke, "Sharecropping, Black Land Acquisition, and White Supremacy, 1868-1900," World Food Policy Center, https://wfpc.sanford.duke.edu/durham-food-history/sharecropping-black-land-acquisition-and-white-supremacy-1868-1900.

Starr, Kevin, *Inventing the Dream*, New York, NY: Oxford University Press, 1985, pp. 42–43.

Steinmetz-Jenkins, Daniel, "The European Intellectual Origins of the Alt-Right," Istanbul University Press, pp. 255–266, https://dergipark.org.tr/tr/download/article-file/679543.

Stenner, Karen, *The Authoritarian Dynamic*, New York, NY: Cambridge University Press, 2005, pp. 17–18 and 31.

Stephens-Dougan, Lafleur, *Race to the Bottom: How Racial Appeals Work in American Politics*, Chicago, IL: University of Chicago Press, 2020, p. 176.

Stokols, Eli, "Trump's Four Dysfunctional Days in Cleveland," July 22, 2016, https://www.politico.com/story/2016/07/rnc-2016-donald-trump-dysfunction-226001.

Sturkey, William, "The Hidden History of the Civil Rights Act of 1960," *Black Perspectives*, https://www.aaihs.org/the-hidden-history-of-the-civil-rights-act-of-1960/.

Tarrow, Sidney, *Movements and Parties*, New York, NY: Cambridge University Press, 2021, pp. 179–180.

Tenpas, Kathryn Dunn, "Tracking Turnover in the Trump Administration," Brookings, January 2021, https://www.brookings.edu/research/tracking-turnover-in-the-trump-administration/.

The Atlantic, "An Oral History of Trump's Bigotry," June 2019, https://www.theatlantic.com/magazine/archive/2019/06/trump-racism-comments/588067/.

The Cook Political Report, "GOP Won the Votes, but Not the Seats," November 15, 2022, https://www.cookpolitical.com/analysis/national/national-politics/gop-won-votes-not-seats.

The Cultural Atlas, "Swedish Cultural," 2022, https://culturalatlas.sbs.com.au/swedish-culture. The Economist, "A New Low for Global Democracy," February 2, 2022, https://www.economist.com/graphic-detail/2022/02/09/a-new-low-for-global-democracy.

The Economist, "Democracy Index 2020: In Sickness and Health?" 2021, p. 44, https://www.eiu.com/public/topical_report.aspx?campaignid=democracy2020.

The Economist, "The Upper Han," November 19, 2016, https://www.economist.com/briefing/2016/11/19/the-upper-han.

The Fresno Bee, "Kevin McCarthy's Tweet is either a Bluff or Really Dangerous," Editorial, June 9, 2023, https://www.fresnobee.com/opinion/editorials/article276258706.html.

The Gallup Poll, "Immigration," https://news.gallup.com/poll/1660/immigration.aspx.

The Gallup Poll, "Presidential Approval Ratings—Donald Trump," January 2017 through January 2021, https://news.gallup.com/poll/203198/presidential-approval-ratings-donald-trump.aspx.

The Guardian, "From Reformer to 'New Sultan': Erdogan's Populist Revolution," March 11, 2019, https://www.theguardian.com/world/2019/mar/11/from-reformer-to-new-sultan-erdogans-populist-evolution

The Guardian, "New PPRI Report Reveals Nearly One in Five Americans and One in Four PPRI, Republicans Still Believe in QAnon Conspiracy Theories," February 24, 2022, https://www.prri.org/press-release/new-prri-report-reveals-nearly-one-in-five-americans-and-one-in-four-republicans-still-believe-in-qanon-conspiracy-theories/.

The Guardian, "Proud Boys Memo Reveals Meticulous Planning for 'Street-Level Violence,'" September 19, 2022, https://www.theguardian.com/world/2022/sep/19/proud-boys-document-jan-6-violence.

The Guardian, "QAnon Explained: The Antisemitic Conspiracy Theory Gaining Traction around the World," August 25, 2020, https://www.theguardian.com/us-news/2020/aug/25/qanon-conspiracy-theory-explained-trump-what-is.

The Guardian, "Trump Disavows the White Nationalist 'Alt-Right' but Defends Steve Bannon Hire," November 22, 2016, https://www.theguardian.com/us-news/2016/nov/22/donald-trump-steve-bannon-alt-right-white-nationalist-disavow.

The Guardian, "Trump Sparks Anger by Calling Coronavirus the 'Chinese Virus,'" March 17, 2020, https://www.theguardian.com/world/2020/mar/17/trump-calls-covid-19-the-chinese-virus-as-rift-with-coronavirus-beijing-escalates.

The Guardian, "War in Wokeness: The Year the Right Rallied around a Made-Up Menace," December 21, 2022, https://www.theguardian.com/us-news/2022/dec/20/anti-woke-race-america-history.

The Hill, "6 in 10 Trump Voters Agree with Core Tenet of Great Replacement Theory: Survey," May 24, 2022, https://thehill.com/homenews/state-watch/3499877-6-in-10-trump-voters-agree-with-core-tenet-of-great-replacement-theory-survey/.

The Hill, "ADL Chief: Trump Post on American Jews 'Sounds like a Threat,'" December 17, 2022, https://thehill.com/policy/international/3692763-adl-chief-trump-post-on-american-jews-sounds-like-a-threat/.

The Hill, "Juan Williams: My Immigrant Story," June 25, 2018, https://thehill.com/opinion/immigration/393887-juan-williams-my-immigrant-story/.

The Hill, "McCarthy told Trump that Jan. 6 Rioters 'were trying to f...... Kill Me': Book," October 11, 2022, https://thehill.com/homenews/house/3682571-mccarthy-told-trump-that-jan-6-rioters-were-trying-to-ing-kill-me-book/.

The Hill, "Supreme Court Clears Way for Louisiana to Redo Congressional Map," June 26, 2023, https://thehill.com/homenews/4067876-supreme-court-clears-way-for-louisiana-to-redo-congressional-map/.

The Hill, "Trump Calls Ex-chief of Staff Mick Mulvaney 'a Born Loser," April 18, 2023, https://thehill.com/blogs/blog-briefing-room/3956541-trump-calls-ex-chief-of-staff-mick-mulvaney-a-born-loser/.

The Hill, "Trump Slams Bill Barr as 'a Coward Who Didn't Do His Job,'" June 11, 2023, https://thehill.com/blogs/blog-briefing-room/4044744-trump-slams-bill-barr-as-a-coward-who-didnt-do-his-job/.

The Independent, "Trump Suggested 'Black vs Whites' Games in *The Apprentice*," July 22, 2019, https://www.independent.co.uk/news/world/americas/us-politics/trump-apprentice-black-vs-white-contest-howard-stern-interview-a9015701.html.

The January 6th Report, New York, NY: Random House, 2023.

The Nation, "Trump's Embrace of QAnon Realizes the Dream of the Religious Right," *The Hill*, September 23, 2022, https://www.thenation.com/article/politics/trump-qanon/.

The New York Times, "77 Days: Trump's Campaign to Subvert the Election," February 1, 2021, https://www.nytimes.com/2021/01/31/us/trump-election-lie.html.

The New York Times, "A 2016 Review: Turnout Wasn't the Driver of Clinton's Defeat," March 28, 2017, https://www.nytimes.com/2017/03/28/upshot/a-2016-review-turnout-wasnt-the-driver-of-clintons-defeat.html.

The New York Times, "A Disturbing New Pattern in Mass Shootings: Young Assailants," June 2, 2022, https://www.nytimes.com/2022/06/02/us/politics/mass-shootings-young-men-guns.html.

The New York Times, "A Jan. 6 Mystery: Why Did It Take So Long to Deploy the National Guard?" July 7, 2021, https://www.nytimes.com/2022/07/21/us/politics/national-guard-january-6-riot.html.

The New York Times, "A Transgender Lawmaker Is Exiled as Montana G.O.P. Flexes New Power," April 27, 2023, https://www.nytimes.com/2023/04/28/us/montana-trans-gianforte.html

The New York Times, "After a Day of Debate, the Voting Rights Bill is Blocked in the Senate," January 19, 2022, https://www.nytimes.com/2022/01/19/us/politics/senate-voting-rights-filibuster.html.

The New York Times, "Assaults Increased When Cities Hosted Trump Rallies, Study Finds," March 16, 2018, https://www.nytimes.com/2018/03/16/us/trump-rally-violence.html.

The New York Times, "Christie Attacks Trump, Calling Conduct Detailed in Indictment 'Awful,'" June 12, 2023, https://www.nytimes.com/2023/06/12/us/politics/chris-christie-trump-cnn-town-hall.html.

The New York Times, "Club for Growth Distances Itself Further From Trump," https://www.nytimes.com/2023/02/06/us/politics/club-for-growth-trump-desantis.html.

The New York Times, "Crossing the Line: How Donald Trump Behaved with Women in Private," May 14, 2016, https://www.nytimes.com/2016/05/15/us/politics/donald-trump-women.html.

The New York Times, "Decades after Infamous Beating Death, Recent Attacks Haunt Asian Americans," June 17, 2022, https://www.nytimes.com/2022/06/16/us/vincent-chin-anti-asian-attack-detroit.html.

The New York Times, "DeSantis Signs Florida Bill That Opponents Call 'Don't Say Gay,'" March 28, 2022, https://www.nytimes.com/2022/03/28/us/desantis-florida-dont-say-gay-bill.html.

The New York Times, "DeSantis Usually Avoids the Press. For Murdoch, He'll Make an Exception," March 3, 2023, https://www.nytimes.com/2023/03/02/business/media/ron-desantis-murdoch-media.html.

The New York Times, "DeSantis, Aiming at a Favorite Foil, Wants to Roll Back Press Freedom," February 10, 2023, https://www.nytimes.com/2023/02/10/us/politics/ron-desantis-news-media.html

The New York Times, "Did a Queens Podiatrist Hep Donald Trump Avoid Vietnam," December 26, 2018, https://www.nytimes.com/2018/12/26/us/politics/trump-vietnam-draft-exemption.html.

The New York Times, "Donald Trump Defiantly Rallies a New 'Silent Majority' in a Visit to Arizona," July 11, 2015, https://www.nytimes.com/2015/07/12/us/politics/donald-trump-defiantly-rallies-a-new-silent-majority-in-a-visit-to-arizona.html.

The New York Times, "Erdogan's Purges Leave Turkey's Justice System Reeling," June 21, 2019, https://www.nytimes.com/2019/06/21/world/asia/erdogan-turkey-courts-judiciary-justice.html.

The New York Times, "Florida Rejects A.P. African American Studies Class," January 19, 2023, https://www.nytimes.com/2023/01/19/us/desantis-florida-ap-african-american-studies.html. "DeSantis 'Review' of Public Records can Add Months of Delays, Newly Uncovered Log Reveals," www.Clickorlando.com, February 28, 2023, https://www.clickorlando.com/news/politics/2023/02/28/desantis-review-of-public-records-can-add-months-of-delays-newly-uncovered-log-reveals/.

The New York Times, "G.O.P Declares Jan. 6 Attack 'Legitimate Political Discourse,'" February 4, 2022, https://www.google.com/search?q=McCarthy+Joins+List+of+Top+Republicans+Trying+to+Mend+Fences+With+Trump&rlz

=1C5CHFA_enUS773US773&oq=McCarthy+Joins+List+of+Top+Republicans+Trying+to+Mend+Fences+With+Trump&aqs=chrome..69i57.30151j0j7&sourceid=chrome&ie=UTF-8.

The New York Times, "How Asian-American Leaders Are Grappling With Xenophobia Amid Coronavirus," April 10, 2020, https://www.nytimes.com/2020/03/29/us/politics/coronavirus-asian-americans.html.

The New York Times, "How the E.U. Standards Allowed Hungary to Become an Illiberal Role Model," January 4, 2022, https://www.nytimes.com/2022/01/03/world/europe/hungary-european-union.html.

The New York Times, "How the Trump Campaign Took Control of the G.O.P.," December 24, 2020, https://www.nytimes.com/2020/03/09/us/trump-campaign-brad-parscale.html.

The New York Times, "How Trump's Billion Dollar Campaign Lost Its Cash Advantage," September 7, 2020, https://www.nytimes.com/2020/09/07/us/politics/trump-election-campaign-fundraising.html.

The New York Times, "'I Answered the Call of My President': Rioters Say Trump Urged Them On," January 22, 2021, https://www.nytimes.com/2021/01/17/nyregion/protesters-blaming-trump-pardon.html.

The New York Times, "In Encounters with Black Leaders, Trump Has Chosen Photo Ops over Substance," September 11, 2020, https://www.nytimes.com/2020/09/10/us/politics/trump-black-leaders.html.

The New York Times, "Inside Trump's Failure: The Rush to Abandon Leadership Role on the Virus," September 9, 2020, https://www.nytimes.com/2020/07/18/us/politics/trump-coronavirus-response-failure-leadership.html.

The New York Times, "Intruder Wanted to Break Speaker Pelosi's Kneecaps, Federal Complaint Says," October 31, 2022, https://www.nytimes.com/2022/10/31/us/pelosi-home-attack-suspect-charged.html.

The New York Times, "Jan. 6 Panel Issues Final Report, Placing Blame for Capitol Riot on 'One Man,'" December 22, 2022, https://www.nytimes.com/2022/03/29/us/politics/trump-tweet-jan-6.html.

The New York Times, "Jan. 6 Panel Outlines Trump's Bid to Coerce Justice Dept. Officials," June 23, 2022, https://www.nytimes.com/2022/06/23/us/politics/jan-6-hearing-trump-justice-department.html.

The New York Times, "Jury Finds Trump Liable for Sexual Abuse and Defamation," May 9, 2023, https://www.nytimes.com/live/2023/05/09/nyregion/trump-carroll-rape-trial-verdict.

The New York Times, "Major Landlord Accused of Antiblack Bias in City," October 16, 1973, https://www.nytimes.com/1973/10/16/archives/major-landlord-accused-of-antiblack-bias-in-city-us-accuses-major.html.

The New York Times, "Mandatory Busing May Go, Even If Races Stay Apart," January 6, 1991, https://www.nytimes.com/1991/01/16/us/justices-rule-mandatory-busing-may-go-even-if-races-stay-apart.html.

The New York Times, "Maps in Four States Were Ruled Illegal Gerrymanders. They're Being Used Anyway," August 8, 2022, https://www.nytimes.com/2022/08/08/us/elections/gerrymandering-maps-elections-republicans.html.

The New York Times, "McCarthy Joins List of Top Republicans Trying to Mend Fences With Trump," January 29, 2021, https://www.google.com/search?q=McCarthy+Joins+List+of+Top+Republicans+Trying+to+Mend+Fences+With+Trump&rlz=1C5CHFA_enUS773US773&oq=McCarthy+Joins+List+of+Top+Republicans+Trying+to+Mend+Fences+With+Trump&aqs=chrome..69i57.30151j0j7&sourceid=chrome&ie=UTF-8.

The New York Times, "McConnell Denounces R.N.C. Censure of Jan. 6 Panel Members," February 8, 2022, https://www.nytimes.com/2022/02/08/us/politics/republicans-censure-mcconnell.html.

The New York Times, "Misinformation Defense Worked in 2020, Up to a Point, Study Finds," April 14, 2023, https://www.nytimes.com/2023/04/13/business/media/misinformation-2020-election-study.html.

The New York Times, "Montana Governor Signs Law Banning Transition Care for Minors," April 28, 2023, https://www.nytimes.com/2023/04/28/us/montana-trans-gianforte.html.

The New York Times, "Myanmar Executes Four Pro-Democracy Activists, Defying Foreign Leaders," https://www.nytimes.com/2022/07/25/world/asia/myanmar-executions.html.

The New York Times, "New Insights into Trump's State of Mind on Jan. 6 Chip Away at Doubts," July 3, 2022, https://www.nytimes.com/2022/07/03/us/politics/new-insights-into-trumps-state-of-mind-on-jan-6-chip-away-at-doubts.html

The New York Times, "New York Sues Trump, Citing Decade of 'Staggering' Fraud," September 22, 2022.

The New York Times, "'No Vacancies' for Blacks: How Donald Trump Got His Start, and Was First Accused of Bias," August 27, 2016, https://www.nytimes.com/2016/08/28/us/politics/donald-trump-housing-race.html.

The New York Times, "Proud Boys Celebrate Trump's 'Stand By' Remarks about them at the Debate," September 29, 2020, https://www.nytimes.com/2020/09/29/us/trump-proud-boys-biden.html.

The New York Times, "Putin Reclaims Crimea for Russia and Bitterly Denounces the West," March 18, 2014, https://www.nytimes.com/2014/03/19/world/europe/ukraine.html.

The New York Times, "Republicans Face Setbacks in Push to Tighten Voting Laws on College Campuses," March 30, 2023, https://www.nytimes.com/2023/03/29/us/politics/republicans-young-voters-college.html.

The New York Times, "'So the Traitors Know the Stakes:' The Meaning of the Jan. 6 Gallows," June 16, 2022, https://www.nytimes.com/2022/06/16/us/politics/jan-6-gallows.html.

The New York Times, "Supreme Court Invalidates Key Part of the Voting Rights Act," June 25, 2013, https://www.nytimes.com/2013/06/26/us/supreme-court-ruling.html#:~:text=WASHINGTON%20%E2%80%94%20The%20Supreme%20Court%20on,laws%20without%20advance%20federal%20approval.

The New York Times, "Supreme Court Rejects Theory That Would Have Transformed American Elections," June 27, 2023, https://www.nytimes.com/2023/06/27/us/politics/supreme-court-state-legislature-elections.html#:~:text=The

%20Supreme%20Court%20on%20Tuesday,maps%20warped%20by%20partisan%20gerrymandering

The New York Times, "Supreme Court Rejects Voting Map That Diluted Black Voters' Power," June 8, 2023, https://www.nytimes.com/2023/06/08/us/supreme-court-voting-rights-act-alabama.html.

The New York Times, "Taking Aim at Trump, Koch Network Wil Back G.O.P. Primary Candidates," https://www.nytimes.com/2023/02/05/us/politics/koch-donors-trump-campaign-finance.html.

The New York Times, "The Mar-a-Lago Machine: Trump as a Modern-Day Party Boss," April 18, 2022, https://www.nytimes.com/2022/04/17/us/politics/trump-mar-a-lago.html.

The New York Times, "The President vs. the Experts: How Trump Downplayed the Coronavirus," March 20, 2020, https://www.nytimes.com/interactive/2020/03/18/us/trump-coronavirus-statements-timeline.html.

The New York Times, "The Story behind DeSantis's Migrant Flights to Martha's Vineyard," October 4, 2022, https://www.nytimes.com/2022/10/02/us/migrants-marthas-vineyard-desantis-texas.html.

The New York Times, "Transcript: Donald Trump's Taped Comments About Women," October 8, 2016, https://www.google.com/search?q=trump%27s+statements+about+women&rlz=1C5CHFA_enUS773US773&ei=9CTfYuWkA8mfkPIPhuaVoAE&start=10&sa=N&ved=2ahUKEwjl7vPMlpX5AhXJD0QIHQZzBRQQ8NMDegQIARBC&biw=1440&bih=719&dpr=1.

The New York Times, "Trump Adds to Playbook of Stoking White Fear and Resentment," July 6, 2020, https://www.nytimes.com/2020/07/06/us/politics/trump-bubba-wallace-nascar.html.

The New York Times, "Trump and Justice Dept. Lawyer Said to Have Plotted to Oust Acting Attorney," October 13, 2022, https://www.nytimes.com/2021/01/22/us/politics/jeffrey-clark-trump-justice-department-election.html.

The New York Times, "Trump Angst Grips Republicans (Again) as 2024 Announcement Looms," https://www.nytimes.com/2022/11/12/us/politics/trump-2024-republicans.html.

The New York Times, "Trump Charged with Rental Bias," March 7, 1978, https://www.nytimes.com/1978/03/07/archives/trump-charged-with-rental-bias.html.

The New York Times, "Trump Disavows Alt-Right in New York Times Interview," November 22, 2016, https://www.pbs.org/newshour/politics/inside-donald-trumps-meeting-new-york-times.

The New York Times, "Trump Embraces Conspiracy Theories He Only Winked at Before," September 2, 2022, https://www.nytimes.com/2022/09/02/technology/trump-conspiracy-theories-truth-social.html.

The New York Times, "Trump Encourages Racist Conspiracy Theory about Kamala Harris," August 14, 2020, https://news.gallup.com/poll/1660/immigration.aspx.

The New York Times, "Trump Gives White Supremacists an Unequivocal Boost," August 15, 2017, https://www.nytimes.com/2017/08/15/us/politics/trump-charlottesville-white-nationalists.html.

The New York Times, "Trump Impeached for Inciting Insurrection," January 13, 2021, https://www.nytimes.com/2021/01/13/us/politics/trump-impeached.html.

The New York Times, "Trump Organization Found Guilty in Tax Fraud Scheme," December 6, 2022, https://www.nytimes.com/live/2022/12/06/nyregion/trump-organization-trial-verdict.

The New York Times, "Trump Put National Secrets at Risk, Prosecutors Say in Historic Indictment," https://www.nytimes.com/2023/06/09/us/politics/trump-indictment-charges-classified-documents.html.

The New York Times, "Trump, Vowing 'Retribution,' Foretells a Second Term of Spite," March 7, 2023, https://www.nytimes.com/2023/03/07/us/politics/trump-2024-president.html.

The New York Times, "Trump Wanted I.R.S. Investigations of Foes, Top Aide Says," November 14, 2022, https://www.nytimes.com/2022/11/13/us/politics/trump-irs-investigations.html/.

The New York Times, "Trump's Latest Dinner Guest: Nick Fuentes, White Supremacist," https://www.nytimes.com/2022/11/25/us/politics/trump-nick-fuentes-dinner.html.

The New York Times, "Trump's Suggestion That Disinfectant s Could Be Used to Treat Coronavirus Prompts Aggressive Pushback," April 20, 2020, https://www.nytimes.com/2020/04/24/us/politics/trump-inject-disinfectant-bleach-coronavirus.html.

The New York Times, "Trumps Words, and Deeds, Reveal Depths of His Drive to Keep Power," February 1, 2022, https://www.nytimes.com/2022/02/01/us/politics/trump-election-jan-6-voting-machines.html.

The New York Times, "Trying to Trademark 'Rigged Election' and Other Revelations From the Jan. 6 Transcripts," January 2, 2023, https://www.nytimes.com/2023/01/02/us/politics/jan-6-committee-transcripts.html.

The New York Times, "Two Men Convicted in Plot to Kidnap Michigan's Governor," August 23, 2022, https://www.nytimes.com/2022/08/23/us/verdict-trial-gretchen-whitmer-kidnap.html and "Jury Convicts Men of Supporting Plot to Kidnap Michigan Governor," *The New York Times*, https://www.nytimes.com/2022/10/26/us/michigan-wolverine-watchmen-trial.html.

The New York Times, "Two Years Later, prosecutions of Jan. 6 Rioters Continue to Grow," January 6, 2023, https://www.nytimes.com/2023/01/06/us/politics/jan-6-capitol-riots-prosecutions.html.

The New York Times, "When Trump Calls a Black Woman 'Angry,' He Feeds This Racist Trope," August 15, 2020, https://www.nytimes.com/2020/08/14/arts/trump-black-women-stereotypes.html.

The New York Times, "With Rising Book Bans, Librarians Have Come under Attack," July 7, 2022, https://www.nytimes.com/2022/07/06/books/book-ban-librarians.html.

The New York Times, "With Watchful Eyes, a Nationwide Network Tracks Antisemitic Threats," May 29, 2023, https://www.nytimes.com/2023/05/29/us/anti-semitic-attacks-jewish-secure-community-network.html.

"The Proud Boys: Chauvinist Poster Child of Far-Right Extremism," *European Center for Populism Studies*, February 1, 2021, https://www.populismstudies.org/the-proud-boys-chauvinist-poster-child-of-far-right-extremism/.

The Seattle Times, "Truman's Racist Talk Cited by Historian," November 3, 1991, https://archive.seattletimes.com/archive/?date=19911103&slug=1314805.

The Texas Monthly, "Why Is Donald Trump Kicking Off His 2024 Campaign in Waco?" March 22, 2023, https://www.texasmonthly.com/news-politics/why-is-trump-kicking-off-2024-campaign-in-waco/.

The Texas Tribune, "Analysis: When 1 in 8 Texas Mail Ballots gets Trashed, that's Vote Suppression," March 3, 2022, https://www.texastribune.org/2022/03/18/texas-rejected-election-ballots/.

The Texas Tribune, "Texas Reduces Black and Hispanic Majority Congressional Districts in Proposed Map, Despite People of Color Fueling Population Growth," September 27, 2021, https://www.texastribune.org/2021/09/24/texas-congressional-redistricting/.

The Wall Street Journal, "Demographic Shift Poised to Test Trump's 2020 Strategy," https://www.wsj.com/articles/demographic-shift-poised-to-test-trumps-2020-strategy-11578047402.

The Wall Street Journal, "Mexico Referendum on Former Leaders Has Low Turnout," August 2, 2021, https://www.wsj.com/articles/mexico-referendum-on-former-leaders-has-low-turnout-11627923776.

The Wall Street Journal, "Putin Speech Takes Swipe at U.S.-Led International Order," February 22, 2022, https://www.wsj.com/articles/putin-address-takes-swipe-at-u-s-led-world-order-11645485419.

The Wall Street Journal, "Putin's Endgame: Undo Post-Cold War Accords," February 22, 2022, https://www.wsj.com/articles/putins-endgame-unravel-the-post-cold-war-agreements-that-humiliated-russia-11645482412.

The Wall Street Journal, "Supreme Court Strikes down Affirmative Action in College Admissions," June 29, 2023, https://www.wsj.com/articles/supreme-court-rules-against-affirmative-action-c94b5a9c.

The Wall Street Journal, "Trump is the Republican Party's Biggest Loser," November 9, 2022, https://www.wsj.com/articles/donald-trump-is-the-gops-biggest-loser-midterm-elections-senate-house-congress-republicans-11668034869.

The Wall Street Journal, "Trump Offers to Buy Out Islamic Center Investor," September 9, 2010, https://www.wsj.com/articles/SB10001424052748704644404575482093330879912.

The Wall Street Journal, "Trump Repeatedly Pressed Ikraine President to Investigate Biden's Son," September 21, 2019, https://www.wsj.com/articles/trump-defends-conversation-with-ukraine-leader-11568993176.

The Wall Street Journal, "Trump Says Judge's Mexican Heritage Presents 'Absolute Conflict,'" June 3, 2016, https://www.google.com/search?q=trump+university&rlz=1C5CHFA_enUS773US773&oq=trump+university&aqs=chrome..69i57j46i131i199i433i465i512j0i512j0i131.

The Wall Street Journal, "Trump's Campaign War Chest Tops $100 Million Heading into Election Year," January 2, 2020, https://www.wsj.com/articles/trump-campaignraised-46-million-infourth-quarter-11577970640.

The Wall Street Journal, "Turkish Court Upholds Politician's Prison Term," May 13, 2022, https://www.wsj.com/articles/turkish-court-upholds-prison-sentence-for-opposition-leader-11652374773.

The Washington Post, "1 in 3 Americans Say Violence against Government can be Justified, Citing Fears of Political Schism, Pandemic," January 1, 2022, https://www.washingtonpost.com/politics/2022/01/01/1-3-americans-say-violence-against-government-can-be-justified-citing-fears-political-schism-pandemic/.

The Washington Post, "4 Final Takeaways from Trump's Impeachment Trial," February 13, 2021, https://www.washingtonpost.com/politics/2021/02/13/takeaways-trump-impeachment-trial-final/.

The Washington Post, "7 Former Communist Countries Join NATO," March 30, 2004, https://www.washingtonpost.com/archive/politics/2004/03/30/7-former-communist-countries-join-nato/476d93dc-e4bd-4f05-9a15-5b66d322d0e6/.

The Washington Post, "A Look at Trump's 'Birther' Statements," April 28, 2011, https://www.theatlantic.com/ideas/archive/2020/05/birtherism-and-trump/610978/.

The Washington Post, "A White Teacher Taught White Students about White Privilege. It Cost Him His Job," December 6, 2021, https://www.washingtonpost.com/education/2021/12/06/tennessee-teacher-fired-critical-race-theory/.

The Washington Post, "Alicia Machado, the Woman Trump called Miss Housing, is Ready to Vote against Donald Trump," September 2016, https://www.washingtonpost.com/news/the-fix/wp/2016/09/27/alicia-machado-the-woman-trump-called-miss-housekeeping-is-ready-to-vote-against-donald-trump/.

The Washington Post, "Behind the Armor: Men Seek 'Purpose' in Protecting Property Despite Charges of Racism," October 5, 2020, https://www.washingtonpost.com/national/behind-the-armor-men-seek-purpose-in-protecting-property-despite-charges-of-racism/2020/10/05/b8496fec-001e-11eb-9ceb-061d646d9c67_story.html.

The Washington Post, "Bipartisan House Probe of Jan. 6 Insurrection Falls Apart after Pelosi Blocks Two GOP Members," July 21, 2021, https://www.washingtonpost.com/politics/pelosi-mccarthy-jan6-committee/2021/07/21/21722d44-ea41-11eb-84a2-d93bc0b50294_story.html.

The Washington Post, "Caught in the Culture Wars, Teachers Are being Forced from their Jobs," June 16, 2022, https://www.washingtonpost.com/education/2022/06/16/teacher-resignations-firings-culture-wars/.

The Washington Post, "CDC to Cut by 80 Percent Efforts to Prevent Global Disease Outbreak," February 1, 2018, https://www.washingtonpost.com/news/to-your-health/wp/2018/02/01/cdc-to-cut-by-80-percent-efforts-to-prevent-global-disease-outbreak/.

The Washington Post, "Censorship Battles' New Frontier: Your Public Library," April 17, 2022, https://www.washingtonpost.com/nation/2022/04/17/public-libraries-books-censorship/.

The Washington Post, "Confident. Incorrigible. Bully. Little Donny was a lot like Candidate Donald Trump," June 22, 2016, https://www.washingtonpost.com/lifestyle/style/young-donald-trump-military-school/2016/06/22/f0b3b164-317c-11e6-8758-d58e76e11b12_story.html.

The Washington Post, "DeSantis Signs Bill to Defund DEI Programs at Fla. Colleges," May 15, 2023, https://www.washingtonpost.com/education/2023/05/15/desantis-defunds-dei-programs-florida-colleges/.

The Washington Post, "DeSantis Spokeswoman Christina Pushaw makes Sure Reporters Feel the Burn," July 27, 2022, https://www.washingtonpost.com/media/2022/07/27/christina-pushaw-desantis/.

The Washington Post, "'Get 'em out!' Racial Tensions Explode at Trump Rallies," March 12, 2016, https://www.huffpost.com/entry/list-racist-things-trump-rallies_n_56d7019ae4b0871f60ed519f.

The Washington Post, "GOP Leaders Fear Damage to Party's Image as Donald Trump Doubles Down," July 8, 2015, https://www.washingtonpost.com/politics/trump-could-damage-the-republican-image-party-leaders-worry/2015/07/08/2ec75b4c-25ab-11e5-b72c-2b7d516e1e0e_story.html.

The Washington Post, "Growth and Opportunity Project," Republican National Committee, December 2012, https://www.washingtonpost.com/politics/all-eyes-will-be-on-trump-at-republican-debate/2016/02/13/bd30bae2-d274-11e5-abc9-ea152f0b9561_story.html.

The Washington Post, "How Donald Trump's 1993 Comments about 'Indians' Previewed much of His 2016 Campaign," July 1, 2016, https://www.washingtonpost.com/news/the-fix/wp/2016/07/01/how-donald-trumps-1993-comments-about-indians-previewed-much-of-his-2016-campaign/.

The Washington Post, "How Harry S. Truman went from being a Racist to Desegregating the Military," July 26, 2018, https://www.washingtonpost.com/news/retropolis/wp/2018/07/26/how-harry-s-truman-went-from-being-a-racist-to-desegregating-the-military/.

The Washington Post, "I Just Want To Find 11,780 Votes': In Extraordinary Hour-Long Call, Trump Pressures Georgia Secretary of State to Recalculate the Vote in His Favor," January 3, 2021, https://www.washingtonpost.com/politics/trump-raffensperger-call-transcript-georgia-vote/2021/01/03/2768e0cc-4ddd-11eb-83e3-322644d82356_story.html.

The Washington Post, "'If you're a Good Worker, Papers don't Matter': How a Trump Construction Crew has Relied on Immigrants without Legal Status," August 9, 2019, https://time.com/4386240/donald-trump-immigration-arguments/.

The Washington Post, "In Colombia's Mass Protests, Indigenous and Black Activists Find Echoes of Colonial History," June 2, 2021," https://www.washingtonpost.com/politics/2021/06/02/colombias-mass-protests-indigenous-black-activists-find-echoes-colonial-history/.

The Washington Post, "Inside Mark Meadows's Final Push to Keep Trump in Power," May 9, 2022, https://www.washingtonpost.com/politics/2022/05/09/inside-mark-meadowss-final-push-keep-trump-power/.

The Washington Post, "'Let's Party Like It's 1933': Inside the Alt-Right World of Richard Spencer," November 22, 2016, https://www.washingtonpost.com/local/lets-party-like-its-1933-inside-the-disturbing-alt-right-world-of-richard-spencer/2016/11/22/cf81dc74-aff7-11e6-840f-e3ebab6bcdd3_story.html.

The Washington Post, "Mar-a-Lago Classified Papers held U.S. Secrets about Iran and China," October 21, 2022, https://www.washingtonpost.com/national-security/2022/10/21/trump-documents-mar-a-lago-iran-china/.

The Washington Post, "Mounting Intimidation against Members of Congress Threatens Us All," October 3, 2022, https://www.washingtonpost.com/opinions/2022/10/03/threats-violence-members-congress-intimidation/.

The Washington Post, "Mueller Complained that Barr's Letter did not Capture the 'Context' of Trump Probe," April 19, 2019, https://www.washingtonpost.com/world/national-security/mueller-complained-that-barrs-letter-did-not-capture-context-of-trump-probe/2019/04/30/d3c8fdb6-6b7b-11e9-a66d-a82d3f3d96d5_story.html.

The Washington Post, "Muslim Woman gets Kicked of Trump Rally—For Protesting Silently," January 9, 2016, https://www.washingtonpost.com/news/post-politics/wp/2016/01/08/muslim-woman-escorted-out-of-trump-rally-in-south-carolina/.

The Washington Post, "New Critical Race Theory Laws have Teachers Scared, Confused and Self-censoring," February 14, 2022, https://www.washingtonpost.com/education/2022/02/14/critical-race-theory-teachers-fear-laws/.

The Washington Post, "Northern Ireland's Troubles began 50 Years Ago. Here's Why they were so Violent," August 22, 2019, https://www.washingtonpost.com/politics/2019/08/22/why-were-troubles-so-bloody-this-helps-explain/.

The Washington Post, "President Trump's 90-Second Rant on Richard Blumenthal and Vietnam," October 3, 3028, https://www.washingtonpost.com/politics/2018/10/03/president-trumps-second-rant-richard-blumenthal-vietnam/.

The Washington Post, "Republican Debate Raises Voices, Name Calling, and Personal Attacks," February 13, 2016, https://www.washingtonpost.com/politics/all-eyes-will-be-on-trump-at-republican-debate/2016/02/13/bd30bae2-d274-11e5-abc9-ea152f0b9561_story.html.

The Washington Post, "Republicans Who Supported Voting Rights Act Now Oppose Bill Democrats Say would Strengthen Its Provisions," January 19, 2022, https://www.washingtonpost.com/politics/2022/01/19/republicans-voting-rights/.

The Washington Post, "Six Times President Trump Said He is the Least Racist Person," January 17, 2018, https://www.washingtonpost.com/news/the-fix/wp/2018/01/17/six-times-president-trump-said-he-is-the-least-racist-person/.

The Washington Post, "The Abnormal Presidency," November 10, 2020, https://www.washingtonpost.com/graphics/2020/lifestyle/magazine/trump-presidential-norm-breaking-list/.

The Washington Post, "The Alt-Right Supported Trump. Now its Members Want Him to Satisfy their Demands," November 10, 2016, https://www.washingtonpost.com/national/the-alt-right-used-to-be-ignored-now-theyre-courting-a-president-elect/2016/11/10/746341d8-a75b-11e6-8fc0-7be8f848c492_story.html.

The Washington Post, "The Biggest Fans of President Trump's Israel Policy? Evangelical Christians," December 18, 2017, https://www.washingtonpost.com/news/made-by-history/wp/2017/12/18/the-biggest-fans-of-president-trumps-israel-policy-evangelical-christians/.

The Washington Post, "The Many Ways in which Donald Trump was Once a Liberal's Liberal," July 9, 2015, https://www.washingtonpost.com/news/the-fix/wp/2015/07/09/ths-many-ways-in-which-donald-trump-was-once-a-liberals-liberal/.

The Washington Post, The Mueller Report, published by *The Washington Post* in 2019.

The Washington Post, "The Race Politics of Ron DeSantis," *The Washington Post*, February 1, 2023, https://www.washingtonpost.com/politics/2023/02/01/desantis-race-politics/.

The Washington Post, "The Tale of a Trump Falsehood: How His Voter Fraud Claim Spread like a Virus," January 31, 2071, https://www.washingtonpost.com/politics/the-tale-of-a-trump-falsehood-how-his-voter-fraud-claim-spread-like-a-virus/2017/01/30/47081e32-e4ed-11e6-ba11-63c4b4fb5a63_story.html.

The Washington Post, "The Washington Post's New Slogan Turns Out to be an Old Saying," February 24, 2017, https://www.washingtonpost.com/lifestyle/style/the-washington-posts-new-slogan-turns-out-to-be-an-old-saying/2017/02/23/cb199cda-fa02-11e6-be05-1a3817ac21a5_story.html.

The Washington Post, "Trump Calls Women's Claims of Sexual Advances 'Vicious' and 'Absolutely False'," October 13, 2016, https://www.washingtonpost.com/politics/multiple-women-accuse-donald-trump-of-making-sexual-advances/2016/10/13/3862fab0-9140-11e6-9c52-0b10449e33c4_story.html.

The Washington Post, "Trump Derides Protections for Immigrants from 'Shithole' Countries," January 12, 2018, https://www.washingtonpost.com/politics/trump-attacks-protections-for-immigrants-from-shithole-countries-in-oval-office-meeting/2018/01/11/bfc0725c-f711-11e7-91af-31ac729add94_story.html.

The Washington Post, "Trump has No Qualms about Calling Coronavirus the 'Chinese Virus.' That's a Dangerous Attitude, Experts Say," March 20, 2020, https://www.washingtonpost.com/nation/2020/03/20/coronavirus-trump-chinese-virus/.

The Washington Post, "Trump Promotes Video of a Supporter Saying 'White Power,'" June 28, 2020, https://www.washingtonpost.com/politics/2020/06/28/trump-promotes-video-supporter-saying-white-power/.

The Washington Post, "Trump Says Presidents can Declassify Docs 'Even by Thinking about It,'" September 22, 2022, https://www.washingtonpost.com/national-security/2022/09/22/trump-hannity-declassify-documents/.

The Washington Post, "Trump Tells Four Liberal Congresswomen to 'Go Back' to their Countries, Prompting Pelosi to Defend Them," July 14, 2019, https://www.washingtonpost.com/politics/trump-says-four-liberal-congresswomen-should-go-back-to-the-crime-infested-places-from-which-they-came/2019/07/14/b8bf140e-a638-11e9-a3a6-ab670962db05_story.html.

The Washington Post, "Trump Threatens to Adjourn Congress to Get His Nominees but Likely would be Impeded by Senate Rules," April 16, 2020, https://www.washingtonpost.com/politics/trump-threatens-to-adjourn-congress-to-get-his-nominees-through/2020/04/15/e3bfc4c6-7f6a-11ea-9040-68981f488eed_story.html.

The Washington Post, "Trump Warns GOP on Immigration: 'They're Taking Your Jobs,'" March 6, 2014, https://www.washingtonpost.com/news/post-politics/wp/2014/03/06/trump-warns-gop-on-immigration-theyre-taking-your-jobs/.

The Washington Post, "Trump-Allied Lawyers Pursued Voting Machine Data in Multiple States, Records Reveal," August 15, 2022, https://www.washingtonpost.com/investigations/2022/08/15/sidney-powell-coffee-county-sullivan-strickler/.

The Washington Post, "Trump's Debate Comments give an Online Boost to a Group Social Media Companies have Long Struggled Against," September 30, 2020, https://www.washingtonpost.com/technology/2020/09/30/trump-debate-rightwing-celebration/.

The Washington Post, "Trump's Outrageous Claim that 'Thousands' of New Jersey Muslims celebrated the 9/11 Attacks," November 22, 2015, https://www.washingtonpost.com/news/fact-checker/wp/2015/11/22/donald-trumps-outrageous-claim-that-thousands-of-new-jersey-muslims-celebrated-the-911-attacks/.

The Washington Post, "U.S. Intelligence Reports from January and February Warned about a Likely Pandemic," March 20, 2020, https://www.washingtonpost.com/national-security/us-intelligence-reports-from-january-and-february-warned-about-a-likely-pandemic/2020/03/20/299d8cda-6ad5-11ea-b5f1-a5.

The Washington Post, "U.S. Investigating Possible Ties between Roger Stone, Alex Jones, and Capitol Rioters," February 20, 2021, https://www.washingtonpost.com/local/legal-issues/stone-jones-capitol-riot-investigation-radicalization/2021/02/19/97d6e6ee-6cad-11eb-9ead-673168d5. NPR, "Members of Right-Wing Militias, Extremist Groups Are Charged in Capitol Siege," January 19, 2021, https://www.npr.org/sections/insurrection-at-the-capitol/2021/01/19/958240531/members-of-right-wing-militias-extremist-groups-are-latest-charged-in-capitol-si. The Washington Post, "What Happened to the 10 Republicans Who Voted to Impeach Trump?" November 23, 2022, https://www.washingtonpost.com/politics/2022/11/23/gop-trump-impeachment-house/.

The Washington Post, "What we know about Donald Trump's Income Tax History, by Year," March 14, 2017, https://www.washingtonpost.com/news/the-fix/wp/2016/10/01/what-we-know-about-donald-trumps-income-tax-history-by-year/.

Thomas, David "Is South African Transformation Dead?" *African Business*, September 1, 2020, https://african.business/2020/09/economy/black-economic-power-matters-is-south-african-transformation-dead/.

Time, "Accidental Poisonings Increased after President Trump's Disinfectant Comment," May 12, 2020, https://time.com/5835244/accidental-poisonings-trump/.

Time, "Here's Donald Trump's Presidential Announcement Speech", June 16, 2015, https://time.com/3923128/donald-trump-announcement-speech/.

Time, "Kellyanne Conway Defends White House's Falsehoods—'Alternative Facts,'" January 22, 2017, https://time.com/4642689/kellyanne-conway-sean-spicer-donald-trump-alternative-facts/.

Time, "President Trump Likes Acting Cabinet Members. Research Shows They May Hurt Them," April 9, 2019, https://time.com/5566733/trump-acting-secretary-concerns-scholars/.

Time, "The Violent History of Waco, the Infamous Site of Trump's Next Rally," March 22, 2023, https://time.com/6265218/waco-texas-history-trump-rally/.

Tomson, Danielle Lee, "The Rise of Sweden Democrats: Islam, Populism, and the End of Swedish Exceptionalism," The Brookings Institution, Washington, DC,

March 25, 2020, https://www.brookings.edu/research/the-rise-of-sweden-democrats-and-the-end-of-swedish-exceptionalism/.

Tourse, Robbie W.C., Johnnie Hamilton-Mason, and Nancy J. Wewiorski, *Systemic Racism in the United States*, Cham, Switzerland: Springer, 2018, pp. 9–11.

Trump, Donald J., with Tony Schwartz, *Trump: The Art of the Deal*, New York, NY: Ballentine Books, 1987, p. 71.

Trump, Mary L., *Too Much and Never Enough*, New York, NY: Simon & Schuster, 2020, p. 15, p. 43 and p. 281.

U.S. News, "From Embrace to 'Replace,'" May 20, 2022, https://www.usnews.com/news/the-report/articles/2022-05-20/the-republican-embrace-of-the-great-replacement-theory.

U.S. News and World Report, "The 10 Most Corrupt Countries, Ranked by Perception," April 13, 2021, https://www.usnews.com/news/best-countries/articles/10-most-corrupt-countries-ranked-by-perception?slide=10.

Ubi, Efem and Vincent Ibonye, "Is Liberal Democracy Failing in Africa or Is Africa Failing under Liberal Democracy?" *Taiwan Journal of Democracy*, Volume 15, Number 2, December 2019, p. 147, http://www.tfd.org.tw/export/sites/tfd/files/publication/journal/137-164-Is-Liberal-Democracy-Failing-in-Africa-or-Is-Africa-Failing-under-Liberal-Democracy.pdf.

UN News, "Fears Grow for Syria Amid Rising Violence, Deepening Humanitarian Crisis," March 9, 2022, https://news.un.org/en/story/2022/03/1113592.

UN News, "Turkey: UN Report Details Allegations of Serious Rights Violations in Country's Southeast," March 10, 2017, https://news.un.org/en/story/2017/03/553062-turkey-un-report-details-allegations-serious-rights-violations-countrys.

United Nations, Department of Economic and Social Affairs, "World Social Report 2020: Inequality in a Rapidly Changing World," file:///Users/gerstondocs/Downloads/World-Social-Report-2020.pdf.

United Nations News, "Syria: 10 years of War has Left at Least 350,000 Dead," September 24, 2021, https://news.un.org/en/story/2021/09/1101162.

UPI, "Trump Plaza Fined $200,000 for Discrimination," June 6, 1991, https://www.upi.com/Archives/1991/06/06/Trump-Plaza-fined-200000-for-discrimination/2869676180800/.

USA Today, "'A Fanciful Reality': Trump Claims Black Lives Matter Protests Are Violent, but the Majority Are Peaceful," October 25, 2020, https://www.usatoday.com/in-depth/news/nation/2020/10/24/trump-claims-blm-protests-violent-but-majority-peaceful/3640564001/.

USA Today, "Donald Trump Courts Jews by Peddling Anti-Semitic 'Disloyalty' Tropes: Today's Talker," August 21, 2019, https://www.google.com/search?q=Donald+Trump+courts+Jews+by+peddling+anti-Semitic+%27disloyalty%27+tropes%3A+Today%27s+talker&rlz=1C5CHFA_enUS773US.

USA Today, "Exclusive: 43% of Americans Say a Specific Organization or People to Blame for COVID-19," March 21, 2021, https://www.usatoday.com/story/news/politics/2021/03/21/poll-1-4-americans-has-seen-asians-blamed-covid-19/4740043001/.

USA Today, "Exclusive: Trump's 3,500 Lawsuits Unprecedented for a Presidential Nominee," October 23, 2017, https://www.usatoday.com/story/news/politics/elections/2016/06/01/donald-trump-lawsuits-legal-battles/84995854/.

USA Today, "Fact Check: 12 of 28 Comments Deemed Racist on Viral List Are Trump's Direct speech," October 30, 2016, https://abcnews.go.com/Politics/federal-judge-rules-children-parents-separated-border-reunited/story?id=56192051.

USA Today, "Far-Right Candidates Struggled in Mid-Term Election. Who's to Blame? Experts Say Trump, GOP," November 12, 2022, https://www.usatoday.com/story/news/politics/2022/11/12/far-right-midterms-trump/8295708001/.

USA Today, "'He was Dumb as a Rock:' Trump Responds to Rex Tillerson Calling Him 'Undisciplined,'" December 7, 2018, https://www.usatoday.com/story/news/politics/2018/12/07/rex-tillerson-donald-trump-remarks/2237327002/.

USA Today, "President Trump Thanks 'Deplorables' for Helping Him Win the 2016 Election," November 8, 2017, https://www.usatoday.com/story/news/politics/onpolitics/2017/11/08/president-trump-thanks-deplorables-helping-him-win-2016-election/844744001/.

USA Today, "This Time, Donald Trump Says He's Running," June 16, 2015, https://www.usatoday.com/story/news/politics/elections/2015/06/16/donald-trump-announcement-president/28782433/.

USA Today, "USA Today/Ipsos Poll: A Majority of Americans Say Cities under Siege by Protesters," September 23, 2020, /politics/2020/09/22/usa-today-ipsos-poll-majority-americans-say-cities-under-siege/3483172001/.

Vanity Fair, "Mitch McConnell to Republicans on Midterms: I Told You These Weirdos Would Lose," December 14, 2022, https://www.vanityfair.com/news/2022/12/mitch-mcconnell-laments-gop-candidate-quality-2022-midterms.

Vanity Fair, "Of Course Fox News Is Fueling Election Denialism," November 9, 2020, https://issueone.org/articles/60-of-president-donald-trumps-post-election-tweets-sought-to-undermine-legitimacy-of-presidential-race/.

Vanity Fair, "Trump Claims Coronavirus Will 'Miraculously' Go Away By April," February 11, 2020, https://www.vanityfair.com/news/2020/02/donald-trump-coronavirus-warm-weather. Vanity Fair, "Trump Claims Teaching Kids about Racism Is 'Child Abuse,' Wants It Abolished From Schools and Replaced With a 'Patriotic Education,'" September 9, 2020, https://www.vanityfair.com/news/2020/09/donald-trump-1776-commission.

Vanity Fair, "Trump's Racist Comments Jeopardize His Miss Universe Pageant," June 25, 2015, https://www.vanityfair.com/news/2015/06/univision-drops-miss-universe-trump-comments.

Verea, Monica, "Anti-Immigrant and Anti-Mexican Attacks during the First 18 Months of the Trump Administration," *Norteamerica*, Volume 13, Number 2, 2018, https://www.revistanorteamerica.unam.mx/index.php/nam/article/view/335.

VOA News, "Trump Attacks on Press Effective, New Study Finds," April 17, 2020, https://www.voanews.com/a/press-freedom_trump-attacks-press-effective-new-study-finds/6187774.html.

Vox, "How the Voting Rights Act Transformed Black Voting in the South, in One Chart," August 6, 2015, https://www.vox.com/2015/3/6/8163229/voting-rights-act-1965.

Vox, "Trump Says China 'Should Have Told Us' about the Coronavirus. He Removed the Official Meant to do that," March 23, 2020, https://www.vox.com/policy-and-politics/2020/3/23/21190713/coronavirus-trump-china-cdc-embed-quick.

Vox, "Trump's Last Rally as President was Supposed to be about the Georgia Runoffs. It wasn't," January 4, 2021, https://www.vox.com/2021/1/4/22214512/trump-dalton-georgia-rally-runoffs-perdue-loeffler.

Waldman, Michael, "2022: Democracy Rises," Brennan Center for Justice, December 27, 2022, https://www.brennancenter.org/our-work/analysis-opinion/2022-democracy-rises.

WalletNews, "2023's States with the Most Racial Progress," January 20, 2023, https://wallethub.com/edu/states-with-the-most-and-least-racial-progress/18428.

Walter, Barbara F., *How Civil Wars Start*, New York, NY: Crown Publishers, 2022, pp. 19–21, 34 and 90–91.

Wang, Tova Andrea, *The Politics of Voter Suppression*, New York, NY: Cornell University Press, 2012, p. 125.

Warren, Katie, "I Visited Trump's Childhood Neighborhood on the Outskirts of NYC and it Didn't Take Too Long to See Why He's called it an 'Oasis,'" *Business Insider*, August 19, 2020, https://www.businessinsider.com/donald-trump-childhood-neighborhood-queens-new-york-city-photos-2018-11.

Washington Examiner, "Exclusive: Trump Urges State Legislators to Reject Electoral Votes, 'You Are the Real Power,'" January 2, 2021, https://www.washingtonexaminer.com/washington-secrets/exclusive-trump-urges-state-legislators-to-reject-electoral-votes-you-are-the-real-power.

Washington Examiner, "Trump Indictment: Mark Levin Rails against Biden's Hand in Document Case, Calls 'An Insurrection,'" June 12, 2023, https://www.washingtonexaminer.com/news/justice/trump-indictment-mark-levin-rails-against-biden-doj-insurrection.

Washington Examiner, "Trump Says He 'Should Get All the Credit' if Republicans Win Midterm Elections," November 8, 2022, https://www.washingtonexaminer.com/news/campaigns/trump-credit-republicans-win-midterms.

Washington Post/ABC Poll, August 20–23, 2017, http://apps.washingtonpost.com/g/page/politics/washington-post-abc-news-poll-aug-16-20-2017/2235/.

Weber, Jim M., "William Jefferson Clinton, 'Racism in the United States,'" 16 October 1995.

"What You Need to Know about the Rise in U.S. Mass Shootings," The Marshall Project, July 6, 2022, "https://www.themarshallproject.org/2022/07/06/what-you-need-to-know-about-the-rise-in-u-s-mass-shootings.

Wheeler, Tom, "The Republican Party Platform: 'L'etat, c'est moi,'" Brookings, August 25, 2020, https://www.brookings.edu/blog/up-front/2020/08/25/the-2020-republican-party-platform-letat-cest-moi/.

Winograd, Morley, Michael Hais, and Doug Rose, "How Younger Voters will Impact Elections: Younger Voters Are Poised to Upend American Politics," Brookings Institution, February 27, 2023, https://www.brookings.edu/articles/younger-voters-are-poised-to-upend-american-politics/.

Winsor, Morgan, "Trump's Victory Buoying White Nationalists, Anti-Discrimination Advocates Say," *ABC News*, November 11, 2016, https://abcnews.go.com/Politics/trumps-victory-buoying-white-nationalists-anti-discrimination-advocates/story?id=43467300.

WNYC Public Radio, "What this White Separatist Expects from the Trump Administration," *On the Media*, November 17, 2016, https://www.wnycstudios.org/podcasts/otm/segments/what-white-separatist-expects-trump-administration.

Woodward, Bob, *Fear: Trump in the White House*, New York, NY: Simon & Schuster, 2018, p. 321.

Woodward, Bob and Robert Costa, *Peril*, New York, NY: Simon & Schuster, 2021, p. 180.

World View, "Syrian Refugee Crisis: Facts, FAQs, and How to Help," July 13, 2021, https://www.worldvision.org/refugees-news-stories/syrian-refugee-crisis-facts.

Wray, Christopher, "Threats to the Homeland: Evaluating the Landscape 20 Years After 9/11," Testimony before the U.S. Senate, September 21, 2021, https://abcnews.go.com/Politics/threats-congress-decreased-after-record-high-2021-police/story?id=96492983.

Wright, Robin, "How the Curse of Sykes-Picot Still Haunts the Middle East," *The New Yorker*, April 30, 2016, https://www.newyorker.com/news/news-desk/how-the-curse-of-sykes-picot-still-haunts-the-middle-east.

YouGov, "Most Americans—But Fewer than in 2021—Disapprove of the January 6 Capitol Takeover," January 2023, https://today.yougov.com/topics/politics/articles-reports/2023/01/04/most-americans-disapprove-january-6-capitol-attack.

YouGov Poll, "Views on Great Replacement Theory," June 1–5, 2022, https://today.yougov.com/topics/politics/articles-reports/2022/06/07/views-great-replacement-theory-yougov-poll-june-1-.

Ziadeh, Radwan, "Countries at the Crossroads 2011: Syria," Freedom House, Washington, DC, 2012, https://www.freedomhouse.org/sites/default/files/inline_images/SYRIAFinal.pdf.

Zitser, Joshua, "Steve Bannon said Trump 'Would Lie about Anything' to Win, New Book Says," *Business Insider*, July 16, 2022, https://www.businessinsider.com/trump-lie-about-anything-win-arguments-steve-bannon-book-2022-7.

Index

9/11 attacks, 72, 135n60
The 1619 Project, 181–82, 259
1807 Act, 65
1871 Enforcement Acts, 76
2001 Muslim terrorist attacks, 71, 82
2018 Helsinki, 35
2020 presidential campaign, 171, 179, 183–84
2021 War Room, 204

Abbott, Greg, 262
Abraham, Henry J., 214n11
Acemoglu, Daron, 28, 39
Aceves, Paula, 58n9
activism, 76, 78, 258, 262, 271
Adams, John, 18, 21n35
adulthood, 92–94, 96–97, 125, 237
affirmative action, 77–78, 81, 85, 89n59, 154
African-American: citizenship, 64; political influence, 253; slaves, 63
African slaves, 56
Afro-Colombians, 50–51, 59n26
Afro-East Indians, 56
Afro-Europeans, 56
al-Assad, Bashar, 53–55, 60n45
al-Assad, Hafez, 53–54, 60n41
Alawites, 53–54
Allen, John R., 89n65

all-male, 158
Almond, Gabriel, 19n16, 20n17, 41n53
al-Qaeda, 55
alternative right, 124, 135, 153–62, 166–68, 171, 182, 185, 203–6, 217n46, 222
Altink, Henrice, 61
America First, 114–15, 122, 150, 204–5, 213, 237
American: democracy, 140; exceptionalism, 20, 35; experiment, 275; Jews, 129–31; revolution, 69, 156, 181; values, 261
American Democracy in Peril, 18n1, 250
American Federalism: A Concise Introduction, 243n45
Americans, Native, 50, 63, 67–68, 85n3, 86, 103, 178
anarchists, 205, 210
Anderson, Terry H., 85
Andrew O. Ballard, 241n14
anti-Asian bigotry, 175
anti-Asian hate crime, 72, 87n39, 252
anti-Black sentiments, 128
anti-corruption law, 24
anti-democratic theme, 2
anti-democratic values, 27
anti-democrats, 260

anti-immigrant, 86n23, 154, 158, 187, 237, 268n10, 272n54
Anti-Immigrant Rhetoric, 86n23
antisemitic, 158–59, 189n59, 237, 260, 268
anti-Semitism, 130, 217n53
The Apprentice, 111, 128, 136n71
Araujo, Blanca, 89n67
Arizona, 68–69, 86, 89n58, 151, 165, 176, 189n58, 215n24, 225, 230, 234, 239, 262
Arizona v. Inter Tribal Council of Arizona, 86n19
Asian Americans, 63, 71–72, 87n38, 236, 252
Asians, 52, 70, 72–73, 79, 81, 87n37, 91, 129
Asiatic Exclusion League, 71
Aspects of Political Development, 38n15, 40n36
assassination, 32, 35, 80, 265
Atlantic City, 101–2, 107n40, 111
The Authoritarian Dynamic, 39, 110, 150, 165n45
authoritarianism, 2, 6, 109–10, 150, 162, 248–49, 277
Authoritarianism & Polarization of American Politics, 110

backsliding, 16, 20, 29
Baker, Peter, 185n6, 187, 214n10
Baker v. Carr, 77
Bakke case, 77, 81
ballot system, 66
Bannon, Steve, 95, 106n14, 115, 124, 133n17, 155, 161, 166, 168n96, 204
Baptiste, H. Prentice, 89n67
Baptist War, 56
Barber, David, 139, 162n1
Barr, William, 142–43, 196
Barrett, Wayne, 95, 106n17
Beaumont, Elizabeth, 19n9
Becoming Black Political Subjects: Movements and Ethno-Rights in Colombia and Brazil, 59n22

Belgium, 20n23, 39n31
The Bell Curve: Intelligence and Class Structure in American Life, 166n55
Bendix, Reinhard, 8, 18n2
Bernhard, Michael, 20n30
Beyond the Melting Pot, 41n55
Biden, Joe, 68, 84, 86, 90n79, 187, 189, 192–93, 219n70, 228–30, 250, 257, 261, 264, 276
Biggs, Andy, 230
Bigotry, 104, 114, 126, 130, 175, 249–51
birtherism, 98, 107, 113, 122, 155, 179
Bitecofer, Rachel, 134n49
Black civilians, killing of, 36
Black civil rights, 76
Black community, 57, 82
Black individuals, 50
Black leaders, 129, 179, 187n35, 188n38
Black Lives Matter movement, 157, 180, 262
Black registration, 67
Black slaves, 56, 85n2
Blankfield, Keren, 132n8
Blinken, Antony, 48
BLIP, 35, 222
Bloomberg, Michael R., 271n47
Bolívar, Simón, 50
The Boogaloo Bois, 205
Borjas, George J., 88n47
The Boston Globe, 145
Bragg, Alvin, 237
Bratspies, Rebecca, 59n23
Brazil, 25, 59n22
Breitbart, Andrew, 154–55
Breitbart News, 124, 154–55
Britain, 52, 54
Brnovich v. Democratic National Committee, 77
Brooker, Russell, 132n2
Brown, N. Derek, 268n5
Brownstein, John S., 186n17
Brown v. Board of Education, 68, 74, 76, 80
Buchanan, Patrick J., 270
Buddhism, 47

Budhos, Marina, 105n3
Bundy, Cliven, 157
Burnham, Walter Dean, 87n41
Burns, Alexander, 218n63
Burns, MacGregor, 90n69
Bush, George H. W., 81, 112
Bush, George W., 19n14, 82, 121, 141, 195
Butler, Jaime Herrera, 207
Butros, Marina, 105n5

California State Supreme Court, 68, 70
Campbell, Travis, 188n39
Cao, Andy, 268n7
Capitalism, Socialism and Democracy, 19n4
Caribbean, 50, 56
Caribbean Sea, 50
Carlson, Tucker, 140, 162n4, 203, 265
Carroll, E. Jean, 227
Carroll, Rory, 38n14
Carson, Ben, 152
Carter, Jimmy, 81
Caryl, Christian, 41
Catholics, 30, 49, 66, 93
Centers for Disease Control (CDC), 173–75, 186
Central Park Five, 97, 106n24
Central Park Jogger, 97
Chao, Elaine, 236
Chavez, Hugo, 25–26, 38
Cheney, Liz, 209, 211, 234
Chervinsky, Lindsay, 218n69
Childress, Sarah, 167n69
Chile, 31–32, 40n39
China, 47–48, 51, 58, 115, 129, 140, 160, 168, 186n16, 236, 242n24
Chinese-American citizens, 72
Chinese Communist Party, 47–48
Chinese Exclusion Act, 70, 73
Chinese government, 48, 58n10, 72, 193
Chinese immigration, 70–71, 73
The Chinese Must Go, 87n29
Chinese Persecution of the Uyghurs, 58n7

Chinese Virus, 72, 87n35, 174, 178, 186n18, 252, 268n7
Christian Whites, 6, 150
chronic poverty, 53
church of Sweden, 13
Cineas, Fabiola, 133n32
Cippolone, Pat, 199
citizenship, 8, 18n2, 47, 52, 70–71, 73, 116, 120, 179, 213
The Civic Constitution: Civic Visions and Struggles in the Path Toward Constitutional Democracy, 19n9
civil discourse, 23
civil disobedience, 10
civilian control, 23
civil liberties, 6, 8, 10–11, 27, 36, 82, 262
Civil Rights Act, 74, 76, 80–81, 87n41, 88n49, 125; 1875, 73–74, 76; 1957, 74, 80; 1960, 74, 87n41, 88n49; 1964, 41n54, 74–75, 87n41, 125, 148, 269n16; 1965, 65, 67–68, 71, 73–75, 80–88, 253
civil rights amendments, 66, 81
The Civil Rights Cases, 76
civil rights crisis, 90n68
Civil war, 2, 6, 14, 19n11, 37n1, 39, 55, 65–67, 189n57, 191, 204, 210, 217n49, 267, 279
Clark, Jeffrey, 197
The Clash of Civilizations and the Remaking of World, 39n31
climate change, 263
Clinton, Bill, 82, 112, 141, 210
Clinton, Hillary, 19n14, 92, 118, 130–31, 134n47, 152–53, 155, 160, 165n48, 192
Clyburn, James, 179
Cohn, Gary, 141
Cohn, Roy, 98
Cold War, 33, 35, 40n45, 73
Collingwood, Loren, 166n51
Colombia, 25, 50–51, 59
Colombian government, 50–51
colonialism, 30, 59n27

Columbus, 56
Comey, James, 141, 143, 163n9, 171, 195
commission of civil rights, 74
Comparative Politics: A Developmental Approach, 20n17, 41n53
Confucianism, 47
Conservative Political Action Conference (CPAC), 127, 276
constitutional decolonization, 56
Corn, David, 107n27
Coronel, Gustavo, 38n12
Costa, Robert, 215n15
The Courage to Be Free, 273n71
COVID-19, 29, 39, 72, 87, 170–71, 173–76, 178, 251–52, 263, 265
Critical Elections and the Mainstreams of American Politics, 87n41
Critical Race Theory (CRT), 257–60, 263, 270n40, 271
Cruz, Ted, 120, 151–52, 158
Cubans, 86n21
Cuccinelli, Ken, 128
culture, definition of, 13
Curiel, Gonzalo, 127
Cutlip, Kimbra, 86n15

Dahike, Ross, 280n5
Daines, Steve, 265
Damascus Spring, 55
Daoism, 47
Dasche, John, 59n29
Declaration of Independence and Constitution, 10
Deferred Action on Childhood Arrivals (DACA), 82, 90, 178
democracies, 7–9, 11–18, 19n8, 21n33, 23–31, 41n57, 43, 109
Democracy Dies in Darkness, 275
democracy rules, 8–9
The Democratic Civilization, 41n54
democratic erosion, 26
democratic governments, 2, 9, 11, 24
Democratic pedophiles, 225
Democratic Republic of Algeria, 15

Democratic Republic of Georgia, 14
Democratic Republic of North Korea, 15
democratic values and institutions, 26
demography, 150, 166n53, 168, 176, 212–13
Department of Homeland Security (DHS), 86n26, 128, 142, 177, 187, 197, 260, 273n76
DeSantis, Ron, 230, 234, 254, 258, 262–63, 272, 273n71
Devil's Bargain: Steve Bannon, Donald Trump, and the Storming of the Presidency, 131, 133n17, 134n39, 166n59, 168n95
Diamond, Jeremy, 137n81
Diamond, Larry, 38n2
Dias, Elizabeth, 137n80
discrimination: Americans, Native, 67–68; Asian-Americans, 87, 174, 176; Chinese, 70–73, 87; Hispanics, 127–28; Japanese, 70–71, 76; Jews, 129–31; Latinos, 63–64, 68–70, 75, 81–82, 86n21, 161, 252; Muslims, 126; Teenage Girls, 103–4; Women, 103–4
The Divider: Trump in the White House, 214n10
Djibouti, 30
domestic terrorism, 265–66, 273n76, 275
Dominicanos, 86n21
Dominion Voting Systems, 193
Donald Trump's childhood, 93–94, 105
DREAM Act, 82
Dred Scott v. Sandford, 75
Ducey, Doug, 262
Duffy, Martin, 20n23
Dukakis, Michael, 81
Duke, David, 237

Eastman, John, 198–99
economic inequality, 23, 28–29, 59n27
The Economist, 5–6, 25, 37, 38n10, 41n59, 58
Edsall, Thomas B., 187

Edwards III, George C., 79, 89n61
Eggers, Andrew C., 269n26
Eisenhower, Dwight, 79–80
El Salvadorans, 91
Emancipation Proclamation, 66
employment, 10, 74, 77, 81, 251
Enemy of the People: Trump's War on the Press, the New McCarthyism, and the Threat to American Democracy, 19n5
Enrique Tarrio, 204
Enyedi, Zsolt, 21n32
equal rights, 11, 89n55
equal treatment, 10
Erdogan, Recep, 27, 48–49, 140
Eritrea, 30
Espionage Act, 229
Ethiopia, 30
ethnic divisions, 23, 27, 29–30, 109
ethnicity, 8, 40, 47, 50, 64, 86n24, 90n83, 270
ethnic minorities, 116, 155, 169
European-American culture, 154
extremist Muslim organization, 55

Fair Housing Act, 100
fair presidential election, 36
Fair Sentencing Act, 83
Farkash, Andrew Tzvi, 59n27
fascism, 181
federal government, 65, 101, 103, 156–57, 162, 228, 233, 267
federal income taxes, 103
Federalism and the Making of America, 88n53
Federal Vacancy Reform Act, 142
Ferguson, Melissa J., 268n3
Filipinos, 70
Fish, M. Steven, 20n21
Fisher, Marc, 105n7, 132n1, 241n16
flawed democracy, 5, 16, 25, 37
Flemish, 30
Florida, 117, 119, 127, 151, 158, 188n45, 254, 258–59, 262–63, 269n21, 272n63, 273

Floyd, George, 147, 180, 258
Ford, Gerald, 81
Four Threats: The Recurring Crises of American Democracy, 18n1, 41n58
Fragile Nation, Shattered Land: The Modern History of Syria, 60n37
France, 36, 54–55
free debate, 10
Freedlander, David, 132n4
Free Press, 8–9, 48, 146, 278
The Fresno Bee, 242n32
Frey, William H., 187
Friedman, Steven, 53, 60n33
Friedman, Thomas L., 33, 40n42
Fuentes, Nick, 204, 237, 245
Fugitive Slave Act, 65, 75
Fukuyama, Francis, 17, 21n34

Gab, 204
Gallup Poll, 132, 151, 173, 178, 186n9, 187n34
The Gallup Poll, 186n9
Garber, Andrew, 88n51
Garber, Megan, 216n41
Garland, Merrick, 212, 228, 230, 276
Garro, Haritz, 269n26
Gashaw, Tasew, 40n35
Gee, Gilbert, 186n17
Genocide Watch, 49, 58n16
Gerston, Larry N., 243n45
Gest, Justin, 20n25
Ghana, 36
Giglio, Mike, 167n73
Giuliani, Rudy, 198–99
Glasser, Susan B., 185n6, 187, 214n10
Glazer, Nathan, 36, 41n55
Glickman, Lawrence, 125, 135n58
global racism, 57
Golan Heights, 54
Gold, Emelia, 271n42
Goldman, Ralph M., 165n38
Goldstone, Lawrence, 89n55
Gonzales, Nathan, 119
Goodman, Ryan, 218n60
Gorchinskaya, Katya, 38n5

Gosar, Paul, 234, 239
Graber, Doris, 144, 164n23
Graham, David A., 133n29
Great Britain, 52
The Great Experiment: Why Diverse Societies Fall Apart and How They Can Endure, 17
Great Replacement Theory, 256–57, 260, 270
Greek Orthodox, 49
Green, Joshua, 131, 133n17, 166n59
Griffin, Rob, 187
Grimmer, Justin, 269n26
Gross, Daniel A., 89n63
Guerrero, Jean, 106n16, 133n18

Haberman, Maggie, 98, 106n25, 238
Haggard, Stephan, 16, 20n29
Hais, Michael, 280n3
Haisa, 31
Haley, Nikki, 151, 230, 234, 264
Hamilton-Mason, Johnnie, 57n1
Hanchard, Michael G., 46, 58n3
Hancock, Jeffrey T., 280n5
Haney-Lopez, Ian, 90n72
Hannity, Sean, 229
harassment, 252
Harriot, Michael, 272n64
Harris, Kamala, 179, 182, 187n36, 224
Harvard Journal of Law and Public Policy, 215n16
Harvard's MBA program, 155
Hassan, Miiad, 60n35
Hassell, Hans J. G., 241n14
hateful, 181, 259, 279
Hawkins, Jared B., 186n17
Hayes, Rutherford, 79
Heikkila, Niko, 166n53
Helmond, Anne, 166n62
Hendrix, Justin, 218n60
Hernnstein, Richard, 166n55
Herrington, Marc, 110
Herrnstein, Richard, 154
Heseltine, Michael, 241n14
Hetherington, Marc J., 110

A Higher Loyalty: Truth, Lies, and Leadership, 163n9
The Hill, 163, 176, 218n59, 269, 270n40, 272
Hindu majorities, 29
Hing, Anna, 186n17
Hirsch, Alan, 59n28
Hispanics, 86n21, 91, 127, 129, 176, 237, 252, 254
Hockstader, Lee, 61n51
Holland, Alisha, 38n13
Holocaust, 35, 58n7, 79, 89n63, 129, 237
Holt, Lester, 122
homogeneous, 13, 29, 61n53, 70, 148
homosexuality, 263
Houdini, Harry, 210
How Civil Wars Start and How to Stop Them, 6, 19n11
How to Be an Antiracist, 259
How Voter Suppression Laws Target Native Americans, 86
Hswen, Yulin, 186n17
Huckabee, Mike, 113
Hudson, William, 18n1
humanity, 13, 55, 58, 91, 139
human rights, 14, 38, 48–49, 55, 58–59
Hungarians, 16
Huntington, Samuel P., 30, 39n31
Huq, Aziz, 89n60
Hutchinson, Asa, 264
Hutchison, Cassidy, 202
hybrid regime, 25
hyper-political epidemic, 2

Iberian Peninsula, 86n21
Ibonye, Vincent, 40n34
Igbo, 31
Ilhan Tohti Wants the Uyghurs to Be Free, 58n9
illegal immigration, 100, 115–16, 127–28, 156, 260–61
illiberal state, 17
Immigrant Control Act, 73
Immigration and Nationality Act, 73

Immigration Equality, 90n77
Immigration Reform and Control Act, 73
impeachment effort, 172
The Impending Crisis, 85
inclusiveness, 26
Independence Party of America, 112
independent journalists, 27
Indian Citizenship Act, 68
Indians, 56, 70, 86, 103, 108
Indigenous Americans, 50, 67–68, 85n3
inequality, 23, 28–29, 39, 46–47, 61, 64, 71, 180, 258, 260–61, 263
inexcusable, 57
Ingraham, Laura, 203
Inherently Unequal: The Betrayal of Equal Rights By the Supreme Court, 89n55
Insurgency: How Republicans Lost Their Party and Got Everything They Ever Wanted, 165n46
Insurrection, 3, 191–93, 217, 234, 239–40, 243, 275–76, 278–79
Internal Revenue Service (IRS), 143, 164, 194–95, 214, 227, 260
international humanitarian law, 55
International Institute for Democracy and Electoral Assistance, 20, 26, 39
Intra-Party Republican Struggles, 118
invasion, 23, 33–35, 41
Inventing the Dream, 87n28
Iran, 55, 177, 242n24
Iraq, 25, 112, 177
Is China Committing Genocide Against the Uyghurs?, 58n6
Isikoff, Michael, 107n27
Islam, 13, 20n19, 126, 152, 155; Islamic terrorism, 117; Islamists, 55; Islamization, 156; Islamophobia, 126, 135, 251; Islamophobic, 82, 90n75, 158; Islamophobic administration, 82, 90n75
Israel, 54, 129–31, 136n79, 236, 244
Israeli policy, 236
Iyengar, Shanto, 19n6

Jacoby-Senghor, Drew S., 268n5
Jamaica, 55–57, 60n48, 61, 93
Jamaican society, 57
Jamaican Stock Exchange, 56
James, Leticia, 227
January 6 Committee, 211, 250
January 6 Rally, 201–2, 204
Japanese, 70–71, 76
Japanese-American citizens, 71, 76
Japanese immigrants, 70–71
Jerusalem, 236
Jews, 63, 66, 79, 129–31, 137n83, 153, 159, 244, 252, 268n12
Jiménez, Tomás R., 86n24
Johnson, Andrew, 210
Johnson, Lyndon, 80–81, 83
Johnson, Ron, 199, 215n27, 257
Johnson, Theodore R., 271n42
Johnson, William Daniel, 161
Jones, Alex, 204, 217n51
Jong-Un, Kim, 140
Jordan, 55, 103, 234
Jordan, Jim, 234
Jordan, Michael, 103
journalists' investigations, 10
Joyce, David, 239
Judeo-Christian creed, 130
Judicial Minimalism, 76
The Judicial Process, 214n11, 232
Jury, Grand, 227, 229, 232
Justice and Internal Revenue Service, 194

Kalb, Marvin, 9, 19n5, 164n24
Kasich, John, 151
Kaufmann, Eric, 20n26
Kaufmann, Robert, 16, 20n29
Keeper, Oath, 157–58, 167, 216n38, 217n49, 231, 243n39
Kelly, Megyn, 119, 134n38
Kelly, Monique D.A., 61n54
Kemp, Brian, 224, 241n6
Kendi, Ibram X., 259
Kennedy, John F., 80, 90n68, 159
Key, V.O., 269n16
kidnapping, 160, 265

Kirisci, Kemal, 39, 58n12
Kitzinger, Adam, 209, 211
Koreans, 70
Kranish, Michael, 105n7, 132n1, 241n16
Kreko, Peter, 21n32
Kroenig, Matthew, 20n21
Ku Klux Klan, 66, 76, 85, 124, 161
Kung Flu, 161, 174
Kurashige, Lon, 86n27
Kurdistan, 49, 54
Kurdistan Workers Party, 49
Kurds, 49, 54–55
Kurtz, Lester, 40n39
Kyi, Aung San Suu, 32

Latino, 63–64, 68–70, 75, 81–82, 86n21, 91, 127, 161, 252, 255
leadership, 29, 51–52, 80, 83, 89, 118–22, 141, 150, 162, 163n9, 215, 234, 239–40
Lebanon, 54–55
Lee, Robert E., 130, 180
Leighley, Jan E., 19n7, 164n22
Levin, Bess, 244n57
Levin, Mark, 203, 230, 243n34
Levitsky, Steven, 36
Levy, Brian, 59n28
Lew-Williams, Beth, 71, 87n29
LGBTQ community, 63, 82
LGBTQ rights, 263
liberal White activism, 262
Lieberman, Robert, 18n1, 37
Lincoln, Abraham, 66
Lindo, Jason M., 268n7
Lipset, Seymour Martin, 29, 39
Lipson, Leslie, 35, 41n54
Loeffler, Kelly, 223, 241n6
Los Angeles, 70, 90n76, 106n24, 217n54, 243n35, 274n81
Louisiana's population, 254
Loving v. Virginia, 77
Lusinchi, Jaime, 25

MacFarquhar, Neil, 60n41
Machado, Alicia, 98, 107n26

mainstream media, 36, 162
Maizland, Lindsay, 40n40
Maltese, John Anthony, 18n1
Manhattan, 93, 97, 101, 111, 222, 227, 237, 240; indictment, 222, 240; projects, 111
Marietta, Morgan, 85n5
Martin, Jonathan, 218n63
mass destruction, 265
Mass Media and American Politics, 164n23
Mass Media and Politics: A Social Science Perspective, 19n7, 164n22
McCain, John, 116, 121, 151
McCarthy, Kevin, 207–9, 211, 218–19, 239, 242n32, 245
McConnell, Mitch, 208–9, 211, 218, 241, 245
McDougall, Gay, 59n19
McGovern, George, 148
McKeever, Amy, 85
Meadows, Mark, 95, 106n15, 199
Media Politics: A Citizen's Guide, 19n6
Mendelberg, Tali, 19n10
Meredith, James, 80, 83
Mesopotamians, 45
Mettler, Suzanne, 18n1, 37
Mexican American, 69, 86n24, 98
Mexican immigrants, 98–99
Mexican immigration, 69
Mexican rapists, 99, 116
Mexico, 24–25, 38, 98–99, 113–16, 147, 215n24, 237, 245, 272n58
Mexico's corruption problems, 25
Michigan Home Guard Militia, 205
Military Coups, 23, 31
Miller, Stephen, 95, 106n16, 115, 124, 133n18
Milley, Mark, 231
minimalism, 76–77
misogynistic, 158
mobility, 25, 28, 51
Moore, Ryan C., 280n5
moral crisis, 80
Morlino, Leonardo, 39

Morris, Alex, 165n41
Morrison, Toni, 82
Mounk, Yascha, 17, 21n33
Movements and Parties: Critical Connections in American Political Development, 168n87
Moynihan, Daniel Patrick, 36, 41n55
Mueller, Robert, 142, 171, 196
multiculturalism, 89n67, 154
Mungiu-Pippidi, Alina, 38n3
Mungo, Monita, 270n40
Muñoz Martinez, Monica, 86n23
Murdoch, Rupert, 234
Murkowski, Lisa, 238
Murray, Charles A., 154, 166n55
Muslim Brotherhood, 54, 60n39
Muslim immigrants, 14
Muslims, 27, 49, 54–55, 63, 91–92, 103, 108n47, 117, 135, 151, 156, 161, 177, 185
Muslim terrorists, 103
Mutz, Diana C., 166n52
Myanmar, 32, 40

Naftali, Tim, 81, 90n70
Naidoo, Vinothan, 59n28
The National Review, 234
Nation-Building and Citizenship, 18n2
native-born White Americans, 74
Nauta, Waltine, 242n29
Nazis, 79, 147, 153, 157, 205, 266
neo-Nazi organization, 205
neo-Nazis, 147, 153, 266
Neustadt, Richard, 163n7
New England-based White supremacist, 205
New Granada, 50
New York Military Academy, 94–95
The New York Times, 20n25, 21n31, 39–40, 219n72, 232, 241, 280
Nguyen, Tina, 133n30
Nigeria, 31
Nixon, Richard, 81, 143
non-Arab Kurds, 54
non-Christian populations, 3

non-Christian religion, 116, 261
non-Hispanic White countries, 74
non-Hispanic Whites, 74, 254–55
nonpartisan, 119, 225, 253, 258
non-Protestant religious, 251
non-White populations, 74
North Atlantic Treaty Organization (NATO), 34–35, 40
Northern Ireland, 30, 39
Norton, Michael I., 268n4
No White Guilt, 205
NSC 131, 205
Nxele, Musa, 59n28

Oath Keepers, 157–58, 167, 216n38, 217n49, 231, 243n39
Obama, Barrack, 79, 82–83, 98–99, 113, 116–17, 120–22, 149, 154, 156–57, 178–79, 195–96
Obari, Chineyer, 39n31
Obrador, Andres Manuel Lopez, 25
O'Brien, Timothy L., 106n8, 132n14
O'Connell, John, 102
O'Donnell, John, 105n2, 107n37
off the reservation, 64
One Earth Future, 40n38
On the Social Contract, 8, 19n3
open dissent, 10
open political culture, 13, 109
Orban, Viktor, 16
ordered authority, 26
Orquhart, Mikhail-Ann, 61n53
Ottoman Empire, 49, 54

Pacific Ocean, 50
Page Act, 73
Pakistan, 29
Parker, Kunal M., 86n16
Paschel, Tianna S., 59n22
Patrick Buchanan, 256, 270n33
patriotic education, 179, 181, 188
Paumgarten, Nick, 107n40
pedophilia, 263
Pelosi, Nancy, 172, 211, 265
Pelosi, Paul, 265, 273n79

PEN America, 258
Pence, Mike, 179, 199, 201–2, 206, 215n27, 216n32, 229
Peters, Jeremy W., 165n46
Pika, Joseph A., 18n1
Pinkett, Randal, 102
Pinochet, Augusto, 32
Plessy v. Ferguson, 66, 76
pluralism, 6, 26, 256
poison, 181
Poland, 20n30, 29, 36, 58
political coalitions, 278
political expression, 10
political parties, 14, 16, 23–27, 148–49, 165n39, 254, 261, 267
Political Parties Matter: Realignment and the Return of Partisan Voting, 165n39
Politico, 20, 113, 132, 163n11, 164, 216, 243n41, 244n52, 274n85
The Politics of Voter Suppression, 87n42
Potok, Mark, 166n54
Potter, David M., 85
Powell, Bingham, Jr., 20n17, 41n53
presidential election: 2012, 112–13, 152; 2016, 35, 92, 97, 100, 104, 111, 113, 115, 117, 122, 124, 131, 140, 158, 171, 192, 226; 2020, 170–71, 182–83, 185, 191, 195–96, 201–2, 205–6; 2024, 3, 230, 233, 255, 260, 263, 277, 279
Presidential Primary Campaign, 116
Protestants, 30, 49, 64, 79, 130, 261
Proud Boys, 147, 158–59, 167n75, 182–83, 216n38, 217n48, 231
Public Religion Research Institute, 187
Puerto Ricans, 86n21
The Pursuit of Fairness: A History of Affirmative Action, 85
Putin, Vladimir, 33–35, 40, 140, 162
Pye, Lucien W., 26, 38n15, 40n36

QAnon, 159–60, 189, 205, 237–38, 241n5, 245n68, 263

Quaranta, Mario, 29, 39

race, 6, 8, 19n10, 43, 63–64, 74–84, 270n40, 271–72
The Race Card: Campaign Strategy, Implicit Messages, and the Norm of Equality, 19n10
racial: discrimination, 36, 51, 55, 63, 70–71, 76–78, 100, 253; gerrymandering, 196, 253–55, 260, 269, 279; science, 71; segregation, 52, 79–80, 93, 206
racism, 2–3, 6, 162, 167, 188n50, 248–49, 251–53, 258–60, 268n4
racism post-Civil War, 79
Racist and Xenophobic Hate Crimes, 58n4
racist behavior, 43, 45–46, 72, 154, 162, 184
racist-dependent political framework, 2
racist-free society, 3
racist rallies, 116
Raffensperger, Brad, 200, 216n30, 224, 226
Rails, Mark Levin, 243n34
Raymundo, Isaac, 268n5
Reagan, Ronald, 81, 90n70, 141
reconstruction era, 76
Red Famine: Stalin's War on Ukraine, 40n43
referendum, 25, 38
reform party, 112, 256
refugee, 27, 55, 59n26, 60, 73, 89, 177
Refugee Act, 73
Regents of the University of California v. Bakke, 77
Reich, Robert, 273n79
Reid, Shannon E., 167n80
Reilly, James A., 54, 60n37
religion, 6, 8, 13, 27, 30, 48, 196, 261, 263, 270, 272n54
religious: discrimination, 6; divisions, 6, 14, 54; hate crimes, 36, 58n4, 72, 84, 90n79, 236, 252, 268
Reny, Tyler T., 166n51

Index

representation, 10–12, 24, 155, 181, 254, 259
Republican Jewish Coalition, 131
Republican Leaders, 72, 120, 213, 238, 240, 257, 262, 265
Republican Party, 2, 92, 116, 118, 148–51, 162, 165n42, 169, 235, 244n48, 263
Republican Voters, 132n6, 152, 209–10
Rettig, Charles, 143, 164n20
Revolutionary Armed Forced of Colombia (FARC), 51
Revolutions of 1989, 16
Rhodes, Stewart, 157–58, 183, 204, 232
Rights in Colombia and Brazil, 59n22
Right-Wing Cable Media, 203
Roberts, John, 78
Robertson, David Brian, 88n53
Robinson, James A., 28, 39
Romney, Mitt, 113, 121, 151
Roosevelt, Franklin, 71, 76, 79
Roosevelt, Theodore, 79
Rose, Doug, 280n3
Rosen, Jeffrey, 197
Rosenstein, Ron, 171, 197
Rothbart, Daniel, 167n79
Rothchild, Mike, 168n83, 189n63
Rothenberg and Gonzales Political Report, 119
Rousseau, Jean-Jacques, 8, 19n3
Ruisch, Benjamin C., 268n3
Ruprecht, Daniel, 90n68
Russia, 23, 25, 33–35, 40–41, 54–55, 121, 140; Russian revolution, 33
Rutherford, James, 105n2, 107n37
Ryan-Kor-Sins, 217n46

Sachs, Jeffrey D., 28, 39
Sanandaji, Tino, 20n18
Sanders, Sarah Huckabee, 264
San Francisco, 70–71, 88n43, 265, 271n51
Saramo, Samira, 133n15
Saudi Arabia, 55
Schaefer, Todd, 132n2
Schudson, Michael, 19n8

Schumpeter, Joseph, 9, 19n4
Schwartz, Tony, 106n13
Scott, Rick, 158
Scott, Tim, 230
separatism, 48
Sessions, Jeff, 115, 143, 171
sexual orientations, 6
Shelby County v. Holder, 77, 253, 255
Shia, 53
Shively, W. Phillips, 18n1
Sides, John, 135n51, 166n50
Silva-Leander, Annika, 39
Sindelar, Daisy, 58n13
slavery, 2, 45–46, 50, 52, 56–57, 58n2, 180–82, 249, 258–59, 263
Slavery's Roots: War and Economic Domination, 58n2
Sloat, Amanda, 39, 58n12
Smith v. Allwright, 76, 85
Social Media, 155–56, 158, 160, 166n62, 183, 225, 238–40, 250, 252, 268n7, 277
Soldak, Katya, 20n22
Somaliland, 30
Sommers, Samuel R., 268n4
South Africa, 51–53, 57, 59
South Africa's Black population, 53
South Africa's transformation, 53
South Sudan, 55
Soviet Union, 14, 16, 40n46, 73
Soyemi, Eniola Anuoluwapo, 40n37
Spanish-controlled territory, 50
Spanish Crown, 56
The Spectre of Race: How Discrimination Haunts Western Democracy, 58n3
Spencer, Nekeisha, 61n53
Spencer, Richard, 130, 154, 161, 166n58, 237
Starr, Kevin, 87n28
Stebbins, David, 167n79
Stefanik, Elise, 234, 257
Steinmetz-Jenkins, Daniel, 166n56
Stenner, Karen, 39, 109–10, 150, 165n45

Stephens-Dougan, Lafleur, 6, 135n52
Stone, Roger, 112, 115, 217n51
Stonecash, Jeffrey M., 165n39
The Storm Is Upon Us, 168n83, 189n63
Sturkey, William, 88n49
Sunni Arabs, 53
Sunni Muslims, 27, 55
Survey, Race, 187
Sweden, 13–15, 20, 39; democrats, 14, 20n19; population, 13; Swedish, 14
symbolism, 52, 81–82, 180
Syria, 27, 49, 53–58, 60, 123, 177; Kurds, 55; nation, 54; population, 53; refugees, 27; state, 54; Syrian Army defectors, 55
systemic racism, 85n1, 129, 181, 258
Systemic Racism in the United States, 85n1

Tarrow, Sidney, 135n57, 160, 168n87
Taylor, John, 21n35
Taylor Greene, Marjorie, 184, 234
Teixeira, Ruy, 187
Tel Aviv, 236
terrorism, 48, 117, 121, 180, 265–66, 273, 275
Tesler, Michael, 135n51, 166n50
Texas, 69, 151, 156, 158, 183, 188n45, 269, 272
Texas Freemen Force, 205
Thomas, David, 60n32
thought transformation, 48
Three Percenters, 156–57, 166n63, 167n66, 205, 231
Todd, Chuck, 145
tolerance, 13, 18, 26, 83
Tomson, Danielle Lee, 20n19
Too Much and Never Enough, 106
Tourse, Robbie W.C., 57n1, 85n1
toxic propaganda, 181
transfer of territory, 69
transgender issues, 263–64
transitional societies, 24
transparency, 36, 144, 275
Treaty of Guadalupe Hildalgo, 69

tribalism, 93
Truman, Harry, 65, 67, 79
Trump: business affairs, 100; ongoing rhetoric, 251; racist-oriented campaign, 152; village, 100
Trump, Fred, 93–94, 96, 100
Trump, Mary L., 93–95, 106n9
Trumpism, 1, 3–4, 43, 132n14, 133n15, 240, 247–50, 260–61, 263, 265, 275–79
Trump Nation: The Art of Being the Donald, 106n8
Trump Revealed, 98, 105n7, 106n10, 108n44, 132n1, 241n16
Trump: The Art of the Deal, 95, 106n13
Trump: The Deals & The Downfall, 106n17
Turkey, 27, 39, 48–51, 54–55, 58–59, 140
Turkey's democracy, 27
Turkish Christian Armenians, 49
Turkish Syriac Christians, 49
Turkish troops, 49
Two Faces of Exclusion: The Untold History of Anti-Asian Racism in the United States, 86n27

Ubi, Efem, 40n34
Ukraine, 23, 33–35, 38n5, 40–41, 214
United Kingdom, 35, 55–56
United Nations Human Rights Commission, 49
United States, 1–3, 5–7, 81–85, 90n83, 91, 98–99, 231–32, 249–52, 264–65
United States Supreme Court, 66–68, 71, 143, 151–52, 178, 196, 253–55, 279
United States vs. Cruikshank, 76
urban populations, 55
Uyghur population, 48
Uyghurs, 47–48, 58

Valasik, Matthew, 167n80
Valenzuela, Ali A., 166n51
vandalism, 252
Vavreck, Lynn, 135n51, 166n50

V-Dem Institute, 17
Venezuela, 25–26, 38, 70, 98
Venezuela's democracy, 25–26
Verea, Monica, 268n10
Viable Institutional Mechanisms, 11
Vietnamese, 70
Vietnam war, 95–96
vocational training, 48
Voting Rights Act, 65, 67–68, 74–75, 77, 88n52, 152, 253, 269n17; 1965, 65, 67–68, 74, 77, 81, 83, 85, 87, 87n41, 125, 152, 253; 2006, 75
Voting Rights laws, 77

Waldman, Michael, 247–48
Walloons, 30
The Wall Street Journal, 21n34, 38n7, 108n46, 135n63, 185n1, 187, 214n8, 234, 244n48, 271n47
Walter, Barbara F., 5, 6, 19n11, 37n1, 39
Wang, Tova Andrea, 87n42
Warnock, Raphael, 224
Warren, Katie, 105n4
Warren Era, 78
The Washington Post, 39–40, 167n70, 168n91, 174, 241n5, 242, 272, 273n70, 274n80, 275, 279n1
Wayne, Stephen J., 79, 89n61
Weber, Jim M., 90n74
Weiler, Jonathan D., 110
Wewiorski, Nancy J., 85n1
White Anglo-Saxon Protestants, 64
Whitely, Patrice, 61n53
White/non-White conflict, 63

White Protestants, 79
white supremacists, 84–85, 164n34, 182, 205, 237, 256, 266, 274n84
White vote, 81, 152, 256
Whitmer, Gretchen, 265
Why Scholars and Activists Increasingly Fear a Uyghur Genocide in Xinjiang, 58n8
Williams, Juan, 261, 272n56
Willis, Fani, 226, 237
Wilson, Woodrow, 40n35, 79
Winograd, Morley, 280n3
Winsor, Morgan, 135n55
wokeness, 260, 262–64, 272
Woodland Wild Dogs, 205
Woodward, Bob, 128, 136n72, 215n15
World Trade Center buildings, 103
World War I, 33, 54, 73
World War II, 33–36, 48, 69, 73, 76, 87n31, 129
Wray, Christopher, 266, 274n83

xenophobia, 87n36, 249, 264, 275
Xu, Xiang, 186n17

Yanukovych, Victor, 34
Yoruba, 31
Youngkin, Glenn, 236

Zelenskyy, Volodymyr, 34, 172, 184, 195
Zhao, Ashley, 271n42
Zhong, Jiee, 268n7
Ziblatt, Daniel, 36
Zitser, Joshua, 106n14

About the Author

Larry N. Gerston, PhD, political science professor emeritus at San Jose State University, examines politics and policy making at the national and state levels of government. Along with his current work, he has written *California's Recall Election of Gavin Newsom: The Politics of Political Reform in the Era of COVID*, co-author, 2022; *Reviving Citizen Engagement: Policies to Renew National Community,* 2014; *Not So Golden After All: The Rise and Fall of California*, 2012; *Confronting Reality: Ten Issues Threatening to Implode American Society (and How We Can Fix it)*, 2009; *American Federalism: A Concise Introduction*, 2007; *Recall! California's Political Earthquake*, co-author, 2004; *Public Policy Making in a Democratic Society: A Guide to Civic Engagement*, 2002; *Public Policy Making: Process and Principles, 1997; American Government: Politics, Process and Policies*, 1993; *California Politics and Government: A Practical Approach*, co-author, 1991; *Politics in the Golden State: The California Connection*, co-author, 1988; *The Deregulated Society*, co-author, 1987; *Making Public Policy: From Conflict to Resolution*, 1983.

Professor Gerston appears twice weekly as the on-air political analyst at NBC Bay Area television and speaks frequently on radio station KCBS. Aside from his local responsibilities, he has been interviewed on NBC Nightly News, CBS Evening News, BBC, CNBC, NPR, CSPAN, MSNBC, CNN's Inside Politics, and *Time* magazine. He also has written more than 150 op-ed articles and has been quoted in virtually every nationally significant newspaper. He has a unique ability to passionately put complex issues into an understandable perspective.